THE ROUGH GUIDE TO
THE LAKE DISTRICT

Written by
Jules Brown

This eighth edition updated by
Norm Longley

**ROUGH
GUIDES**

Contents

A NOTE TO READERS

At Rough Guides, we always strive to bring you the most up-to-date information. This book was produced during a period of continuing uncertainty caused by the Covid-19 pandemic, so please note that content is more subject to change than usual. We recommend checking the latest restrictions and official guidance.

OPPOSITE: A LONE HIKER AT HELM CRAG **PREVIOUS PAGE:** GRASMERE

Introduction to

The Lake District

There's nothing in England to match the splendour of the Lake District, a tight knot of romantic peaks, moors – and yes, lakes – up in England's northwesternmost corner. For a nation reared on the tales of Beatrix Potter and Arthur Ransome, the pastoral images of a misty-eyed English past could hardly be more familiar: lush fields enclosed by dry-stone walls; warm, weatherbeaten and time-worn inns; shepherds gathering their flocks on green hillsides. Adventure-seekers, meanwhile, come to explore the country's largest lakes and highest mountains, or to immerse themselves in full-on outdoor activities from mountain-biking to fell-walking and kayaking. Whatever attracts you to the country's most famous, largest and most picturesque National Park, one visit won't be enough.

While **rural tradition** and the **great outdoors** loom large on any Lake District trip, it's not all sheepdog trials, hiking boots, timewarp pubs and flowery B&Bs. For such a small region (36 miles from east to west), there's an astonishing number of glam places to stay and eat – from boutique hotels to organic tearooms, gastropubs to yurt-filled campsites – and you're often closer to an artisan bakery or microbrewery than a tractor and a field full of sheep. Farming, in fact, accounts for just ten percent of the National Park's working population, with up to to fifty percent of all jobs attributable in some way to tourism, rather than the more traditional occupations you might expect.

But wherever you stay, and whatever you do, the **scenery** certainly makes a play for your attention, whether it's the glacial lakes and forested valleys or the steeply pitched mountains and their tumbling waterfalls. There's nowhere else quite like it in Britain and even on the busiest of summer days it's relatively easy to escape the crowds by climbing to the higher fells or exploring the more remote valleys.

WINTER WALK IN THE CENTRAL FELLS

AVERAGE DAILY TEMPERATURES AND RAINFALL

	Jan	Feb	Mar	Apr	May	Jun	Jul	Aug	Sep	Oct	Nov	Dec
Max/min (°C)	4/1	5/1	8/1	11/2	14/5	16/7	19/10	18/9	15/7	12/5	8/2	6/0
Max/min (°F)	39/34	41/34	46/34	52/36	57/41	61/45	66/50	65/48	59/45	54/41	46/36	43/32
Rainfall (mm)	230	200	135	91	90	83	70	98	110	180	164	206

The region's **literary connections** are also justly famous – William Wordsworth and the Lake Poets feature, of course, but also many others, from John Ruskin to Norman Nicholson, whose houses, haunts and places of inspiration form the backbone of many a lakeland literary trail. Perhaps surprisingly for such a rural area, a long **industrial history** manifests itself in scattered mining works, scarred quarry sites, surviving mills and a couple of old railway lines – Ravenglass to Eskdale, and Lakeside to Haverthwaite – now converted to tourist use.

In the end though, for all the renowned literary sites, local museums or big-ticket family-friendly attractions, many visitors take home a more personal memory of their trip. A lakeside stroll and a pint in front of a roaring fire; valley panoramas from scenic peaks such as Cat Bells; or a night's star-gazing in spectacularly clear skies – they all guarantee that one day you'll be back for more in England's most ruggedly lovely holiday region.

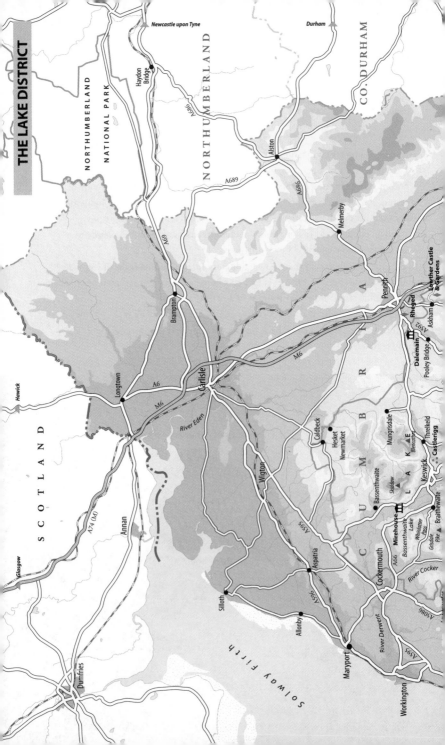

THE LAKE DISTRICT

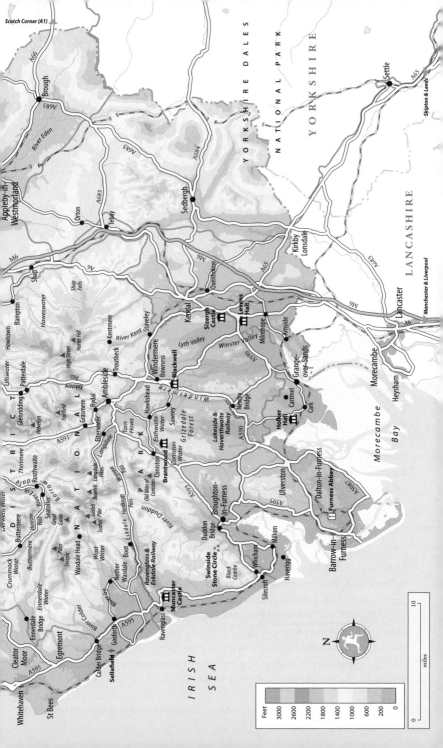

LAKELAND PLACE NAMES AND TERMS

Many lakeland **place names**, **geographical features** and **dialect words** have origins that go back to Norse, Saxon or even Celtic times. The most common are appended to features you'll see every time you stride out into the countryside – like "fell" (hill, mountain, or high common land), "mere" (lake), "holme" (island), "beck" (stream), "force" (waterfall) and "tarn" (small mountain lake).

With other names, it helps to know the derivation in order to figure out exactly what you're looking at: such as place names ending in "-thwaite" (signifying a clearing), or those incorporating the words "ghyll" or "gill" (narrow ravine or mountain stream), "hause" (summit of a pass), "how" or "howe" (rounded hill), "pike" (peak), "raise" (summit of a ridge), "rake" (natural rock passage) or "wyke" (bay).

Farming language is deeply rooted in the past – words like "heaf" (grazing area), "garth" (enclosed land or field) or "lath" (barn) have ancient roots – and there is still an entire dialect counting system for keeping tabs on sheep (yan, tyan, tethera, or one, two, three …), not to mention scores of other local words for describing traditional skills and pastimes, from basket-weaving to wrestling.

Where to go

It's easy to see a great deal of the Lake District in just a few days, even if you're travelling by public transport or hiking from place to place. In fact, there's a lot to be said for getting out of the car and seeing places under your own steam, whether it's on foot, by bike or boat.

Windermere is the largest lake (10.5 miles long), featuring a cruise service which calls at all points north and south. The lake's towns – Windermere, Bowness and, especially, **Ambleside** – are among the region's busiest settlements and, given their choice of accommodation, cafés, restaurants and pubs, they make obvious bases. Even if they don't plan to stay there, most people at least pass by Windermere on the way to **Grasmere** and the famous Wordsworth houses, or to impossibly pretty **Hawkshead** and Beatrix Potter's house at nearby **Hill Top**.

Coniston Water boasts the Brantwood home of John Ruskin, plus cruises on the lake's idiosyncratic wooden launches and steam yacht. Away from the literary trail, there are renowned hikes, peaks and tarns in central **Langdale** – and, arguably, the finest hikers' inn in Britain (the *Old Dungeon Ghyll*) from which to explore them.

The scenery is even more dramatic in the north, where four peaks top out at over 3000ft – including England's highest mountain, **Scafell Pike** (3210ft) – while the quite different lakes of **Derwent Water** and **Ullswater** provide superb backdrops for a day's cruising and walking. **Keswick**, the main town in the north, is the one major lakeland settlement with real year-round character, and it makes a handy base for exploring – from delightful **Borrowdale**, a valley for which the word picturesque might have been invented, to **Bassenthwaite** and its ospreys, nature reserves and animal park.

On the western side of the National Park, gentle **Buttermere** is perhaps the best-known destination, while awesome **Wast Water** (incidentally, England's deepest lake)

FEMALE MORRIS DANCERS OUTSIDE A PUB IN CARTMEL

and remote **Ennerdale Water** lie further off the beaten track. Keep heading west and you find the only part of the **Cumbrian coast** that lies within the National Park. This stretches twenty miles south from **Ravenglass**, an undistinguished village with a Roman past, which provides a bucolic route into the heart of dramatic **Eskdale** via the charming Ravenglass & Eskdale Railway.

Outside the somewhat arbitrary National Park boundaries, most visitors make time for the southern gateway town of **Kendal**, the revitalized Georgian port of **Whitehaven** and the peripheral historic market towns of **Ulverston**, **Penrith** and **Cockermouth**, the last also famous as the birthplace of Wordsworth. Foodies meanwhile increasingly make their way to the highly attractive village of **Cartmel**, which is rapidly becoming a something of a boutique getaway.

When to go

It rarely pays to second-guess the weather in the Lake District. You can get varying conditions – or even several seasons – on the same day sometimes. But there are a few generalizations that can be made, as well as some observations about the best time of year for a trip to England's northwestern corner.

High **summer** may be the warmest season – usually – but it isn't the ideal time to visit the Lakes. July and August can see accommodation (and the roads) stretched to

SENSATIONAL SAUSAGES

The humble breakfast sausage is hardly so humble in the Lake District, where the traditional highly spiced, spiral-shaped **Cumberland sausage** is king. Its origins are obscure, though some trace its ancestry to the arrival of German miners in the Lake District in the sixteenth century. Whatever the truth, Cumbrian butchers zealously guard their secret recipes for the perfect blend of pork, herbs and spices, and the matter is taken so seriously that there's a celebratory **Sausage Day** every July. Meanwhile, in 2011, following years of campaigning by the Cumberland Sausage Association and others, the traditional Cumberland sausage was finally awarded the same **protected status** as Parma ham, champagne, Stilton cheese and Melton Mowbray pork pies; if you want to guarantee your breakfast banger has been made in Cumbria to a strictly traditional recipe, look for the European PGI mark.

---

capacity as the bulk of the annual visitors descend. If you're thinking of swimming in the lakes, it's worth knowing that late August and September see the waters at their warmest, as they've had time to soak up the summer sun. To be honest, though, you'll barely notice the difference: the inland waters are pretty cold, at best, year-round.

Other busy periods include **Easter week**, the few days around **New Year** and school **half-term holidays** (February and October). Fewer people visit the Lakes in the **late autumn, winter** and **early spring**, so if you're looking for relative peace and quiet, these are the seasons to choose. Many of the indoor sights and attractions remain open year-round, so you shouldn't be unduly inconvenienced, and while some hotels, guesthouses and campsites are closed, those that do stay open tend to offer reduced rates.

Spring usually arrives a little later than in the south of England, though in mild seasons you sometimes get the famous **daffodils** flowering as early as February. Mostly, though, before May you might get bright, blue skies, but you can also expect chilly mornings, overnight frosts and cold conditions (snow can linger on north-facing slopes as late as June). December has the shortest and rainiest days; November and January aren't much better.

Author picks

Our authors have explored every corner of the Lake District over several editions of this guide to uncover the very best the region has to offer. Here are some of their personal favourites.

Romantic weekend Lounge in luxury at the cunningly named *Randy Pike*, a former gentleman's hunting lodge converted into a gorgeous boutique B&B (see page 77).

Spectacular views Latrigg (see page 151) for a quick dash and a lake vista; Kentmere Horseshoe (see page 81) for a long walk with sweeping panoramas.

A walk, a fire and a pint Toddle around Loweswater and fall gratefully into the *Kirkstile Inn* (see page 196).

King for a day Muncaster (see page 182) and Lowther (see page 216) offer very different castle experiences, but for noble life in a nutshell Wray Castle (see page 72) gets the nod.

Off-road biking What a backdrop for a bike ride, and what a choice of experiences – first-timers shouldn't miss the exhilarating Eskdale Trail (see page 184).

Glamping When it comes to camping the Lakes can't be beat, from woodland pods at *Grizedale Campsite* (see page 134) to the mountain-view yurts at *Great Langdale* (see page 107).

Quirky museum You want to see lion's teeth and bang some musical stones? You want Keswick Museum (see page 144).

Adrenaline rush When hiking and biking simply won't cut it, accept the challenge of Honister's Via Ferrata (see page 163).

Gourmet picnic Artisan bread from *More?* (see page 83), farmhouse cheese from *Cartmel Cheeses* (see page 234), organic fruit and veg from *Low Sizergh Barn* (see page 230) and a gourmet pizza to share from the *Woolpack Inn* (see page 188).

Wild swimming It's against the spirit of the thing to make a specific recommendation, but pick a tarn and take the plunge – you may just discover your new best outdoor hobby.

> Our author recommendations don't end here. We've flagged up our favourite places – a perfectly sited hotel, an atmospheric café, a special restaurant – throughout the Guide, highlighted with the ★ symbol.

BIKING TOWARDS THE DERWENT FELLS

SWIMMING IN THE RIVER DUDDON

15

things not to miss

It's not possible to see everything that the Lake District has to offer in one trip – and we don't suggest you try. What follows, in no particular order, is a selective taste of the highlights of the region: hidden beauty spots, lake cruises, family days out and mountain activities. All highlights are colour-coded by chapter and have a page reference to take you straight into the Guide, where you can find out more.

1 CASTLERIGG STONE CIRCLE
See page 147
The dramatically sited standing stones at Castlerigg, above Keswick, are the most prominent reminder of the Lake District's ancient inhabitants.

2 COOL CAMPING
See page 77
It's glamping all the way with cool tree tents, safari tents and pods at wonderfully rustic sites like Windermere's *Low Wray*.

3 MUNCASTER CASTLE
See page 182
A perfect family destination, featuring ghosts, gardens and flying owls.

4 GRIZEDALE FOREST
See page 132
Whether it's biking, hiking or tree-scrambling, Grizedale Forest makes a great day out.

5 HARDKNOTT ROMAN FORT
See page 188
The finest Roman remains in the Lakes stretch across a blustery hillside.

6 WILD OSPREYS, BASSENTHWAITE LAKE
See page 168
A viewing platform above Bassenthwaite allows you to see these majestic birds at close quarters.

7 AIRA FORCE
See page 206
This sparkling waterfall with a 70ft drop is a cherished location – Wordsworth "wandered lonely as a cloud" among the neighbouring daffodils.

8 DOVE COTTAGE, GRASMERE
See page 93
The most famous literary house in the Lake District, pretty Dove Cottage was the early home of William and Dorothy Wordsworth.

9 THE JOURNEY THROUGH BORROWDALE
See page 157
The Lakes' most scenic road flanks Derwent Water and runs through the stunning valley of Borrowdale.

10 LEVENS HALL
See page 229
The extraordinary topiary gardens at Levens Hall present a cornucopia of curious shapes.

11 GREAT LANGDALE

See page 108

For the best rugged walking in the central fells, head for the peerless Langdale Valley.

12 RAVENGLASS & ESKDALE RAILWAY

See page 182

A ride on "La'al Ratty", as the train is known, makes a happy family outing, with easy walks possible straight off the platforms of the tiny Eskdale stations.

13 CARTMEL

See page 232

The south lakeland village of Cartmel is a firm foodie favourite with its artisan producers, great restaurants and farmers' market.

14 VIA FERRATA, HONISTER

See page 163

There's no more thrilling day out than the fixed-rope and zip-wire challenge of England's first "Iron Way".

15 A CRUISE ON ULLSWATER

See page 207

Steamer trips depart all year from Glenridding for walks and visits around lovely Ullswater.

11

12

Itineraries

The Lake District might only be a small region but it packs a lot in, not least England's highest mountain and the country's deepest and longest lakes. A tour of the major highlights could be done in a week, but ten days is better. Come for the weekend and you'll still be able to sample some of the region's most alluring tastes and attractions. They also give a flavour of what the region has to offer and what we can plan and book for you at www.roughguides.com/trips.

LAKES GRAND TOUR

❶ **Windermere** A cruise on Windermere up to the main National Park Visitor Centre at Brockhole starts you off on the right foot. See page 58

❷ **Grasmere** Wordsworth's village grave and his famous Dove Cottage lure visitors. See page 86

❸ **Keswick and Skiddaw** From Keswick, the main resort town in the north, you can conquer Skiddaw, easiest of the Lake District's famed 3000ft mountains. See page 151

❹ **Borrowdale** South of Keswick lies the Lakes' most handsome valley, with its Derwent Water vistas and hardcore hiking trails. See page 157

❺ **Buttermere** Cross Honister Pass – where adventures await at Honister Slate Mine – and descend to Buttermere, the most spectacularly sited of the western lakes. See page 197

❻ **Cumbrian coast** Top attraction is the narrow-gauge Ravenglass & Eskdale Railway, which steams from the Cumbrian coast into the heart of the western fells. See page 182

❼ **Eskdale** The glorious Eskdale valley is overlooked by a stupendously sited Roman fort, after which comes a dramatic, zigzag drive over the notorious Hardknott Pass. See page 184

❽ **Coniston Water** Inspiration for Arthur Ransome's *Swallows and Amazons* – take a cruise on the magnificent Steam Yacht *Gondola* to evoke memories of bygone days. See page 118

❾ **Holker Hall** Top stately home is a tough call, but for wonderful gardens, and a tearoom and food hall to boot, our vote is for Holker. See page 233

LITERARY LAKES

❶ **Wordsworth House** See where it all began – birthplace and family home of William Wordsworth, in the agreeable Georgian town of Cockermouth. See page 245

❷ **Aira Force** Away from Wordsworth's houses are more gentle reminders of his inspired genius – like the dancing Gowbarrow daffodils near Ullswater's Aira Force waterfall. See page 206

Create your own itinerary with Rough Guides. Whether you're after adventure or a family-friendly holiday, we have a trip for you, with all the activities you enjoy doing and the sights you want to see. All our trips are devised by local experts who get the most out of the destination. Visit **www.roughguides.com/trips** to chat with one of our travel agents.

❸ **Orrest Head** The very first lakeland hill climbed by fell-walker extraordinaire, Alfred Wainwright; chances are you'll have one of his walking guides with you. See page 51

❹ **Armitt Library and Museum** The best place to investigate the contributions of writers and artists to Lake District life. See page 71

❺ **Allan Bank** Complement Grasmere's famous Wordsworth houses with a visit to the National Trust's fascinating Allan Bank. See page 91

❻ **Brantwood** John Ruskin built a beautiful house above the shores of Coniston Water – come by boat for a complete experience. See page 123

❼ **Hill Top** Beatrix Potter's favourite Lakeland spots feature in her timeless children's stories – not least the farmhouse where she wrote many of her books. See page 130

TASTING THE LAKES

❶ **Staveley** The craft-foodie businesses at Mill Yard range from artisan bakery to microbrewery and beer hall. See page 80

❷ **Pooley Bridge Farmers' Market** A pretty village location for a spring and summer farmers' market. See page 212

❸ **Old Crown** The out-of-the-way village of Hesket Newmarket has a landmark pub in the *Old Crown*, the first cooperatively owned pub in the UK. See page 173

❹ **Syke Farm** Farmhouse tearoom at glorious Buttermere, with ice cream made from the milk of their own Ayrshire cows – that's food inches, not miles. See page 198

❺ **Keswick Market** Hit Keswick on Thursday or Saturday, when Market Place fills with stalls offering everything delicious. See page 144

❻ **Drunken Duck Inn** The Hawkshead country inn that sets the local benchmark, with boutique rooms, gourmet food and an award-winning brewery out back. See page 129

❼ **Cartmel** Medieval village that's centre of the epicurean scene, from Michelin-starred *L'Enclume* restaurant to the world's best sticky toffee pudding from the village shop. See page 232

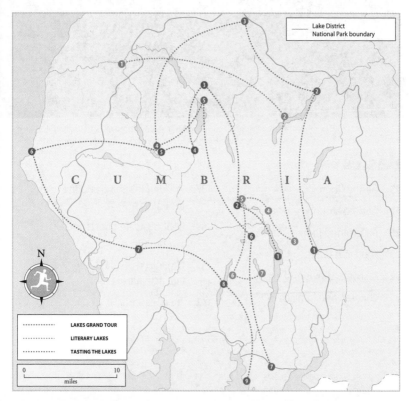

POSTBOX NEAR GLENRIDDING

Basics

Getting there

The Lake District is in the county of **Cumbria, in the northwest of England, eighty miles north of Manchester and 270 miles from London. The M6 motorway gets you within a few miles' drive of the eastern side of the region, while public transport links are good, with trains or buses providing reasonably direct services from most major British cities (and from Manchester Airport). The main points of access are Lancaster, Kendal and Windermere to the south, and Penrith and Carlisle to the north.**

This section tells you how to reach the Lake District by bus, train or car, and gives all the contact details you'll need for planning routes and booking tickets. Touring around the Lakes by either public transport or car is covered in "Getting around" (see page 22). Large-scale package-tour operators tend to concentrate on whirlwind trips through the region, bussing passengers in to see the famous lakes and literary sites. Generally speaking, you can do much better on your own – either using public transport or booking local tours. But for **outdoor activities or pastime-based holidays** – from cycle touring to art appreciation – we've picked out some of the more interesting options in the "Walking, climbing and the mountains" (see page 37) and "Organized holidays, courses and outdoor activities" sections (see page 40).

For more guidance on holidaying in the Lake District – including full transport details – contact **Cumbria Tourism** (☎01539 822222, ☻golakes. co.uk). At the time of writing, there were some limitations on regular services due to ongoing Covid-19 pandemic restrictions, but these are not intended to be permanent.

By train

The main train access is via the **west-coast main-line service** between London and Glasgow. For the Lake District, you change either at Lancaster or **Oxenholme** for the branch-line service to Kendal (4min from Oxenholme) and Windermere (20min). The only other places in the region directly accessible by train are **Penrith** (also on the west-coast main line) and **Carlisle** (west-coast main line, plus connections from Newcastle upon Tyne). There are also direct services from Manchester to Kendal and Windermere; and from Manchester, Preston and Lancaster along the **Cumbrian Coast line** to Ulverston, Barrow-in-Furness, Ravenglass, Whitehaven and Carlisle, providing a leisurely approach to the western Lakes. Various train operators provide these services: check **National Rail Enquiries** (☻nationalrail.co.uk) for timetable, route and service information – the website has a journey planner and links to ticket-sale sites.

From London (Euston Station) trains depart roughly hourly to Lancaster and Oxenholme and the trip usually take around two hours and forty-five minutes. There are some very good deals if you book in advance (the earlier the better), with one-way fares starting at around £28, or around £55 return. If you buy your ticket on the day, or travel at more popular times, expect to pay more like £90 one way (£112 return), and a lot more if you intend to travel on a Friday or during peak commuter hours. To reach Keswick and the northern Lakes, either take the train from Oxenholme to Windermere and continue from there by bus or stay on the main-line service to Penrith or Carlisle, from where buses also run to Keswick.

From Manchester Piccadilly, the quickest trains to Windermere take two hours (advance one-way fares from £8); note that some services from or via Manchester might require a change of trains either at

---

GETTING TO THE LAKE DISTRICT FROM OVERSEAS

From **Manchester Airport**, northern England's major airport, there are direct train services to Kendal and Windermere.

Travelling from Ireland by **ferry**, the most logical port to use is Liverpool (sailings from Belfast and Dublin), from where it's an easy train ride to Manchester and on to the Lakes. Using the Belfast or Larne service to Cairnryan in Scotland, you'll need to travel first by train from nearby Stranraer to Glasgow then head south from there on the west-coast main line; arriving in Holyhead from Dublin, take the train via Crewe to Oxenholme. From the rest of Europe, using the North Sea crossings makes most sense. Docking at Hull (from Rotterdam and Zeebrugge), take the train to York and Manchester, changing for the onward service to the Lakes; from Newcastle (Hamburg, Amsterdam, Norway and Sweden), take the train to Carlisle, changing for the service south to Penrith and Oxenholme.

DISTANCES IN MILES FROM MAJOR CITIES

	WINDERMERE	KESWICK	PENRITH
London	270	305	290
Birmingham	150	190	175
Manchester	80	115	100
York	100	115	95
Newcastle upon Tyne	90	80	75
Edinburgh	145	135	115
Glasgow	140	135	115

Lancaster or at Oxenholme, the station for the Lakes on the west-coast main line. Coming from Yorkshire, a longer, more scenic approach is provided by the famous **Settle–Carlisle Railway** (connections from Leeds and Bradford), which runs through stunning Yorkshire Dales countryside. At Carlisle, you'll have to switch to local buses to get you to Keswick, Penrith or Cockermouth.

Services **from Glasgow** (2hr 15min–3hr) and **Edinburgh** (2hr 30min–3hr 15min) run to Oxenholme for connections to Windermere, with stops en route at Carlisle and Penrith. Advance one-way fares to Windermere from either city start at £13.50, though considerably more if you buy on the day, or travel on a Friday or at peak times.

If you're visiting Cumbria as part of a wider northern-England trip, you'll find that Northern Rail rover tickets (Ⓦnorthernrailway.co.uk) offer the best deals on getting to the Lakes: the **North Country Rover** ticket (any four days in eight; £104.50) or the **North West Rover** (any four days in eight £83.90; seven consecutive days £100.10), are both valid for unlimited travel within Cumbria and the northwest and further afield (as far as Manchester, Newcastle and the Scottish borders). Other regional rover tickets are good value for travel between Lancaster, Carlisle, the Cumbrian coast and the Lakes (see page 23). You can also buy Day Ranger tickets, allowing you to jump on and off trains as much as you like for a day (£48.40 for an adult without a railcard).

By bus

National Express (Ⓦnationalexpress.com) buses from London's Victoria Coach Station run once daily to Windermere, via Birmingham, Preston and Lancaster (8h 30min; from £28 single). This service continues from Windermere on to Ambleside (15min), Grasmere (30min) and Keswick (45min). There's also a once-daily service to Windermere and the same onward stops **from Manchester**, via Preston (3hr; from £9 single). National Express services from Birmingham, York, Newcastle and Scotland route via Manchester or Carlisle to the Lakes; from the south, east and west you'll have to change in London or Birmingham. The website has all sorts of ticket offers and discounts; it's usually cheapest to book in advance and travel midweek.

From nearby cities, **Stagecoach** (Ⓦstagecoachbus. com) has the most useful direct daily services: the #554 from Carlisle to Keswick; the #104 from Carlisle to Penrith; and the #555 from Lancaster to Kendal, Windermere, Ambleside, Grasmere and Keswick.

By car

The Lake District lies to the west of the **M6 motorway**, which – as it approaches the hills and troughs of the Lakes and the Eden Valley – displays one of the best feats of road engineering in the country: the section between Kendal and Penrith is as impressive as major highways get in England. For Keswick and Penrith, come off at junction 40; for Kendal and Windermere, take junction 38 (north) or 36 (south); for Cartmel and Ulverston, take junction 36.

Count on a **driving time** of five hours from London and the southeast, an hour and a half from Manchester or Newcastle, two and half hours from York or Birmingham, and three hours from Glasgow or Edinburgh. Once you leave the motorway, the nature of the roads and the summer traffic can slow you right down, so allow plenty of time if you're aiming for the central fells or the western Lakes. Local radio stations carry regular traffic and weather reports.

Getting around

Too many people bring cars to the Lake District and, as a consequence, once-quiet valleys and villages can be adversely

affected by the amount of traffic. However, over the last few years – recognizing the damage that's being done to the environment – the local authorities have made great improvements to the public transport network within the National Park to encourage people to leave their cars at home. Many of the local bus and lake cruise or ferry services are fully integrated, so you can get around the major destinations easily in a day, and there are lots of very good value "day rider" and other discount tickets available. Bus, boat and train combinations can get you to the start of some of the best-known hikes and mountain climbs, while loading your bike onto a "bike bus" helps cyclists get around the Lakes in a more sustainable fashion.

The southern, central and northern band – from Windermere and Coniston through Ambleside and Grasmere to Keswick – is the easiest section of the Lakes to tour by **public transport**. In summer especially, when services are at their peak, there's no longer any real excuse not to use buses or trains for at least some journeys. In the western Lakes and valleys, and in the far north beyond Keswick, getting around by bus becomes trickier, though nearly everywhere is connected by some sort of service, however limited.

Timetables and information

Major **routes** and service **schedules** are listed within each chapter of the Guide. Otherwise, the best single source of information is the **Go Lakes website** (Ⓦ golakes.co.uk/travel/timetables.aspx), which covers the main bus routes, trains and ferry services in the Lakes, plus links to ticket offers and discounts. You can also pick up individual bus, train and ferry timetables from tourist information centres, as well as themed brochures combining bus routes with things like scenic tours, local walks or pub crawls.

For all public transport enquiries in Cumbria – bus, coach, rail and ferry services – check **Traveline** (Ⓣ 0871 200 2233, Ⓦ traveline.info). Its telephone enquiries service is available daily 7am to 8pm, while the website gives access to a searchable database of all public transport services in the area.

By bus

Stagecoach (Ⓦ stagecoachbus.com) is the biggest bus operator in the Lakes and Cumbria, though it also works with other agencies to ensure services to areas that wouldn't otherwise be economically viable. Routes connect every major town and village, and although travel frequencies vary you can usually count on being able to reach most places at least once a day throughout the year. The most frequent services on all routes are between Easter and the end of the school holidays in the first week of September, though some peak-period timetables continue into September and October (often at weekends only).

You can buy **tickets** on the bus as you go, though the best deal is the **North West Explorer** (one-day £11.50, family £32.70), which is valid on the entire network and available on any bus from the driver. For a week's unlimited travel within Cumbria there's also the **North West Megarider Gold** card (£29, available on the bus), while other special **day-rider tickets** offer really good deals on specific bus routes (as in Borrowdale) or on **bus-and-boat** combinations for Windermere, Coniston and Ullswater – details are included throughout the Guide.

Cross Lakes Experience

The best integrated transport service, when it's operating, is the excellent **Cross Lakes Experience**, which combines boats, minibuses and scheduled buses to connect Bowness-on-Windermere with the Beatrix Potter house at Hill Top, and then on into Hawkshead. You're also invited to "take your bike or boots" so you can connect with bike trails and footpaths for a full day out, whether you're starting

---

A BETTER KIND OF TRAVEL

At Rough Guides we are passionately committed to travel. We believe it helps us understand the world we live in and the people we share it with – and of course tourism is vital to many developing economies. But the scale of modern tourism has also damaged some places irreparably, and climate change is accelerated by most forms of transport, especially flying. We encourage all our authors to consider the carbon footprint of the journeys they make in the course of researching our guides.

ALL ABOARD

Quite apart from the Cumbrian coastal route, and the rustic ride from Oxenholme to Windermere down the Lake District branch line, there are a couple of other highly scenic private train lines in the Lakes. The **Lakeside & Haverthwaite Railway** (Ⓦ lakesiderailway. co.uk) might only be a short steam-pulled jaunt at the southern end of Windermere but it's a lovely trip from the lake and along the River Leven. Meanwhile the narrow-gauge **Ravenglass & Eskdale Railway** (Ⓦ ravenglass-railway.co.uk) is a fantastic way to explore the more remote western valleys – again, with regular steam services through a gorgeous part of the countryside. And if you're really taken with train travel, think about coming or going on the **Settle-Carlisle Railway** (Ⓦ settle-carlisle.co.uk), a 72-mile route through the Yorkshire Dales that links with the Cumbrian county capital.

from Bowness or Hawkshead – there are bike racks on participating buses and boats. Ticket prices range from £11.95 adult return for the boat-and-bus trip from Bowness to Hill Top, up to £43.80 for a family ticket valid as far as Coniston Water including a cruise on the lake.

The service runs daily from April to October, but is suspended for 2021 due to the Covid-19 pandemic and need for social distancing. It will hopefully resume in 2022; contact Mountain Goat (☎ 01539 445161, Ⓦ mountain-goat.com).

By train

The only place actually in the Lake District National Park you can reach on a regular train service is **Windermere** town, on the branch line from Oxenholme (on the London–Manchester–Glasgow west-coast main-line route) via Kendal and Staveley. Outside the National Park, but still a handy approach to the northern Lakes, **Penrith** is also a stop on the west-coast main-line route, while the Furness and **Cumbrian Coast** branch line from Lancaster runs via Ulverston, Barrow-in-Furness, Millom, Ravenglass and the Cumbrian coastal towns to Carlisle.

Good-value rail passes include the **Cumbria Day Ranger** (£48.40), the **Cumbria Round Robin** (£33.70) and the **Cumbria Coast Day Ranger** (£22). There are discounts on all these for children or those with family railcards, and the passes are valid on any train – buy them at the stations or from conductors on board trains. They all cover slightly different sections of the Cumbrian train network, but you can easily figure out which is most appropriate by checking with Northern (Ⓦ northernrailway.co.uk) or National Rail Enquiries (Ⓦ nationalrail.co.uk). Northern Rail also offers "Duo" tickets (basically a second adult return ticket for half-price when two adults travel together), which save you money on the coastal line between Barrow and Carlisle.

By ferry

Windermere, Coniston Water, Derwent Water and Ullswater have **ferry or cruise services**, all of which are covered in detail in the Guide. Windermere (Ⓦ windermere-lakecruises.co.uk) and Ullswater (Ⓦ ullswater-steamers.co.uk) are the most popular choices for a round-trip cruise; the service on Derwent Water (Ⓦ keswick-launch.co.uk) is extremely useful for hopping around the lake and accessing Borrowdale walks; while the Coniston launches and *Gondola* steam yacht (Ⓦ nationaltrust. org.uk/steam-yacht-gondola) are also great for local walks and for reaching Ruskin's house, Brantwood. The Windermere boats also run from Bowness and Ambleside to the main National Park Visitor Centre at Brockhole, and down to the bottom of Winder-mere for the attractions at Lakeside. Combination bus, boat and entry tickets are widely available – basically, if you're planning to take the bus to Windermere or Ullswater, then go on the lake or visit Lakeside's aquarium, Haverthwaite steam train or Brantwood on Coniston, you can save money with an all-in ticket.

By car

While driving around the Lakes might seem conven-ient, it soon loses its attraction on July and August weekends when the roads are busy: it takes ages to get from village to village and you can't find anywhere to park once you arrive. Leave the car at home, or at your accommodation, whenever you can and you'll get more enjoyment out of the region.

Parking can be difficult throughout the Lakes, especially in the towns and villages. There is free on-street parking in Ambleside, Windermere, Bowness, Coniston, Grasmere and Keswick, but there's not very much of it and it's usually limited to thirty minutes or an hour. Most places have a **disc parking** scheme, so to park on the street you'll have to nip into a local shop or tourist office and pick up a disc for your dashboard. For longer stays, the best advice, every time, is to follow the signs to the official car parks. Expect to pay £2–4 for up to four hours' parking, and up to £7 or £8 for a full day, even in car parks on National Park Authority and National Trust land in out-of-the-way places. Most town and village hotels and some B&Bs have private parking; we mention in our accommodation reviews when parking is available. If the establishment is rural, you can take it as read there'll be somewhere free to park. In 2021, the Lake District National Park has provided additional temporary car parks, thanks to the area's even greater than usual popularity, with much of the country holidaying at home for a second year.

Most **roads** in the region are in good condition, though single-track driving is common – don't park in the passing places. Surfaces on high ground and off the beaten track tend to deteriorate rapidly, being little more than unmetalled tracks in places: many routes can be adventurous at the best of times and downright treacherous in winter or bad weather. The steepest road gradients and most difficult driving are on the high **lakeland passes between valleys**, with Hardknott Pass (between Eskdale and Duddon Valley) and The Struggle (Ambleside and Kirkstone Pass) being particularly notorious.

By bicycle

Local cycle businesses do much to promote responsible **cycling** within the National Park, and by following agreed routes, exercising caution and respecting walkers' rights of way you'll help to ensure continued cooperation.

The going rate is around £25 for a full day's rental of a mountain bike, with helmets, locks and route maps usually included in the price. Children's bikes, tagalong trailer bikes and tandems are also often available, while the current push is to get people who otherwise might not cycle on to **electric bikes** (around £35 a day) – a low-impact way to get up all those Lake District hills with minimal effort. Several visitor attractions and local businesses have electric bikes available (full details on Ⓦelectricbicyclenetwork.com), including the National Park's Brockhole Visitor Centre and Coniston Boating Centre, while other good places to go for cycling include Whinlatter and Grizedale forest parks, which have dedicated bike rental outlets and special mountain-bike trails. The Eskdale Trail, meanwhile, is a great (and mostly flat or downhill) introduction to the western Lakes.

A **Bike Bus service** (#599; bike £1) connects Windermere train station with Ambleside, Grasmere and Bowness. It runs on weekends and bank holidays from May to September, plus a daily service in school summer holidays – basically, it will pick you up and drop you off with your bike (normal bus fare plus a small charge for the bike), meaning that you can reach the start of loads of off-road trails without using a car.

Several long-distance routes also cut through Cumbria and the Lake District, including the 72-mile **Cumbria Way Cycle Route** (Ⓦcumbriawaycycleroute.co.uk) from Ulverston to Carlisle and the well-known **Sea-to-Sea (C2C)** cycle route, a 140-mile trip between Whitehaven/Workington and Sunderland/Newcastle (Ⓦc2c-guide.co.uk). Other parts of the National Cycle Network – like the Hadrian's Wall Cycleway or the Reivers Cycle Route – also

---

THE LAKES' FIVE BEST DRIVES

Mountain views, lakeshore vistas, rolling farmland and dappled forests – the Lake District has some of England's most beautiful routes. Just watch out for the sheep!

Borrowdale and the B5289 From the shores of Derwent Water to the base camps for climbing England's highest mountains, the winding B5289 is a beauty – and you can do it by bus too. See page 157

Grizedale and beyond Into the woods from Hawkshead you're soon in a different Lake District, where forest glades and hidden hamlets beckon. See page 132

Hardknott and Wrynose Pass The tortuous, narrow, soaring zigzags are not for faint hearts, but this classic route takes you from the western wilds of Eskdale towards the central tourist fleshpots. See page 189

Honister Pass to Buttermere On a bright, sunny day there's no more thrilling drive as you wind down from slate mine to serene waters, shadowed by high fells on all sides. See page 162

Whitehaven to Silloth The west Cumbrian coast at its best, especially the section from Maryport to Silloth, with views of the salt marshes, dunes and glistening waters of the Solway Firth. See page 240

pass through the region. Route details are available from the eco-conscious transport charity Sustrans (W sustrans.org.uk).

There's lots of useful cycling information on the Lake District National Park website (W lakedistrict. gov.uk), and for more **mountain-bike routes** and off-road cycling in the Lakes, check out W mountain-bike-cumbria.co.uk.

Accommodation

The Lake District has no shortage of accommodation, though it sometimes seems like it at peak periods. At New Year, Easter, public holidays and school holidays (particularly the six-week summer break from late July to the end of August) it's wise to book ahead – though tourist information centres will always be able to find a room for anyone arriving without a reservation. Accommodation listed in the Guide is open year-round unless otherwise stated, though note that, even so, many places close for a few days over Christmas and New Year.

Local information offices all offer a **free room-booking** service where you'll be charged a deposit (usually ten percent) that's then deducted from your accommodation bill. Or you can book accommodation **online** through the Cumbria Tourism website (W golakes. co.uk), which also offers short breaks, special deals and late-availability bookings.

Hotels, guesthouses and B&Bs

Bed-and-breakfast (B&B) rates start at around £30 per person per night. Even in the most basic of places, you should get a sink, a TV and a kettle in the room. These days, though, nearly all B&Bs and guesthouses have rooms with en-suite facilities, but in a few cases, you might still have to share or use a bathroom that's down the hall.

Once above these prices – say from £40–50 per person – you can expect fancier services and facilities, from fresh flowers and gourmet breakfasts to king-sized beds and handmade toiletries. Many traditional B&Bs and small guesthouses have raised their game in recent years – some are truly excellent – while others have retained the cosy familiarity of a B&B but gone down the boutique road, so while you might pay up to £200 a night at places like Ambleside's *Randy Pike* (see page 77) you're getting a highly individual B&B experience.

Hotels in the Lakes start at around £80–120 a night, though you can easily spend £200–300 or even more for a room in one of the famous country-house hotels, like *Miller Howe* (see page 54), *Sharrow Bay* (see page 213) or the *Gilpin* (see page 58). Again, overall standards are improving, as lots of places have had boutique makeovers, adding things like designer fabrics, handmade local furniture, roll-top baths, iPod docks and spa facilities. You no longer have to stay in a flouncy, frilly country-house hotel unless you really want to – more typical of the modern lakeland experience are hotels like Ambleside's townhouse-style *Waterhead* (see page 76) or Grasmere's seriously stylish *Moss Grove Organic* (see page 97).

Rooms are also available in most **pubs and inns**. Often this is traditional B&B in old-fashioned or modernized rooms, starting at around £30 per person, rising to more than £50 in the best-known traditional hikers' inns, like Langdale's *Britannia Inn* (see page 106) and the *Old Dungeon Ghyll* (see page 108), and Wasdale's *Wasdale Head Inn* (see page 193). However, several country inns in particular have gone contemporary, with sharp styling, snappy service and good food now the norm at places

---

ACCOMMODATION PRICES

We give a room price for all establishments reviewed in this guide. Unless otherwise stated, this represents the price of the **cheapest available double or twin room in high season** (ie, usually Christmas/New Year, Easter, and June to August). Prices are often higher at weekends, and over public holidays: conversely, it's always worth asking about off-season **discounts**, which might shave a couple of quid off a B&B room, or up to fifty off a hotel. **Breakfast** is included, and rooms are **en suite**, unless otherwise stated.

For **youth hostels**, and anywhere else with **dorm beds**, we also give the per-person overnight high-season rate, unless otherwise stated. YHA hostel rates often come down to as little as half of the quoted price out of season, and members can save up to a further £3 per night (see W yha.org.uk). **Campsites** can charge per person or per tent, usually with added costs for bringing in a vehicle – we've made it clear in each review what the quoted price is for.

like the *Drunken Duck Inn* (see page 129) outside Hawkshead, the *Punch Bowl Inn* (see page 68) at Crosthwaite, the *Wild Boar* (see page 59) near Bowness, Loweswater's *Kirkstile Inn* (see page 196) and Clifton's *George and Dragon* (see page 217).

At weekends, many places insist upon two- or (over public holidays) even three-night **minimum stays**. There again, staying more than a couple of nights in many places brings the standard price down by a few pounds a night. There aren't a great many **single rooms** available, and solitary hikers or holiday-makers won't often get much knocked off the price of a double room if that's the only option. Finally, many guesthouses, inns and hotels offer a discounted **dinner, bed and breakfast (D, B&B) rate** that – provided you want to eat there in the first place – is always a better deal than the standard B&B rate. Note, though, that some hotels *only* offer stays on a D, B&B basis, while others are so remote that there's nowhere else to eat anyway.

Farm stays

Not surprisingly, one of England's most rural regions offers plenty of opportunity to see country life at close quarters by **staying on a farm**. At its most basic this might be simple farmhouse B&B, offered on many farms as a way of boosting income. Accommodation might be in the farmhouse itself or in cottages on the land, and you can expect to pay standard bed-and-breakfast rates. Some offer a very special experience – at Coniston's *Yew Tree Farm* (see page 161) or *Crake Trees Manor* (see page 253) near Penrith, for example, you can expect a glamorous night's stay that's more about chic than sheep. Although there's no obligation, some farms provide a lot more opportunity to muck in, either feeding the animals or finding out more about farming life.

Around twenty farms on **National Trust** land in the Lakes offer B&B. Some of the best are reviewed in the Guide, though the full list and booking details are on the NT website (⦿nationaltrust.org.uk; click on "Holidays" and then "Hotels & B&Bs"). Alternatively, check out **Farm Stay UK** (⦿farmstay.co.uk) for more farmhouse options in Cumbria, including a group of superior farm stays marketed as "Luxury in a Farm" (⦿luxuryinafarm.co.uk).

Hostels

There are twenty Youth Hostel Association (YHA) **youth hostels** (⦿yha.org.uk) in the Lake District, and a couple more just outside the park boundaries including a summer-only hostel in the county

> ### BEST FOR...
> **Brilliant breakfast** *Howe Keld*, Keswick. See page 149
> **Budget grandeur** *YHA Wasdale Hall*, Seascale. See page 191
> **Cool camping** *Low Wray Campsite*, Low Wray. See page 77
> **Country elegance** *Armathwaite Hall*, Bassenthwaite. See page 169
> **Farm fancy** *Yew Tree Farm*, Coniston. See page 121
> **Inn style** *Punch Bowl Inn*, Crosthwaite. See page 68
> **Old-school charm** *Old Dungeon Ghyll*, Langdale. See page 108
> **Romantic getaway** *Randy Pike*, Ambleside. See page 77
> **Room with a view** *Linthwaite House*, Windermere. See page 59
> **Rough and remote** *YHA Black Sail*, Cleator. See page 195
> **Veggie retreat** *Yewfield*, Hawkshead. See page 129

capital of Carlisle. Several, including those in Ambleside, Keswick and Grasmere, are among the most popular in the country, so advance booking is a good idea at any time of the year. Gone are the days of tasks and sackcloth comforts: many hostels have refurbished rooms of two to six beds (duvets and linen provided) and nearly all have kitchen, laundry, drying-room and wi-fi, while others have licensed restaurants, outdoor activities and rental services. There are still two or three fairly basic hostels based in prime walking country, like *Skiddaw House* (see page 172) in the Back o'Skiddaw and *Black Sail* (see page 195) in Ennerdale, but these too have a charm all of their own.

You don't have to be a member to use a YHA hostel, though non-members pay a £3 supplement for accommodation (under-18s £1.50) and aren't eligible for any other hostel discounts or benefits. If you choose to, you can join the YHA in person at any affiliated hostel on your first night's stay. Overseas visitors who belong to any **International Youth Hostel Federation (IYHF)** association in their own country have automatic membership of the YHA.

YHA **hostel prices** start at around £10 per night for an adult bed in low season, though you can pay up to £25 a night at popular hostels in summer. Many hostels have twin or **family rooms** available (sometimes even with double beds): couples will pay the current overnight per-person bed price while a typical four-bed family room costs between £60 and £80. Breakfast costs around an extra fiver, as does a packed lunch. Lots of hostels now also offer **dinner** (two courses from around £10), often using locally sourced ingredients and with Cumbrian beers and organic wines available, while others may have, for example, pizza night once a week. You can book any YHA hostel online on the website, or call or email the hostels direct. The major YHA hostels are open daily, year-round, though many others have restricted **opening periods** in the winter, which are detailed in the Guide.

The number of **independent backpackers' hostels** in the Lake District has grown in recent years – some of these are well-known former YHA properties now under new management, including *Derwentwater* (see page 156) near Keswick and *Thorney How* (see page 98) in Grasmere. These and others have similar facilities and are pitched at roughly the same prices as the higher-grade YHA hostels. Bear in mind, however, that there are no membership requirements for independent hostels.

Bunkhouses and camping barns

Lakeland **bunkhouses** (some operated by the YHA, others privately owned) provide simple accommodation for hikers and backpackers. At their most basic, there's a mattress on the floor and a shower room, though others have bunk beds, kitchens, stoves and open fires. You'll have to provide your own sleeping bag and cooking gear, and prices run from £6 to £10 per person per night. In a similar vein, there's a series of ten **camping barns** in and around the National Park, mostly self-catering converted farm buildings with communal facilities and which sleep between eight and eighteen people The cost is £12 per person per night, and although mattresses are provided you'll need your own sleeping bag, foam mat and cooking equipment – some of the farms offer breakfast. For reservations, contact the **Lakeland Camping Barn Booking Office** (☎017687 74301, ⓦ lakelandcampingbarns.co.uk).

TOP FIVE HOSTELS

YHA Keswick Great for families. See page 149
Black Sail Hiker's heaven. See page 195
Elterwater Country calm. See page 106
Ennerdale Eco-retreat. See page 195
Keswick Townhouse lodgings. See page 149

Holiday property rental

Lake District **holiday properties** range from simple stone cottages to large country houses, by way of barn conversions, former mills, townhouses and shooting lodges. There are lots of companies vying for your custom but all offer the same kind of basic deal. The minimum rental period is usually a week, though outside the summer season and especially in the winter you may be able to negotiate a three-day/long-weekend rate – except, that is, at Christmas, New Year and Easter when prices are at their highest. All properties come with a fully equipped kitchen and many (but not all) provide bed linen and towels. Prices vary dramatically – from around £300 a week for the smallest places to £1000+ for a week in a large, luxury property with admission to the local pool and health club thrown in.

HOLIDAY PROPERTY AGENCIES

Coppermines and Coniston Lakes Cottages ⓦ coppermines. co.uk. Specialist in the Coniston area, with unique properties in Coppermines Valley as well as around Coniston Water and the Duddon Valley.
Goosemire Cottages ⓦ lake-district-cottages.com. Forty barn conversions or traditional cottages, some with lake views, in the Ullswater, Haweswater, Bassenthwaite, Windermere and Wast Water regions.
Heart of the Lakes ⓦ heartofthelakes.co.uk. Excellent choice of more than 300 quality properties in all corners of the National Park.
Keswick Cottages ⓦ keswickcottages.co.uk. A good selection of cottages in and around Keswick, Braithwaite and Portinscale in the northern Lakes.
Lakeland Cottages ⓦ lakelandcottages.co.uk. Period cottages and farmhouses in the northern Lakes, from the Keswick area, through Borrowdale, Lorton Vale, Bassenthwaite and Cockermouth.
Lakeland Hideaways Cottages ⓦ lakelandhideaways.co.uk. Cottages, barn and farm conversions in Hawkshead, Sawrey and around Esthwaite Water.
Lakelovers ⓦ lakelovers.co.uk. A large range of quality properties mainly in the western and southern Lakes, with accommodation generally on the chintz-free side.
National Trust ⓦ nationaltrust.org.uk/holidays. Twenty-eight lakeland properties, from lakeside cottages to remote farmhouses – mainly around Ambleside, Little Langdale, Eskdale, Loweswater and Penrith.
Wheelwright's ⓦ wheelwrights.com. Best starting place for cottages in and around Elterwater, Chapel Stile, Langdale, Grasmere and Ambleside.

Camping and glamping

The Lake District has scores of **campsites**, ranging from back-to-basics hikers' favourites to family-style holiday parks – we've tended to recommend those

TOP FIVE CAMPSITES

Caslerigg Farm Peace and quiet. See page 149

Great Langdale Hiking hot spot. See page 107

Grizedale Farm and forest. See page 134

Low Wray Lakeside glamp. See page 77

Wasdale Campsite Mountain glory. See page 193

Food and drink

There's been a quiet revolution in Cumbrian food and drink over the last few years, and renowned restaurants, chilli festivals, gastropubs, artisan bakeries and cookery schools are now just as much part of the scene as the good old cream tea and Cumberland sausage. Pub and café meals in particular have improved immeasurably, while restaurants right across the region pride themselves on using locally sourced ingredients, whether it's farmhouse cheese, organic vegetables or fell-bred lamb.

that favour tents over the large caravan-RV parks. Cumbria Tourism (Ⓦ golakes.co.uk) has a searchable database of campsites and holiday parks on their website, or consult Ⓦ lakedistrictcamping.co.uk, a really useful resource giving more in-depth details about Lake District campsites. Many sites close between November and March, while in July and August it's always worth booking a pitch in advance if you can (not all accept advance bookings). Prices vary considerably, from a few quid for a field site with toilet and cold tap to £15–20 a night for a pitch at one of the big resort sites, complete with washrooms, leisure facilities, shop and bar. Note that some places charge per person, some charge per tent and some charge for both – while others may charge for your vehicle as well.

The **National Trust** (Ⓦ nationaltrust.org.uk/features/lake-district-camping) maintains five campsites – *Great Langdale* (see page 107), *Low Wray* (see page 77), *Wasdale Head* (see page 193), *Hoathwaite* (see page 121) on Coniston Water, and *Eskdale* (see page 188) – in fantastic locations. These are incredibly popular and you'll need to book ahead or get there early, especially around summer and bank holiday weekends.

As for **glamping**, you can now choose between **yurts**, **tipis** and walk-in **bell tents** on many campsites. Some are stand-alone sites, like the yurts at *Rydal Hall* (see page 102), while others put glampers in separate areas on established sites, as at the National Trust's *Low Wray* site (see page 77). You can expect such luxuries as futon beds, wood-burning stoves, rugs and hammocks, barbecue pits and even kitchens, though you may well have to use the campsite shower-block. Options are usually rented in part- or full-week periods, and prices reflect the facilities, from around £250 (part-week) to £450 (week) for something that sleeps four or more people. **Camping pods** are also creeping onto many sites, which are eco-friendly, insulated wooden shelters sleeping two or three people, for around £35–50 a night.

Traditionally, **fine dining** in the Lakes was very much a silver-service roast-and-veg affair, or heavily Anglo-French in character, and this is still the case in some old-fashioned lakeland hotels. But many local chefs have married contemporary tastes and trends with well-sourced local ingredients to produce something slightly different – if not a specific lakeland style of cuisine then at least a welcome change from old-school menus. At the more adventurous places expect to see plenty of pan-searing, chargrilling and slow roasting, together with ethnic and fusion menu twists, using fresh, local, home-made ingredients. The Lake District currently offers some of the finest **country dining** experiences in England, including seven Michelin-starred foodie locations, including the terrific, Asian-inspired *HRiSHi* restaurant at the Gilpin Hotel in Windermere (see page 58) and Simon Rogan's extraordinary restaurant *L'Enclume* (see page 234) in Cartmel, which has few peers in Britain, never mind the Lakes – Rogan also owns the one-star *Rogan & Co* in the same village. For sheer style, panache and invention, it's hard to beat a Rogan restaurant.

Elsewhere, you're as likely to come across good Cumbrian food in a farmhouse **tearoom** or village **café** as in a restaurant, and some of your best memories will be unexpected ones – say a scoop of Buttermere ice cream straight from the farm or fresh-baked organic bread in the Mill Yard at Staveley (see page 81).

Information, events and courses

The Cumbria Tourism website (Ⓦ golakes.co.uk) is a good place for general **information**, from local food producers to farmers' markets, restaurant news to food festival dates.

Annual events showcasing regional food and drink producers include the **Westmorland Country**

THE LAKES' BEST...

Bar meal *Old Crown*, Heskett Newmarket. See page 173

Casual dining *Jumble Room*, Grasmere. See page 99

Deli *Cartmel Cheeses*, Cartmel. See page 234

Dress-up dinner *HRiSHi* at the *Gilpin Hotel*, Bowness-on-Windermere. See page 58

Fish supper *Hooked*, Windermere. See page 54

Foodie pilgrimage *L'Enclume*, Cartmel. See page 234

Gourmet inn *Drunken Duck Inn*, Hawkshead. See page 129

Organic meal *George and Dragon*, Clifton. See page 217

Post-hike recharge *Strands Inn*, Nether Wasdale. See page 191

Restaurant with rooms *The Plough*, Lupton, Kendal. See page 230

Romantic treat *Lucy's on a Plate*, Ambleside. See page 78

Tearooms *Bluebird Café*, Coniston. See page 122

Veggie dining *Fellinis*, Ambleside. See page 77

Fest at the end of May (ⓦ westmorlandshow.co.uk) and the **Cumbria Sausage Festival** at Muncastle Castle in May, while **Taste Cumbria** (ⓦ tastecumbria.com) organises festivals in different destinations across the Lake District throughout the year, including Kirkby Lonsdale, Ulverston and Cockermouth. Offbeat foodie fests include the celebratory **Damson Day** in the Lyth Valley each April (ⓦ lythdamsons.org.uk), Dalemain's **Marmalade Festival** (ⓦ dalemain.com/marmalade-festival) in March – patron, Paddington Bear, obviously – and the **Chilli Fest** at Holker Hall (ⓦ holker.co.uk) in September.

Time was, a **cookery course** in the Lakes might have instructed you in the subtle arts of the microwave, but no more. There's now a real interest in broadcasting the best of Cumbrian cuisine to a wider public.

Local specialities

The classic pork **Cumberland sausage** (see page 10) is the mainstay of every breakfast menu in the Lakes, and a staple in pubs and restaurants too.

Otherwise, beef and pork tend to be overshadowed by the local lamb, particularly by **Herdwick lamb**, the traditional lakeland breed which forms the basis of the "tattie pot", a lamb stew topped with potato. One of the region's most respected **meat** producers is the three-thousand-acre Lowther Park Farm (ⓦ lowther.co.uk), which supplies restaurants and shops across the district, as well as its own *George and Dragon* inn near Penrith. In the south, Holker Hall estate (ⓦ holker.co.uk) specializes in farm-produced cheese, home-reared venison, shorthorn beef and salt-marsh lamb (reared on the salt marshes of Morecambe Bay).

For fish, it's usually **local trout** (farmed on Ullswater and elsewhere, as well as found wild) and Morecambe Bay shrimps, though keep an eye out for lake-caught **char**, a trout-like fish which, in the UK, is peculiar to the Lake District. Landlocked in the Lakes after the last Ice Age, it thrives in the deep, cold waters of Windermere (Daniel Defoe recommended potting this "curious fish" and sending it to your best friend).

Bread is at its best from a growing number of organic, artisan-style bakeries, including the long-standing Village Bakery, Melmerby, near Penrith and More? in Staveley (ⓦ moreartisan.co.uk). Many outlets also stock **cheese** from the Thornby Moor Dairy, in Thursby near Carlisle (ⓦ thornbymoordairy.co.uk), either made plain (a smooth, creamy variety), smoked, or flavoured with garlic and herbs.

You should also keep an eye out at roadside stalls, craft outlets and village shops for locally made **honey and preserves** – the Lyth Valley's **damson** harvest, for example, ends up in jams, ice cream, chocolate, even beer, gin and vinegar. The Hawkshead Relish Company (ⓦ hawksheadrelish.com) and others supply locally made **chutneys and pickles**, often served as part of a ploughman's lunch, and Alston in northern Cumbria provides many outlets with its speciality Cumberland mustards.

The prince of lakeland puddings is Cartmel Village Shop's **sticky toffee pudding** (ⓦ cartmelvillageshop.co.uk), though plenty of other places claim the title. People also travel miles for **Grasmere gingerbread** (ⓦ grasmeregingerbread.co.uk), made to a traditional recipe dating from the 1850s, and **Penrith fudge and toffee** (ⓦ thetoffeeshop.co.uk), while other old Cumbrian recipes that have been dusted off in shops, cafés and restaurants include things like Borrowdale Teabread (a dried-fruit cake), Cumberland Rum Nicky (a date, ginger and rum pie or tart) and rum butter (with rum, nutmeg, cinnamon and brown sugar). **Windermere Ice Cream** (ⓦ windermereicecream.co.uk) is made with milk from Low Sizergh Barn (where you can see the cows being milked daily) and comes in more than thirty flavours.

Vegetarians

These days, most B&Bs and hotels at least make a stab at a non-meat breakfast, while several places provide a wholly **vegetarian** overnight experience, including *Lancrigg* in Grasmere (see page 97) and *Yewfield* at Hawkshead (see page 129). There is also a fair number of strictly vegetarian cafés and restaurants in the Lakes, particularly in the main towns – and at places like the gourmet *Quince & Medlar* in Cockermouth (see page 248), *Fellinis* fine dining (see page 77) or *Zeffirelli's* pizza and Italian joint (see page 78), both in Ambleside, veggies are certainly not getting second best.

Pubs and beer

If you like your pubs with oak beams, slate floors, log fires and country beer gardens, you're in the right part of England. There's a fine selection of old **pubs and inns** throughout the Lakes, many dating back several hundred years. Some have become very well known, either as hikers' bars – like the *Old Dungeon Ghyll* in Langdale (see page 108) or Elterwater's *Britannia Inn* (see page 106) – or for the quality of their **food**; indeed, some places are more like restaurants-with-rooms these days, such as the classy *Punch Bowl Inn* (see page 68) at Crosthwaite or Hawkshead's *Drunken Duck* (see page 129). If you were to visit just one pub in the Lakes for its beer, it should probably be the *Watermill Inn* at Ings (see page 83), between Windermere and Staveley, which not only brews its own but has up to sixteen real ales on at any one time.

Otherwise, the main **brewery** is **Jennings** (⦿ jenningsbrewery.co.uk), once independent, now owned by Marston's. You'll come across its beers everywhere, and they also offer brewery **tours** at their base in Cockermouth. Meanwhile, the local branches of the **Campaign for Real Ale** (links at ⦿ cumbri-acamra.org.uk) have useful websites listing real-ale pubs and carrying news about breweries and beer festivals.

HERE FOR THE BEER: CUMBRIA'S BEST BREWERIES

There are more than forty **independent microbreweries** in Cumbria – probably a higher number than in any other comparable region in the UK. Some are little more than single-pub craft brewers; others sell their beers at increasing numbers of pubs across the region. Here's our pick of the best – you'll just have to taste your way around Cumbria to see if you agree.

Barngates Brewery ⦿ barngatesbrewery.co.uk. In-house brewery at the fabulous *Drunken Duck Inn* near Hawkshead (see page 129), serving beers (Cracker Ale, Tag Lag, Chester's Strong and Ugly) named after dogs that have lived at the inn.

Bitter End Brewery ⦿ bitterend.co.uk. Based at the *Bitter End* pub in Cockermouth (see page 248), and bravely brewing a great range of beers on Jennings' home soil.

Coniston Brewing Company ⦿ conistonbrewery.com. Produces its award-winning Bluebird bitter, Old Man Ale and Bluebird XB pale ale at Coniston's excellent *Black Bull* pub (see page 119).

Cumbrian Legendary Ales ⦿ cumbrianlegendaryales.com. Makes great-tasting ales for Loweswater's *Kirkstile Inn* (see page 196) among others – including "Loweswater Gold", the UK's champion golden ale of 2011.

Hardknott ⦿ hardknott.com. Passionate local brewer Dave Bailey produces contemporary beers from his Millom base – and he's keen to prove that they go just as well with food as fine wines do.

Hawkshead Brewery ⦿ hawksheadbrewery.co.uk. Founded by former BBC journalist Alex Brodie, now with a brewery (tours available) and great beer-hall in Staveley near Windermere (see page 83).

Hesket Newmarket Brewery ⦿ hesketbrewery.co.uk. Full-flavoured ales from Britain's first cooperatively owned pub, the *Old Crown* in Hesket Newmarket (see page 173).

Keswick Brewing Company ⦿ keswickbrewery.co.uk. There are tours of Keswick's independent brewery, while every pint of Thirst Rescue sold – try it at Keswick's *Dog and Gun* – includes a donation to local mountain-rescue teams.

Festivals, shows and events

There must be more unique festivals, sports and events in the Lake District than in any other region in England. From sheep shows to open-air wrestling, scarecrow festivals to face-pulling competitions, the region shows off its age-old traditions and rugged characteristics in a year-round series of events that often defy description. Most are rooted firmly in the countryside, with the local agricultural show being the annual village highlight in many places, although there's also a thriving arts and culture scene that promotes some internationally recognized festivals.

Many festivals traditionally take place on fixed days (often fairly convoluted), so for exact **dates** either check the websites or contact local information offices or Cumbria Tourism (ⓦgolakes.co.uk). Be aware, too, that the traditional outdoor agricultural shows are particularly susceptible to cancellation due to bad weather – even some of the most famous shows have been postponed in recent years. There are hundreds of other events held throughout the year – from guided walks and lectures to craft demonstrations and children's entertainment – many sponsored by the **National Park Authority** (ⓦlakedistrict.gov.uk), based at the Lake District Visitor Centre at Brockhole (ⓦbrockhole.co.uk).

FESTIVALS AND EVENTS CALENDAR

FEBRUARY TO APRIL

Keswick Film Festival (End Feb; ⓦkeswickfilmclub.org). A showcase of Cumbrian short films, competing for the Osprey Awards.

Words By The Water (First and second week March; ⓦwayswithwords.co.uk). Keswick's ten-day-long literature festival, based at the Theatre By The Lake, features high-profile names.

Hawkshead Beer Festival (Third weekend March; ⓦhawksheadbrewery.co.uk). What better way to spend a blustery, wet spring day than in Staveley, testing some of the best brews on offer in the Lakes?

Damson Day (Third week April; ⓦlythdamsons.org.uk). Head to the Lyth Valley, heart of local plum production, for ale, craft demonstrations, archers, dog agility contests, Morris dancers and all things damson.

Ulverston Walking Festival (End April; ⓦulverstonwalkfest. co.uk). Ten days of guided, graded walks in and around Ulverston – from simple strolls to exerting treks – plus evening talks by hiking and fell-running luminaries.

MAY

Cumbria Life Sausage Festival (First bank holiday weekend; ⓦmuncaster.co.uk). Cumbria's famous coiled sausages are out on show at Muncaster Castle.

Keswick Jazz and Blues Festival (First or second week; ⓦkeswickjazzandbluesfestival.co.uk). Renowned event that turns the whole town into a carnival for four days of gigs and street performances.

Keswick Mountain Festival (Third week; ⓦkeswickmountainfestival.co.uk). Biking, hiking, canyoning, rock climbing, moonlight canoeing... a full-on, extreme-sports blowout.

Cartmel Races (Last bank holiday weekend; ⓦcartmel-racecourse.co.uk). Dress up for an afternoon of picnics and ponies – not to mention the Grand Veterans Chase.

JUNE

Westmorland Country Fest (First weekend; ⓦwestmorlandshow.co.uk). Held at County Showground, Lane Farm, Crooklands, this classic country show features sausage making, dog trials and a "young shepherd" event.

Ulverston International Music Festival (Second week; ⓦulverstonmusicfestival.co.uk). Nine days of music, featuring everything from opera to jazz and barber-shop quartets.

Keswick Beer Festival (First weekend; ⓦkeswickbeerfestival. co.uk). Two days of the finest ale, cider and bands that the Lake District can offer, at this longest running of the regional beer festivals.

Boot Beer Festival (First or second week; ⓦbootbeer.co.uk). Small community-oriented beer fest, held in Eskdale.

Cockermouth Live! (Fourth week; ⓦcockermouthfestival.org). Family-oriented events, talks, music, workshops and shows all around town.

Woolfest (Last weekend; ⓦwoolfest.co.uk). Crafts festival, held in Cockermouth, that celebrates all things woolly, including the sheep.

Ullswater Country Fair (Last Sun; ⓦullswatercountryfair.co.uk). Patterdale is the base for fell races, dog competitions and all manner of country events.

JULY

Ambleside Rushbearing Festival (First Sat). Traditional religious festival with accompanying bands, hymns, children's sports and races.

Ulverston Carnival (First Sat; ⓦulverstoncouncil.org.uk). Floats, dancers, and bands parade through the town centre, with entertainment laid on in Ford Park.

Skelton Agricultural Show (First Sat; ⓦskeltonshow.com). Held near Penrith, there's the usual parade of cattle, horses, vintage cars, dogs, wrestling and home-made jams at this lively show.

Derwentwater Regatta (First weekend; ⓦkeswick.org). Revived in 2014 after a two-century hiatus, this madcap event now features boats, bathtubs, Viking longships and a stone-skimming contest – but not, sadly, the original attack on Derwent Island.

Grasmere Rushbearing (Second Sat). Traditional festival similar to that in Ambleside (see above).

Furness Tradition Folk Festival (Second or third week; ⓦ furnesstradition.org.uk). Three days of folk music, storytelling and dancing at Ulverston.

Hawkshead Beer Festival (Second or third week; ⓦ hawkshead brewery.co.uk). Rerun of the March event, held at Staveley.

Cumberland County Show (Third Sat; ⓦ cumberlandshow.co.uk). One of the largest county shows in the region, held in Carlisle.

Coniston Country Fair (Third or fourth Sun; ⓦ coniston countryfair.co.uk). Another chance to take a look at traditional rural Cumberland life at this entertaining agricultural show.

Ambleside Sports (Last Thurs; ⓦ amblesidesports.co.uk). Major sports event, featuring running, cycling and wrestling (see page 34).

Potfest in the Park (Fourth week; ⓦ potfest.co.uk). The first of Penrith's two annual festivals of ceramics, held in the grounds of a stately home in Hutton-in-the-Forest.

Ryedale Show (Last Tues; ⓦ ryedaleshow.org.uk). More livestock competitions, sheep-dog trials, farm produce and stick-carving contests.

North Lonsdale Agricultural Show (Fourth week; ⓦ ulverstonandnorthlonsdaleshow.com). All the usual agricultural-fair suspects, plus sheep shearing, alpacas and noted horse events.

Penrith Show (Third Sat; ⓦ penrithshow.co.uk). Another big rural show, increasing in popularity each year.

Cockermouth & District Show (Last weekend or first weekend Aug; ⓦ cockermouthshow.co.uk). Good excuse to visit the northwestern Lakes; includes wrestling events open to members of the public – "if you are fit".

Cumbria Steam Gathering (Last weekend; ⓦ steamgathering. org.uk). All manner of steam-driven vehicles, from antique tractors to home-built go-karts, are on show at this annual event held at Flookburgh.

Kendal Calling (Last weekend; ⓦ kendalcalling.co.uk). This four-day indie, dance and new music fest, held in the Lowther Deer Park grounds, gets bigger and better each year.

Lake District Summer Music Festival (Last weekend; ⓦ ldsm. org.uk). International line-up of talent at venues across the region, from early music recitals to big-stage opera.

AUGUST

Potfest in the Pens (First week; ⓦ potfest.co.uk). Penrith's second ceramics celebration of the year, held in the cattle mart just outside town.

Cartmel Agricultural Show (First Wed; ⓦ cartmelagriculturalsociety.org.uk). Another superb parade of all things agricultural – with a foodie bent.

Lake District Sheepdog Trials (First Thurs). If you are a fan of such things – along with wrestling matches and plenty of food and drink – then this is the one not to miss. Held at the Ings, Staveley.

Rydal Sheepdog Trials (Second Thurs; ⓦ rydalshow.co.uk). Another good opportunity to see collies put through their paces, rounding up sheep into pens at the call and whistle of their owner.

Threlkeld Sheepdog Trials (Third Wed; ⓦ threlkeldweb.co.uk). Definitely more locals than tourists at this good-natured event.

Langdale Country Fair (Third Sun). Probably the nicest location of any of the Lakes' agricultural shows, held in a stunning valley at Great Langdale.

Grasmere Sports and Show (Third or fourth Sun; ⓦ grasmeresports.com). The major sporting event in the Lakes region (see page 99).

Hawkshead Show (Penultimate Tues; ⓦ hawksheadshow.co.uk). Great event, though the tiny village becomes even more crowded than usual.

Ennerdale Show (Last Wed; ⓦ ennerdaleshow.co.uk). Despite the rural location this popular agricultural show – which even features wrestling – has been held annually for more than a century.

Millom and Broughton Show (Sat before bank holiday Mon; ⓦ millomandbroughtonshow.com). Featuring everything you'd expect from one of the region's prime agricultural events.

Patterdale Dog Day (Sat before bank holiday Mon; ⓦ patterdaledogday.co.uk). Sheepdog trials, similar to those held in Rydal (see above).

Cartmel Races (Bank holiday weekend; ⓦ cartmel-racecourse. co.uk). A rerun of the May event.

Solfest Music Festival (Bank holiday weekend; ⓦ solfest.org. uk). A great family-friendly bash, taking Bplace on a farm close to Silloth on the Cumbrian coast.

Keswick Agricultural Show (Bank holiday Mon; ⓦ keswickshow. co.uk). One of the region's biggest shows.

SEPTEMBER

Ulverston Beer Festival (First week; ⓦ furness.camra.org. uk). More ale, stout, porter and bitter than it's safe to be left alone with.

Ambleside Summer Flower Show and Craft Fair (First week). Brighten up a trip to Ambleside with this exhibition of local horticulture and crafts.

Loweswater Agricultural Show (First Sun; ⓦ loweswatershow. com). Sheepdog trials, fell racing, horse and livestock competitions, wrestling... it's all here.

Westmorland County Show (Second Thurs; ⓦ westmorlandshow.co.uk). Major county show held in Crooklands, Kendal.

Holker Chilli Fest (Second weekend; ⓦ holker.co.uk. Two-day festival featuring all things chilli, cooking demonstrations and the dreaded chilli-eating contest.

Egremont Crab Fair (Third weekend; ⓦ egremontcrabfair. com). Eccentric show, held annually since 1267 and featuring the unmissable World Gurning Championship.

Borrowdale Shepherds' Meet (Third Sun; ⓦ borrowdaleshow. org.uk). Traditional shepherds' meet (see below), based in Rosthwaite.

WOODSTOCK, GLASTONBURY, KENDAL, SILLOTH...

The Cumbrian summer music scene is now an annual fixture on the festival circuit. Check out in particular **Kendal Calling** (see page 33), **Solfest** (see page 33) and Keswick's superb **Jazz Festival** (see page 34).

Eskdale Show (Last Sat; Ⓦ eskdaleshow.co.uk). Shepherds' meet, held at Eskdale Green.

Ullswater Walking Festival (Last week; Ⓦ lakedistrict.gov.uk). Eight days of guided hikes up through local valleys for all levels of fitness and ambition.

Kendal Torchlight Carnival (Last weekend; Ⓦ kendaltorchlightcarnival.co.uk). Carnival floats, bands and dance troupes parade through the town streets after dark.

OCTOBER TO DECEMBER

Wasdale Head Show and Shepherds' Meet (Second Sat Oct; Ⓦ wasdaleheadshow.co.uk). Traditional shepherds' meet.

Comics Art Festival (Second or third week Oct; Ⓦ comicartfestival.com). International convention at Kendal devoted to comics and graphic novels.

Buttermere Show and Shepherds' Meet (Third Sat Oct). Shepherds' meet (see below).

Kendal Mountain Festival (Third week Nov; Ⓦ kendalmountainfestival.com). Screenings, lectures and events all related to films, books and art about the world's mountains.

World's Biggest Liar Competition (Third Thurs Nov; Ⓦ santonbridgeinn.com). Head to Santon Bridge, Wasdale, and join porky-tellers from all over the world in this century-old event that celebrates the tallest of tales (see page 191).

Ulverston Dickensian Christmas Festival (Fourth weekend Nov). Period costumes, carol-singing, street stalls and strolling Santas.

Keswick Victorian Fair (First Sun Dec; Ⓦ keswick.org). A Christmas fair, much like Ulverston's (see above).

Festivals and events

The main towns host the biggest variety of annual festivals. **Ulverston** in particular – the self-billed "Festival Town" – has something on every month, while **Cockermouth** follows its spring Georgian Fair with a long Midsummer Festival that starts in June and runs right through until the agricultural show at the beginning of August. **Kendal**, too, parties throughout the summer, not least during the long-established Torchlight Carnival parade (September). Winter, meanwhile, sees popular **Christmas and Victorian fairs** in Ulverston and Keswick.

Lake District **literary, film and music** festivals are starting to acquire an international reputation, notably Keswick's Words By The Water in March, the Keswick Film Festival (February), the Summer Music Festival (July) and Kendal's Mountain Festival (November). Naturally, the **great outdoors** is celebrated too, from Ulverston Walking Festival (May), or the similar Ullswater Outdoor Festival (September), to the Keswick Mountain Festival (May).

Cumbria's burgeoning independent breweries have promoted a growing attendance at local **beer festivals** – Keswick Beer Festival (June) is the main one, but Eskdale's Boot Beer Festival (June) is hard to beat for local atmosphere.

Shows, meets and sheepdog trials

Cumbria's most loved annual events take the form of **agricultural shows**, featuring farming equipment, trade and craft displays (including dry-stone walling), food stalls, vegetable-growing and sheepshearing competitions, and prize-winning animals. The **Cumberland** (Carlisle, in July) and **Westmorland** (Kendal, September) shows are the largest examples – relics of the days when they were the annual county shows – but smaller shows (nearly all in July or August) are highly enjoyable affairs where it's still very much a case of local communities coming together.

Some very traditional autumn shows are termed **shepherds' meets**, since that's what they once were – opportunities for shepherds to meet once a year, return sheep belonging to their neighbours, catch up on local gossip and engage in competitions, sporting or otherwise. The mainstays of these events are sheep- and dog-judging competitions, bouts of hunting-horn blowing and displays of decorated shepherds' crooks. In addition, there are several annual **sheepdog trials** in August, the main ones at Rydal and Patterdale.

Sports, races and traditional pastimes

Some annual shows specifically announce themselves as **Sports**, such as those at Ambleside (July) and Grasmere (August), the two most important gatherings. At these (but in practice at all of the agricultural shows and meets too) you'll encounter a whole host of special Cumbrian sports and activities, as well as bicycle and track events, carriage-driving, gymkhanas, ferret- or pigeon-racing and tugs-of-war.

Cumberland and Westmorland wrestling is the best known of the local sports, probably dating back to Viking times: two men, dressed in embroidered trunks, white tights and vests, grapple like Sumo wrestlers and attempt to unbalance each other – the first to touch the ground with anything except their feet is the loser, and if both men fall, the winner is the one on top. It's a best-of-three contest that is hugely technical, yet strangely balletic, and has its own vocabulary of holds and grips, like the "hype", the "hank" and the "cross buttock". The winner is declared "World Champion".

Fell-running is basically cross-country running up and down the fells (news and local club links on ⓦ fellrunner.org.uk). It's a notoriously tough business, dominated by local farm workers and shepherds who bound up the fells like gazelles. The famous Joss Naylor of Wasdale is typical of the breed: in 1975 he raced over 72 peaks in under 24 hours; in 1986 he ran the 214 Wainwright fells in a week; and to celebrate his 60th birthday he did the sixty highest lakeland peaks in 36 hours. The sports show races are shorter than these trials, but no less brutal. In a similar masochistic vein is the challenge known as the **Bob Graham Round** (ⓦ bobgrahamclub.co.uk), named after Bob Graham of Keswick who in 1932 completed a traverse of 42 Lake District peaks (and 72 miles) within 24 hours (starting and finishing at Keswick's Moot Hall); more than 2500 people have undertaken the round since records started being kept in 1960, with the current record holder being Kilian Jornet, who completed the feat in 2018 in an astonishing 12 hours and 52 minutes. Moreover, the most extreme competitors have extended the round to include as many peaks as possible in 24 hours (the current record is 77).

Hound trailing dates back to the eighteenth century and is derived from the training of foxhounds for hunting. A trail is set across several miles of countryside using a paraffin-and-aniseed-soaked rag and the dogs are then released, with the owners calling them in across a finish line at the show. Trailing (and the heavy betting that accompanies it) occurs most weeks during spring and summer outside the shows – the season runs from April to October, with five main events a year (starting on May Day) and scores of smaller meetings. As in other English rural areas, **fox-hunting** proper was long a Cumbrian pastime (on foot in the Lakes, not on horseback), though the controversial 2005 ban on hunting with hounds is supposed to have put paid to the practice. However, the traditional Lake District hunts still meet throughout the autumn and winter, all now claiming to work within the restrictions – ie, the hunts gather for trail-hunting, rather than pursuing foxes.

Rushbearings and scarecrow festivals

The oldest festivals – dating back to medieval times – are the annual **rushbearings**, harking back to the days when church floors were covered in earth rather than stone. The rushes, or reeds, laid on the floors (on which churchgoers knelt or stood) would be renewed once a year. Now the rushes are fashioned into crosses and garlands, decorated with mosses and flowers, and carried in symbolic procession around the village and into the church: the most famous rushbearing festivals are held in July at Ambleside and Grasmere. Lots of Cumbrian villages also go in for summer **scarecrow festivals**, with the streets filled with Carnival-style scarecrows big and small.

Children and families

There are few better places in England than the Lakes for children and families. The whole region is something of an outdoor playground, and most of the traditional activities and pursuits – from paddling to rambling – are free. Many festivals and events are timed to coincide with school holidays, and even the capricious weather needn't be a hindrance. Most kids are far less bothered by the rain and mud than their parents, while in any case Cumbria has a terrific selection of wet-weather attractions.

Admissions and restrictions

Children pay half-price or go free at most museums, sights and attractions, and there are nearly always discounted **family tickets** available too. The same applies to public transport, boat rides, steam-train trips and other activities – it's always worth asking about child/family discounts. Not all **hotels and B&Bs** are so accommodating, and quite a few in the Lakes specifically exclude the under-12s (or children of any age), so you should always check before booking your brood into that dream holiday destination. On the other hand, we've picked out many places in the Guide that are particularly family friendly. Children might also be excluded from some **pubs and restaurants** after a certain time (say 6 or 9pm) – there should always be a sign warning you – and in many country-house hotels you might find that smaller children (again, say the under-12s, however

TOP SIX FAMILY EXCURSIONS

Brockhole There's something to see and do every day at the Lake District Visitor Centre. See page 61

Lake District Wildlife Park The animal park with a difference. See page 167

Lakeside, Windermere Cruise, aquarium, steam-train ride and picnic grounds. See page 63

Muncaster Castle The most haunted house in England? See page 167

South Lakes Safari Zoo Tiger-feeding and kangaroo-spotting in darkest Cumbria. See page 237

World of Beatrix Potter No real fan – or anyone under 5 – will want to miss this. See page 55

well behaved) are not encouraged to eat dinner with everyone else. If you don't like this attitude, there's no reason to stay at such a place; there are many others where your children will be welcomed.

Outdoor activities

It's hard to look beyond the **lakes and fells** for keeping active youngsters occupied. The steamers on Ullswater (see page 207) and the solar-powered launches on Coniston Water (see page 118) are particular family favourites, while there are boxed features throughout the Guide on local walks, climbs and rambles, including a list of the dozen best lakeland walks in the section on "Walking, climbing and the mountains" (see page 37). For routes specifically designed for those in **wheelchairs or with strollers**, consult the excellent "Miles Without Stiles" section of the National Park Authority website (🌐lakedistrict.gov.uk).

There's always the **beach**, never very far away from the hills of the southern and western Lakes, particularly around Millom and Silecroft, or at the sweeping

TOP FIVE FAMILY STAYS

Castle Green Hotel Kendal. See page 230

Coachman's Quarters Muncaster. See page 183

Lakeside Hotel Lakeside. See page 67

Lodore Falls Derwent Water. See page 156

Low Wood Bay Windermere. See page 76

sands of St Bees Head (see page 242). The two forest parks at **Whinlatter** (see page 165) and **Grizedale** (see page 132) are excellent stand-alone destinations with their high-ropes adventure courses (for over-10s only), bike rental and off-road trails, playgrounds and picnic areas. The **Ravenglass & Eskdale Railway** (see page 182) is another great day out, as you can walk and cycle right off the platforms. For wildlife-spotting don't miss **viewing the ospreys** at Bassenthwaite (see page 168). Local industry is entertainingly covered at places like **Stott Park Bobbin Mill** (see page 65) and **Threlkeld Quarry** (see page 164), while hardcore mine tours and daring mountain adventures await at **Honister Slate Mine** (see page 162).

Whether you visit the famous historic houses and literary sites probably depends on your children's tastes, though **Wordsworth House** in Cockermouth (see page 245) is excellent for families, while places like Wray Castle (see page 72), Holker Hall (see page 233), Dalemain (see page 212), Muncaster Castle (see page 182), Hutton-in-the-Forest (see page 252) and Levens Hall (see page 229) also have extensive grounds and plenty of year-round activities on offer. For clambering around old ruins and prehistoric sites, consider **Furness Abbey** near Ulverston (see page 237), **Castlerigg Stone Circle**, Keswick (see page 147) and **Hardknott Roman Fort**, Eskdale (see page 188).

Outdoor activity operators can take you and your family mountain biking, ghyll-scrambling, kayaking, sailing or horseriding. Otherwise, the best single stop is the National Park Visitor Centre at **Brockhole** (see page 61), which coordinates hundreds of year-round activities, from guided walks to craft days, and also offers kayak sessions, bike rental, a family-oriented high-ropes adventure course and other child-friendly attractions.

Indoor activities

The skies are dark, the clouds are gathering and it's starting to pelt down – not so good if you're halfway up a mountain, not such a disaster if you head for one of the region's many indoor attractions. At Lakeside's **Lakes Aquarium** (see page 65) you can learn all about lakeland river habitats without setting foot outside – even the otters and ducks are under cover – while Maryport's **Lake District Coast Aquarium** (see page 243) lets kids feed the fish. For fascinating local lore and life there's a range of excellent museums with children's activities, like Coniston's **Ruskin Museum** (see page 117), Kendal's **Museum of Lakeland Life and Industry** (see page 228), Keswick's **Derwent Pencil Museum** (see page 144), Whitehaven's **The Beacon** (see page 241) and the **Dock Museum** in

Barrow-in-Furness (see page 237). There are shops, crafts and giant-screen 3D movies at **Rheged** Visitor Centre (see page 251), just outside Penrith, while in Ambleside you can browse and shop in the region's best selection of **outdoors stores**.

Walking, climbing and the mountains

The Lake District was the birthplace of British fell-walking and mountaineering, and hundreds of thousands of people still come to the Lakes every year to get out on the hills. Whatever your level of fitness or expertise, you can find a Lake District walk to suit – from an hour's stroll up to a local waterfall to an all-day circuit, or "horseshoe" route, around various peaks and valleys. If you're not confident about being able to find your own way, or simply want someone else to do the organizing, then it's probably best to join a guided walk or a tour. Various operators run Lake District walking holidays, while local schools and instructors can also introduce you to the arts of rock-climbing, mountain navigation and winter hill-walking.

Footpaths and walks

Of the long-distance paths, Wainwright's Coast-to-Coast – which starts in St Bees, near Whitehaven – spends its first few sections in the northern Lakes, and the Dales Way finishes in Windermere, but the only true Lake District hike is the seventy-mile **Cumbria Way** between Ulverston and Carlisle, which cuts through the heart of the region via Coniston and Langdale. The fifty-mile **Allerdale Ramble**, from Seathwaite (Borrowdale) to the Solway Firth, spends around half its time in the National Park area, running up Borrowdale and across Skiddaw, while the 182-mile **Cumbria Coastal Way** runs from Silverdale on Morecambe Bay, all round the Lake District peninsulas and Solway Firth to the Scottish border town of Gretna.

The **walks detailed in this Guide** aim to provide a cross-section of lakeland experiences, from valley bottom to fell top. Some of the most famous mountain ascents are included, as well as gentle round-the-lake strolls. It's vital to note that the brief descriptions in the Guide are not in any sense to be taken as specific route guides, rather as providing start and finish details and other pieces of local information.

We have picked our dozen best walks in the Lakes (see page 37); for more ideas visit the **Cumbria Tourism** website (Wgolakes.co.uk) where you can download things like Wainwright podcasts, Jennings' pub-based "ale trails" (from day walks to four-day trips) or bike and hike routes from major lakeland towns.

USEFUL WALKERS' WEBSITES

W **lakedistrictwalks.com** John Dawson's incredibly detailed Lake District hiking site features more than forty classic walks, complete with route descriptions, photos and a distance calculator.

W **lakelandcam.co.uk** Beautiful shots of lakeland scenery and the weather in all seasons and conditions from the roving digital camera of Tony Richards. Updated daily.

W **stridingedge.net** Sean McMahon's stunning photo diary of fell walks gives a useful first look at the 214 Wainwright and 541 Birkett fells, from route descriptions to summit photos.

W **walklakes.co.uk** Excellent all-round site detailing dozens of walks throughout the Lakes, from easy to challenging, as well as information on local accommodation.

Equipment, skills and support

Experience isn't always necessary but for any walk you should have the proper **equipment** – Ambleside and Keswick are the best places in the Lakes to shop for outdoor gear (and some outdoor stores can rent you a pair of boots and a day-pack). Wear strong-soled, supportive walking shoes or boots – you can turn your ankle on even the easiest of strolls. Even in apparently good weather, warm, wind- and water-proof layered clothing, a watch, water and something to eat are all essential; in winter, make sure you are fully equipped for the conditions.

Bad weather can move in quickly, even in the height of summer, so before starting out you should check the **weather forecast** – hotels, hostels and most outdoor shops post a daily forecast, or check with the official forecasting service (see page 38). Be aware that weather conditions in the valleys are completely different from mountain-top conditions. Above all, take a **map** and, for up on the fells, a **compass** – and be sure you know how to use them. A handheld **GPS** is useful, but can't be relied upon on its own (due to battery failure or loss of satellite signal, for example); similarly, carrying a **mobile phone** is no guarantee of safety in the event of trouble as reception in the Lakes is patchy. You might want to join a guided walk or attend a map-and-compass course instead – the National Park Authority (NPA) runs both in spring and summer, while any of our recommended climbing schools and instructors (see page 37) offer instruction courses on all aspects of mountain skills and safety.

The NPA also does a huge amount of work in the Lakes on **improving access to the countryside**, repairing paths and maintaining rights of way. For the latest news, check with the NPA website (Ⓦ lakedistrict.gov.uk) or Fix the Fells (Ⓦ fixthefells.co.uk).

HIKING SUPPORT SERVICES

Coast-Coast Packhorse Ⓦ c2cpackhorse.co.uk. Daily, door-to-door baggage and passenger service on the Coast-to-Coast route, plus left-luggage storage for overseas visitors. Easter until end Sept.

Sherpa Van Ⓦ sherpavan.com. Daily door-to-door baggage service for walkers and cyclists between overnight stops on the Coast-to-Coast, Sea-to-Sea, Cumbria Way and Dales Way. Easter–Oct.

WEATHER FORECASTING

Lake District National Park Weatherline ☎ 0844 846 2444, Ⓦ lakedistrictweatherline.co.uk. Five-day Met Office advance forecast for fells and valleys, including hiking conditions.

Walking holidays

The operators we list (see below) are a good place to start looking for an organized walking holiday in the Lakes – all are either locally based or have specialist knowledge of the area. Some holidays are self-guided (ie the arrangements are made for you, but you're given a map and walking instructions to follow), while others are fully guided, but there are always baggage transfers and emergency back-up services provided where appropriate. The prices we quote give an idea of what you can expect to pay for certain types of holiday, but note that transport to and from the Lake District is not included (though some operators may be able to arrange it); these holidays are generally available April to September.

WALKING-TOUR OPERATORS

Contours Holidays Ⓦ contours.co.uk. Large variety of self-guided walking holidays along the Cumbria Way, Dales Way and Coast-to-Coast, plus Lake District short-break walking holidays, starting at £370 for four nights' B&B, walking from 10 to 12 miles a day.

Discovery Travel Ⓦ discoverytravel.co.uk. Self-guided walking tours, following the Cumbria Way (seven nights, from £625), a Lakeland Round circuit (eight nights, £790) or the Coast-to-Coast (fifteen nights, £1095). Prices include B&B accommodation, maps and guides, baggage transfer and emergency support.

Mac's Adventure Holidays Ⓦ macsadventure.com. Self-guided hiking tours (five to nine days) along established trails, such as the Coast-to-Coast (seven nights, from £585) and Lake District Round (seven nights, £765); includes accommodation (anything from pubs to award-winning hotels), breakfast, maps, baggage transfer and emergency support.

Walking Women Ⓦ walkingwomen.com. Women-only guided walking and wild swimming trips to suit all abilities in places like

---

TWELVE OF THE BEST LAKE DISTRICT WALKS

Whether you're a couch potato or a mountain goat, here's our pick of the dozen best walks in the Lakes – tick them all off and you'll have experienced some of Europe's finest hikes and rambles.

High-altitude circuit Keep your head in the clouds on the Coledale Horseshoe. See page 166

Pub walk Circle pretty Loweswater and stop off at the *Kirkstile Inn*. See page 195

Mountain peaks Langdale's most exciting walk is up Crinkle Crags and Bowfell. See page 108

Round-lake There are more famous lakes, but the long ramble around Haweswater gets you right off the beaten track. See page 217

Panoramic views From Cat Bells – everyone's favourite scramble – you can see for miles. See page 154

Waterfall hike Stock Ghyll force is dramatic in spate and an easy walk from Ambleside. See page 70

Family stroll There are woodland paths, glistening water and idyllic picnic spots at Tarn Hows. See page 128

Only for experts Early start, late finish, guts and stamina required – it's the gruelling Woolpack Walk. See page 186

Into the valley Strike off up glorious Grisedale from near Patterdale on Ullswater, with Grisedale Tarn your destination. See page 208

Wordsworth's footsteps A tramp in the poet's backyard around Grasmere and Rydal Water. See page 96

Crowd-free ramble You'll be on your own in the heart of the Duddon Valley. See page 136

3000-footer A must for list-tickers, England's highest mountain, Scafell Pike, tops out at 3205ft. See page 161

MOUNTAIN RESCUE

If you get into trouble on the mountains and someone dials ☎ 999, one of twelve Cumbrian **mountain rescue** teams is likely to swing into action. It's an entirely voluntary service, funded by donation – members all live locally, on call 24 hours a day, and each year they save many lives in all weather conditions. Three basic rules, to avoid having to call them: be prepared, check the weather and don't be too ambitious. There's a useful information video and lots more news and advice on the Lake District Search and Mountain Rescue Association website ⓦ ldsamra.org.uk.

Borrowdale and Grasmere. Three- to four-night tours (£400–550) on a B&B or full-board basis.

Rock-climbing, mountain and outdoor skills

There's probably no better place in England to learn some rock-climbing and mountain skills, and certainly no better pool of climbing talent available to teach, at either introductory or advanced level. The **schools and instructors** in our list (see below) offer sessions or courses to individuals, families and groups – it's always best to call first to discuss your requirements. Prices vary wildly, depending on the number in the group, the level of training and length of the course, but for a guided walk in the company of someone hugely experienced in the mountains, or a day's rock-climbing instruction or abseiling for beginners, you'll pay from around £150 per day (split between your party). A day learning bushcraft skills costs around £60 per person, while a night's wild camping starts at £75.

If all you want is a climbing taster, then the indoor **climbing walls** at Kendal (ⓦ kendalwall.co.uk) and Keswick (ⓦ keswickclimbingwall.co.uk) offer introductory training sessions for around £15.

CLIMBING SCHOOLS, SKILLS AND INSTRUCTORS

Carolclimb ⓦ carolclimb.co.uk. Based in Wasdale, Carol Emmons and Richard Sagar offer beginners' courses, guided climbs, ghyll scrambles, winter skills training and kayaking. Beginners, children and families welcomed.

Glenridding Walking Guides ⓦ glenriddingguides.com. Guide-led walks, climbs and mountain-skills courses for individuals, families and friends, based at the foot of Helvellyn.

Highpoint ⓦ mountainguides.co.uk. Courses throughout the year – in Langdale and elsewhere – concentrating on hill-walking, navigational skills and rock climbing, as well as things like Lake District bushcraft. Suitable for beginners and improvers as well as more advanced walkers and climbers.

Lake District Guiding ⓦ lake-district-guides.co.uk. Hiking, biking and navigation courses and trips run on low-impact lines, including guided wild-camping adventures that get you right into the Lake District wilderness.

Boating, watersports and swimming

Apart from the ferry and cruise services on Windermere, Derwent Water, Coniston Water and Ullswater, a dozen or so outlets and operators rent out all sorts of craft, from rowing boats to sailing boats, kayaks to windsurfers. Most places offer instruction as well as rental.

Windermere, Coniston Water, Derwent Water and Ullswater have an overall 10mph **speed limit** (6mph in certain clearly marked zones on Windermere). Powerboats are allowed on the lakes (with the exception of Bassenthwaite), but operators must stick to the speed limits. Any boat with an engine (including an outboard motor) also needs to be registered with the National Park Authority (NPA). For more information about what you can and cannot do on the Lakes, contact the **Lake Wardens** (☎ 015394 42753, ⓦ southlakeland.gov.uk) who enforce the restrictions on Windermere, or the NPA for the other lakes.

Rentals, lessons and courses

There are places to rent **rowing boats** on all the major lakes, with prices starting at around £10 per hour; boats usually aren't available in the winter. For something a bit more adventurous, seek out one of the region's **boating and watersports centres** (see below) – the outlets on Coniston Water and at Brockhole Visitor Centre are operated by the National Park Authority, and Brockhole is especially geared towards taster sessions for families and beginners.

Rental prices are broadly similar: canoes and kayaks (from £20–35 for a couple of hours), dinghies and sailing boats (from £60/half-day, £90/day), and small, self-drive motorboats and electric boats (from £75/half-day, £90/day). At most places you can expect to pay around £50 for a couple of hours' windsurfing instruction, or £100 a day, and around £80 for an introductory two-hour sailing lesson, or from £180 for a two-day sailing course.

CONISTON WATER

Coniston Boating Centre Lake Rd, Coniston ☎ 015394 41366, Ⓦ conistonboatingcentre.co.uk. Rent electric boats, dinghies, rowing boats, kayaks, Canadian canoes and paddleboards – there are also sailing lessons and two-day sailing courses available, and a lakeside café. Closed mid-Oct to Feb.

DERWENT WATER

Derwentwater Marina Portinscale, Keswick ☎ 01768772912, Ⓦ derwentwatermarina.co.uk. Sailing, kayaking, canoeing, windsurfing and paddleboarding – both rental and tuition.
Nichol End Marine Portinscale, Keswick ☎ 01768773082, Ⓦ nicholend.co.uk. Windsurfing, sailing, canoeing, kayaking, motorboats and rowing boat rental; there's a café here too.
Platty + Lodore Boat landings, Keswick ☎ 016973 71069, Ⓦ plattyplus.co.uk. Canoeing, kayaking, paddleboarding and sailing, rental and tuition, plus things like raft-building and dragon-boating. Closed Nov–Feb.

ULLSWATER

Glenridding Sailing Centre The Spit, Glenridding ☎ 017684 82541, Ⓦ glenriddingsailingcentre.co.uk. Canoes, kayaks and dinghies; introductory sailing lessons, plus weekend and five-day tuition courses. Closed Nov–March.
St Patrick's Landing Glenridding Pier ☎ 017684 82393, Ⓦ stpatricksboatlandings.co.uk. Rowing boats, motorboats and electric boats. Closed Nov–Feb.

WINDERMERE

Brockhole Visitor Centre Brockhole ☎ 015394 46601, Ⓦ brockhole.co.uk. Rowing boats, sit-on kayaks, Canadian canoes, paddleboards and motor boats for rent. Closed Oct–Easter.
Low Wood Bay A591, Windermere, 1 mile south of Ambleside ☎ 015394 39441, Ⓦ englishlakes.co.uk/low-wood-bay/watersports. Rowing boat rental plus sailing, kayaking and motorboat rental or tuition. It's also the only surviving waterski/wakeboard centre on Windermere (within the 10mph limits), suitable for beginners. Closed Nov–March.
Windermere Canoe & Kayak Ferry Nab Rd, Bowness-on-Windermere ☎ 015394 44451, Ⓦ windermerecanoekayak.com. Canoe, kayak and paddleboard rental; instruction also available.

Swimming

Swimming in the Lakes isn't as straightforward as you might think, since the presence of water craft and other restrictions put some areas off-limits for bathers – Loweswater, for example, might seem very tempting but it's classed as a reservoir so there's no swimming allowed. Even where **lake swimming** is permitted, it can be very dangerous, owing to the extremely cold water and steeply shelving sides – people do drown, even on the sunniest, calmest days, and you should always heed the warning signs.

If you think that coming to the Lakes and sticking to the local **swimming pools** (in Windermere, Keswick, Kendal and Ulverston) is a bit of a waste, there are a couple of other options – either take part in one of the mass swims, like those in Windermere each year (see page 55), or join the increasing number of people seeking out magical **wild swimming** spots in the Lakes. The Ⓦ wildswim.com website has some great suggestions.

Organized holidays, courses and activities

Once you've been out on the fells, climbed the mountains and splashed on the lakes, there's still plenty of scope for an eventful day out in what's billed by the tourism authority as "Adventure Capital UK". Local tourist offices have details of all sorts of outdoor activities, from horseriding and pony-trekking to fishing and go-karting, or check out ideas on the Cumbria Tourism website Ⓦ golakes.co.uk.

Individuals and small groups are always welcome, though bear in mind that some of the activity days are aimed at the corporate or group market, so you may have to fit in around larger groups. Some operators are particularly good for family days out and can tailor their activities to most ages and levels of experience.

Prices vary wildly, though you can expect to pay from around £25 for an hour's pony-trekking, £50 for a half-day's activity session, £60–90 for a full day's activity, and up to £200 for a day off-roading or a balloon flight over the Lakes.

Many of the same operators offer residential courses, while other businesses offer all-inclusive organized holidays based around various themes, from cycle touring and sketching to cooking and pottery. Note that the prices for organized holidays don't include transport to and from the Lakes, which you'll usually be expected to arrange for yourself.

ARTS AND CRAFTS

Gosforth Pottery ☎ 019467 25296, Ⓦ potterycourses.co.uk. Formal instruction in pottery (wheel-throwing, handwork and decoration), followed by working at your own pace, or opportunities for local rambling and exploring. The pottery – based in Gosforth, in the western Lakes – runs two-night weekend courses (£385) and one-week courses (£760) on a full-board basis, tuition and materials included.

Higham Hall ☎ 017687 76276, 🖥 highamhall.com. Residential and day-courses at an adult education centre on Bassenthwaite Lake. A huge variety of courses on offer, from local history or art appreciation talks (£20) to a three-night Winter Watercolours course (£328) or a four-night Jazz Masterclass (£485).

Rothay Manor Hotel ☎ 015394 33605, 🖥 rothaymanor.co.uk. Two- to five-night themed activity breaks at this agreeable Ambleside hotel include landscape photography, painting (oil and watercolours), music appreciation, gardening and antiques. Available mainly in winter, spring and autumn, and costing up to around £800 per person on a dinner, bed-and-breakfast basis.

CYCLE TOURS

Country Lanes ☎ 015394 44544, 🖥 countrylaneslakedistrict. co.uk. Bike-hire specialist also offering guided cycle rides with a Level 2 qualified mountain bike leader (£180 per day).

EQUESTRIAN CENTRES

Cumbrian Heavy Horses Baystone Bank Farm, Whicham Valley ☎ 01229 777764, 🖥 cumbrianheavyhorses.com. Lets you get up close and personal with Clydesdale, Shire and Ardennes horses, on anything from morning farm rides (£75/90mins) to longer (half- and full-day) beach and fell treks (from £145).

Holmescales Riding Centre Holmescales Farm, Old Hutton, near Kendal ☎ 01539 729388, 🖥 holmescalesridingcentre.co.uk. Riding instruction, pony-trekking and hacking at a 350-acre riding school with indoor and outdoor facilities.

Murthwaite Green Trekking Centre Silecroft ☎ 01229 770876, 🖥 murthwaitegreen.co.uk. Offers beach (£75/2hr, £160/day) and combined beach and fell (£150/day) rides from their beachside stables on the Cumbrian coast.

Park Foot Trekking Pooley Bridge, Howtown Rd, Ullswater ☎ 017684 86696, 🖥 ponytrekkingullswater.co.uk. One- or two-hour treks on the northeastern fells, longer trips on request. Closed Nov–March.

FISHING

Esthwaite Water Trout Fishery ☎ 015394 36541, 🖥 hawksheadtrout.com. Boat-fishing on Esthwaite Water, with tuition for beginners (free on certain days), plus equipment rental/ purchase, BBQ and picnic areas (to cook your own catch).
🖥 **lakedistrictfishing.co.uk**. A useful resource for all aspects of fishing in the Lakes, with links to courses, clubs and information.

OFF-ROAD

Kankku ☎ 015394 47414, 🖥 kankku.co.uk. Off-road 4x4 expeditions on rough and rocky terrain in Grizedale Forest, Tarn Hows, Langdale and Coniston, with an emphasis on promoting sound driving skills and techniques. Individuals and families welcome; two- to five-hour guided expeditions (from £45/person)

as well as self-drive day trips costing £225/vehicle (for up to four people). Based in Windermere; pick-ups available.

OUTDOOR ACTIVITIES

Country Adventures ☎ 01254 690691, 🖥 countryadventures. co.uk. A varied programme in the Lakes, from a day's scenic walking or cycling to sailing weekends, gorge-scrambling/climbing and multi-activity sessions. Many holidays are youth-hostel-based in places like Ambleside, Buttermere, Elterwater and Borrowdale.

Keswick Canoe and Bushcraft ☎ 07950 559623, 🖥 keswickcanoeandbushcraft.co.uk. Half- and full-day lake paddles and river trips, plus an overnight wilderness canoe journey – or release your inner Ray Mears on the bushcraft days and learn about shelter-building, fire-lighting and other wilderness skills. Usual locations are Derwent Water and Whinlatter, with children and families particularly welcome.

Lake District National Park Authority ☎ 0845 272 0004, 🖥 lakedistrict.gov.uk. A huge programme of day events throughout the year, mostly but not always free. Highlights include mountain-biking with the park rangers, falconry displays, dry-stone-walling and watersports weekends. Contact the events team or check the events diary on the website.

River Deep Mountain High ☎ 015395 28666, 🖥 riverdeepmountainhigh.co.uk. Multi-activity holidays (weekend/week-long, self-catering or fully inclusive) incorporating guided walking, canoeing and mountain-biking, plus activity days, river trips, raft-building, etc.

Rookin House Farm ☎ 017684 83561, 🖥 rookinhouse.co.uk. Huge range of activities, from archery to zip wires, via go-karting, quad-biking, horseriding, pony-trekking, archery and clay-pigeon shooting.

Summitreks ☎ 015394 41212, 🖥 summitreks.co.uk. Established adventure company offering a year-round programme of activities, from climbing to canoeing, aquasailing (abseiling down waterfalls) to canyoning (descending gorges). Children's multi-adventure days in the school holidays usually incorporate mountain-biking, gorge-scrambling and canoeing; adults can learn orienteering or join guided walks.

Youth Hostel Association 🖥 yha.org.uk. One of the biggest organizers of holidays in the Lakes, the YHA uses its hostels for weekend breaks or longer holidays, with the emphasis on hill-walking, rock-climbing, kayaking, mountain-biking and orienteering. Accommodation is in bunk rooms (twins and family rooms often available) and most hostels serve budget meals, though self-catering is also available.

PHOTOGRAPHY

Bill Birkett Photography Courses ☎ 015394 37420, 🖥 billbirkett.co.uk. The respected lakeland writer and photographer runs small-group photography courses throughout the year in Langdale and further afield, involving daily walks, mountain photography and technical assistance (bring your own camera and laptop). Either contact Bill directly or check his weekend courses available though Highpoint, 🖥 mountainguides.co.uk.

Travel essentials

Climate

England's northwest – and Cumbria in particular – has a not entirely undeserved reputation for being **wet**; it is, after all, called the "Lake" District, which suggests the presence of a certain amount of water. But it's also relatively mild for the UK along the Cumbrian coast and in the inland valleys, and annual temperatures, while hardly spectacular, are reasonably consistent. All of this of course seems laughable on one of those baking hot March days or during a June hailstorm, and the best advice for outdoors types is to pack for a season either side of the one you're actually visiting in. This goes double for anyone venturing onto the mountains, who should be prepared for dramatic changes in the weather at any time.

Costs and discounts

If you're counting the cost, there are plenty of ways to keep to a budget. Nearly all **accommodation** options – from simple B&Bs to luxury hotels – offer special off-season deals or discounts for longer stays. It always pays to ask when booking. Youth hostels and self-catering cottages – the Lakes has the most extensive network of either in the country – mean you can save money by cooking for yourself. **Children and senior citizens** get discounts on most forms of transport in the Lakes, and on entrance to the sights, museums and historic houses, and nearly every attraction has a discounted family ticket available. **YHA members** qualify for discounts and special deals on all sorts of activities and at attractions and retail outlets.

As far as **events and activities** go, many of the traditional festivals or local attractions are free, while the National Park Authority organizes free or low-cost activities, courses, walks and events throughout the year. And if you join the **National Trust** (membership ⓦ nationaltrust.org.uk) or **English Heritage** (ⓦ english-heritage.org.uk), you'll get free entry to all their sights and attractions.

Hospitals and pharmacies

For minor complaints, you'll find **pharmacies** in the main towns and villages (all listed in the Guide). These are open standard shop hours, though local newspapers and all pharmacy windows list the pharmacies that stay open an hour or two later on some nights of the week (usually on a rota basis).

HOSPITALS

There are accident, emergency and minor injury services at all the following hospitals.

Barrow-in-Furness Furness General Hospital, Dalton Lane (☎ 01229 870870, ⓦ uhmb.nhs.uk).

Carlisle Cumberland Infirmary, Newtown Rd (☎ 01228 523444, ⓦ ncic.nhs.uk).

Kendal Westmorland General Hospital, Burton Rd (☎ 01539 732288, ⓦ uhmb.nhs.uk).

Keswick Keswick Community Hospital, Crosthwaite Rd (☎ 01768 245678, ⓦ ncic.nhs.uk).

Penrith Penrith Community Hospital, Bridge Lane (☎ 01768 245555, ⓦ ncic.nhs.uk).

Whitehaven West Cumberland Hospital, Homewood Rd, Whitehaven (☎ 01946 693181, ⓦ ncic.nhs.uk).

Internet

You'll find that almost all accommodation providers, plus most cafés and restaurants, offer free wi-fi even if it can be a little patchy in places. Alternatively, you can always try the local library, which is usually free or inexpensive for short periods.

Laundry

Most youth hostels have washing and drying facilities of some sort, and B&B owners can sometimes be persuaded (or offer) to help out. There are **self-service laundries** in Keswick, Cockermouth, Windermere and other towns (though none in Grasmere or Coniston), with details included in the relevant Directory sections of this Guide.

Left luggage

Hotels, B&Bs and hostels will all mind guests' **luggage** for the day (or longer), but there's a distinct shortage of places where you can simply turn up in town and leave your bag or pack for the day. Tourist offices are understandably reluctant to help, given the number of visitors; the only railway stations in the Lakes (at Kendal and Windermere) don't have the facilities; and bus stations are usually little more than roadside stops. Usually, your best bet is to ask nicely at local shops, cafés or hotels – buying something first sometimes helps.

Mail

Each town and major village in the Lakes has a **post office** (branch finder on ⓦ postoffice.co.uk). Normal opening hours are Monday to Friday from 9am to 5.30pm and Saturday from 9am to 12.30pm, though

ROUGH GUIDES TRAVEL INSURANCE

Rough Guides has teamed up with WorldNomads.com to offer great travel insurance deals. Policies are available to residents of over 150 countries, with cover for a wide range of adventure sports, 24hr emergency assistance, high levels of medical and evacuation cover and a stream of travel safety information. Roughguides.com users can take advantage of their policies online 24/7, from anywhere in the world – even if you're already travelling. And since plans often change when you're on the road, you can extend your policy and even claim online. Roughguides.com users who buy travel insurance with WorldNomads.com can also leave a positive footprint and donate to a community development project. For more information, go to ⓦroughguides.com/travel-insurance.

smaller offices may have restricted hours. It's worth noting that not all post offices are stand-alone businesses – the smaller ones, especially, are often housed in village stores.

Maps

The best general map of the National Park area is the Ordnance Survey (ⓦordnancesurvey.co.uk; OS) Travel Map, Tour no. 3 (1:110,000), with hill shading and principal footpaths illustrated. For more detail of Cumbria as a whole (including Carlisle and the coast), you'll need the (1:50,000) **OS Landranger** series of maps (nos. 85, 89, 90, 96 and 97).

Essential for hikers are the orange (1:25,000) **OS Explorer** series – four maps (nos. 4, 5, 6 and 7) which cover the whole Lake District National Park. There are rugged, plastic-coated versions of these available too. Some prefer the **Harvey Superwalker** (ⓦharveymaps.co.uk) series of four waterproof maps (also 1:25,000) covering north, east, west and southeast Lakeland. There's also a good, compact, ring-bound Harvey Lake District **National Park Atlas** (1:40,000), useful for cyclists and general walkers, as well as detailed (1:40,000) fold-out Harvey **route maps** for the Cumbria Way, Dales Way and Coast-to-Coast long-distance paths that all pass through the Lake District.

Most bookshops, outdoors stores and tourist information offices sell the full range of maps, as well as various **local walk guides and leaflets**. For a waterproof, foldaway, stick-in-your-pocket walking guide and map, you can't do better than the very cute HandiHike range of eighteen walking guides with clear OS mapping, covering sixty of the best Lake District walks, from family strolls to high peaks; although the company no longer operates, you should still be able to obtain these maps. Other recommended series include the packs of Lakeland Leisure Walks (five assorted walks in each of the major areas), local fell expert Paul Buttle's various walking

booklets and the National Park Authority's *Walks in the Countryside* leaflets.

Markets

Local **markets** are held on: Monday, Cockermouth and Kendal; Tuesday, Broughton-in-Furness and Penrith; Wednesday, Ambleside and Kendal; Thursday, Ulverston and Keswick; Saturday, Kendal, Keswick, Penrith and Ulverston.

The best regional **farmers' market** is at Orton in the Eden Valley (ⓦortonfarmers.co.uk), two miles off the M6 (junction 38; 17 miles north of Kendal), held on the second Saturday of the month. The Orton farmers are also at Pooley Bridge in the summer (April–Sept last Sun) and Rheged Visitor Centre in the winter (Oct–March last Sun). But it's a growing scene and there are also farmers' markets at Carlisle (first Fri of the month), Cartmel (Feb–Dec third Fri), Keswick (second Thurs, plus others), Ulverston (third Sat), Kendal (last Fri), Whitehaven (second Sat), Cockermouth (first Sat) and Penrith (March–Dec third Tues).

Media

Two **daily papers** carve up the region between them: *The Mail* (southern Cumbria; ⓦnwemail.co.uk) and the *News and Star* (northern Cumbria; ⓦnewsandstar. co.uk). Otherwise, there are weekly papers for each region: the *Westmorland Gazette* (ⓦthewestmorlandgazette.co.uk), which covers eastern Cumbria and the southern and central Lakes; the *Cumberland & Westmorland Herald* (Penrith, Keswick and eastern Cumbria; ⓦcwherald.com); the *Keswick Reminder* (covering just Keswick; ⓦkeswickreminder.co.uk).

Magazines include *Cumbria* (ⓦcumbriamagazine. co.uk), a small-format monthly magazine, and the bigger, glossier *Cumbria Life* (ⓦcumbrialife.co.uk), both of which concentrate on the history, culture and social and natural fabric of the Lakes. *Lakeland Walker* (ⓦlakeland-walker.com), published six times

PUBLIC AND BANK HOLIDAYS

January 1
Good Friday (late March or early April)
Easter Monday (late March or early April)
First Monday in May
Last Monday in May
Last Monday in Aug
December 25
December 26
Note that if January 1, or Dec 25 or 26 falls on a Saturday or Sunday, the next weekday becomes a public holiday.

a year, is a chatty periodical aimed at hikers and lakeland lovers, featuring walks, news, reviews and equipment-testing.

LOCAL RADIO STATIONS

The Bay Ⓦ thebay.co.uk; North 96.9 FM; Lakes/South 102.3 FM; Cumbria 103.2 FM.
BBC Radio Cumbria Ⓦ bbc.co.uk/radiocumbria; North Cumbria 95.6 FM; West Cumbria 104.1 FM; South Cumbria 96.1 FM.
Lakeland Radio Ⓦ lakelandradio.co.uk; South Lakes area 100.1/100.8 FM.

Money

Normal **banking hours** are Monday to Friday from 9.30am to 3.30pm, with some branches in the major towns open on Saturday morning too. Conversely, in smaller lakeland villages, bank branches sometimes only open a couple of days a week. Most settlements in the Lakes have at least one branch of the major banks with an **ATM**, though more are closing year-on-year, while stand-alone ATMs are found in most village shops and petrol stations; some of these, however, charge a fee for withdrawing cash with your card. You can exchange foreign currency at major post offices.

Credit cards are widely accepted in shops, hotels, restaurants and service stations, but don't count on being able to use plastic in B&Bs, guesthouses, and some pubs and cafés: we indicate all those that don't accept credit cards in the Guide. Be aware, however – even those that do accept credit cards often don't accept American Express.

Opening hours and public holidays

Full opening hours are given in the Guide for sights, tourist offices, restaurants, bars and shops. **Shops and businesses** follow the standard pattern for the UK (Monday to Saturday 9am to 5.30pm or 6pm), though you'll find some village stores and local shops open an hour or so earlier or later than these times. **Early closing day** (when the shops shut for the afternoon) is still observed in some towns and villages, usually on Thursday.

Phones

Mobile phone coverage is generally pretty good around the Lakes. However, the nature of the terrain means you sometimes can't get a signal (though you're usually all right in the main towns and villages), which is one reason why it's not recommended that hikers rely solely on their phones – rather than their navigational skills – to get them out of trouble on the fells. Although there are now fewer of them, you will find the occasional public **telephone boxes** throughout the Lake District, even in isolated rural areas, and most take phonecards and credit cards.

Police and emergencies

Dial ☎ 999 for all emergencies: in relevant circumstances ask for Mountain Rescue. If you want to speak to the police but it's not an emergency, call ☎ 101. The addresses of local police stations are given in the relevant town listings in this Guide – most are only open for limited weekday hours. There's more information about stations and services at Ⓦ cumbria.police.uk.

Shopping

There's a fantastic range of local **crafts**, workshops and galleries in Cumbria, from cottage candle-makers to furniture carvers, chutney producers to ceramics studios. We've picked out some highlights in the Guide, whether it's artisan food producers at Staveley or Cartmel, art and antiques at Low Newton's Yew Tree Barn, carved slate at Honister or the changing exhibitions of regional crafts on show at Rheged. The website Ⓦ madeincumbria.co.uk is a great resource, dedicated to Cumbrian crafts, gifts and food, with information and links to craftspeople and local suppliers throughout the region. The website also lists outlets where their recommended products are sold.

Tourist information

Both Cumbria Tourism and the Lake District National Park Authority (NPA) have very useful **websites** for visitors, while the Cumbria County Council website is the place to go for local community, transport, leisure and business information, with handy links to other sites.

In the Lake District itself, a number of visitor information offices provide help on the ground – all are listed in the Guide – with the main **National Park Visitor Centre** situated at Brockhole on Windermere (see below). The other offices are funded and run by the tourist board and the NPA, or by local councils and volunteers: opening hours vary, though in the summer most of the main offices are open daily from 10am to 6pm, sometimes an hour earlier in the morning and an hour later in the evening. Opening hours are reduced in winter and, in some offices, may be restricted to weekends only (usually Fri to Sun) from 10am to 4pm. Local budgetary constraints also sometimes restrict hours and services, but at each office, when it's open, you'll be able to book accommodation, check on local weather conditions and buy guides and maps.

USEFUL CONTACTS

Cumbria County Council The Courts, Carlisle, Cumbria, CA3 8NA (🕸 cumbria.gov.uk).

Cumbria Tourism Windermere Rd, Staveley, Kendal, Cumbria, LA8 9PL (☎ 01539 822222, 🕸 golakes.co.uk).

Lake District National Park Authority Murley Moss, Oxenholme Rd, Kendal, Cumbria, LA9 7RL (☎ 01539 724555); for events and visitor information contact the NPA at Brockhole, Windermere, Cumbria, LA23 1LJ (☎ 015394 46601, 🕸 lakedistrict.gov.uk).

Western Lake District Tourism Partnership ☎ 01539 822222, 🕸 western-lakedistrict.co.uk.

Windermere

BOATS FOR HIRE ON WINDERMERE

1 Windermere

England's largest and most famous lake rarely fails to impress. The rocky inlets, secluded bays, grassy banks and wooded heights of Windermere form the very core of most people's image of the Lake District. And on bitingly cold winter days, or in the dappled spring and autumn sun, there are few finer places in England to soak up the scenery. The three most popular destinations – the small towns of Windermere, Bowness and Ambleside – group together on its northeast shore, and contain the bulk of the visitor facilities and a wide range of accommodation. It's these places, in fact, that many people first think of when they consider the Lakes. However, the southern and western reaches of the lake are still remarkably underdeveloped, and their small hamlets, rustic attractions, waterside walks and hilltop scrambles provide some of the most inviting destinations in the southern Lakes.

Most people approaching the central lakes and fells from the south funnel through **Windermere town**, getting their first glimpse of the lake at nearby **Bowness** – formerly a medieval lakeside village, though now the National Park's largest resort and boating centre. This also has the pick of the local cultural attractions, most notably the Arts and Crafts mansion of **Blackwell** to the south.

William Wordsworth himself thought that "None of the other Lakes unfold so many fresh beauties" and it makes sense to get out on the water as soon as possible. The cruise-boat ride south from Bowness provides access to **Lakeside** and its aquarium, and to the picnic lawns of **Fell Foot Park**, while combined boat-and-train tickets are available for steam trips on the **Lakeside & Haverthwaite Railway**. North of Windermere town there are landings at **Brockhole** – whose magnificent gardens form the backdrop for the National Park's Lake District Visitor Centre – and at Wray, where lake and fells are overlooked on the far shore by the wonderfully sited National Trust property of **Wray Castle**. At the head of the lake, meanwhile, Waterhead is the pier for nearby **Ambleside**, a handily sited hiking and touring base that's also the busiest settlement on Windermere.

Away from the lake, **Troutbeck Bridge** sits at the mouth of a gentle valley running north between Windermere and Ambleside, where the quiet hamlet of **Troutbeck** and **Townend** house are appealing targets. There's good walking from here, as there is from the neighbouring **Kentmere** Valley, where the River Kent tumbles down through the old mill village of **Staveley**. This is only four miles east of the hubbub at Windermere but it seems like a world apart up on the fell tops or in the even quieter reaches of neighbouring **Longsleddale**.

Windermere town

The completion of the railway from Kendal in 1847 changed the face of Windermere for ever, providing direct access to the lake for Victorian day-trippers and holiday-makers. The hillside hamlet of Birthwaite, lying a good mile from the water, was entirely subsumed within a newly created town, soon named **Windermere** to emphasize the link with the lake itself. Not everyone welcomed the development. William Wordsworth, ever more conservative in his old age, feared the effects of

WRAY CASTLE

Highlights

❶ The view from Orrest Head The summit of Orrest Head, a short climb from Windermere town, provides stunning views up and down the lake. See page 51

❷ Brockhole The National Park HQ, set in acres of gardens, makes a great family day out. See page 61

❸ Blackwell Stunning Arts and Crafts house overlooking Windermere, with a handcrafted interior of immense style. See page 62

❹ Lakes Aquarium Dodge the diving ducks in the underwater tunnel at the entertaining Lakes Aquarium. See page 65

❺ Armitt Library and Museum, Ambleside The lowdown on lakeland literary and artistic life – from the writings of John Ruskin to watercolours by Beatrix Potter. See page 71

❻ Wray Castle Stunning views, and a family-friendly experience at the magnificent mock-Gothic mansion on the shores of Windermere. See page 72

❼ A night out in Ambleside A romantic dinner at *Lucy's*, or a meal, a movie or a jazz gig at *Zeffirelli's* – Ambleside is the best place in the Lakes for a big night out. See page 78

HIGHLIGHTS ARE MARKED ON THE MAP ON PAGE 50

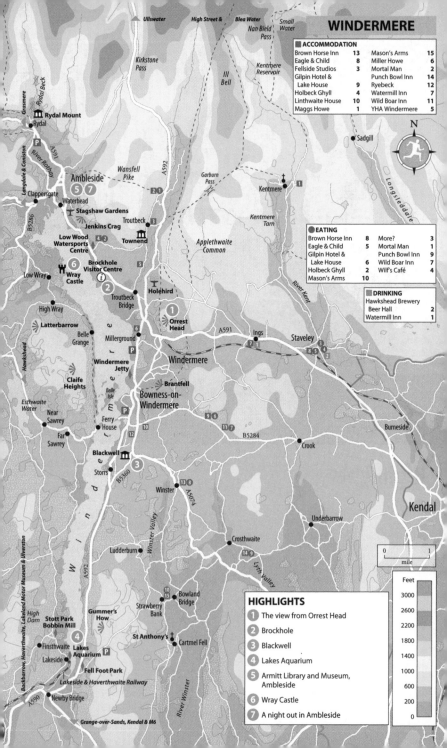

WINDERMERE

ACCOMMODATION

Brown Horse Inn	13	Mason's Arms	15
Eagle & Child	8	Miller Howe	6
Fellside Studios	3	Mortal Man	2
Gilpin Hotel &		Punch Bowl Inn	14
Lake House	9	Ryebeck	12
Holbeck Ghyll	4	Watermill Inn	7
Linthwaite House	10	Wild Boar Inn	11
Maggs Howe	1	YHA Windermere	5

EATING

Brown Horse Inn	8	More?	3
Eagle & Child	5	Mortal Man	1
Gilpin Hotel &		Punch Bowl Inn	9
Lake House	6	Wild Boar Inn	7
Holbeck Ghyll	2	Wilf's Café	4
Mason's Arms	10		

DRINKING

Hawkshead Brewery	
Beer Hall	2
Watermill Inn	1

HIGHLIGHTS

1. The view from Orrest Head
2. Brockhole
3. Blackwell
4. Lakes Aquarium
5. Armitt Library and Museum, Ambleside
6. Wray Castle
7. A night out in Ambleside

Feet	
3000	
2600	
2200	
1800	
1400	
1000	
600	
200	
0	

0   mile   1

1

the railway (while conveniently forgetting that his own *Guide to the Lakes* had done much to popularize the district in the first place). The poet attempted to keep out the hordes by means of a sonnet – "Is then no nook of English ground secure from rash assault?" – and by penning rambling broadsides which must have sorely tested the patience of their recipient, the editor of the *Morning Post*. Wordsworth's defence of the "picturesque" had reason behind it, and he can hardly be said to have been wrong in fearing the "railway inundations [of an] Advance of the Ten Thousand". But (like most gentlemen of his day) his real fear was that of the great unwashed, the "imperfectly educated", sullying his back yard with their "wrestling matches, horse and boat races … pot houses and beer shops".

Most of the villas and guesthouses built for the Victorians still stand, and Windermere town remains the **transport hub** for the southern and central Lakes, but there's precious little else to keep you in the slate-grey streets. Instead, all the traffic pours a mile downhill to its older twin town, lakeside Bowness (see page 55), and the only reason for not doing the same is to take time to climb the heights of **Orrest Head** (784ft), just to the north of Windermere town.

Orrest Head

An easy 20min walk from Windermere town: the signposted path begins just to the left of the *Windermere Hotel* on the A591, just up from the train station

The bare summit of **Orrest Head** gives a famous 360° panorama, sweeping from the Yorkshire fells to Morecambe Bay, the Langdale Pikes to Troutbeck Valley. This was the very first lakeland climb made by a young Alfred Wainwright (see page 227), on his earliest visit to the Lake District in 1930 – one that, in his own words, cast a spell that changed his life. Ten minutes up the path, in shaded Elleray Wood, you'll pass the cottage-studio of **blacksmith** Steve Hicks (⊚ hicksironcraft.co.uk), where on most days you can grab a cup of tea and browse his creative, handcrafted ironwork.

ARRIVAL AND DEPARTURE   **WINDERMERE TOWN**

BY CAR
The A591 between Kendal and Ambleside runs across the northern side of town, past the train station. There's a car park inside the train station yard and another down in the town on Broad St by the library; otherwise on-street parking is usually limited to 30min.

BY BUS
All bus services stop outside the train station; bus #599 runs year-round down to the lake at Bowness. A one-day Central Lakes Dayrider ticket (buy from the driver; £8.50, family £23.50) gives unlimited travel on any service running between Windermere/Bowness and Grasmere/Coniston/Langdale, while the Bus & Boat ticket (from £12.90) combines the #599 bus service with a Windermere lake cruise.
Bus #505 "Coniston Rambler" to: Brockhole (7min); Ambleside (15min); Hawkshead (35min); Coniston (51min). Service operates Easter–Oct roughly hourly.
Bus #508 "Kirkstone Rambler" to: Troutbeck *Queen's Head* (12min); Kirkstone Pass (25min); Brothers Water

(40min); Patterdale (47min); Glenridding (52min); Pooley Bridge (1hr 14min); Penrith (1hr 32min). Service operates March–Oct 5–7 daily, Nov–Feb Sat, Sun & bank holidays only.
Bus #555 to: Brockhole (7min); Waterhead (12min); Ambleside (15min); Rydal (26min); Grasmere (34min); Keswick (1hr 5min); also to Staveley (9min) and Kendal (20min). Service operates hourly.
Bus #599 to: Bowness (10min); also to Troutbeck Bridge (4min); Brockhole (7min); Waterhead (12min); Ambleside (15min); Rydal (26min); Dove Cottage (30min); Grasmere (34min). Service operates Easter–Oct daily every 20–30min; Nov–Easter (only to Bowness or Ambleside) Mon–Sat hourly.

BY TRAIN
Windermere is as far into the Lakes as you can get by train, on the branch line from Oxenholme, via Kendal. Windermere train station is just off the main A591, on Station Precinct.
Destinations Kendal (hourly; 14min); Oxenholme (hourly; 19min), for onward services to Lancaster, Preston and Manchester, or to Penrith and Carlisle; Staveley (hourly; 5min).

1

GETTING AROUND

By bike Country Lanes, The Railway Station (Easter–Oct daily 9am–5pm; Nov–Easter 10am–4pm most days but call in advance; ☎015394 44544, ⓦcountrylaneslakedistrict. co.uk). Bikes from £22–30/day, plus tandems, tag-alongs and trailers; helmet, lock, maps and routes provided.

By taxi Windermere Taxis (☎015394 44144).

INFORMATION AND TOURS

Tourist office Windermere TIC, Victoria St (daily: April–Oct 8.30am–5.30pm; Nov–March 9am–4.30pm; ☎015394 46499, ⓦwindermereinfo.co.uk), 100 yards from the train station, opposite NatWest bank.

Tours Mountain Goat, near the tourist office on Victoria St (☎015394 45161, ⓦmountain-goat.com), offers minibus tours (from £35 for half a day) that get off the beaten track, with daily departures from Windermere, plus pick-ups in Bowness, Grasmere and Ambleside. There's also Lakes Supertours, operating from the *Lakes Lodge*, 1 High St (☎015394 42751, ⓦlakes-supertours.com), which has a variety of half- and full-day tours – lakes and mountains

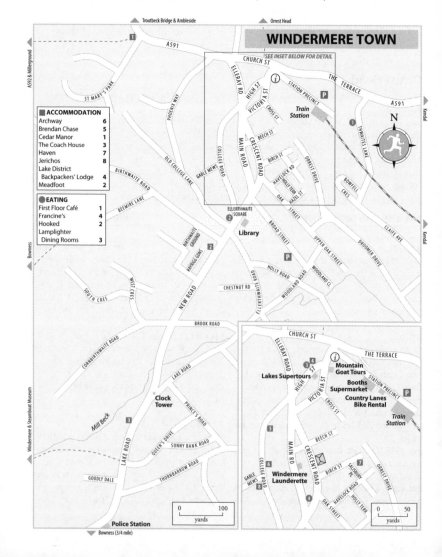

ACCOMMODATION

Archway	6
Brendan Chase	5
Cedar Manor	1
The Coach House	3
Haven	7
Jerichos	8
Lake District Backpackers' Lodge	4
Meadfoot	2

EATING

First Floor Café	1
Francine's	4
Hooked	2
Lamplighter Dining Rooms	3

or literary themes – with some cruises and house entrance fees included. Alternatively, Kankku, next to Mountain Goat on Victoria St (☎ 015394 47414, ⓦ kankku.co.uk) organizes guided self-drive 4x4 safaris from £45/person.

ACCOMMODATION

SEE MAPS PAGES 50 AND 52

Good places to look for **B&Bs** are on High Street and neighbouring Victoria Street, with other concentrations on College Road and Oak and Broad streets. At the bottom of town, halfway to Bowness, Lake Road and its offshoots have a line of mid-range **guesthouses** and hotels, but these are a fair walk (or bus ride) from either Bowness or Windermere. Further out still is a selection of very grand **country-house hotels**, which make the most of their secluded locations, lake views and extensive grounds. Although there's a backpackers' hostel in Windermere itself, the nearest YHA youth hostel is at Troutbeck (see page 53).

WINDERMERE

★ **Archway** 13 College Rd, LA23 1BU ☎ 015394 45613, ⓦ archwayguesthouse.co.uk. A great B&B with four trim rooms (two double, two twin) in a homely slate-built Victorian house. You get the best light, and (distant) mountain views, in the two rooms at the front – in "Coniston" you can also wallow in a sparkling bathroom with freestanding tub and walk-in rain shower. The two rear-facing rooms are slightly smaller and slightly cheaper. You know you're in good hands when you get home-made bedside biscuits, and the *Archway* also serves a splendid breakfast – options include blueberry pancakes, home-made granola, muesli and yoghurt, and, of course, the traditional full English. Parking. **£80**

Brendan Chase 1 College Rd, LA23 1BU ☎ 015394 45638, ⓦ brendanchase.co.uk. A popular place with backpackers and overseas travellers, who get a warm welcome and a good breakfast. There are eight reasonably priced rooms (some en suite), and if you can fill the spacious family/group rooms, which can sleep up to five, you'll bring the price down to around £30/person a night. Parking is available and bikes can be stored in the basement of the house. **£60**

Cedar Manor Ambleside Rd, LA23 1AX ☎ 015394 43192, ⓦ cedarmanor.co.uk. This restored Victorian gentleman's holiday residence goes for a contemporary country look, mixing soft, soothing colours, elegant fabrics and handmade wooden furniture with vintage wallpaper, burnished panelling and original stained glass. The separate duplex coach-house suite (from £295) is magnificent, featuring a designer bathroom with mood lighting and a great sense of style. With mature gardens and just a short stroll from the lake, it all makes for a quiet retreat, despite being just off the main road. Parking. **£175**

★ **The Coach House** Lake Rd, LA23 2EQ ☎ 015394 44494, ⓦ coachhousewindermere.co.uk. Comfort and contemporary design join hands in this stylish conversion of a Victorian coach house. Five classy double rooms with wrought-iron beds, gleaming bathrooms and elegant touches are complemented by a relaxed breakfast with the morning papers and the use of a local leisure club. Parking. **£80**

Haven 10 Birch St, LA23 1EG ☎ 015394 88583, ⓦ the havenwindermere.co.uk. Big windows let the light into this handsomely refurbished Victorian house, with the choice of four comfortably appointed rooms. Walkers are welcome to use the books, maps and drying facilities. Parking. **£80**

★ **Jerichos** College Rd, LA23 1BX ☎ 015394 42522, ⓦ jerichos.co.uk. Chris and Jo Blaydes' acclaimed guesthouse is known as much for their fantastic breakfast as breakfasts for the smart accommodation. The building's a refit of the old Victorian *Waverley Temperance Hotel*, and the ten resulting rooms (eight doubles and two singles) are modish but unpretentious, keeping the original cornicing and sash windows, for example, but adding black leather beds, designer fabrics, iPod docks and gleaming boutique bathrooms. Rooms rated deluxe (add another £15) are slightly bigger and a little more desirable – with maybe a fell view, a full bath as well as shower, or a king-sized bed. Parking. Closed Dec (except last week) & Jan. **£106**

Lake District Backpackers' Lodge High St, LA23 1AF ☎ 015394 46374, ⓦ lakedistrictbackpackers.co.uk. Nineteen beds in small dorms, a laidback atmosphere and good facilities, including kitchen with washing machine, satellite TV, bike storage and lockers. The two four-bed rooms are mixed dorms, but there's a six-bed women-only dorm, plus a double (two beds) and a three-bed room available for exclusive use. It's undoubtedly a squeeze when full, but the price includes breakfast (cereal, tea/coffee and toast), and there's information about local tours and work opportunities. No credit cards. Dorms **£16.95**, double **£39**

Meadfoot New Rd, LA23 2LA ☎ 015394 42610, ⓦ mead foot-guesthouse.co.uk. One of the rooms at this friendly family villa opens directly onto the secluded garden, while the others overlook it – as does the dining room and deck where you take breakfast. It makes for a comfortable touring base, with five pine-furnished rooms (two with carved four-posters), plus patio and summerhouse. Parking. **£88**

AROUND WINDERMERE

Holbeck Ghyll Holbeck Lane (off A591), LA23 1LU, 3 miles north of Windermere ☎ 015394 32375, ⓦ holbeck ghyll.com. One of the stalwarts of the local country-house hotel scene, with elegantly presented rooms either in the main house (once a hunting lodge for the Earl of Lonsdale) or in detached lodges, suites and cottages in the grounds. Decor and furnishings vary from room to room – country-house antique to a splash of bespoke designer style –

1

and not all have lake views (those that do start at £300, midweek). Other choices to ponder include amenities like spa baths, panoramic balconies and private gardens. There are also seven acres of gardens and woodland, plus a gym and spa, while the refined restaurant (see below) is one of *the* Lake District dining destinations – the inclusive D, B&B packages (see page 26) are the way to go. Parking. £275

★ **Miller Howe** Rayrigg Rd (A592), LA23 1EY, 0.5 mile west of Windermere ☎015394 42536,

Ⓦmillerhowe.com. This gorgeous Edwardian house, high above Windermere, has long been a byword for lakeland indulgence. As well as Arts and Crafts furniture and plump armchairs in fire-warmed lounges, there's also an up-to-the-minute sheen throughout and lake views to die for – from classy rooms with their own balconies, or from the bird's-eye terraces and landscaped gardens. Room rates include a rather lavish breakfast. Closed Jan. Parking. £225

EATING

SEE MAPS PAGES 50 AND 52

You don't need to make the trek down to Bowness to get a good meal – there are plenty of **cafés and restaurants** in Windermere, as well as more formal dining in the nearby country-house hotels of *Holbeck Ghyll* and *Miller Howe* (see above). Both of these are open to non-residents – and both, incidentally, are great places for a slap-up afternoon tea with a lake view (around £27). The main **supermarket** is Booths, by the train station, which also has its own café.

First Floor Café Lakeland Ltd, Alexandra Buildings, LA23 1BQ, behind the train station ☎015394 47116, Ⓦ1stfloorcafe.co.uk. Occupying the first-floor gallery of the kitchen/home-furnishings/design store, this superior café's breakfasts, brunches and lunches keep hungry shoppers happy. There are always filled baguettes, tortilla wraps, soups, meat and cheese platters, salads, cakes and puddings, alongside a selection of unusual and exciting dishes like cod tacos, and honey mustard ham hock. Most dishes £6.50–10. Mon–Fri 9am–5.30pm, Sat 9am–5pm, Sun 10.30am–4pm.

Francine's 27 Main Rd, LA23 1DX ☎015394 44088, Ⓦfrancinesrestaurantwindermere.co.uk. During the day you can drop into this easy-going café-restaurant for anything from a *pain au chocolat* to a big bowl of mussels. Dinner sees the lights dimmed for a wide-ranging continental menu of such dishes as confit duck with prune terrine or seared turbot fillet with dauphinoise potatoes, with most mains around £17. Café Tues–Sun 10am–2.30pm, restaurant Tues–Sun 6–11pm.

★ **Holbeck Ghyll** Holbeck Lane (off A591), LA23 1LU, 3 miles north of Windermere ☎015394 32375, Ⓦholbeckghyll.com. The restaurant at *Holbeck Ghyll*, under chef William DiMartino, remains one of the most consistently

excellent places in the region for a fab special-occasion meal, whether leisurely lunch or romantic dinner. We're talking lake views from an elegant oak-panelled dining room, a smartish dress code and artfully presented food that puts a refined spin on local flavours and ingredients, from Cartmel smoked salmon with pickled vegetables to Cumbrian lamb with lentils, swede purée and haggis beignets. Four-course Gourmet menu (£72) and an eight-course tasting menu (£92, plus another £50 for the accompanying fine wines; available evenings only), plus a three-course Sunday lunch menu (£35). Reservations essential. Daily 6.30–9.30pm, plus Fri & Sat noon–1.30pm & Sun noon–2pm.

★ **Hooked** Ellerthwaite Square, LA23 1BU ☎015394 48443, Ⓦhookedwindermere.co.uk. Top quality fish is all that's served at *Hooked*, with the catch of the day delivered straight from the Fleetwood boats and dished up in an upbeat style, brimming with Mediterranean and Asian flavours. Whitebait with a smoked paprika mayo is a typical starter and then, depending on availability, expect anything from hake with chorizo, fava beans and garlic to Thai-style sea bass (starters £6–8, mains £22). Reservations advised. Daily 5.30–9pm.

Lamplighter Dining Rooms High St, LA213 1AF ☎015394 43547, Ⓦlamplighterdiningrooms.com. Very popular local choice for bistro meals, served in the hotel's bar-cum-dining room. Expect classics (fish and chips, Lancashire beef suet pudding) plus a bit of sophistication (rump of Lakeland lamb, grilled salmon), all with locally sourced products, and in big portions (most dishes £15–20). There's also a cracking carve-your-own three-course Sun lunch (£16.95). April–Oct Mon–Thurs 4–9pm, Fri 4–9.30pm, Sat noon–9.30pm, Sun noon–9pm; check website for off-season hours.

DIRECTORY

Banks NatWest (High St) and Barclays (Crescent Rd) have ATMs, and there's an ATM outside Booths supermarket by the station.

Hospital The nearest hospital is in Kendal: Westmorland General Hospital, Burton Rd (☎01539 732288, Ⓦuhmb.nhs.uk).

Laundry Windermere Launderette, 19 Main Rd (Mon & Thurs 8.30am–5pm, Tues, Wed & Fri 8.30am–5.30pm, Sat

9am–5pm; ☎015394 42326).

Pharmacy Boots, 10–12 Crescent Rd (Mon–Sat 9am–5.30pm; ☎015394 43093); David Carter, 16 Crescent Rd (Mon–Fri 9am–1pm & 2–6pm; ☎015394 43417).

Police station Lake Rd, just beyond the war memorial (☎101, Ⓦcumbria.police.uk).

Post office 21 Crescent Rd Mon–Sat 9am–5.30pm.

Bowness and the lake

Bowness-on-Windermere – to give it its full name – is undoubtedly the more attractive of the two Windermere settlements, spilling back from its lakeside piers in a series of terraces lined with guesthouses and hotels. Set back from the thumbprint indent of Bowness Bay, a village has existed here since at least the fifteenth century and a ferry service across the lake for almost as long. On a busy summer's day, crowds swirl around the trinket shops, cafés, ice-cream stalls and lakeside seats, but you can easily escape onto the lake or into the hills, and there are several scattered attractions around town to fill a rainy day. Come the evening, when the human tide has subsided and the light fades over the wooden jetties and stone buildings, a promenade around Bowness Bay can even conjure visions of the Italian Lakes.

St Martin's church

Lake Rd, LA23 3DF • Apr–Sept daily 10.30am–3pm, call at other times; churchyard always open • ☎ 015394 44176, ⓦ stmartin.org.uk

What's left of the oldest part of Bowness survives in the few narrow lanes around **St Martin's church**, consecrated in 1483. The church is notable for its stained glass, particularly that in the east window, now very difficult to make out but sporting the fifteenth-century arms of John Washington, a distant ancestor of first American president George Washington. Outside in the churchyard is the grave of one Rasselas Belfield (d. 1822), "a native of Abyssinia" who was born a slave – and found himself shipped to England – but as a free man became servant to the Windermere gentry.

The World of Beatrix Potter

Old Laundry, Crag Brow, LA23 3BX • Daily 10am–4.30pm; closed last two weeks in Jan • £7.95, family ticket £22, all-year family Freedom Pass £35 • ☎ 015394 88444, ⓦ www.hop-skip-jump.com

Most tourists bypass the church and everything else in Bowness bar the lake for the chance to visit **The World of Beatrix Potter**, a major attraction devoted to the iconic children's author. It's unfair to be judgemental – you either like Beatrix Potter or you don't – but it is safe to say that the displays here find more favour with children than the more formal Potter attractions at Hill Top and Hawkshead. Heralded by a 15ft-high bronze outdoor sculpture symbolizing the Potter oeuvre, inside all 23 tales are featured in 3D form (complete with sounds and smells), and there are virtual walks to the places that inspired the author, plus interactive children's attractions, a gift shop, a garden and a themed tea room.

COOL SWIMMINGS

It might be cold, but it's also cool – swimming in Windermere, that is, now firmly entrenched as part of England's wild swim circuit (see ⓦ outdoorswimmingsociety.com). The British Long-Distance Swimming Association (ⓦ bldsa.org.uk) organizes two official **Windermere swims** every September – a short dash across the lake (first Thurs of the month) and the far more serious ten-mile, length-of-the-lake endurance route (first Sat), which people use as training for the iconic English cross-Channel swim. There's more of a carnival air to the weekend-long, mass-participation **Great North Swim** (ⓦ greatrun.org/great-swim), in June, when thousands plunge in for a series of races ranging from half-a-mile all the way up to 10k. It's the UK's biggest outdoor swim and, like the equivalent road marathons, attracts a mix of charity swimmers and medal-winners – you need to register well in advance to take part.

1

Windermere Jetty

Rayrigg Rd, LA23 1BN • Daily: March–Oct 10am–5pm; Nov–Feb 10am–4pm; closed two weeks mid-Jan • £9, family ticket £27 • ☎ 01539 637940, ⓦ windermerejetty.org

A fifteen-minute walk north of Bowness centre is the shiny new **Windermere Jetty (Museum of Boats, Steam and Stories),** formerly the Steamboat Museum. The lakeside here has long been the setting for the museum's peerless collection of Victorian and Edwardian steam launches, yachts and historic water craft, among them the 1850 *SL Dolly*, claimed to be the world's oldest mechanically driven boat, *Margaret*, the world's oldest yacht, and exhibits relating to children's author Arthur Ransome and his *Swallows and Amazons* stories (notably Ransome's own boat, *Coch-y-Bondhu*, which became the boat *Scarab* in *The Picts and the Martyrs*). The museum also hosts various

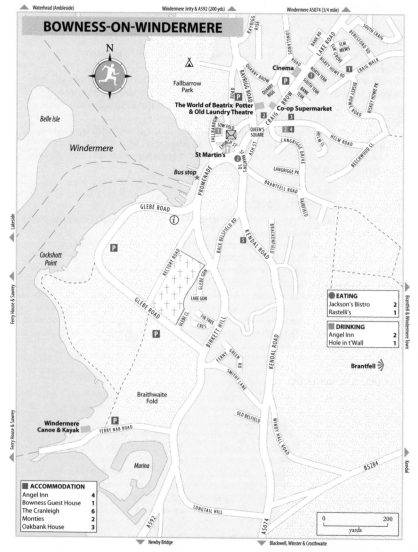

exhibitions, there's a model boating pond (bring your own boat if you've got one), while, for another £9, you can hop aboard the heritage boat Osprey for a forty-five minute jolly around the lake.

1

The lake

All the attractions in Bowness come second-best to a boat trip on **Windermere** itself – the heavyweight of Lake District lakes, at ten and a half miles long, a mile wide in parts and a shade over 200ft deep. As so often in these parts, the name derives from the Norse ("Vinandr's Lake") and since "mere" means lake, references to "Lake Windermere" are tautologous. The views from the water tend towards the magnificent: north to the central fells, or south along a wooded shoreline that is mostly under the protection of the National Trust. The seasons are reflected in the changing colours and tree cover around the lake. Autumn can be a real treat, though global warming has put paid to the spectacular freezing winters of yesteryear – in the 1890s, excursion trains brought astonished sightseers to skate on the lake and marvel at the icicles hanging from the trees.

Belle Isle

Many of the private lakeside mansions built for Victorian Lancashire mill owners are now hotels, though **Belle Isle** – the largest of eighteen islets in the lake at a mile long – is still privately owned. Believed to harbour the site of a Roman villa, for more than two hundred years (until the 1990s), its guardians were various members of the Curwen family who built the island's eye-catching Georgian round house, one of the first of its type in England. The current owners don't allow public access to the island, though the house is visible through the trees if you get close enough on a boat.

ARRIVAL AND DEPARTURE   BOWNESS

BY CAR
The A592 from the south runs into Bowness along the lake, past the piers, and then continues to meet the A591 northwest of Windermere town. There's free two-hour parking on Glebe Rd, but otherwise you're going to have to put up with the car park charges, either at Glebe Park or in town (all well signposted).

BY BUS AND BOAT
Buses (including the #599 from Windermere train station) stop by the Bowness piers. For onward routes to Ambleside and Grasmere you have to return first to Windermere station, though the very useful Cross Lakes Experience (daily April– Oct; ☎015394 48600, ⊛mountain-goat.com/transport-services/525-cross-lakes-experience) provides a direct connecting boat-and-bus service, whereby you catch a boat from Bowness pier 3 to Ferry House, before a connecting

minibus (#525) transports you to Hill Top (£11.80 return/ family £33.10) and Hawkshead (£13.60/£38.10). From Hawkshead, there's a further bus connection to Coniston Water, in addition to walking and biking trails to Grizedale Forest and Tarn Hows.
Bus #6/X6 to: Newby Bridge (18min); Haverthwaite (21min); Ulverston (33min); or to Windermere (10min). Service operates Mon–Sat 5 daily.
Bus #508 "Kirkstone Rambler" to: Windermere (12min); Troubeck *Queen's Head* (22min); Kirkstone Pass (32min); Brothers Water (42min); Patterdale (49min); Glenridding (55min); Pooley Bridge (1hr 14min); Penrith (1hr 35min). Service operates end March–Oct 4 daily.
Bus #599 to: Windermere train station (10min). Service operates Easter–Oct daily every 20–30min; Nov–Easter Mon–Sat hourly.

INFORMATION AND ACTIVITIES
Bike, boats and kayak rental Windermere Canoe & Kayak, Ferry Nab Rd (March–Oct daily 9am–5pm: Nov, Dec & Feb closed Tues & Wed; ☎015394 44451, ⊛windermere canoekayak.com) have sit-on kayaks to rent from £27 for 3hr,, and stand up paddleboards from £20 for 2hr, plus guided tours and tuition available from £30; they also rent out bikes (£20). Otherwise, rowboats (from £15/hr) and

motorboats (from £21/hr) are available at Bowness piers, usually daily from April to Oct.
Tourist office Bowness Bay Information Centre, near the piers on Glebe Rd (daily: April–Oct 9.30am–5.30pm; Nov– March 10am–4.30pm; ☎0845 901 0845, ⊛lakedistrict. gov.uk).

1

WINDERMERE BOAT SERVICES AND CRUISES

There are plenty of ways to get out on the water, from short cruises and cross-lake ferries to hop-on, hop-off services that run the length of the lake from Bowness, calling at Lakeside (south) and Ambleside (north). There are also **combination boat tickets** available for the Lakeside & Haverthwaite Railway (Ⓦlakesiderailway.co.uk) and the Lakes Aquarium (Ⓦlakesaquarium.co.uk) – you can pick up more information from the pier-side ticket office or respective websites. Services on all routes are very frequent between Easter and October (every 30min–1hr at peak times and weekends), and reduced during the winter – but there are sailings every day except Christmas Day. There's discounted **parking** for customers at Bowness (Braithwaite Fold), Ambleside (Waterhead) and Lakeside.

Cross Lakes Shuttle Between Bowness piers and Ferry House, Sawrey. This useful pedestrian launch service (every 40min; return £5.40, family £15.50) saves you the walk down to the car ferry.

Windermere Ferry Ferry Nab, Bowness to Ferry House, Sawrey. The traditional cross-lake ferry service is this chain-guided contraption a 10min walk south from the cruise piers (every 20min; Mon–Sat 6.50am–10pm, Sun 8.50am–10pm, final departure in winter 9pm; pedestrian £1, cyclist £2, cars £5). The ferry provides access to Beatrix Potter's Hill Top and to

Hawkshead beyond, but as it can take only eighteen cars at a time, queues soon form in summer.

Windermere Lake Cruises ☎015394 43360, Ⓦwindermere-lakecruises.co.uk. Services from Bowness to Lakeside ("Yellow Cruise"; return £12.30, family £35.50; 1hr 30min), Bowness to Ambleside via Brockhole ("Red Cruise"; return £11.80, family £34; 1hr 10min), and a 45min Islands Cruise (£9, family £24). The Freedom-of-the-Lake ticket (one-day £16.30, family £44) is valid on all routes.

ACCOMMODATION

SEE MAPS PAGES 50 AND 56

Be warned that a **lake view** doesn't come cheap – most places in Bowness with even a glimpse of the water set their prices accordingly, while the local country-house hotels are in uniformly desirable locations. Apart from the places recommended below, Kendal Road has a line of other B&B possibilities, while you have to travel up to Ambleside for the nearest youth hostel.

BOWNESS

Angel Inn Helm Rd, LA23 3BU ☎015394 44080, Ⓦthe angelbowness.com. Eleven chic rooms – all burnished wood and black leather – above a smooth bar bring a bit of metropolitan style to Bowness. There are also a couple of rooms in the Gatehouse annexe including a huge suite with a help-me-out-of-here sofa, corner bath and a distant lake view. You get breakfast too (their "Full Cumbrian" should set you up for the day). Parking. **£100**

★ **Bowness Guest House** 80 Craig Walk, LA23 2JS ☎015394 43584, Ⓦbownessguesthouse.co.uk. Quiet townhouse offering five rather dramatic, earth-toned rooms with a contemporary sheen; they're all en-suite doubles (one of which is dog-friendly), each with a small library and smart TVs featuring Netflix. Street parking nearby. **£90**

The Cranleigh Kendal Rd, LA23 3EW ☎015394 43293, Ⓦthecranleigh.com. Indulge yourself in the "guest house with a difference" – the difference being the pampering on offer in super-stylish rooms and suites. They are all different,

but share a common core (vibrant fabrics, designer beds, massive TVs, iPod docks and space-station-like showers), while larger superior/luxury rooms and suites have private terraces, sitting areas and splash-proof bathroom TVs – the eye-popping "Sanctuary" even has a sleek glass bath and outdoor hot tub. Note that some rooms are in adjacent annexe buildings. Parking. **£145**

★ **Monties** Crag Brow, LA23 3BX ☎015394 42723, Ⓦmontiesbnb.co.uk. Over the years most of the rooms here have been given a stylish shot in the arm, with strong colours, good beds and decent bathrooms. Prices are pretty reasonable for the Lakes and all rooms are en suite, save a bargain room with private bathroom that sleeps three and goes for £120. Breakfast is served in the fab *Monties* café downstairs. Parking. **£90**

Oakbank House Helm Rd, LA23 3BU ☎015394 43386, Ⓦoakbankhousehotel.co.uk. A cut above your usual traditional B&B – think rugs and flowers, scatter cushions and coordinated furniture, and a welcoming sherry decanter for guests. Some of the rooms have the cherished lake views, and five superior rooms (around £10 extra) provide a bit more elegance. Parking. **£100**

AROUND BOWNESS

Gilpin Hotel & Lake House Crook Rd, LA23 3NE, 2 miles southeast of Bowness on B5284 ☎015394 88818, Ⓦthegilpin.co.uk. The relatively small size and long family ownership have a lot to do with *Gilpin's* success, and warm personal service underpins all that's good here. The Georgian main house has been handsomely restyled, with contemporary interior design much to the fore, not least in the elegant, individually styled rooms, some with four-posters, others with whirlpool baths or private patios – six contemporary suites (from £465) have glass-fronted lounges leading to individual gardens with cedarwood hot tubs, while five cedar-clad spa lodges (£635) feature oval stone baths and private en-suite spas. Then there are the designer "Lake House" suites (£465), a mile away in the grounds, with their own spa and heated pool. Rates include an extraordinarily bountiful breakfast. Parking. **£285**

★ **Linthwaite House** Crook Rd, LA23 3JA, 1 mile south of Bowness on B5284 ☎ 015394 88600, ⓦ leeu collection.com. An absolute boutique beauty, grafting contemporary style onto an ivy-covered country house set high above Windermere. Rooms are superbly detailed – rich muted fabrics, Shaker-style furniture, king-sized beds with canopies – while in the Loft Suite there's the most beautiful bathroom, a retractable glass roof panel and telescope provided for star-gazing. A conservatory and terrace offer grandstand lake and fell views, and you can work up an appetite for dinner with a walk in the extensive gardens to the hotel's private tarn. Room rates vary according to outlook and size, and also depend upon whether dinner is included. Parking. **£230**

Ryebeck Lyth Valley Rd, LA23 3JP, 1 mile south of Bowness on A5074 ☎ 015394 88195, ⓦ ryebeck.com. Refurbished Victorian country-house B&B, sporting a range of bright, conservatively furnished rooms with heavy drapes, fresh flowers and plump cushions. There's a friendly, personal welcome, and though their standard rooms are best described as "snug", with limited views, others are fairly spacious and overlook the grounds or lake, or come with private patios; a number of rooms are dog-friendly. Packages (from £199) include a really good dinner in genteel, candlelit surroundings. Closed two weeks in Jan. Parking. **£140**

★ **Wild Boar Inn** Crook Rd, LA23 3NF, 3 miles southeast of Bowness on B5284 ☎ 0333 220 3108, ⓦ englishlakes. co.uk. Good things await at this traditional-inn-with-a-twist, not least the dining experience (see page 59), though the *Wild Boar* is also a lovely rustic overnight stop for anyone who doesn't mind being away from the lake. What was once a series of woodland cottages centred on a basket-weaving workshop is now a fancy country inn with regulation oak beams, slate floors and a selection of agreeable "classic" rooms, but also with some sumptuous "feature" rooms (up to £300), where you can pad from swagged canopy bed past cast-iron wood-burner to hardwood-floor bathroom for a soak in a deep, freestanding, designer copper bathtub. It's a classy operation all round, from greeting to farewell, while outside are 70 acres of private woodland (with "green gym" exercise trail). **£180**

EATING
SEE MAPS PAGES 50 AND 56

There are lots of places in Bowness to get a pizza, fish and chips, a Chinese stir-fry or a budget **café** meal – a stroll along pedestrianized Ash Street and up Lake Road shows you most of the possibilities. Finer dining is available at a couple of local **restaurants**, as well as in the dining rooms of the major hotels – the *Gilpin*, in particular, gets rave reviews, while for a rustic treat drive out to the *Wild Boar Inn*. If you're looking for something more casual, you have the choice of two good pubs in Bowness (see page 60).

BOWNESS

Jackson's Bistro St Martin's Square, LA23 3EE ☎ 015394 46264. The long-standing local choice for a family dinner or romantic night out, with intimate dining on two floors. Mussels, onion tart, grilled trout and confit of duck provide a classic bistro experience, or choose from the good-value three-course *table d'hôte* menu (£18.95), available all night. Otherwise mains range from £12 to £18. Mon–Fri & Sun 5.30–11pm, Sat 5.30pm–midnight.

Rastelli's Lake Rd, LA23 3AP ☎ 015394 44227, ⓦ rastellis.co.uk. No surprises, just proper, authentic pizza and pasta (£9–11) in an amiable family-run restaurant decked out in cheery red, white and green – it's good value, so you can expect to have to wait for a table in summer. Mon & Wed–Sun 5–10pm.

AROUND BOWNESS

★ **Gilpin Hotel & Lake House** Crook Rd, LA23 3NE, 2 miles southeast of Bowness on B5284 ☎ 015394 88818, ⓦ thegilpin.co.uk. The *Gilpin* offers two exceptional, and very contrasting, dining options: first up is the Michelin-starred HRiSHi under the helm of Hrishikesh Desai, who conjures up magical Modern British dishes like pressed terrine of Cartmel Valley game with camomile and sweet wine jelly, and chilli-glazed lobster with avocado mousse and tobiko caviar; if it's too tricky deciding on something from the main menu, then the tasting menu (£95) offers a great introduction. Secondly there's *Gilpin Spice*, which, as the name suggests, veers towards Asian-influenced dishes with soups, snacks and flatbreads complemented by small and large sharing plates (£6–18) like Thai-style octopus, and marinated sea bream with a lemongrass and green chilli rub. Whichever restaurant you plump for, you won't be disappointed. Daily noon–2pm & 6–9.30pm.

★ **Wild Boar Inn** Crook Rd, LA23 3NF, 3 miles southeast of Bowness on B5284 ☎ 015394 45225, ⓦ englishlakes. co.uk. The first place in the Lakes with its own smokehouse, the *Wild Boar* makes merry on the menu with its unique cooking style flavoured by cherry, chestnut and oak from its own woods – expect home-smoked meat and fish on the deli platters, delicately smoked steaks and chops, and

1

WALKS FROM BOWNESS

While Bowness gets very busy in summer, there are plenty of quieter lakeside spots in the vicinity. Even on the east shore, near the town, you can escape the crowds fairly quickly for an hour or two's stroll, while if you cross to Sawrey using the car-ferry or launch, the whole of the wooded west side as far as Wray Castle (where you can pick up another cross-lake service) makes for an enjoyable circuit.

RAYRIGG MEADOW AND MILLERGROUND

A mile north of Bowness (along the A592), past the Windermere Jetty Museum of Boats, Steam and Stories, a path cuts west across **Rayrigg Meadow** to the lakeside and then traces the wooded shore for half a mile to the **Millerground** piers (there's parking here), where you can rejoin the main road. If you're not too muddy, then morning coffee or afternoon tea at nearby *Miller Howe* is a treat. The round trip from Bowness, including walking along the road, is two and a half miles, though from Millerground you can walk up through the woods to Windermere town, a mile away, if you want to make a circuit of it.

BRANTFELL

Best viewpoint is from **Brantfell** (626ft) – "steep hill" – about a mile southeast of Bowness, which takes an hour or so, there and back. Follow Brantfell Road up the hill from St Martin's Square and keep on the path (signposted as the "Dales Way") until you see the diversion up the hillside at Brantfell Farm. The views from the rocks at the top are all-embracing – Belle Isle to Morecambe Bay – and if you rejoin the Dales Way at the farm you could then follow the path east and north all the way into Windermere town (3.5 miles; 2hr from Bowness) – though it's actually an easier, and nicer, route *from* Windermere to Bowness and the lake, diverting up Brantfell on the way.

LATTERBARROW AND CLAIFE HEIGHTS

The Victorians liked to cross the lake to take tea on the shore below the woods on the west side, and if you're up for an afternoon's walk away from the crowds, this is still the best idea. Cross by car-ferry or launch to Ferry House at Sawrey, from where a gentle path runs two miles north along the shore to Belle Grange. From here you can climb up to **Latterbarrow** (800ft) for lake views before returning along the paths of **Claife Heights** and back to Sawrey. The steep descent through the woods from Far Sawrey to the ferry pier passes the ruins of **The Station**, a castellated viewing platform from which eighteenth-century tourists would view the lake and mountains through a "claude-glass" (named after Romantic landscapist Claude Lorraine), a convex mirror used to "frame" their view. These viewing stations were very popular until well into the nineteenth century and formed part of any tour of picturesque Lakeland, but the views from this one have been lost to the overarching trees.

---

anything from hot-smoked sausage to wild-boar pastrami (all-day menu dishes £5–16, dinner starters £6–12, mains £15–30). The rambling restaurant and bar is a convivial space of stone floors, exposed wood, duck-your-head beams and vintage leather armchairs, and there's a real sense of theatre from the open kitchen and grill – cranked up another notch if you opt for the prime-positioned "chef's table". Better still, they've even got their own microbrewery, which staff are happy to show visitors around. Mon–Sat noon–5pm & 6.30–9pm, Sun 12.30–2.30pm & 6.30–9.30pm.

DRINKING

SEE MAP PAGE 56

BOWNESS

Angel Inn Helm Rd, LA23 3BU ☎ 015394 44080, ⓦ ange bowness.com. The contemporary bar at the *Angel* is mostly about location, with a great hillside terrace for views over town and lake. Light bites, lunchtime sandwiches and posh pub food (sandwiches £7–10, most mains under £14) are served, either in the bar or with waiter service in the back restaurant for dinner. Daily 8.30am–11pm; kitchen 11.30am–4pm & 5–9pm.

★ **Hole in t'Wall** Fallbarrow Rd, LA23 3DH ☎ 015394 43488, ⓦ holeintwall.co.uk. How did the town's oldest hostelry get its name (it's officially the *New Hall Inn*)? Apparently after the hole through which ostlers once had their beer passed to them. The crowded interior features stone-flagged floors, open fires, dark wooden furniture and real ales; outside, the terrace-style beer garden is a popular spot on summer evenings. The usual bar meals (£9–12) include a daily curry special (£10.75). The best village pub by far. Mon–Sat 11am–11pm, Sun noon–11pm; kitchen Mon–Fri noon–2.30pm & 6–8pm, Sat noon–3pm & 4–8pm, Sun noon–2.30pm.

ENTERTAINMENT

Old Laundry Theatre Crag Brow, LA23 3BX ☎ 015394 40872, ⓦ oldlaundrytheatre.co.uk. Sharing the same building as the World of Beatrix Potter attraction, Bowness's cultural hub hosts – occupying a one-time laundry – offers a varied programme of theatre, music, comedy, film and spoken word throughout the year.

The Royalty Lake Rd, LA23 3BJ ☎ 015394 43364, ⓦ windermere.nm-cinemas.co.uk. Three screens showing the latest releases; screen one is the original 1930s auditorium, while the cinema also possesses a fully refurbished – and very rare Wurlitzer theatre organ dating from 1927.

DIRECTORY

Banks NatWest (Lake Rd) has an ATM and there's a Barclays ATM (though no bank) on Crag Brow, Lake Rd.

Hospital The nearest hospital is in Kendal: Burton Rd (☎ 01539 732288, ⓦ uhmb.nhs.uk).

Pharmacy Lakeland Pharmacy, 5 Grosvenor Terrace, Lake Rd (☎ 015394 43139).

Post office 2 St Martin's Parade (Mon–Sat 8am–5.30pm, Sun 8am–1pm).

Brockhole

Brockhole, LA23 1LJ, 3 miles northwest of Windermere on A591 • Daily: Easter–Oct 10am–5pm; Nov–Easter 10am–4pm • Free; parking £3/2hr, £8/day • ☎ 015394 46601, ⓦ brockhole.co.uk • Buses #555 and #599 stop outside, or take Windermere Lake Cruises boat from Bowness or Ambleside (see page 58)

The **Lake District National Park Authority** has its main visitor centre at **Brockhole**, a late Victorian mansion set in lush grounds on the shores of Windermere, to the north of Bowness. It's the single best place to get to grips with what there is to see and do in the Lakes, with some excellent displays, lovely gardens and a big range of activity sessions, including electric-biking, watersports and treetop adventures. Families, especially, will find Brockhole to be a great day out – quite apart from everything else, there's a huge adventure playground, mini-golf course and putting green, indoor play area, pushchair-friendly trails and other child-oriented attractions. Undoubtedly the best way to arrive is by boat, with year-round services on the cruises from Bowness or Ambleside – you're dropped at the Brockhole jetty from where it's a ten-minute walk up through the gardens to the house and visitor centre.

Brockhole Visitor Centre

The all-singing, all-dancing **Brockhole Visitor Centre** occupies a house built originally for a Manchester silk merchant but much expanded and refitted since then. Besides the permanent natural history and geological displays, the centre hosts guided walks, children's activities, tours, farmers' markets, special exhibitions, lectures and film shows – the centre, and any local tourist office, can provide a schedule. There's also a shop – good for local guides, maps, arts and crafts – and a café with an outdoor terrace looking down to the lake.

1

GETTING HIGH, GETTING WET AND GETTING AROUND

The two big activities at Brockhole are the **watersports** down on the lake and the **high-ropes adventure course**. Advance bookings are advised for either, especially in school holidays.

Bike rental Information and bookings from lakeshore office ☎ 015394 46601. Hiring a bike (half-day £25, full day £30) is a great way to explore the area, and while cycling is not permitted within the Brockhole grounds themselves, you can go for an off-road ride in the woods and lanes on the other side of the lake, reachable via the Brockhole to Bark Barn boat (included in bike hire price). April–June Sat & Sun (Easter hols daily); July & Aug daily.

Treetop Trek ☎ 015394 47186 ⓦ treetoptrek. co.uk; bookings also at Brockhole Visitor Centre (see page 61). Brockhole's treetop high-ropes course (through the magnificent ancient oaks) is a bit more whole-family-oriented than the Go Ape courses at Grizedale and Whinlatter – kids as young as 5 can take part and there's a continuous belay system (meaning you're always attached to a safety line). But it's no less exciting, featuring 36 aerial obstacles built into the trees (the highest platform is at a dizzying 43ft) and a 250m-long (820ft) triple (ie three people at once) zip wire. There's also Treetops Nets, a combination of walkways, slides and trampolines (under-5s permitted if supervised), and a cool climbing wall. Sessions operate daily during Brockhole opening hours. Mini treetop trek (1hr course £22 adult/£18 aged five upwards); Full treetop trek (2hr course £33 adult/£25 under-16); Treetop Nets (2 hours £20); Climbing Wall (30mins £15).

Watersports Information and bookings from lakeshore office ☎ 015394 46601. Head down to the lakeside for rowing boats (from £20/1hr for two people), sit-on kayaks (£15/1hr, £25/2hr) and Canadian canoes, seating two or three people (£20/1hr, £30/2hr), plus stand-up paddle boards (£15/1hr, £25/2hr). April–June Sat & Sun (Easter hols daily); July & Aug daily.

The gardens and grounds

On a warm day, Brockhole's 30 acres of **gardens and grounds** are a treat, with their little arbours, lakeside paths, grassy lawns, wild-flower meadow and picnic areas – the website tells you what's flowering month by month, while woodpeckers, deer, rabbits, foxes and badgers are all regular visitors. The landscaping is among the finest in the Lakes, the work of the celebrated Lancastrian garden architect **Thomas Mawson** (1861–1933), who also designed the grounds for other Victorian piles at Holehird, Langdale Chase, Holker Hall and Rydal Hall.

Blackwell

Blackwell, LA23 3JT, 1.5 miles south of Bowness on the B5360, just off the A5074 • Daily: March–Oct 10.30am–5pm; Nov–Feb 10.30am–4pm; closed two weeks in mid-Jan; introductory talk Tuesday 2pm • £8.90, free entrance to tearoom and shop; free parking • ☎ 015394 46139, ⓦ blackwell.org.uk

A mile and a half south of Bowness, in an elevated position above the lake, stands the superbly restored mansion of **Blackwell**. It's the masterpiece of **Mackay Hugh Baillie Scott** (1865–1945) – an architect less celebrated than his contemporaries, Sir Edwin Lutyens and Charles Voysey, but just as influential in the Arts and Crafts Movement that emerged from the ideas of John Ruskin and William Morris.

The house is hugely significant as the only major Arts and Crafts house in such remarkable condition open to the public in Britain. Most are still in private hands, and Blackwell itself has had a variety of owners: from World War II until the 1970s the house was a girls' school, and was then leased by English Nature until it was bought and restored by the Lakeland Arts Trust. Today, Blackwell is the starting point of an engaging **Arts and Crafts Trail** that links other period houses and sights in the southern Lakes – pick up a leaflet at the house or check the website.

1

YOU DON'T ALWAYS GET WHAT YOU WANT...

Blackwell's origins – as with so many houses on the shores of Windermere – lie in the nineteenth-century explosion of wealth in the industrial cities. Given free rein by Mancunian brewer and Lord Mayor **Sir Edward Holt**, who wanted a holiday home in the Lakes, architect **Baillie Scott** grasped the opportunity to design an entire house, and Blackwell was completed to his specifications between 1898 and 1900. Taking his cue from Ruskin and Morris, who had championed the importance of traditional handicrafts allied with functionalism, Baillie Scott let Blackwell speak for his ideas and principles – from the almost organic nature of the free-flowing layout to the decorative emphasis on natural motifs and handcrafted designs. The use of **natural light**, in particular, is revealing, with the family rooms all south-facing, even though this orientates them away from the lake views for which, presumably, Sir Edward had paid a premium. Indeed, there's evidence that the Holts were never entirely comfortable in their designer holiday home. The family (of five children and six servants) soon cluttered Baillie Scott's harmonious interlinked rooms with the paraphernalia of the Victorian gentry – an old photograph shows the main hall encumbered with a heavy chandelier, potted ferns and a stuffed moose's head – and by the end of World War I, as the Arts and Crafts Movement lost its fashionable edge, the Holts visited Blackwell less and less.

The house

The house grabs your attention from the very first, as you proceed from the entrance down an oak-panelled corridor, off which is the **main hall**. Baillie Scott's idealized baronial design provides the sort of things you might expect to see in a showpiece country house – vast fireplace, oak panelling, minstrels' gallery and heraldic crests – but lightens the experience with huge dollops of inventive flair. An open-plan room with nooks and corners of varying proportions sports a peacock wallpaper frieze, a bluebell-and-daisy hessian wall hanging, copper lightshades, Delft tiles and – above all – the recurring carved rowan leaves and berries from the Holt family coat of arms. At the end of the corridor, sun streams into the **white drawing room** and here, and elsewhere in the house, you can sit in the cushioned bay windows and enjoy the garden and lake views.

The **bedrooms** upstairs contain changing exhibitions of contemporary and historic applied Arts and Crafts, though the contents of the entire house are display pieces in their own right, from the early twentieth-century carved oak furniture by Simpson's of Kendal to the modern earthenware that is positioned throughout. But it's Baillie Scott's naturalistic touches that perhaps sum up the whole – such as the door handles shaped like leaves or the lakeland birds and flowers that are ever-present in the stained glass and stonework.

If you're visiting on a Tuesday, try and coincide it with the informative **introductory talk** at 2pm. There's also a rather fine **tearoom**, and a garden terrace – overlooking the Coniston fells and the waters of Windermere – where lunches, cream teas and lemonade are served on summer days. A **craft shop** sells contemporary works by leading designers, including jewellery, ceramics, scarves and handbags, as well as specialist books on architecture and the Arts and Crafts Movement.

Lakeside and around

From Bowness, cruise boats head five miles down the lake to the piers at **Lakeside**, where gentle wooded hills frame Windermere's serene southern reaches. Combination tickets are available for the boat ride and the two big family

1

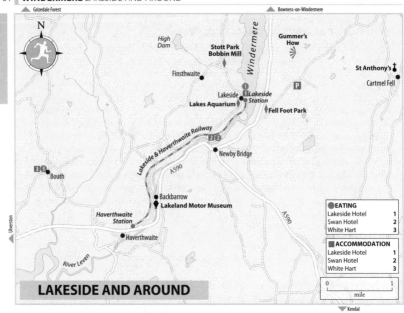

LAKESIDE AND AROUND

attractions on the quayside, namely the **steam train** and **aquarium**, and the three things together would fill a day. The **Lakeland Motor Museum**, not far from Haverthwaite railway station, is the focus of another good combined day out. But you can also hike up through the local woods for some views, or catch a launch across the water to **Fell Foot Park** for a picnic. Other than Lakeside itself, where there's a car park and cafés at both the aquarium and railway station, the only other local facilities are at the nearby hamlet of **Newby Bridge**, distinguished by a couple of large hotels and a seventeenth-century five-arched stone, bridge.

Lakeside & Haverthwaite Railway

Haverthwaite station, LA12 8AL, on A590 • April–Oct 6 services daily, Feb half-term 4 services daily, plus winter weekend special services; tearoom closed Jan & Feb • Return £7.10, family ticket £20.50; combined rail and boat fares to Bowness (return £17.50, family £49.50) or Ambleside (£24.80/£68) • ☎ 015395 31594, ⓦ lakesiderailway.co.uk • Pay-and-display car parks at both stations; otherwise boat to Lakeside or buses to Haverthwaite (#6/X6 from Kendal/Ulverston, or #618 from Ambleside/Bowness/Ulverston)

The southern Windermere quayside is the terminus of the **Lakeside & Haverthwaite Railway**, whose steam-powered engines puff gently along four miles of track along the River Leven and through the woods of Backbarrow Gorge; boat arrivals at Lakeside connect with train departures throughout the day.

It's the only surviving remnant of a railway line that once used to stretch all the way to Ulverston and Barrow. There's a billowing rush of smoke in the tunnel – very atmospheric – as you arrive at Haverthwaite, where you'll find a cute station tearoom. If you get a chance, explore the engine shed, where (when it's not out on duty) Britain's oldest working standard-gauge loco, built in Manchester in 1863, is kept; if you've still got time on your hands (and kids), then there's an excellent woodland adventure playground for them to muck around in. The annual **events calendar**, meanwhile, incorporates steam gala weekends, Victorian evenings, Thomas the Tank Engine days and Santa specials – there's more information on the website.

Lakes Aquarium

Lakeside, LA12 8AS • Daily 10am–4.30pm; last admission 1hr before closing; feeding of the otters daily 10.30am & 3pm • £7.50, children £5.50, family ticket from £17.95; discounts for online bookings • ☎ 015395 30153, Ⓦ lakesaquarium.co.uk • Pay-and-display car park at Lakeside, or take boat to Lakeside

The best rainy day children's attraction around Windermere is the **Lakes Aquarium**, centred on the fish and animals found in and along a lakeland river, on the Cumbrian coast, and in other habitats from lake to rainforest. There's a pair of frisky otters, plus rays from Morecambe Bay and a terrific walk-through tunnel aquarium with huge carp and diving ducks. Educational exhibits, documentaries and daily presentations give the low-down on everything from cockles to pike and leeches to lobsters. Enthusiastic staff are on hand to explain what's going on, and afterwards you can grab a drink in the adjacent 1872 café and enjoy watching the comings and goings of the boats.

Stott Park Bobbin Mill and around

Colton, LA12 8AX • Easter–May Wed–Sun 10am–5pm; June–Sept daily 10am–5pm; last tour 30min before closing • £8.40, family ticket £21.80, parking free; EH • ☎ 015395 31087, Ⓦ english-heritage.org.uk/visit/places/stott-park-bobbin-mill

Half a mile up the hill from Lakeside, below Finsthwaite Heights, stands one of England's few working mills, **Stott Park Bobbin Mill**. It was founded in 1835 to supply the British textile industry with bobbins – rollers or spools for holding thread – and at one stage employed as many as 250 men and boys. When the cotton industry declined, the mill later diversified, manufacturing pulleys, hammers, mallets, spade handles, yo-yos and even duffel-coat toggles. Commercial production finally ceased in 1971, at a time when plastic had replaced wood for most bobbins. Former workers guide visitors on a 45-minute tour through the processes of cutting, roughing, drying, finishing and polishing on machinery that hasn't changed since it was introduced in the mid-nineteenth century. Note that the steam engine driving the water wheel doesn't operate every day – call for details if you want to catch it.

High Dam and Finsthwaite

From a car park above Stott Park Bobbin Mill (follow the road to Finsthwaite) there's a pleasant walk up through the woods to **High Dam**, the reservoir whose water used to drive the mill machinery – allow an hour or so to circle the water and return. Alternatively, if you head for **Finsthwaite** hamlet itself, half a mile above the mill, you can clamber up through the woods of **Finsthwaite Heights** to the naval commemorative tower.

BOBBINS AND COPPICING

For a time in the nineteenth century the south Lakes' **bobbin mills** formed an important part of the national economy, supplying up to half of all the bobbins required by the booming British textile mills. There were two reasons for the industry's strength in the Lakes: the fast running water from lakeland rivers to drive the mills and the seemingly inexhaustible supply of wood. To make bobbins and other items, **coppiced** wood was required, from trees cut to stumps to encourage the quick growth of long poles, which were then harvested for use. It's a technique that's been used for more than five thousand years, and ash, beech, birch, chestnut, hazel and oak were all grown in this way. The bark was peeled off and used in the tanneries, while coppiced wood was also used widely in charcoal-making (another key local industry), thatching and the production of tent pegs, cask bindings, fencing, agricultural implements (such as rakes) and so-called "swill" baskets (cradle-shaped Cumbrian panniers).

1

Fell Foot Park and around

Newby Bridge, LA12 8NN, access from the A592 (Bowness road), a mile north of Newby Bridge • Daily 8am–7pm or dusk; tearoom April–Oct Mon–Fri & Sun 10am–5pm, Sat 9am–5pm; Nov–March Mon–Fri & Sun 10am–4pm, Sat 9am–4pm • Free, though parking fee charged; NT • ☎ 015395 31273, ⊕ nationaltrust.org.uk/fell-foot • Bus #6 from Windermere and Bowness stops outside

Across from Lakeside, **Fell Foot Park**, on Windermere's southeastern reach, makes a relaxed picnic spot, where you can lounge on the Victorian landscaped lawns and explore the rhododendron gardens and oak and pine plantations; there's an adventure playground for kids too. There was also once a private mansion here, to go with the grounds, though that's long gone. But the mock-Gothic boathouse still stands and offers rowing boats, kayaks and paddleboards for hire, while doubling as a rather superior **tearoom** – from the tables outside you can watch the Lakeside & Haverthwaite trains chuff into the station just across the lake. In spring and summer, Windermere Lake Cruises (see page 58) runs launches across to the park from Lakeside, usually every twenty minutes depending on demand and the weather.

Gummer's How

An ancient packhorse route from Newby Bridge to Kendal, now a steep and winding minor road, passes to the northeast behind Fell Foot. A mile up, there's free parking by the start of the footpath to **Gummer's How**, the gorse-topped fell that peers over the southern half of Windermere. It's an easy walk up to the little stone trig point on the summit – it'll take an hour there and back, including a rest at the top to gaze down at the Fell Foot marina and the snaking River Leven.

Lakeland Motor Museum

Old Blue Mill, Backbarrow, LA12 8TA, on A590 • Daily 9.30am–4.30pm • £9, family ticket £26, parking free • ☎ 015395 30400, ⊕ lakelandmotormuseum.co.uk • Bus #6/X6 (from Barrow, Ulverston, Grange and Kendal); also seasonal bus transfers from the boat at Lakeside, or the museum is just 1 mile from Haverthwaite station

After thirty years located in the old shire-horse stables at Holker Hall, the splendid **Lakeland Motor Museum** now has a purpose-built home at Backbarrow, near Newby Bridge, to show off its thirty-thousand-plus motoring history exhibits. The landmark riverside blue building is a dream for petrol-heads and nostalgia buffs alike, as it's simply stuffed with vintage vehicles and memorabilia, from boneshaker bikes and Bentleys to DeLoreans and Dinky toys.

There are digressions into the local industries that used to dominate this part of the Lakes – the museum itself occupies the converted packing shed of Backbarrow's former "Dolly Blue" works, where ultramarine pigment (used in laundry powder, paint and crayons, among other things) was once boxed up for export around the world. There are also some re-created vintage shop windows and an authentically greasy 1930s motor garage, while a separate hangar houses an exhibition space devoted to the speed-racer Campbells, Sir Malcolm and son Donald, where you can view life-sized replicas of their record-breaking Bluebird machines. There's also a riverside **café** with an outdoor deck.

ARRIVAL AND DEPARTURE

LAKESIDE AND AROUND

By car There's a large pay-and-display car park at Lakeside, which is around 9 miles (25min drive) from Bowness down the A592.

By boat The best way to visit Lakeside is by boat (⊕ windermere-lakecruises.co.uk), with the aquarium and railway just a step or two away from the quayside and other

attractions easily reachable on foot. There's also a seasonal launch from Lakeside across to Fell Foot Park (Easter–Oct daily 11am–5pm, usually every 30min; £1.75 return).

By bus The #6/X6 (Mon–Sat 5 daily; from Ambleside, via Windermere and Bowness) calls at Newby Bridge, Backbarrow (for the Motor Museum) and Haverthwaite station.

ACCOMMODATION AND EATING

SEE MAP PAGE 64

There's limited **accommodation** at Lakeside itself, which is dominated by one big namesake hotel. A mile south of

the foot of the lake, down the River Leven at Newby Bridge, the *Swan Hotel* has a fine riverside location. From here, it's another couple of miles southwest along the A590 to the village of Haverthwaite, which also has a selection of B&Bs. All the major attractions have their own **cafés** for daytime snacks and drinks – you'll have to pay for parking to use those at Lakeside, though it's free to park at Haverthwaite station and the Lakeland Motor Museum.

★ **Lakeside Hotel** Lakeside, LA12 8AT ✆015395 30001, ⊚lakesidehotel.co.uk. A very hospitable four-star hotel with a great location on the lapping shores of Windermere. Some rooms have private gardens or their own terrace, and most overlook the water – they are all country house in feel, with elegant fabrics and marble bathrooms, while eight family rooms (some with separate bunk room for the kids) offer more space. A conservatory runs the length of the hotel, opening onto lakeside lawns and gardens (the ducks are fed daily at 11am), and there's a large family-friendly indoor pool, a hot tub and classy spa facilities. You can eat in the conservatory, with its lovely views; alternatives include the contemporary *John Ruskin's Brasserie* or the elegant but unstuffy *Lakeview Restaurant* (evenings only) – both restaurants have dedicated menus for under 14s. Closed first three weeks in Jan. Parking. Kitchen daily noon–3pm & 6.30–9pm. **£215**

Swan Hotel Newby Bridge LA12 8NB, a mile south of Lakeside ✆015395 31681, ⊚swanhotel.com. This classic old inn has undergone extensive refurbishment to get it up to four-star standard, with modern rooms (including king-sized beds and a sitting room in the executive suites), up-to-date facilities including indoor pool and spa and a contemporary bar that's more Manchester than muck-and-country. Sat-night stays are typically £20 more expensive, while school-holiday prices can be as high as £290 a night. Fusion rules in the *River Room* restaurant (breaded scampi, chimichurri chicken, lamb kofta with mint, coriander and honey; most dishes around £14), or there's a wide bar menu that you can eat at riverside tables by the five-arched bridge. Parking. Bar daily 10am–11pm, food served till 9.30pm; restaurant Mon–Sat 5–9pm, Sun noon–2pm. **£140**

★ **White Hart** Booth, LA12 8JB, off A590, 1.5 miles northeast of Haverthwaite ✆01229 861229, ⊚whitehart-lakedistrict.co.uk. It's a short, winding drive off the A590 to this cosy seventeenth-century country inn, known for its unfussy but extremely tasty food, typically steak and Guinness pie with veg and chips, and spicy Cumbrian sausage with onion and cranberry gravy (rustic sandwiches at lunch £6, otherwise mains £11–16). There's also a great choice of real ales, and a kids' playground opposite the pub, while five sympathetically upgraded en-suite guest rooms are an absolute bargain – two with green-field views (£80), and three cheaper ones under the eaves in the older part of the pub, including a large family room with a double bed and two singles. Parking. Mon–Sat noon–11pm, Sun noon–10.30pm; kitchen Mon–Sat noon–2pm & 6–8.45pm, Sun noon–8.45pm. **£70**

The Winster and Lyth valleys

You don't have to travel far from the shores of the lake to get off the beaten track into some lovely – and largely unheralded – country, but you do need a car or a bike. Make a night of it in one of several wonderful local country inns, and the **Winster and Lyth valleys** might just turn out to be your new secret place away from the crowds.

Strawberry Bank and Winster Valley

From near the foot of Windermere and Fell Foot Park, a minor road runs three miles up to the brow of a hill at **Strawberry Bank**, where the celebrated *Mason's Arms* (see page 68) is impeccably sited overlooking the low stony outcrops and tidy plantations of the **Winster Valley**. The pub's terrace is a great place for a beer – there are two hundred on offer, from all corners of the globe, including a damson beer made on the premises. Arthur Ransome moved to the Winster Valley in 1925 and it was here that he wrote *Swallows and Amazons*. His house, known as **Low Ludderburn** (not open to the public), can be seen if you take the tortuous bracken- and bramble-lined road north from the pub for a couple of miles.

St Anthony's church

Cartmel Fell, LA11 6NH • Daily, hours vary; Sun service 9.30am • ⊚ crosthwaiteandlyth.co.uk

A mile south of the *Mason's Arms* (follow the signposts), **St Anthony's church** lies tucked into a hollow on the side of Cartmel Fell, resplendent with wild daffodils in spring. The church dates from 1504 – it was built as an isolated, outlying chapel of Cartmel

1

priory – and preserves a characterful seventeenth-century interior with exposed rafters, a triple-decker pulpit and twin "box" pews once reserved for the local gentry.

Crosthwaite and the Lyth Valley

From Strawberry Bank, the road drops a mile to **Bowland Bridge**, beyond which a minor road makes its way north along the upper Winster Valley, before joining the A5074 (Bowness road). Where the roads meet there's a sign pointing you northeast towards the tiny village of **Crosthwaite**, whose parish church and adjacent seventeenth-century *Punch Bowl Inn* (see below) nestle in the gentle **Lyth Valley**. Lyth Valley **damsons** are a staple of the local early summer fruit crop, used in these parts in desserts and preserves (and to flavour beer and gin) – they are a relic of the former textile industry, when the fruit was used to make cloth dyes.

ACCOMMODATION AND EATING

SEE MAP PAGE 50

Brown Horse Inn Winster, LA23 3NR, on A5074 ☎015394 43443, ⓦthebrownhorseinn.co.uk. A revamped country inn doing great things with home-produced food from their own Winster Valley family farm, just half a mile away from the pub – beat that for food miles. There's a seasonally changing menu, from beef, lamb and pork to chicken, game and garden veg (mains £14–20; D, B&B rates available), served under oak beams in the handsome bar and restaurant. They brew their own beer too, so you might well fancy an overnight stay in one of nine refurbished rooms, four of which are more contemporary in style and have lovely valley views. They also offer four luxury self-catering cottages nearby, sleeping two to ten people (contact the pub for rates). Parking. Daily 11am–11pm; kitchen Mon–Fri noon–2.30pm & 6–9pm, Sat noon–9pm, Sun noon–8pm. **£115**

Mason's Arms Strawberry Bank, Cartmel Fell, LA11 6NW ☎015395 68486, ⓦmasonsarmsstrawberrybank. co.uk. One of those places you're delighted to have happened upon, especially on a sunny day at lunchtime, when you can look forward to an alfresco "posh pub" meal, from peppered squid with pickled coleslaw and crisp pork belly (mains £15–20). The stylish country inn has tables in the stone-flagged bar as well as a contemporary upstairs dining room, and there's also accommodation in two decidedly chic cottages (which sleep four to six, midweek

nights £155, otherwise £175) and five variously furnished and equipped suites for couples, all available by the night. You'll pay £20 less for three of the suites midweek, and around £50 more at weekends for the two most exclusive ones (four-poster bed, standalone bath, private walled garden). Parking. Mon–Sat noon–11pm, Sun noon–10.30pm; kitchen Mon–Fri noon–2.30pm & 6–9pm, Sat & Sun noon–9pm. **£105**

★ **Punch Bowl Inn** Crosthwaite, LA8 8HR, next to St Mary's church ☎015395 68237, ⓦthe-punchbowl. co.uk. One of the best lakeland gastro-inns, with a fistful of awards to prove it and a loyal clientele who keep returning year after year. The *Punch Bowl's* nine gorgeous earth-toned rooms (all quirkily named after past vicars of the next-door church) feature exposed beams, clunky retro bedside radios and superb bathrooms with underfloor-heated limestone floors, clawfoot bathtubs and quite possibly the largest bath towels in Britain. Room rates vary wildly (£145–320/night, depending on day and season), but include a superb breakfast and afternoon tea. The scrumptious food, meanwhile, is modern but unpretentious, locally sourced and seasonal (pot-roast wood pigeon to local lamb; mains £14–20) and you can eat either in the bar or the restaurant (which also has an a la carte menu). Parking. Daily 11am–11pm; kitchen noon–9pm. **£145**

Ambleside and around

Ambleside, five miles northwest of Windermere, at the head of the lake, lies at the hub of the central and southern Lakes region. It's a popular, if commercial, base for walkers and tourers, but has lost most of its traditional market-town character over the years. The original market square and associated buildings were swept away in a typically vigorous piece of Victorian redevelopment (though the market cross still stands) and today's thriving centre – more a retail experience than a lakeland town – consists of a cluster of grey-green stone houses either side of the babbling gully of **Stock Ghyll**,

VIEW OF LAKE WINDERMERE FROM ORREST HEAD

1

AMBLESIDE

ACCOMMODATION

Ambleside Manor	6
Brantfell House	5
Compston House	4
Hillsdale	3
Rooms at the Apple Pie	1
The Waterwheel	2

Armitt Library and Museum

Grasmere

Bridge House

Spar Supermarket

Co-op Supermarket

Ghyllside Cycles Bike Rental

Cinema

Rothay Park

St Mary's

Cinema

White Platts Recreation Ground

Bus stops

Library

Ambleside Climbing Wall

Waterhead, Campsite & Coniston

Waterhead, Windermere & Bowness

EATING

Apple Pie	2
Doi Intanon	4
Fellinis	7
Fulling Mill	1
Lucy's On A Plate	6
Rattle Ghyll Café	3
Zeffirelli's	5

DRINKING & NIGHTLIFE

Golden Rule	1
Zeffirelli's Jazz Bar	2

and more outdoors shops, pubs, B&Bs and cafés than you can shake a hiking pole at. Huge car parks soak up the day-trip trade, but actually Ambleside improves with time, boasting some enjoyable local walks as well as the best selection of accommodation and restaurants in the area. It's also only a short trip from town down to the pier at **Waterhead** for a lake cruise, including the jaunt across to the majestic National Trust property of **Wray Castle**.

Stock Ghyll

The river through town – **Stock Ghyll** – once powered Ambleside's fulling and bobbin mills, whose buildings survive intact on either side of Bridge Street, as do a couple of restored water wheels. Straddling Stock Ghyll is the town's favourite and most photogenic building, tiny **Bridge House**, originally built as a covered bridge-cum-summerhouse and used by a local family to access their orchards across the stream. It's had many other uses over the years, mainly for storage, though records show that in the nineteenth century it was briefly home to a family of eight. The traditional walk in town is to follow Stock Ghyll up to the nearby waterfall (see page 75).

Armitt Library and Museum

1

Rydal Rd, LA22 9BL • Tue–Sat: Apr–Oct 10am–5pm; Nov–Mar 10.30am–4pm • £5 • ☎ 015394 31212, ⓦ armitt.com

For a rundown of Ambleside's history, head a couple of minutes along Rydal Road to the **Armitt Library and Museum**, the town's acclaimed literary museum and historic library, which celebrated its centenary in 2012. Founded by society intellectual Mary Louisa Armitt, the collection catalogues the very distinct contribution to lakeland society made by writers and artists from John Ruskin to Beatrix Potter: others, like the abstract artist Kurt Schwitters (see page 106) and the redoubtable Harriet Martineau (see box), made their homes in the town, and the museum contains cases full of memorabilia – from a life-mask of Martineau to a lock of Ruskin's hair. There's plenty, too, on the life and work of Herbert Bell (1856–1946), pharmacist of Ambleside turned pioneering lakeland photographer. And anyone driven to distraction by the bunny-and-hedgehog side of Beatrix Potter should be prepared to revise their opinion on viewing the changing selection of her early scientific watercolour studies of fungi and mosses – a beautifully painted sequence donated by Potter herself.

St Mary's church

Vicarage Rd, LA22 9AD • Daily 9am–5.30pm • ⓦ stmarysambleside.org.uk

At the southern end of Ambleside, **St Mary's church** has a rocket-shaped spire that is visible from all over town. Completed in 1854, the church was designed by George Gilbert Scott – the architect responsible for London's Albert Memorial and St Pancras

---

A MOST SINGULAR WOMAN

Harriet Martineau, a delicate child and hard of hearing, was born into a Nonconformist East Anglian manufacturing family in 1802. Left penniless by the death of her father in 1826, Harriet began to earn a living by writing moral and devotional tales, which she called "**Illustrations**", addressing such weighty matters as slavery, the Poor Laws, taxation, education and emigration. Martineau produced these on a monthly basis between 1832 and 1834 – and, much to the surprise of her publisher, they made her famous overnight. She subsequently travelled widely (with ear trumpet in tow), when it was not easy for a woman of her background to do so, and produced two successful books on America – *Society In America* (1837), lauded by Charles Dickens, and *A Retrospect of Western Travel* (1838). But, never fully well, she collapsed on a visit to Venice in 1839 and remained prone and weak for five years. Often dismissed as a "hysteric", like many Victorian women, Martineau had in fact suffered a prolapse of the uterus, which seriously curtailed her work and travel.

Devoted to the supposed powers of mesmerism, a popular "alternative medicine" of the 1840s, she recovered enough to tour the Middle East and, on her return, visited the Lake District, where she settled, building a house, **The Knoll**, in Ambleside, in which she lived for the rest of her life. Never an orthodox woman, Martineau cut a notable figure in lakeland society. Smoking a pipe or a cigar, she tramped around the fells in men's boots, picking plants for her garden, much to the amusement of the locals. It was said she bathed in the lake by moonlight; certainly she mixed with the lower orders (lecturing in Ambleside to a working-class audience) and harried local officials and churchmen. All this, of course, put her at odds with the conservative Wordsworths – with William, she would argue ferociously, while Mary Wordsworth couldn't stand Martineau and left Rydal Mount every time she came to call.

Martineau continued to write at The Knoll – her *Complete Guide to the English Lakes* (1855) followed the example of Wordsworth – with later works reflecting her loss of faith and turn to humanism. But she continued to suffer from periodic bouts of illness and, after 1855, rarely left her house. By 1866 she was taking opium to relieve the pain of an ovarian cyst; she died at The Knoll in 1876 and was buried in Birmingham with members of her family.

1

PEOPLE AND PLACES: FIRST LOVES

The Lake District grabs people in different ways. For photographer **Stuart Clarke** (born in Hertfordshire, studied in London) it was the wildness and unpredictability of the ancient, golden-brown landscape that dominated his first visit, which he then married to his first true love – football.

His work started out as a peripatetic exhibition – recording games, grounds, clubs and fans from the Premier League down to the smallest amateur teams – and later Clarke maintained a "Homes of Football" gallery in Ambleside for many years, before moving his archive online (W homesoffootball.co.uk). Clarke's view? It's not too grand to say that he sees football as a window on life, but his adopted Lakes keep creeping in and so other photography champions the people and landscapes of this "magic lantern of a place". And this die-hard Watford fan now has other passions. "My heart leaps when I see Cumberland and Westmorland wrestlers so politely going about their craft", admits Clarke, while these days you're as likely to encounter him snapping away at a Cumbrian music festival as the World Cup. The clue is in the subtitle of his book *Cumbria Surrounded – Somewhere Across A Promised Land*, which charts the dreams and realities of Clarke's "perfect place", his own backyard of Cumbria.

Station – and contains a mural of the town's annual **rushbearing ceremony**, its figures resplendent in their 1940s finery. The ceremony itself dates from medieval times and derives from the custom of replacing the worn rushes (or reeds) on unflagged church floors. In Ambleside, the event takes place on the first Saturday in July, with a procession of decorated rushes through town and the church congregation singing the specially commissioned *Ambleside Rushbearers' Hymn*.

Waterhead

The Ambleside piers lie a mile south of town at **Waterhead**, a harbour on the shores of Windermere that's filled with ducks, swans and rowing boats, and overlooked by the grass banks and spreading trees of **Borrans Park**. Waterhead was known as Galava to the Romans, who first built a turf-and-timber fort on the lake edge in 90 AD, later superseded by a larger stone structure housing five hundred auxiliary soldiers; it was finally abandoned at the end of the fourth century. The Roman scholar Robin Collingwood excavated the two forts in separate digs between 1913 and 1920 (the Armitt collection holds many of the objects recovered), though there's little left to see *in situ* as the foundations of various buildings, including a large granary with hypocaust, are now largely grass-covered. But it's an emotive spot, backed by glowering fells and with views across the rippling Windermere waters – the perfect place for sunset-watching or star-gazing.

Wray Castle

Low Wray, LA22 0JA, 4 miles south of Ambleside, signposted off B5286 • mid-Feb to March daily 10am–4pm; Apr–Oct daily 10am–5pm, last admission 4pm • £10, family ticket £25, parking £5/2hr; NT • ☎ 015394 33250, W nationaltrust.org.uk/wray-castle • Bus #505 to Low Wray turn-off and 1 mile walk; or take Windermere Lake Cruises service from Waterhead (see page 58)

For a great day out, take the boat across to Wray and walk up through the grounds to magnificent **Wray Castle**, a castellated, mock-Gothic mansion built in the 1840s by a wealthy couple as their retirement home and taken on by the National Trust in 2012. With its glorious oak-panelled interior and the gardens and terraces with their superlative views of lake and mountains, appealingly, it's not presented as a period piece but rather a family-friendly attraction where you are positively begged to walk on the grass and sit on the chairs. Children get to play at kings and queens in the dressing-up room, and there are corridors to run in and below-stairs areas to explore.

1

House **tours** (every hour or so) are available to explain the finer points of the architecture and history (Beatrix Potter used to spend her holidays here, for example), but in the end it's the freedom to play and picnic in lovely surroundings that's the real draw.

There's a **café** inside the house (you don't have to pay for entrance to use this) and to make a full day of it, consider the walk down along the lakeshore to Sawrey (about an hour), where you can catch an alternative boat service back to Bowness instead of Ambleside.

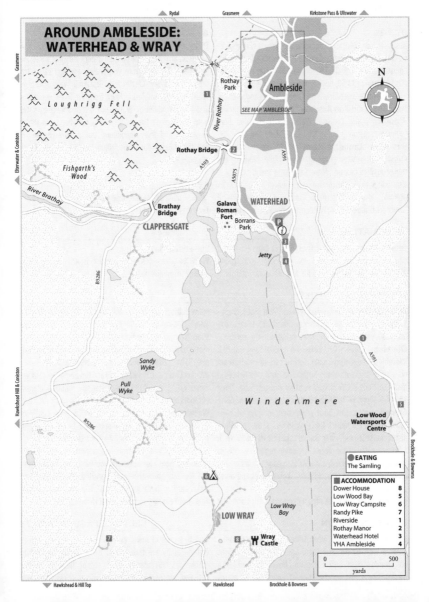

AROUND AMBLESIDE: WATERHEAD & WRAY

Rydal · Grasmere · Kirkstone Pass & Ullswater

Grasmere

Elterwater & Coniston

Hawkshead Hill & Coniston

Loughrigg Fell

Rothay Park

Ambleside

River Rothay

SEE MAP 'AMBLESIDE'

N

Rothay Bridge

A593

A5075

A591

Fishgarth's Wood

River Brathay

Brathay Bridge

CLAPPERSGATE

Galava Roman Fort

Borrans Park

WATERHEAD

P
i

Jetty

B5286

Sandy Wyke

Pull Wyke

B5286

W i n d e r m e r e

A591

Low Wood Watersports Centre

Brockhole & Bowness

LOW WRAY

Low Wray Bay

Wray Castle

● **EATING**
The Samling   1

■ **ACCOMMODATION**
Dower House   8
Low Wood Bay   5
Low Wray Campsite   6
Randy Pike   7
Riverside   1
Rothay Manor   2
Waterhead Hotel   3
YHA Ambleside   4

0   500
yards

Hawkshead & Hill Top · Hawkshead · Brockhole & Bowness

ARRIVAL AND DEPARTURE

BY CAR

Ambleside is around 13 miles (20min drive) from Kendal, or 16 miles (25min) from Keswick. The A591 runs right through town and drivers are best advised to make straight for the signposted car parks, though be warned that these fill quickly in summer – you may not find a space on your first pass through.

BY BUS

Buses stop on Kelsick Rd, opposite the library, with regular services to Windermere, Grasmere, Keswick, Hawkshead, Coniston and Langdale. The Central Lakes Day Rider ticket (£8.50, family £23.50; buy on board) gives unlimited travel as far as Windermere/Bowness, Coniston and Langdale.

Bus #505 "Coniston Rambler" to: Hawkshead (20min); Waterhead Hotel (Coniston Water) for Brantwood boat (30min); Coniston (35min). Mon–Sat 5 daily, Sun 4

Bus #516 "Langdale Rambler" to: Skelwith Bridge (10min); Elterwater (17min); Chapel Stile (20min); Old Dungeon Ghyll (30min). Mon–Sat 5 daily, Sun 4

Bus #555 to: Rydal (6min); Grasmere (13min); Keswick (44min); also to Waterhead (3min); Brockhole (7min); Troutbeck Bridge (9min); Windermere train station (14min);

AMBLESIDE AND AROUND

Staveley (28min); Kendal (40min). Mon–Sat hourly, Sun 6.

Bus #599 to: Waterhead (4min); Brockhole (9min); Troutbeck Bridge (11min); Windermere train station (15min); Bowness pier (25min); also to Rydal (5min); Dove Cottage (10min); Grasmere (14min). Service operates Easter–Oct daily every 20–30min; Nov–Easter (Bowness only) Mon–Sat hourly.

BY BOAT

There are year-round boat services from Bowness and Lakeside, arriving at the piers at Waterhead and Ambleside (see page 58), and from Waterhead, and you can catch services to Wray Castle and Brockhole Visitor Centre. Walking up to Ambleside town from the ferry piers takes about 15min, though a trolley-bus shuttle service operates from the piers to the *White Lion* pub in the town centre (weather- and ferry-dependent, but usually Easter–Oct daily, Nov–Easter Sat & Sun, 10am–4.30pm, roughly every 30min; £2.50).

BY TAXI

Abacus (male and female drivers; ☎015394 88285); John's Taxis (☎07759 143423); Kevin's Taxis (☎015394 32371).

INFORMATION

Tourist office Central Buildings, Market Cross (Mon–Sat 9am–5.30pm, Sun 10am–5pm; ☎015394 32582/0844 2250544, ⓦgolakes.co.uk), with post office and internet in the same building.

Website ⓦamblesideonline.co.uk is an irreverent but useful community website.

TOURS AND ACTIVITIES

Bike rental Ghyllside Cycles, The Slack (Mon–Sat 9.30am–5.30pm; ☎015394 33592, ⓦghyllside.co.uk). Daily rental from £30, with maps for day rides included in the price.

Climbing wall 101 Lake Rd (☎015394 33794, ⓦamblesideadventure.co.uk). Somewhere to let off steam on a rainy day, with walls for all ages and experiences – taster sessions (£20) as well as other courses. Mon–Thurs 12.30–9.30pm, Fri 10.30am–9.30pm, Sat & Sun 9am–6pm.

Guided walks The hugely experienced guys at Lake District Walker, 2 Kelsick Rd (☎0844 693 3389, ⓦthelakedistrictwalker.co.uk), offer guided Lake District walks (from £25) every day of the year – including regular ascents of Scafell Pike and Helvellyn via Striding Edge – plus a wide range of navigation training days, skills courses and other outdoor activities.

Outdoor gear There are almost permanent sales on in the

many outdoors stores. For mountain boots there's F.W. Tyson (Market Place; ☎015394 33329) as well as The Climber's Shop (Compston Corner; ☎015394 30122; walking-boot rental available) and Stewart R. Cunningham (Rydal Rd; ☎015394 32636), while large retailers include Black's (Market Cross; ☎01539 760197) and Gaynor Sports (Market Cross; ☎015394 33305), the latter the country's biggest outdoors store.

Watersports Low Wood, on A591, a mile south of Ambleside (April–Oct daily, otherwise by arrangement; ☎015394 39441, ⓦenglishlakes.co.uk/low-wood-bay/watersports), is a lakefront watersports centre at *Low Wood Bay* hotel, for anything from sit-on kayaking (from £15 for 1hr) and canoeing (£20/hr) to water-skiing and wakeboarding (£60/30mins, £80/hr lesson), plus rowing boat (from £25/hr) and motorboat (from £30/hr) rental.

ACCOMMODATION

SEE MAPS PAGES 70 AND 73

Lake Road, running between Waterhead and Ambleside, is lined with **B&Bs**, and there are other concentrations on Church Street and Compston Road, as well as a **backpackers** just on the edge of town. Fancier places tend to lie out of town, especially a mile to the south at Waterhead by the lake, which is also where you'll find Ambleside's YHA **hostel**. This is one of the most popular in the country and advance reservations are essential most

WALKS FROM AMBLESIDE

Ambleside is impressively framed – **Loughrigg Fell** to the west, the distinctive line of the **Fairfield Horseshoe** to the north and **Wansfell** to the east – and even inexperienced walkers have plenty of choice. Lake District Walker (see page 74) in town offers some excellent **guided walks**.

STOCK GHYLL

The stroll up Stock Ghyll Lane starts behind the *Salutation Hotel* and leads through the leafy woods of Stock Ghyll Park (with wonderful daffs in spring) to the tumbling waterfall of **Stock Ghyll Force**, which drops 60ft through a narrow defile. Allow an hour there and back if you linger on the viewing platform and rest on the benches.

WANSFELL

Those with loftier ambitions can regain the lane by Stock Ghyll Park and, a little way further up, look for the signposted path (over a wall-ladder) up Wansfell to **Wansfell Pike** (1581ft) – an hour all told to the top, from where there are superb views of Windermere and the surrounding fells. Circular hikers either cut due south from the summit to Skelghyll and return via Jenkins Crag (2hr), or head east across a clearly defined path to Troutbeck and Townend before cutting back (4hr).

LOUGHRIGG FELL

Behind St Mary's church in town, the green pastures of **Rothay Park** stretch down to the River Rothay, while above loom the heights of **Loughrigg Fell** (1101ft). The climb to the summit is signposted from near the humpback bridge at the foot of Rothay Park. Count on an hour to the top, though this is one of those walks that you can make last all day if you combine it with a Grasmere-and-Rydal Water circuit.

JENKINS CRAG AND STAGSHAW GARDENS

The viewpoint of **Jenkins Crag**, a mile from Waterhead, gives a glimpse of the lake as well as the central peaks of the Langdales and the Old Man of Coniston – *Country Life* magazine once reckoned this was Britain's most romantic picnic spot. From Ambleside, walk down Lake Road (though there's a handy car park near Hayes Garden World) and follow the signs up Skelghyll Lane, a thirty-minute walk. On the way back you can detour to the National Trust's woodland **Stagshaw Gardens** (Easter–June daily 10am–6.30pm; £2), at its best in spring for the shows of rhododendrons, camellias and azaleas.

FAIRFIELD HORSESHOE

The classic hiker's circuit from Ambleside is the **Fairfield Horseshoe** (11 miles; 6hr), which starts just out of town, off Kirkstone Road, and climbs up via High Sweden Bridge and **Dove Crag** (2603ft) to the flat top of **Fairfield** itself (2864ft), before dropping back along the opposing ridge to Nab Scar and Rydal, outside Grasmere. From Rydal, you can avoid most of the road back to Ambleside by following the footpath through the grounds of Rydal Hall. This really is a superb walk on a clear day, not too difficult yet encompassing eight different peaks.

of the year. The nearest **campsite**, *Low Wray*, is 3.5 miles south and also right by the lake – with its pods, bell tents, yurts and tipis, it's fully embracing the cool camping culture.

AMBLESIDE

Ambleside Manor Rothay Rd, LA22 0EJ ☎ 01539432062, ⌨ ambleside-manor.co.uk. This Victorian grey-slate pile sits in its own quiet grounds just on the edge of the town. Inside it's a tastefully updated period piece; all rooms are spacious, while pricier "superior" options feature elegant wooden furniture, marble fireplaces and oriental-style furnishings. The manor bills itself as a "vegetarian country guesthouse", which in this case means that it's the latest offering from *Zefferelli's* management (see page 78); packages include three-course meals at either of their restaurants, or two courses and a cinema ticket. Ample parking. **£110**

1

Brantfell House Rothay Rd, LA22 0EE ☎015394 55219, ⊛brantfell.co.uk. Soft tones, uncluttered rooms and fell views are the hallmark of this fetching makeover of a Victorian house on the edge of town. Six decent-sized double rooms make up the accommodation, all with serious showers. Breakfast is a big deal too – choose from traditional, continental or options like smoked salmon, bagels and cream cheese, hash browns, pancakes and kippers. Parking. **£100**

★ **Compston House** Compston Rd, LA22 9DJ ☎015394 32305, ⊛compstonhouse.co.uk. This traditional lakeland house conceals six immaculately renovated rooms, while a further three (which still retain the American-themed decor from the previous owners) are to be similarly upgraded in the future. If you really don't feel like leaving the property, kick back in the warming lounge with a cuppa and a book or a board game or two, with the resident German Shepherd, Mia, for company. A stay here also grants complementary access to the recreation ground opposite, with mini-golf and tennis. Free parking permit available. **£95**

Hillsdale Church St, LA22 0BT ☎015394 33174, ⊛hillsdaleambleside.co.uk. Chintz-free B&B, where the refurbished rooms have bold colours, flatscreen TVs and mini-fridges for fresh milk (room 7 has a thoroughly fancy shower room too). Weekend prices are typically £20 higher. Parking. **£80**

★ **Riverside** Under Loughrigg, LA22 9LJ, 0.5 mile west of Ambleside ☎015394 32395, ⊛riverside-at-ambleside.co.uk. A charming Victorian house on a quiet lane facing the River Rothay, a 10min walk from town – on foot, take any path across the park, cross the bridge and turn left. Six large, light country-pine-style rooms (a couple with whirlpool baths) include a river-facing four-poster room (£155). Sit outside on the garden deck and plan your day's walking with the library of guides, and then build yourself up with the magnificent breakfast, which includes home-made preserves, potato cakes and fruit smoothies. Parking. **£135**

★ **Rooms at the Apple Pie** Rydal Rd, LA22 9AN ☎015394 33679, ⊛applepieambleside.co.uk. The well-known Ambleside bakery also has some lovely boutique guest rooms – think specially commissioned artwork, designer light fittings, iPod docks, slatted wooden blinds and woven bed-throws. Two loft rooms also have baths as well as showers – good for cyclists, hikers and families. And while the rooms are as nice and boutiquey as they sound, there's also a welcome attention to detail, so you get real coffee, wine glasses and corkscrew, and the *Apple Pie's* own home-made gingerbread, plus fresh milk (and other drinks) are available in a lobby fridge. Breakfast isn't included but is available (with a ten percent discount) in the next-door bakery (see below). Parking. **£90**

Rothay Manor Rothay Bridge, LA22 0EH, 0.5 mile south of Ambleside ☎015394 33605, ⊛rothaymanor.

co.uk. Honed to perfection over many years, this impressive Regency-style mansion has been in the hands of the same amiable but unobtrusive family for nearly four decades (and in the *Good Hotel Guide* for as long). The nineteen rooms are larger than average (including decent-sized beds and spacious bathrooms), but the most sought-after "superior" rooms (£165) at the front have their own private balcony, while three suites in the grounds (£190) provide more space for families. Dinner's a treat, with a contemporary country-house menu served in the candlelit dining room. Parking. **£145**

★ **The Waterwheel** 3 Bridge St, LA22 9DU ☎015394 33286, ⊛waterwheelambleside.co.uk. An ancient, teeny-tiny Ambleside cottage revamped as a romantic bolthole. There are just three rooms, accessed up a steep staircase, whose signature style is contemporary Victorian – underfloor-heated bathrooms with clawfoot baths, brass bedsteads and flatscreen TVs. Stockgyhll is the priciest (£100) and nicest, but the second-floor Loughrigg and Rattleghyll rooms offer hill views, and in each room is a welcome-back decanter of port and some Kendal Mint Cake. Guests also receive complimentary access to the nearby Ambleside Salutation Spa. Parking permit provided. **£90**

WATERHEAD AND AROUND

Low Wood Bay Windermere, LA23 1LP, on A591, 1.5 miles south of Ambleside ☎0330 404 2676 or ☎015394 33338, ⊛englishlakes.co.uk/low-wood-bay. Framed by green hills behind and fronted by marina and lake, *Low Wood Bay* is every inch the Lake District resort hotel. Part of the same group as the *Waterhead*, it's a four-star, family-friendly place, with its own watersports centre over the road (where kids can take out a sit-on kayak) plus indoor pool, gym, sauna and outdoor hot tub for grown-ups. There's a separate family-oriented bar and bistro, with a smarter, more contemporary bar and restaurant inside the main hotel – breakfast here comes with sparkling views through the bristling yacht masts to the lake. Parking. **£160**

Waterhead Hotel Waterhead, LA22 0ER, on A591, 1 mile south of Ambleside ☎0330 404 2676 or ☎015394 32566, ⊛englishlakes.co.uk/waterhead. Lakeshore city-chic pretty much sums up this designer townhouse-style hotel opposite the Waterhead piers. White high-ceilinged rooms feature boutique fabrics and furnishings, with no detail left unattended – from king-sized beds with suede headboards to monogrammed cups for morning tea and a champagne menu in the sparkling slate-and-marble bathrooms. Guests get to use the pool and spa at nearby *Low Wood Bay*, and then it's back for a Pimms in the swanky garden-bar and dinner in the positively metropolitan restaurant. Parking. **£175**

YHA Ambleside Waterhead, LA22 0EU, on A591, 1 mile south of Ambleside ☎0845 371 9620, ⊛yha.org.uk/

hostel/ambleside. Ambleside's bustling lakeside affair is aimed squarely at the younger international backpacker market, rather than the grizzled, weather-beaten domestic hikers who haunt remoter hostels. Some 250 beds are divided among neatly furnished small dorms, twins and family rooms (most have a water view), with plenty of toilets and showers found down the corridors. There are also two rooms with double beds and a couple more with a double bed and a single bunk on top. Facilities are first-rate – whether it's swimming off the private jetty, hanging out in the licensed lakeside bar and restaurant, or renting a bike or kayak – and all the usual hostel stuff is well taken care of too (kitchen, laundry, drying room etc); there's an all-day restaurant and bar too. Per-person prices vary according to season, but range from £10 to £35. Parking. Dorms **£25**, doubles/twins **£56**

WRAY AND AROUND

Dower House Wray Castle, LA22 0JA, off B5286 (Hawkshead road), 3 miles south of Ambleside ☎015394 33211, ⊕www.dowerhouselakes.co.uk. Sleep the sleep of the just at this very peaceful country house on the Wray Castle estate, and then revel in the view at breakfast – right across the glinting lake waters to the fells. There are four traditionally furnished rooms, including one spacious single – aching hikers should ask for "Fairfield", the only one with a bath (rather than shower). If you've got soaked you can get your walking gear dried, and there's also an optional dinner served (all-inclusive rate £79/person, BYO wine). Alternatively, groups of up to five could opt for their charming, very comfortably appointed self-catering cottage, set in its own gardens

(from £435). To find Dower House, follow signs for Wray Castle and turn into the castle grounds. Parking. No credit cards. **£102**

★ **Low Wray Campsite** Low Wray, LA22 0JA, off B5286, 3.5 miles south of Ambleside, campsite ☎015394 32733, ⊕nationaltrust.org.uk/holidays/low-wray-campsite-lake-district. The beautiful National Trust site on the western shore of the lake is great for bikers, hikers and kayakers, but it's also a glam-campers' haven – as well as tent pitches in various grassy locations there are also woodland camping "pods" for couples and families (from £52) and fully furnished safari tents sleeping up to six (three nights from £330). There's a decent shop plus gourmet catering van in school holidays (breakfast and dinner, farmhouse cakes to handmade burgers). Bus #505 (to Coniston) passes the turn-off to the site, and from the stop it's a mile's walk down a country lane, with Wray Castle nearby. Closed Nov–Easter. Prices include one tent and a vehicle. Per person **£16**

★ **Randy Pike** LA22 0JP, on B5286 (Hawkshead road), 3 miles south of Ambleside, just past Low Wray turn-off ☎015394 36088, ⊕randypike.co.uk. Andy and Chrissy Hill (of Grasmere's Jumble Room restaurant) offer two amazing light-filled B&B suites opening out onto the gardens of what was once a Victorian gentleman's hunting lodge. You could live in the stunning designer bathrooms alone, while the handcrafted beds, pitch-pine floors and quirky furnishings add up to something very special. It's a grown-up, romantic retreat, and you can either stay put – munching from the snack-larder, mooching around terrace and gardens – or be whizzed down to the Jumble Room (see page 99) for dinner. Parking. **£200**

EATING

There's more choice in Ambleside for eating than just about anywhere else in the Lakes, from **cafés** and takeaways to gourmet **restaurants**, which is one of the reasons the town makes such a good base. The two small local **supermarkets**, Spar and Co-op, are both on Compston Road.

CAFÉS

★ **Apple Pie** Rydal Rd, LA22 9AN ☎015394 33679, ⊕applepieambleside.co.uk. The best café and bakery in town has a secluded patio-garden and plenty of room inside for lounging around. Breakfast is served until 11am (with free tea/coffee refills); they also have BLTs, soup and quiche, along with trademark home-made pies that come savoury (say, broccoli and Stilton or sausage and cider) or sweet (a luscious Bramley apple variety laced with cinnamon and raisin). Dishes around £8. Mon–Fri 9am–5.30pm, Sat & Sun 8.30am–5.30pm; closes 4.30pm in winter.

Rattle Ghyll Café 2 Bridge St, LA22 9DU ☎015394 34403, ⊕rattleghyll.com. Squeeze into this little

streamside café by the old water wheels for veggie wholefood dishes, salads and doorstop sandwiches (£5.50–7). They also bake their own bread and whisk up great smoothies. Daily 10am–4pm.

RESTAURANTS

Doi Intanon Market Place, LA22 9BU ☎015394 32119, ⊕ambleside-thai-restaurant.com. Ambleside's popular Thai restaurant makes a welcome change, with a standard stir-fry and curry menu bolstered by specials such as a fiery vegetable jungle curry or marinated chicken wrapped in pandan leaves (most mains £9–12). It was here that Renée Zellweger and co had their wrap party after filming the Beatrix Potter movie Miss Potter. Daily 6–10pm, Fri & Sat til 10.30pm.

Fellinis Church St, LA22 0BT ☎015394 33845, ⊕zeffirellis.com. With dishes like pumpkin risotto with goat's cheese and fresh cranberries, we're talking the gourmet end of veggie dining here. Prices are sensible (starters £6.95, mains £13.95) and, as it's part of the

Zeffirelli's family (see below), no surprise to learn there's a digital arthouse cinema on the premises too (meal and movie deal £24.75, reservations essential). Daily 5.30–10pm.

Fulling Mill Rydal Rd, LA22 9AN ☎015394 32137, ⊚thefullingmill.com. A very handsome bar and bistro, with open mezzanine floors chiselled out of a sixteenth-century mill complete with water wheel and sunny courtyard. The all-day menu is Modern British (pan-fried sea bass, slow-cooked lakeland lamb, confit of duck leg, fish pie), with sandwiches and light lunches (including tapas) from £5, sharing platters for two around £16, and mains £12–18. Daily noon–9pm.

★ **Lucy's On A Plate** Church St, LA22 0BU ☎015394 32288, ⊚lucysofambleside.co.uk. Quirky doesn't even begin to describe Lucy's hugely enjoyable and informal restaurant. If you book in advance, you'll probably find yourself namechecked in the daily personalised menu, which includes a variety of both locally and globally dishes, ranging from Cumbrian beef and lamb to South African bobotie (mains £12–30), as well as fish and vegan choices. The Queen of Desserts, meanwhile, boasts over thirty proper puddings (£7–10). Dinner reservations are pretty much essential. Daily 5pm–late (last orders 9.30pm).

★ **The Samling** Ambleside Rd, LA23 1LR, off the A591 about a mile south of Waterhead ☎015394 31922, ⊚thesamlinghotel.co.uk. Within a secluded luxury country hotel, this is rapidly becoming one of the most renowned places to dine in the Lakes. Dish names – exquisite tasting and artistically-prepared dishes are the order of the day here: for example cured mackerel and caviar with wasabi, venison with beetroot and damson, and chocolate mille-feuille with Laphroaig – with most of the herbs and veg (plus all the hen and quail eggs) from the restaurant's own kitchen garden. The three-course evening Choice Menu (£70) is complemented by a five-course Tasting Menu (£90), but if you don't fancy such a wallet-bashing, there's a three-course Table d'Hote lunch menu for £27.50. Daily noon–2pm & 6.30–9pm.

★ **Zeffirelli's** Compston Rd, LA22 9AD ☎015394 33845, ⊚zeffirellis.com. Zeff's is a star – famous for its wholemeal-base pizzas, but also serving Italian-with-a-twist starters, pastas and salads, all of it vegetarian (pizzas and mains around £12). The menu's available for lunch and dinner, but the funky dining room and conservatory are also open morning and afternoon for cakes, sandwiches and light meals; dinner reservations advised, especially for the popular meal-and-movie special (£22.75) at *Zeff's* own cinema. There's also a great upstairs bar (see below). Daily 10am–10pm.

DRINKING AND NIGHTLIFE

SEE MAP PAGE 70

Gratifyingly, **pubs** are as plentiful as restaurants in Ambleside, with a couple showing real character – the nicest alfresco drinking, however, is down at Waterhead.

Golden Rule Smithy Brow ☎015394 32257, ⊚robinsons brewery.com/goldenrule. The beer-lovers' and climbers' favourite pub – this is a cosy place for a post-hike pint (six real ales usually available) and a read of the Wainwright, with no jukebox, pool table, meals or other distractions (well, except for the dart board). Daily 11am–midnight.

Zeffirelli's Jazz Bar Compston Rd, LA22 9AD ☎015394 33845, ⊚zeffirellis.com. The shiny black fashionable space above *Zeffirelli's* restaurant and main cinema is a contemporary jazz and world music bar, with live music most Fri and Sat nights (often free). You'll catch anything from a local trio to an international act – see the website for schedules – and you can eat here too, from a shorter version of the restaurant menu. Daily, opens 1hr before first film, closes 11pm.

ENTERTAINMENT

Ambleside hosts two annual **festivals** – the Rushbearing in July (see page 32) and Ambleside Sports also in July (see page 33).

Zeffirelli's ☎015394 33845, ⊚zeffirellis.com. Five screens at three locations in town – the main building on Compston Rd (where the Italian restaurant is), *Zeffs by the Park* further down Compston Rd (by the church) and also at *Fellinis*, their veggie restaurant on Church St. Films are a mixture of mainstream releases and indie, arthouse fare, and there are lots of special events, such as live and recorded screenings from opera houses and festivals around the world. Good-value meal-and-movie deals include a meal at either restaurant with a film at any of the screens, but you'll need to book.

DIRECTORY

Banks Barclays (Crescent Rd) has an ATM.
Doctor Ambleside Group Practice, Rydal Rd (☎015394 32693, ⊚amblesidegrouppractice.co.uk).
Hospital The nearest is in Kendal (Burton Rd; ☎01539 732288, ⊚uhmb.nhs.uk).
Pharmacies Thomas Bell, Lake Rd (☎015394 33345);

Boots, 8–9 Market Cross (☎015394 33355).
Police station Rydal Rd (open limited hours, four days a week; ☎101, ⊚cumbria.police.uk).
Post office Inside the tourist office, "Hub of Ambleside", Central Buildings, Market Cross (Mon–Thu 8.30am–5.30pm, Fri & Sat 9am–5.30pm).

Troutbeck Valley

1

Troutbeck Bridge, three miles southeast of Ambleside along the A591 (and just a mile or so from Windermere town), heralds the start of the gentle **Troutbeck Valley** below Wansfell. It's a couple of miles up Bridge Lane, past Windermere youth hostel and the National Trust's **Townend** house, to the namesake **Troutbeck village**, which has a couple of aged inns as a target. The other route is the main A592, from Bowness to Patterdale, which runs north into the valley, passing **Holehird Gardens** before crossing over the bleak **Kirkstone Pass**.

Holehird Gardens

A592, Patterdale Rd, LA23 1NP • Daily 10am–4pm, visitor information open April–Oct; guided walks May–Sept Wed 11am • Free, though £5 donation requested • ☎ 015394 46008, ⊕ holehirdgardens.org.uk

The Lakeland Horticultural Society maintains its splendid gardens at **Holehird**, a mile up the Patterdale road. Seventeen acres of hillside gardens encompass various different habitats, from rock and alpine zones to rose gardens and shrubberies, all kept in perfect order by a willing army of volunteers. In addition to the guided walks, there's usually someone around to answer botanical and horticultural questions.

Townend

Bridge Lane, Troutbeck, LA23 1LB • Easter–Oct Wed–Sun plus bank hols 1–5pm, last admission 4.30pm; guided tours 11am & noon • £8, family ticket £20, cash only; NT • ☎ 015394 32628, ⊕ nationaltrust.org.uk/townend

Just before Troutbeck village, up Bridge Lane, is **Townend**, a seventeenth-century house. It was built in 1626 for George Browne, a wealthy yeoman farmer, one of that breed of independent farmers known in these parts as "statesmen", after the estates they tended. Remarkably, the house remained in the hands of eleven generations of the Browne family, for more than three hundred years, until 1943 when the National Trust took it over. Extensively renovated in 2016, it's an extraordinary relic of seventeenth-century vernacular architecture, with its round chimneys (of the sort admired by Wordsworth) surmounting a higgledy-piggledy collection of small rooms, some added as late as the nineteenth century. The house is well known for its woodcarvings and panelling, and lavishly embellished beds, fireplaces, chests, chairs and grandfather clocks are scattered around the various rooms. You'll also see the surviving laundry room (complete with ancient mangle), dairy, library and parlour.

Troutbeck village

Troutbeck village itself is really just a straggling hamlet with a post office (which sells cups of tea and ice cream). Several hikes pass through village and valley, with the peaks of Yoke (2309ft), Ill Bell (the highest at 2476ft) and Froswick (2359ft) on the east side forming the barrier between Troutbeck and Kentmere. The most direct route into Kentmere is the easy track over the **Garburn Pass**, while many use Troutbeck as the starting point for the five-hour walk along **High Street**, a nine-mile range running north to Brougham near Penrith. The course of a Roman road follows the ridge, probably once linking the forts at Brougham and Galava in Waterhead.

Kirkstone Pass

North of Troutbeck, the A592 makes a gradual ascent to **Kirkstone Pass**, four miles from the village, at the head of which there's a superbly sited pub, the *Kirkstone Pass Inn*, whose picnic tables (across the road) offer terrific views. A minor road from here

1

cuts down directly to Ambleside – so precipitous that it's known as "The Struggle" – while the A592 continues over the pass and down the valley to Ullswater.

ARRIVAL AND DEPARTURE

By bus Public transport to Troutbeck is limited to the seasonal "Kirkstone Rambler" bus #508, which runs (4 daily; late July to early Oct; Easter to late July Sat, Sun & bank hols)

TROUTBECK VILLAGE

from Bowness piers to Windermere train station (10min), and then up the A592 to Troutbeck (24min) and Kirkstone Pass (37min), with onward service to Ullswater and Penrith.

ACCOMMODATION AND EATING

Traditional **accommodation** in Troutbeck is at the famous old inn, the *Mortal Man* but there's also superior studio accommodation and some cheaper village B&Bs – local tourist offices can check on space for you. Budget accommodation is at the valley's self-catering **youth hostel**, confusingly called *YHA Windermere*, which is a mile up the steep road from the bus stop at Troutbeck Bridge.

★ **Fellside Studios** Fellside, LA21 1PE ☎015394 34000, ⓦ fellsidestudios.co.uk. A tranquil base for walkers who can set off each day straight from the door of these two excellent self-contained studios (one double, one twin, both £10 more expensive at weekends). They're decorated in contemporary style, with oak floors, slate-tiled kitchens and shower rooms, while attractive living/sleeping areas open directly on to outside terraces. A generous continental breakfast (cold meats, smoked fish, cheese etc) is brought to your door each morning. Parking. **£90**

Mortal Man Bridge Lane, LA23 1PL ☎015394 33193, ⓦ themortalman.co.uk. For glorious valley views, it's hard to beat the tidy rooms and serene gardens of the famous old *Mortal Man*, whose name derives from the doggerel written on the inn's sign ("O Mortal Man, that lives by bread, What

is it makes thy nose so red? Thou silly fool, that look'st so pale, 'Tis drinking Sally Birkett's ale"). The public bar's an age-old beauty, with pub food (curried bubble & squeak to Cumberland sausage with apple and mustard mash, mains £13–19) served in the bar, gardens or valley-view restaurant. There are walks from the doorstep (and some handwritten walking guides to borrow), while Sun night is Folk Night, Tues is Open Mic night, and Thurs is spoken word night. Parking. Daily noon–11pm; kitchen Mon–Thurs & Sun noon–9pm, Fri & Sat noon–9.30pm. **£100**

YHA Windermere High Cross, Bridge Lane, LA23 1LA ☎0845 371 9352, ⓦ yha.org.uk/hostel/windermere. Built originally as a private mansion, the house revels in magnificent lake views, while a major refit has smartened up rooms and facilities. Families like it for its woodland trails, bike rental and outdoor activities (and a family of four can usually get a room for around £60), while the food gets good reviews – you can also buy bottled Cumbrian beers and organic wines. There are also tipis sleeping four (£99) and bell tents sleeping up to five (£99), while it's also possible to camp here year-round. Parking. Dorms **£21**, twin rooms **£35**, camping **£15**

Staveley and around

Four miles east of Windermere, the little village of **Staveley** lies tucked away on the banks of the River Kent. The river has powered mills in Staveley for more than seven hundred years, and in the eighteenth and nineteenth centuries there was prosperity of sorts as first cotton was produced and then wooden bobbins were manufactured here in sizeable quantities. These wood-turning skills have survived into modern times, with Staveley furniture and woodwork still a thing of beauty. The craft workshops and businesses in the former mill buildings in Mill Yard are the main draw today, though Staveley is also the jumping-off point for fantastic hikes and off-road bike rides in the adjacent hideaway valleys of **Kentmere** and **Longsleddale**.

Staveley

An easy half-hour stroll around **Staveley** starts by the restored tower of **St Margaret's** on Main Street, all that survives of Staveley's original fourteenth-century church. Follow the path at the side of the church tower down to the river, turn left and walk along the riverside path and road to the old bridge, from where you return through the village, passing the replacement nineteenth-century church of **St James**, inside which is a superb Burne-Jones-designed stained-glass window depicting a star-clustered heavenly choir surmounting the Crucifixion.

Mill Yard

Mill Yard, off Main St, LA8 9LR • Business hours vary • Free parking • ⓦ staveleymillyard.com

Staveley's old mill buildings have been developed over the years into **Mill Yard**, a thriving enclave of cottage craft and food businesses, which makes a great target for browsers and buyers whether you're after a scoop of organic lakeland ice cream or a hand-carved piece of furniture. There's also bike rental, as well as a café, artisan bakery, and brewery – it's a pretty good pit stop for food and drink (see page 83).

A visit to **Hawkshead Brewery** (Mon–Thurs noon–7pm, Fri & Sat noon–11pm, Sun noon–8pm; ☏ 01539 825260, ⓦ hawksheadbrewery.co.uk) is a great introduction to brews with names such as "Lakeland Gold" or "Brodie's Prime" – tours (daily 1pm; £10, booking advised) of the brewery include a short film, a 45min tour and a free pint. Otherwise, try and make it here for one of their two annual beer festivals, one in late March and another in mid-July.

Kentmere

North of Staveley a narrow road runs its dappled way alongside the River Kent, widening out after three miles into the splendid broad valley of **Kentmere**, with its isolated chapel perched on a bluff in the distance. Houses are few and far between, but the valley has been settled for more than a thousand years – remains of a Viking Age farmstead have been identified near the valley head. A later building, **Kentmere Hall**, a couple of hundred yards up the country lane from the chapel, retains a remarkably well-preserved fourteenth-century turreted pele tower, which you can see from the lane. The heather moorland further up the valley provides a habitat for ground-nesting birds like red grouse, curlew and – uniquely for a bird of prey – merlin, while on the high fells, if you're lucky, you'll see wild ponies grazing. Needless to say, it's fabulous **walking** country, with various challenging routes available in the valley, including one of the best of all lakeland circular – or "horseshoe" – hikes.

WALKS FROM STAVELEY AND KENTMERE

Staveley makes a good target for a day on the **local fells**. Walkers come past on the Dales Way, which follows the River Kent from Kendal, steers just south of the village and then cuts west across the low fells to Bowness. You can also walk or cycle into Kentmere easily enough from Staveley or Troutbeck, and into Longsleddale from Kentmere, with Kentmere itself sited at the junction of several more strategic paths and bridleways. However, there's only extremely limited parking by the Kentmere Institute hall, behind the chapel, so you'll need to get there early.

LOCAL ROUTES AND WALKS

Easy hiking routes from Kentmere head west to Troutbeck (via the relatively gentle **Garburn Pass**) or east to Sadgill and **Longsleddale** – you can make a six-mile circuit of the latter route by going one way via Green Quarter and Cocklaw Fell. A signposted route also runs up the valley bottom to **Kentmere Reservoir**, a little over two miles from the chapel, which is hemmed in by a ring of dramatic, steep-sided fells.

THE KENTMERE HORSESHOE

The excellent full-day hike known as the **Kentmere Horseshoe** (12 miles; 7hr) is a fairly strenuous peak-bagging route along ridges and saddles high above Kentmere Reservoir, taking in Kentmere Pike, Harter Fell, Mardale Ill Bell, Froswick, Ill Bell and Yoke. At one point, crossing Nan Bield Pass, four bodies of water are in view (Haweswater, two tarns and the reservoir), and if you walk the circuit anticlockwise (most people don't) then you'll have magnificent views of Windermere and Morecambe Bay on the home stretch.

1

BRITAIN'S FAVOURITE POSTIE

As millions of British preschoolers know, the postie's job starts "early in the morning, just as day is dawning" – and don't even think of trying to deliver letters without a black-and-white cat in tow. **Postman Pat**'s village of "Greendale" was originally inspired by the rolling countryside and wandering sheep of **Longsleddale**, which author John Cunliffe got to know well during his time in nearby Kendal. Cunliffe used to live on Greenside in Kendal, just down from which was the Beast Banks post office (next to the *Riflemans' Arms* pub), where he used to chat to the postmaster. It's closed as a post office now (though there's a plaque) but this is where Cunliffe envisaged Pat picking up the mail each morning from Mrs Goggins, in tales that were a big hit on the BBC as soon as they were aired in the early 1980s. Thirty years on, instead of drawing his pension, Pat's been given a new lease of life – the latest programmes have transferred him out of sleepy Greendale to the Special Delivery Service in the busy town of "Pencaster" and given him a helicopter and motorbike (don't worry, Jess the cat gets a sidecar).

Longsleddale

Next valley to the east after Kentmere is **Longsleddale** (pronounced "Longsleddle"), which is about as quiet a corner of the Lakes as can be imagined. There's only one road, as ridiculously pretty as it is narrow: it peters out after six miles at graceful **Sadgill Bridge**, which is as far as you can go by car. Beyond here rise the encircling fells, where hikers can make their way up to the abandoned Wrengill Quarry and its waterfall and then along the old packhorse trail over Gatesgarth Pass and down to Haweswater. Most of the year you'll not see another soul, although wildlife's another matter – red squirrels and deer abound, while buzzards circle above the looming fells.

ARRIVAL AND DEPARTURE
STAVELEY AND AROUND

By car Staveley is bypassed by the A591 – follow the signs in to Mill Yard, where there's masses of free parking (though, as the only such parking in town, it's often full). The narrow roads of Kentmere and Longsleddale require careful driving; also note that parking is very limited, but there are usually spaces at the various walk access points.

By bus Bus #555 stops in Staveley; there's an hourly service from Windermere train station or from Kendal. There are sometimes summer Sun and bank holiday buses into Kentmere, but they don't always run.

By train There's an hourly train service to Staveley from Kendal (9min) and Windermere (5min).

ACTIVITIES

Mountain biking Wheelbase in Mill Yard, Staveley (Mon & Wed–Sat 9am–5.30pm, Tues 10am–5.30pm, Sun 10am–4pm; ☎ 01539 821443, ⊛ wheelbase.co.uk) is the UK's biggest bike store, and rents bikes from £20/day, electric bikes from £30. The bridleways and trails of Kentmere Valley are easily accessible from here, as are the gentler Crook and Winster fells, and the mountain-bike centre has showers and changing rooms for cyclists.

ACCOMMODATION
SEE MAP PAGE 50

Note that the excellent **Watermill Inn**, 1.5 miles away in Ings (see page 83), also offers accommodation.

Eagle & Child Kendal Rd, Staveley, LA8 9LP ☎ 01539 821320, ⊛ eaglechildinn.co.uk. The village's nicest inn – right in the centre – has five smallish, but tastefully decorated rooms, some overlooking the River Kent, along with a loft apartment (£95). Good food, too. Parking. **£90**

Maggs Howe Lowfield Lane, Green Quarter, Kentmere, LA8 9JP ☎ 01539 821689. Half a mile or so east of the chapel (signposted from the bridge) there's either straightforward B&B in three double rooms in the house or bunks (plus mattresses on the floor) in the camping barn next door, which has a couple of showers and a fully equipped kitchen. The nearest shop and pub is down in Staveley, but you can arrange to have a big cooked breakfast (£8) or an evening meal (from £15) at the B&B, and walkers can drop in for afternoon tea. Parking. No credit cards. Bunkhouse (per person) **£12**, doubles **£70**

EATING

Eagle & Child Kendal Rd, Staveley, LA8 9LP ☎ 01539 821320, ⊕ eaglechildinn.co.uk. This great old inn has a riverside garden, where you can sip a Cumbrian beer, and good bar meals (using ingredients from village or local suppliers), including home-made soups and pies, Kentmere lamb shanks or the local butcher's bangers with mash (mains £10.50–13). Friday is fish night (including fish and chips), then on Sunday there's a cracking roast going for £12.95. Daily 11am–11pm; kitchen Mon–Fri noon–2.30pm & 6–9pm; Sat & Sun noon–9pm.

More? Mill Yard, Staveley, LA8 9LR ☎ 01539 822297, ⊕ moreartisan.co.uk. Mill Yard's artisan bakery makes all kinds of real bread in a wood-fired oven, and cakes get an honourable mention too, not least the fab squishy choccie "muddees". It's a good place for a quick snack or lunch (most dishes around the £5 mark), from a bowl of soup to a hot beef sandwich or a pork belly sausage roll, and there are a few outdoor tables. Daily 7.30am–4pm, Sat & Sun till 5pm.

★ **Wilf's Café** Mill Yard, Staveley, LA8 9LR ☎ 01539 822329, ⊕ wilfs-cafe.co.uk. The classic café for outdoor enthusiasts, cyclists and hikers has expanded over the years, but the heart of *Wilf's* was once the bobbin loft of an old wood mill – now there's dining on two floors and terraces out the back overlooking river and weir. The food is good value (most dishes £4.50–7), hearty and mostly veggie – big breakfasts, rarebits, chillis, filled baked potatoes, salads and home-made cakes and puddings are mainstays, though there's a blackboard list of daily specials. Daily 9am–5pm.

DRINKING

★ **Hawkshead Brewery Beer Hall** Mill Yard, Staveley, LA8 9LR ☎ 01539 825260, ⊕ hawksheadbrewery.co.uk. The showcase bar for the excellent beers of the independent Hawkshead Brewery (see page 31) – the stylish main bar is built around the massive fermenting vessels, and there are views into the brew-house and cellars. They'll let you taste the brews before ordering, and there's a whole range of other guest beers, organic juices, and wines by the glass – not to mention quality beer-matched bar bites that are largely Stateside inspired, for example sliders and loaded fries (dishes £4–15). Regular gigs and events include the weekly musical "Sunday Sesh", while two annual beer fests (March & July) offer scores of nationwide brews. Mon–Thurs noon–7pm, Fri & Sat noon–11pm, Sun noon–8pm; kitchen Mon–Thurs noon–3pm, Fri & Sat noon–8.30pm, Sun noon–6pm.

Watermill Inn Ings, LA8 9PY, on A591 1.5 miles west of Staveley ☎ 01539 821309, ⊕ lakelandpub.co.uk. No beer fan should miss the *Watermill*, which has up to sixteen real ales available on tap at any one time, and even more during its various festivals. Add a sun-trap garden and popular bar food and it's no wonder it's won just about every beer award going. The pub was once an old bobbin mill, now imaginatively restored – the bar is fashioned from church pews – and there's a craft brewery on site, as well as eight good-value bedrooms (two with balconies; £89). It's also the venue for regular music nights, plus monthly tall tales (first Tues) when the long-standing South Lakeland Storytelling Club meets. Parking. Mon–Sat 11am–11pm, Sun 11.30am–10.30pm; kitchen daily noon–9pm.

Grasmere and the central fells

THE VILLAGE GREEN IN ELTERWATER

Grasmere and the central fells

Grasmere – lake and village – is the traditional dividing line between the north and south Lakes, between the heavily touristed Windermere region and the more rugged fells on either side of Keswick. Rather than for its own charms (which are considerable), Grasmere owes its wild popularity to its most famous former resident, William Wordsworth, who first moved here in 1799 and lived in a variety of houses in the vicinity until his death in 1850. Two in particular are open to the public: Dove Cottage, where he first set up home in the Lakes with his sister Dorothy; and Rydal Mount, on nearby Rydal Water, the comfortable family home to which he moved at the height of his fame.

The museum and interpretation centre at **Dove Cottage** is the Lake District's most important cultural attraction, an essential visit for anyone interested in the English Romantics. It's centred on Wordsworth, of course, but the influence of other famous **literary names** hangs heavily on Grasmere, too, notably those of Thomas De Quincey, who lived here for more than twenty years and married a local girl; and of the dissolute Coleridges – father Samuel Taylor and son Hartley, whose separate periods of residence often tried the Wordsworths' patience.

Just a few miles west of Grasmere lie the **central fells**, including some of the Lake District's most famous peaks and valleys. Minor roads from Grasmere and Ambleside twist into the superb valleys of Great and Little **Langdale**, overlooked by the prominent rocky summits of hikers' favourites like the **Langdale Pikes**, **Bowfell** and **Crinkle Crags**. It's not all hard going though: there are easier walks to tarns and viewpoints in the bucolic surroundings of **Easedale** and Little Langdale, while hamlets such as **Skelwith Bridge** and **Elterwater** provide classic inns and country B&Bs for an isolated night's stay.

Grasmere and around

Four miles northwest of Ambleside, the pretty village of **Grasmere** consists of an intimate cluster of grey-stone houses beside the babbling River Rothay. With a permanent population of under a thousand, and just a handful of roads which meet at a central green, it would be the archetypal, slow-paced, rustic village were it not for the **Wordsworth** connection – **Dove Cottage**, home to the poet and his sister Dorothy, sits just outside Grasmere. The presence of one of the country's key literary sites certainly brings in the crowds and tour buses and accounts for the assorted gift shops, galleries, cafés and hotels. But even in the poet's day curious visitors to Grasmere were common, and even before Wordsworth put down roots here, the "white village" on the water in this "unsuspected paradise" had entranced the poet Thomas Gray (of "Elegy" fame), whose journal of his ground-breaking tour of the Lakes did much to bring the region to wider attention.

Look beyond the crowds, however, or come out of season, and Grasmere slowly seduces, whether it's for **walks** by the alluring lake or rambles among the surrounding crags and fells. These days, the village is also a rather upmarket retreat, with a fair choice of **boutique accommodation** – ideal for a pampered weekend away, if not the sort of thing of which the plain-living Wordsworth would have approved.

THE GARDENS AT RYDAL HALL

Highlights

❶ Visiting Wordsworth's grave, Grasmere One of England's most famous literary pilgrimages is to the simple grave of the poet Wordsworth. See page 90

❷ Dove Cottage, Grasmere It's an obvious tourist attraction, but you shouldn't miss Wordsworth's first home in the Lake District. See page 93

❸ Rydal Hall and Rydal Water Lovely gardens, woodland walks and a top tearoom, followed by a gentle stroll around a pretty lake. See page 101

❹ Cakes and walks at Skelwith Bridge Indulge your sweet tooth at fabulous *Chesters By The River* after viewing the local waterfall. See page 105

❺ Elterwater Stay the night in one of the Lake District's most attractive hamlets. See page 105

❻ Walking in Great Langdale Routes up the famous Langdale Pikes, Crinkle Crags and Bowfell could keep serious hikers occupied for a week. See page 108

❼ Old Dungeon Ghyll After a day on the fells, recover with a beer or two in the stone-flagged hikers' bar of this atmospheric Langdale inn. See page 109

HIGHLIGHTS ARE MARKED ON THE MAP ON PAGE 88

GRASMERE AND THE CENTRAL FELLS

HIGHLIGHTS

1. Visiting Wordsworth's grave, Grasmere
2. Dove Cottage, Grasmere
3. Rydal Hall and Rydal Water
4. Cakes and walks at Skelwith Bridge
5. Elterwater
6. Walking in Great Langdale
7. Old Dungeon Ghyll

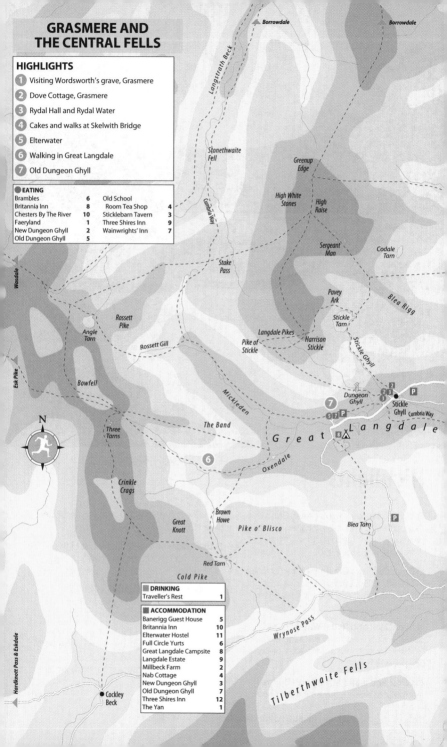

by Oswald (later St Oswald), King of Northumbria. Inside, the church's unique twin naves are split by an arched, whitewashed wall. Wordsworth described its "naked rafters intricately crossed" in *The Excursion*, while **Thomas De Quincey** married a farmer's daughter, Margaret Simpson, here in 1817 (see page 94) – a match disapproved of by the snobbish Wordsworths. Associations aside, it's a rather plain church, though there is a memorial plaque to Wordsworth ("a true philosopher and poet") on the wall to the left of the altar, as well as his prayer book on display in a small case in the nave. Also in the case is a medallion likeness of **Sir John Richardson**, surgeon, naturalist and Arctic explorer who accompanied John Franklin on the heroic, but futile, expedition of 1819 to discover the Northwest Passage. Richardson later came into possession of a Grasmere country house, Lancrigg in Easedale (now a hotel), where he supervised the laying out of the woods and gardens with specimens collected on his travels. He's also buried in Grasmere churchyard (a few paces to the right from the rear entrance).

2

The Wordsworth graves

A couple of hundred thousand people a year traipse through the church grounds, following the signposts to the **Wordsworth graves** – William is buried alongside his wife Mary and sister Dorothy, his beloved daughter Dora (buried in her married name Quillinan) and two of his much younger children, Catherine and Thomas, whose deaths marred the Wordsworths' early years in Grasmere. A worn Celtic cross behind the Wordsworth plots marks the grave of Hartley Coleridge, Samuel Taylor's son. Like his father, Hartley possessed an addictive personality, though – unlike his father – his lapses never produced a formal break with the Wordsworths, with whom Hartley remained a family favourite.

Sarah Nelson's Gingerbread Shop

Church Cottage, LA22 9SW • Daily 9.15am–5.30pm, winter hours may be reduced • ☎ 015394 35428, ⓦ grasmeregingerbread.co.uk

Right at the rear entrance to St Oswald's churchyard stands **Sarah Nelson's Gingerbread Shop** – you'll smell the shop before you see it. It was formerly the village schoolhouse, where Wordsworth taught for a time in 1812, but Grasmere gingerbread has been made on the premises since the mid-nineteenth century and the recipe is a closely guarded secret (kept locked in an Ambleside bank vault).

Heaton Cooper Studio

Grasmere, LA22 9SX • Daily 9am–5pm • ☎ 015394 35280, ⓦ heatoncooper.co.uk

The **Heaton Cooper Studio**, opposite the green, is a showcase for the works of one of the Lakes' most durable and talented artistic families, headed by the landscapes and village scenes of Alfred Heaton Cooper (1864–1929). Cooper became a well-known illustrator of guidebooks, especially in the first two decades of the twentieth century, and was succeeded in this by his son, William Heaton Cooper (1903–95), who climbed with the pioneering lakeland mountaineers. William produced paintings and sketches for four topographical Lake District guidebooks and then virtually ensured a dynastic succession by marrying the sculptor Ophelia Gordon Bell. Examples of all their work are on show in the gallery, together with those of current family members – Alfred's grandson Julian Heaton Cooper (born 1947) is the most notable, a climber-artist who produces huge oil paintings of the world's more remote locations.

Allan Bank

Allan Bank, LA22 9QB • Mid-Feb–Oct daily 10.30am–5pm, Nov to mid-Dec Fri–Sun 10.30am–4pm • £7.50, family ticket £18.25; NT • ☎ 015394 35143, ⓦ nationaltrust.org.uk/allan-bank-and-grasmere • Follow the lane up by the side of *Miller Howe Café*, a 10min walk from the village

2

SOUL, MIND AND SPIRIT – COLERIDGE IN THE LAKES

Samuel Taylor Coleridge (1772–1834) already knew both Robert Southey and William Wordsworth by the time he moved to the Lake District. With Southey, he shared an enthusiasm for the French Revolution and an unfulfilled plan to found a Utopian community in America; and in 1795 he'd married Sarah Fricker, the sister of Southey's fiancée Edith. Later, while living in Somerset, Coleridge and Wordsworth wrote *Lyrical Ballads* together, which contained Coleridge's *The Rime of the Ancient Mariner*. Coleridge sang Wordsworth's praises at every opportunity; a favour returned by the enamoured Dorothy, who thought Coleridge a "wonderful man ... whose conversation teems with soul, mind and spirit".

Thus, when Wordsworth moved to Grasmere in 1799, Coleridge needed little prompting to follow. Having toured the Lakes, he settled on the newly built **Greta Hall** in Keswick, leasing it for 25 guineas a year. The Coleridges – Samuel Taylor, his wife Sarah, and 4-year-old son Hartley – were installed by July 1800; a third son, Derwent, was born in the house that September (the Coleridges' second son, Berkeley, had died in 1798); and daughter Sara followed in 1802.

Coleridge spent much of his first two years at Keswick helping Wordsworth prepare a new edition of the *Lyrical Ballads*, but found plenty of time to explore. His notebooks detail the **walks** he took, and in the summer of 1802 he embarked on a nine-day walking tour of the Lakes (see page 277).

Despite his first flush of excitement at lakeland living, Coleridge wasn't happy. He'd been taking **opium** for years – if *Kubla Khan* didn't spring from an opium-induced dream no poem ever did – and was in poor health, suffering from rheumatism. What's more, his relationship with his wife was deteriorating – spurred by the fact that Coleridge had fallen hopelessly in love with Wordsworth's sister-in-law, Sara Hutchinson (his "Asra"), by now living at Grasmere. Indeed, his last great poem, *Dejection: an Ode*, was originally sent to Sara as a letter in April 1802.

In September 1803, Southey and his wife arrived to share Greta Hall. As the Southeys had just lost a child Coleridge hoped that the two sisters might comfort each other, but he was also looking for a way to escape so that he might regain his health and inspiration. He left for **Malta** in June 1804 (where for two years he was secretary to the Governor) and never lived with his family again. Southey assumed full responsibility for Coleridge's wife and children, who remained at Greta Hall.

When Coleridge returned to the Lakes it was to live with the Wordsworths at **Allan Bank** in Grasmere, where he produced a short-lived political and literary periodical, *The Friend*, helped by Sara Hutchinson. When she left, to go and live with her brother in Wales, a depressed Coleridge – once more dependent on drugs – departed for London. Wordsworth, sick of having him moping around the house, described Coleridge to a friend as an "absolute nuisance", which Coleridge came to hear about: after this breach in 1810, Coleridge only ever made perfunctory visits to the Lakes, avoiding Wordsworth (though the two were later reconciled). He died in London on July 25, 1834, and is buried in that city's Highgate Cemetery.

William Wordsworth spent most of his Grasmere years living in two (now very famous) houses outside the village – Dove Cottage and Rydal Mount – but the years in between these residences (1808–13) saw the Wordsworth family occupying two other houses. One, the Old Rectory (opposite St Oswald's) in the village, is closed to the public, but the more imposing **Allan Bank** is now open again after years as a strictly private residence, and it's a remarkable place to visit.

The **Wordsworths** moved here from Dove Cottage in 1808 and stayed until 1811 – two more children were born to them while they lived here, and **Samuel Taylor Coleridge** was a guest in the house for almost two years, producing his literary and political periodical, *The Friend*, from a room in the house while sinking ever further into drug-induced decline (see box). Allan Bank has undergone several refurbishments since Wordsworth's day – it was remodelled in a Victorian Gothic Revival style in the mid-nineteenth century and was later owned by Canon Rawnsley, co-founder of the National Trust, whose family then gave it to the organization.

The house was opened to the public for the first time in 2012, after being sorely neglected for decades (and nearly burning down), and is something of an ongoing restoration project. You may be surprised by the way the National Trust has encouraged participation in reopening Allan Bank – it's quite something to sit in a chair and gaze out at the lake from Coleridge's room, for example, or let the children paint and draw in Wordsworth's bedroom, while cups of tea in front of the fire and a chat with the staff are positively encouraged. Outside, marked trails take you on a circuit through the garden and surrounding woodland (allow 45 minutes), rewarding you with some lovely views over Grasmere and its lake.

The lake

Rowing boat rental from *Faeryland* tea garden, Redbank Rd • March–Oct daily 10.30am–5pm • Per hour: one or two people £15, three or four people £20 • ☎ 015394 35060

It's a ten-minute walk from the centre of Grasmere down Redbank Road to the western side of the fell-fringed **lake** itself, also called Grasmere. Renting a rowing boat is a nice idea in good weather – you can take a picnic out to the wooded islet in the middle of the lake. Or, if you're in the mood for a walk and a view, continue the mile to the southern reaches of the lake where **Loughrigg Terrace** sits under the crags of Loughrigg Fell (look for a track off the road through Redbank Woods, signposted "Loughrigg Terrace and YHA"). From the terrace there are tremendous views back up the lake and across the broad valley, culminating in the pass of Dunmail Raise. Other walks include a climb up Loughrigg Fell itself, or the excellent round-lake circuit (see page 96).

Dove Cottage

Town End, LA22 9SH, just outside Grasmere on A591 • Daily: March–Oct 9.30am–5.30pm; Nov–Feb 9.30am–4.30pm; closed early Jan to early Feb • £8.25 • ☎ 015394 35544, ⊛ wordsworth.org.uk • Limited parking, though it's an easy walk from the village; buses #555 and #599 pass by

One of the world's most famous places of literary pilgrimage stands on the southeastern outskirts of Grasmere village, in the former hamlet of Town End – **Dove Cottage**, home to **William and Dorothy Wordsworth** from 1799 to 1808 and the place where the great man wrote some of his finest poetry. The cottage – kept as it was in Wordsworth's day – forms part of a complex administered by the Wordsworth Trust, whose unrivalled collection amounts to some seventy thousand manuscripts, first editions, books, letters, portraits and other items. A selection is always on show in the separate Wordsworth Museum, with the rest stored in the adjacent **Jerwood Centre**, a £3-million facility opened in 2005 by Seamus Heaney, and which is accessible to scholars and researchers. Dove Cottage also is the headquarters of the **Centre for British Romanticism**, which together with the Wordsworth Trust sponsors major exhibitions on cultural themes, as well as a respected poetry programme, family activities, residential conferences, and talks and workshops attracting some top names.

Brief history

Wordsworth first saw the house in November 1799 while on a walking tour with his friend Samuel Taylor Coleridge, with whom he had published *Lyrical Ballads* the previous year. Keen to have a base in the Lakes, Wordsworth negotiated a rent of £8 a year for what had originally been an inn called the Dove & Olive-Bough; he and his sister moved in just before Christmas of that year. It was a simple stone house with a slate roof – Wordsworth at this time was far from financially secure – where the poet

2

SEX, DRUGS AND CONFESSIONS – THOMAS DE QUINCEY IN THE LAKES

The direct object of my own residence at the lakes was the society of Mr Wordsworth.
Thomas De Quincey, *Recollections of the Lakes and the Lake Poets*

The young **Thomas De Quincey** (1785–1859) was one of the first to fully appreciate the revolutionary nature of Wordsworth's and Coleridge's collaborative *Lyrical Ballads*, and as a student at Oxford in 1803 he had already written to **Wordsworth** praising his "genius" and hoping for his friendship. In reply, Wordsworth politely invited him to visit if he was ever in the area. It took De Quincey four years (and two abortive visits, abandoned out of shyness) to contrive a meeting, eventually through the auspices of Coleridge, a mutual friend.

De Quincey first came to **Dove Cottage** in November 1807 to meet his hero, trembling at the thought: the meeting is recorded in one of the more self-effacing chapters of his *Recollections*. When the Wordsworths moved to **Allan Bank** the following year, De Quincey – by now a favourite with the Wordsworth children – went too, staying several months. His small private income enabled him to take over Dove Cottage in February 1809, which he filled with books (in contrast to Wordsworth, who had very few). He also demolished the summerhouse and made other changes in the garden that annoyed the Wordsworths; the relationship further cooled after 1812 following the deaths of young Catherine and Thomas Wordsworth. De Quincey was particularly badly affected by the loss of **Catherine**, his "sole companion", and for two months after her death passed each night stretched out on her grave in Grasmere churchyard.

The truth is, De Quincey wasn't a well man. Since his university days, he had been in the habit of taking opium in the form of **laudanum** (ie dissolved in alcohol), and at Dove Cottage he was taking huge, addictive doses – the amount of alcohol alone would have been debilitating enough. He closeted himself away in the cottage for days at a time, complaining that Wordsworth was spoiling the books he borrowed from him, and began an affair with **Margaret (Peggy) Simpson** of nearby Nab Cottage, a local farmer's daughter who bore him an illegitimate child. The drug-taking was bad enough for the upright, snobbish Wordsworths, but when De Quincey married Peggy in 1817 (at St Oswald's church, Grasmere) any intimate relationship was at an end.

De Quincey was never suited to regular employment, and following a disastrous stint as editor of the *Westmorland Gazette* he became a freelance critic and essayist for various literary periodicals. His **Confessions of an English Opium-Eater** (1821) first appeared in the *London Magazine* and made his name, and he had sufficient resources to take on another house (Fox Ghyll, south of Rydal) for his growing family (he eventually had eight children), retaining Dove Cottage as a library. Growing success meant De Quincey spent less and less time in the Lakes, giving up Fox Ghyll in 1825 and finally abandoning Dove Cottage in 1830 to move to Edinburgh, where he lived for the rest of his life. It was only between 1834 and 1839 – long after he'd left the area – that De Quincey started writing his Lake "recollections", offending Wordsworth all over again.

could live by his guiding principle of "plain living but high thinking". But its main recommendation as far as he was concerned was one that is no longer obvious: the views he had enjoyed to the lake and fells were lost when new housing was erected in front of Dove Cottage in the 1860s.

Wordsworth married in 1802 and his new wife, Mary Hutchinson, came to live here; three of their five children were later born in the cottage (John in 1803, Dora in 1804 and Thomas in 1806). Sister Dorothy kept a detailed journal of daily life and the endless comings and goings of **visitors**, notably Coleridge and his brother-in-law Southey, but also Walter Scott, William Hazlitt and, once he'd plucked up the nerve to introduce himself, Thomas De Quincey (see box). And yet with all this going on, Wordsworth produced a series of odes, lyric poems and sonnets that he would never better, relying on Dorothy and Mary to make copies in their painstaking handwriting.

After eight years at Dove Cottage it became clear that the Wordsworths had outgrown their home and, reluctantly, the family **moved** to a larger, new house above Grasmere called **Allan Bank** (see page 91) – Wordsworth had watched it being built and referred to it as a "temple of abomination". They were never as happy there, or in the Old Rectory to which they later relocated, and it wasn't until 1813 and the move to Rydal Mount that the Wordsworths regained the sense of peace they had felt at Dove Cottage.

When the Wordsworths left in 1808, their friend **Thomas De Quincey** took over the lease and Dove Cottage is as much a monument to his happiest days in Grasmere (he married from here) as it is to Wordsworth's plain living; the house has been open to the public since 1917.

The cottage

Wordsworth Trust staff, bursting with anecdotes, lead you on a **guided tour** around the cottage rooms, little changed since the poet's day but for the addition of electricity and internal plumbing. That said, a major overhaul of the cottage was underway at the time of research, which was due for completion some time in 2020. There's precious little space and – downstairs, at least – hardly any natural light: belching tallow candles would have provided the only illumination. William, not wanting to be bothered by questions of a domestic nature, kept to the lighter, upper rooms or disappeared off on long walks to compose his poetry. De Quincey later reckoned that Wordsworth had walked 175,000 to 180,000 miles in the course of his poetry writing – "a mode of exertion which, to him, stood in the stead of wine, spirits, and all other stimulants whatsoever to the animal spirits".

Most of the furniture in the cottage belonged to the Wordsworths, while in the **upper rooms** are displayed a battered suitcase, a pair of William's ice skates and sister Dorothy's sewing box, among other possessions. There are surprisingly few reminders of De Quincey's long tenancy, save a pair of opium scales, yet he lived here far longer than did the Wordsworths.

The **garden** behind the cottage is also usually open for visits, weather permitting. This was a real labour of love for Wordsworth and Dorothy, a half-wild hillside where William chopped wood for the fire, planted runner beans, built a summerhouse and hid the disliked cottage whitewash behind a train of roses and honeysuckle.

Wordsworth Museum

The Dove Cottage ticket also gets you into the **Wordsworth Museum**, housed in the former coach house, near the cottage – and like Dove Cottage, a major overhaul was underway at the time of research, which will eventually result in four new themed galleries. Inevitably, there will be masses of fantastic stuff pertaining to Wordsworth's life and times, including paintings, portraits and original manuscripts (including *Daffodils*) alongside more personal items – such as pages from Dorothy's journals and, perhaps most poignantly, Mary's wedding ring. The museum ticket also allows entry to any special **exhibitions** currently running, which usually have either a lakeland or literary theme.

ARRIVAL AND DEPARTURE   **GRASMERE AND AROUND**

BY CAR

Grasmere lies west of the main A591 (Ambleside–Keswick road), with its centre just a few hundred yards down the B5287, which winds through the village. The main car park is on Redbank Rd at the southern end of the village, by the garden centre. There's a second car park on Stock Lane, on the east side as you come in from Dove Cottage.

2

WALKS FROM GRASMERE

Grasmere makes a good base for a wide selection of **walks**, from lazy round-the-lake rambles to full-on day-hikes requiring a bit of experience. A decent cross-section is detailed below; note that you can also walk the Fairfield Horseshoe circuit (see page 75) clockwise from nearby Rydal.

AROUND GRASMERE AND RYDAL WATER

This is an easy circuit (4 miles; 2hr) that skirts the lake and Loughrigg Fell. From Loughrigg Terrace, the route heads east above **Rydal Water**, passing the dripping maw of Rydal Caves, a disused slate quarry (used as a film location in Ken Russell's *The Lair of the White Worm*), before crossing the A591 to Rydal Mount. Above the house **"Coffin Trail" bridleway** runs back high above the northern shore of Rydal Water, via **White Moss Tarn** (look out for butterflies), and emerges at Dove Cottage.

LOUGHRIGG FELL

There are all sorts of possible ascents of **Loughrigg Fell** (1101ft) – and it's also easily climbed from Ambleside – but the simplest ascent is straight up the hillside from Loughrigg Terrace: the views are fantastic. A six-mile circuit from the terrace, over the undulating top to Ambleside and then back along the lower slopes via Rydal, takes three to four hours.

SILVER HOWE

The best direct climb from the village is up to the top of **Silver Howe** (1292ft), above the west side of the lake, from where the views take in the Langdale Pikes, Helvellyn and High Street. The easiest signposted route up from the village passes Allan Bank – it's a two-hour walk, climbing to the summit and then circling round via Dow Bank and down to the lakeside road, emerging just outside the village opposite the *Faeryland* tea garden and boat-rental place.

HELM CRAG AND HIGH RAISE

A reasonably tough high-level circuit to the west of Grasmere (10 miles; 6hr) starts with the climb up to **Helm Crag** (1299ft) – follow the signs from the end of Easedale Road – whose distinctive summit crags are known as **The Lion and The Lamb**, and have thrilled visitors since Wordsworth's day. It's around an hour from the village to the top, after which an undulating ridge walk runs west to Greenup Edge, and up to **High Raise** (2500ft), popularly regarded as the Lake District's most centrally sited fell. Stay a while for the magnificent views from the summit (marked on maps as High White Stones), before turning back for Grasmere via **Sergeant Man** (2414ft) and then descending past Easedale Tarn (see below) and Sourmilk Ghyll.

EASEDALE

The first version of Wordsworth's autobiographical work, *The Prelude*, was composed after long hours tramping up and down **Easedale** Valley (northwest of the village), while the tragic deaths of George and Sarah Green of Easedale – who died in a blizzard, leaving behind six children – prompted a lovely memorial poem. ("Who weeps for strangers? / Many wept for George and Sarah Green; / Wept for that pair's unhappy fate, / Whose graves may here be seen.") A brisk hike (follow Easedale Road, past the *YHA*), up the tumbling, fern-clad, Sourmilk Ghyll to **Easedale Tarn** and back, takes around two hours – while from the bridge across Easedale Beck at the start of the path you can wander up the drive to *Lancrigg Vegetarian Country House Hotel*, which has an organic café and veggie restaurant open to the public (walkers are welcome).

BY BUS

Bus #555 (between Kendal and Keswick) and the open-top #599 (from Kendal, Bowness, Windermere and Ambleside) both stop on the village green. A Central Lakes Day Rider ticket (buy from the driver; adult £8.50, family £23.50) allows unlimited stops on the return journey between Bowness and Grasmere, allowing you to visit the Wordsworth houses as a day-trip.

Bus #555 to: Dove Cottage (3min); Rydal (8min); Ambleside (13min); Brockhole (20min); Windermere train station (36min); Kendal (1hr); or to Keswick (30min). Service operates hourly.

Bus #599 to: Dove Cottage (3min); Rydal (8min); Ambleside (13min); Brockhole (20min); Windermere train station (31min); Bowness piers (45min). Service operates Easter–Oct every 20–30min.

BY TAXI

Grasmere Taxis (☎015394 35506).

ACCOMMODATION

SEE MAPS PAGES 88 AND 90

You should book well in advance for accommodation at any time of year, especially the **boutique** places and the popular **youth hostel** and **backpackers' accommodation**. You can walk into Grasmere village and to Wordsworth's Dove Cottage from any of the recommended choices in and around Grasmere. If you stay out at **Rydal** (see page 101) you'll be handily placed for the other Wordsworth house, Rydal Mount, though you'll need to drive or catch the bus to the village for food and other services. Grasmere itself has no **campsite**, though the yurts at Rydal Hall (see page 101) are only a couple of miles south, or it's 7 miles west to the excellent Great Langdale National Trust campsite (see page 107).

★ **Banerigg Guest House** Lake Rd, LA22 9PW, 1 mile south of Grasmere, on A591 ☎015394 35204, ⓦbanerigg.co.uk. Grasmere lake views are like hen's teeth, so the selling point of this lakeside B&B (a 15min walk from the village, past Dove Cottage) is obvious. There are six rooms (five doubles and a single), most with water views, and even a house canoe that you're welcome to use. Fewer guests take up the option of a morning swim in the lake with your host on his daily plunge. Walkers and cyclists are welcome (there are drying facilities and a garage for bikes), fuelled by a good breakfast. Parking. **£100**

Beck Allans College St, Grasmere, LA22 9SZ ☎015394 35563, ⓦbeckallansguesthouse.co.uk. A quality B&B in a modern but traditionally built house in the centre – the more you pay, the larger the room, but all five are smartly furnished and well equipped, with baths in the en-suite bathrooms. Most rooms have a view over the riverside gardens. Self-catering apartments, run by different people, are also available. Bike storage too. Parking. **£90**

Daffodil Keswick Rd, Grasmere, LA22 9PR ☎015394 63550, ⓦdaffodilhotel.co.uk. This huge slate Victorian-era lakefront hotel, the landmark at the southern village entrance (for many years previously the *Prince of Wales*), has been given a complete contemporary makeover. Its lakeview rooms and suites, restaurant-with-a-view and up-to-the-minute spa add another string to Grasmere's increasingly boutique bow. **£175**

Heidi's Grasmere Lodge Red Lion Square, Grasmere, LA22 9SP ☎015394 35248, ⓦheidisgrasmerelodge. co.uk. Not so much B&B as a boutique "retreat for adults", offering five rustic-chic double rooms, each with its own theme and touch of Swiss-German mountain style. Everything is set up for a cosy getaway, from duck-down duvets and underfloor heating to jacuzzi baths. While all the rooms have a view, a couple also have patios and the duplex suite (up to £135) has a private sun terrace. Breakfast is served in cheery owner Heidi's downstairs namesake deli and coffee house – the boy in the Alpine photo on the back wall is her father. Parking. **£99**

★ **How Foot Lodge** Town End, LA22 9SQ ☎015394 35366, ⓦhowfootlodge.co.uk. The position – a few yards from Dove Cottage – couldn't be better for Wordsworth groupies, and you won't get a better deal on good-quality accommodation in Grasmere than in this light-filled Victorian villa. Thoughtful touches abound (wineglasses and corkscrew provided, fresh milk available for tea and coffee), and there's a charming mix of rooms with views over the well-kept gardens, including a very appealing room with French windows (£85) opening onto its own garden-side sun lounge. Parking. **£82**

Lancrigg Vegetarian Country House Easedale Rd, LA22 9QN, 0.5 mile northwest of Grasmere ☎015394 35317, ⓦlancrigg.co.uk. The isolated country house is a rustic gem, with trimmed lawns and wildlife-filled woods, while ten idiosyncratic rooms have been carved from the well-worn interior. The highlight of the house, however, is the newly installed Poet's Bar, occupying the former library of naturalist John Richardson, where you can kick back with a local ale and a bite to eat. More upscale fare is available in the restaurant. Parking. **£125**

★ **Moss Grove Organic** Grasmere, LA22 9SW ☎015394 35251, ⓦmossgrove.com. Rarely does a Victorian-era hotel look so stunning, from the luminous lighting that throws a blue glow upon the exterior slate to the luxurious high-concept rooms complete with underfloor heating and Bose sound systems. It's been designed on organic, low-impact lines, so the extraordinary handmade beds are of reclaimed timber, the wallpaper coloured with natural inks, duvets made from duck down and the windows screened by natural wood blinds. The feel is less hotel and more private house party – there are only eleven rooms and you're encouraged to forage in the kitchen for a buffet-style breakfast (produce largely local, the drinks Fair Trade) and take it back to your room. Weekend visits typically cost £20–50 more/night. Parking. **£159**

Raise View White Bridge, Grasmere, LA22 9RQ ☎015394 35215, ⓦraiseviewhouse.co.uk. There are lovely fell views from every corner of this superior B&B, plus a warm welcome and five very comfortable rooms;

2

the Silver How Suite is the pick, with a luxurious bed and mountain views and just a touch too many furnishings. Decor is contemporary country house – think fluffy towels, bold feature walls and fetching fabrics – and the traditional lakeland breakfast (sausage, bacon, toast and free-range eggs) is great. Parking. **£126**

Rothay Garden Broadgate, Grasmere, LA22 9RJ ☎015394 35334, ⓦrothaygarden.com. A classy mix of town and country, set in quiet grounds by the Rothay River on the edge of Grasmere village. It's four-star standard, and there are three grades of rooms in soothing earth tones with dark wood furniture, designer-print wallpaper, thick drapes, and velvet seats and sofas; smart bathrooms have walk-in showers and big, curvy baths. The cheapest rooms don't have much of an outlook, and it's more like £200 a night for the urban-style attic "loft suites" or the bright first-floor "Grasmere" rooms that open out onto a terrace by the babbling river. A separate riverside spa building plonks you in a hot tub with views to the hills through floor-to-ceiling windows. Dining, meanwhile, is by candlelight in the conservatory restaurant. Parking. **£150**

★ **Thorney How Independent Hostel** Off Easedale Rd, LA22 9QW, 0.75 mile north of Grasmere ☎015394 35597, ⓦthorneyhow.co.uk. The first property bought by the YHA (back in 1931) now trades as an eager-to-please indie hostel, with around fifty beds overseen by friendly live-in family owners. There are four- to six-bed bunk rooms (all en suite) and three en-suite doubles in the main house – a 350-year-old farmhouse, recently spruced up – and slightly cheaper bunkhouse accommodation in the form of four, four-bed dorms (£21/person) in an annexe. Rates for the main house include continental breakfast, otherwise there's a cooked breakfast available, plus drinks and other meals in the café-bar – which also hosts film screenings, art shows and the like. Facilities include self-catering kitchen, snug lounge, bike storage and drying room. It's a little further along the road beyond *Butharlyp Howe* – look for the signposted right turn and then follow the track up to your left. Limited parking;

no dogs. Dorms per person £27.85, doubles per person **£42.25**

Wordsworth Hotel College St, Grasmere, LA22 9SW ☎015394 35592, ⓦthewordsworthhotel.co.uk. If you're after a more traditional experience, the four-star "grande-dame" choice in the village presses all the right buttons, from the antique-laden lounge to big, sometimes flouncy rooms with a largely country-house decor and character. It's not a complete time warp – room facilities have kept up with the times, and some are positively stylish – while the real bonus is the heated indoor pool, jacuzzi, gym and sauna. For more room space or any kind of view, you're looking at up to £380 a night. There are two good dining options on site – *Dove* bistro and bar (see below), and the more formal *Signature* restaurant – so the D, B&B deals are worth a look. Parking. **£190**

★ **The Yan** Broadrayne Farm, LA22 9RU, 1.3 miles north of Grasmere on A591, beyond Traveller's Rest pub ☎015394 35055, ⓦtheyan.co.uk. Swish and dog-friendly boutique residence harbouring seven rooms sleeping between two and four, and all manifesting a definite Nordic feel in the minimalist pine-and-white decor. They've also got a top-drawer bistro offering the likes of chicken stew and chorizo dumplings, and Parmesan and fresh herb polenta cake; the bonus is that the nearest pub is just a few hundred yards down the road. Parking. **£100**

YHA Grasmere Butharlyp Howe Easedale Rd, Grasmere, LA22 9QG ☎0845 371 9319, ⓦyha.org.uk/hostel/grasmere-butharlyp-howe. The big, eighty-bed YHA hostel is the closest budget accommodation to the centre of Grasmere, just a 5min walk north of the green. It's a handsome, refurbished Victorian mansion with modern bunk rooms, plentiful showers and decent facilities throughout, as well as a restaurant (dinner available) overlooking grassy gardens. There's also a children's play area and outdoor games, and some of the rooms are suitable for couples and families (four-bed, from £60). Small camping area at the front of the hostel too. Parking. Dorms £22, doubles £49, camping **£15**

EATING

SEE MAPS PAGES 88 AND 90

There are plenty of **tearooms and cafés** in Grasmere catering for the mass of tourists that descends every day, and hikers can get sandwiches made up at a couple of places. If you're Helm Crag- and mountain-bound, it's good to know that the *Thorney How* hostel (see above) serves walk-in hiker's breakfasts, though a call first to check wouldn't hurt. One nearby country tearoom that is worth a special visit is the *Old School Room* at Rydal Hall (see page 101), where you can combine cakes with a gentle walk. Outside Grasmere's hotels and pubs, good independent **restaurants** are thinner on the ground, though there's enough choice to ring the changes over a few days' stay.

Dove Bistro Wordsworth Hotel, College St, Grasmere, LA22 9SW ☎015394 35592, ⓦthewordsworthhotel. co.uk. This hotel bistro is more like an independent bar and restaurant, with a pubby feel, a choice of local ales and a short but reasonably priced menu featuring the likes of green Thai fishcakes, and confit duck with rocket, walnut and beansprouts (mains £13–17). Mon–Thurs noon–3pm & 6–10pm, Fri & Sat noon–11pm, Sun noon–10.30pm; kitchen daily noon–2pm & 6–9pm.

Faeryland Redbank Rd, LA22 9PU, by the lake ☎015394 35060, ⓦfaeryland.co.uk. The prettily sited tea garden, in a glade by the lake, a 5min walk out from the village, is where people come to rent rowing boats (all

RUSHES, WRESTLING, TALL TALES AND FINE ART

Grasmere's two big annual summer **events** are the village's rushbearing ceremony and the traditional sports festival, held a month apart. The **rushbearing** (mid-July), centred on St Oswald's church, dates back to the medieval practice of renewing the church's reed-covered earth floor once a year – not strictly necessary any more, of course, but still an excuse to celebrate. Not quite as old, the **Grasmere Sports and Show** (late Aug; ⓦgrasmeresports. com) has nonetheless been held pretty much every year since 1868, world wars excepted, and is the spiritual home of lakeland wrestling, fell-running, hound-trailing and other arcane pastimes. Also unique to Grasmere is the **Storytellers' Garden** (ⓦtaffythomas.co.uk) at the Northern Centre for Storytelling, which is located in the former National Trust shop opposite the church. Traditional tale-teller and raconteur Taffy Thomas presents open-air events throughout the year (story walks, firelight tales, music and juggling) – call in or check the website for details. Finally, the big art show of the year is the summer exhibition of the **Lake Artists Society** (late July to early Sep; ⓦlakeartists.org.uk) held at Grasmere Hall on Broadgate and founded in 1904 by local writer and artist W.G. Collingwood. The work displayed is varied, but the society's members are mostly resident in, and take their inspiration from, Cumbria and the Lake District.

cutely named and nicely painted), but even if you're not game for that it's worth the walk. The views are lovely, and they can serve you an organic hot chocolate or mulled apple juice and a slice of carrot cake (£2–5) or authentic Sicilian cannoli. March–Oct daily 10am–5pm; also open some winter days, varied hours.

★**Jumble Room** Langdale Rd, Grasmere, LA22 9SU ☎015394 35188, ⓦthejumbleroom.co.uk. Top restaurant in the village is this funky, relaxed dining spot, run with a light touch by an amiable Grasmere couple. With close-packed tables overlooked by sister-in-law Thuline's dramatic animal oil paintings, the locally sourced menu spans the globe – fried feta-stuffed fig, Scottish queeny scallops, Asian pork loin with pak choi, and so on. Once ensconced, awash in the chilled-out atmosphere and great music, no one's in any hurry to leave. Mains £14–20. Dinner reservations advised. Wed–Sun 5.30–9.30pm, plus Mon in summer; Nov–Feb Fri & Sat only.

DRINKING
SEE MAPS PAGES 88 AND 90

1769 Bar The Inn at Grasmere, Red Lion Square, Grasmere, LA22 9SS ☎015394 35456, ⓦtheinnatgrasmere.co.uk. As the only pub actually in the village, this age-old inn's adjoining bar packs 'em in, especially at weekends. There are a good stable of regional beers on tap (Hawkshead, Jennings, Black Sheep), decent pub grub all day (chunky sandwiches £8, mains around £15), and a queue of local Fast Eddies waiting to drub you at pool. Daily 10am–11pm; kitchen noon–9.30pm.

Traveller's Rest Keswick Rd, LA22 9RR, 1 mile north of Grasmere on A591 ☎015394 35604. Old roadside coaching inn that's a popular place for Jennings' beers and decent bar meals (from Cumberland sausage and mash to Thai curry, £10–15). There's a beer garden with views, though traffic noise intrudes a bit, and a warming log fire inside in winter. Daily noon–11pm; kitchen noon–9.30pm.

★**Tweedies Bar** Langdale Rd, Grasmere, LA22 9SW ☎015394 35300, ⓦtweediesgrasmere.com. Although part of the hotel of the same name, there's more of a country pub feel here than anywhere else in Grasmere, from the stone-flagged floors and wood-burning stove to the big beer garden. It's a CAMRA award-winner for its hand-pumped beers (the "Grasmere Guzzler" real ale fest is held here on the first weekend in Sept), though if you're after a Pinot or a Prosecco you'll be fine. The locally sourced menu is definitely on the gastropub side of things, from wood pigeon with black pudding and root veg to saddle of wild rabbit with cider cream (mains £14–28). The same menu is also served in the hotel's Lodge restaurant, if you want a bit more formality. Live music most Fridays and Saturdays. Mon–Thurs & Sun noon–11pm, Fri & Sat till midnight; kitchen Mon–Wed noon–2.45pm & 6–9pm, Thurs–Sun noon–5pm & 6–9pm.

SHOPPING
SEE MAP PAGE 90

Sam Read Booksellers Junction College St and Broadgate, Grasmere, LA22 9SY ☎015394 35374, ⓦsamreadbooks.co.uk. A fine independent bookshop, especially good for local interest books, guides and maps, and the works of the Lake Poets. Feb–Dec daily 9am–5pm.

DIRECTORY

Banks There's no bank in Grasmere, though there is an ATM inside the post office.
Doctor Ambleside Surgery (Rydal Rd ⓣ015394 32693, ⓦwww.centrallakesmedicalgroup.co.uk).
Hospital The nearest hospital is in Keswick (Keswick Community Hospital, Crosthwaite Rd ⓣ01768 245678).
Pharmacy Grasmere Pharmacy, 1 Oak Bank, Broadgate (ⓣ015394 35553).
Post office Stock Lane (Mon–Wed & Fri 9am–5pm, Thurs & Sat 9am–12.30pm/Mon–Fri 9.30am–5pm, Sat 9.30am–4.30pm, Sun 10am–4pm).

2

Rydal Mount

Rydal, LA22 9LU • April–Oct daily 9.30am–5pm; Nov, Dec, Feb & March Wed–Sun 11am–4pm; tearoom daily 10am–5pm • £7.50, garden only £5, family ticket £20 • ⓣ015394 33002, ⓦrydalmount.co.uk • Buses #555 & #599 stop at Rydal church, 200 yards from the house; parking (on the road alongside Rydal Hall) is minimal

Following the deaths of their young children Catherine and Thomas in 1812, the **Wordsworths** couldn't bear to continue living in Grasmere's Old Rectory. In May 1813 they moved a couple of miles southeast of the village to the hamlet of Rydal, little more than a couple of isolated cottages and farms set back from the eastern end of Rydal Water. Here William rented **Rydal Mount** from the Flemings of nearby Rydal Hall, where he remained until his death in 1850.

Brief history

Rydal Mount is a fair-sized family home, a much-improved-upon Tudor cottage set in its own grounds, and reflects **Wordsworth's changed circumstances.** At Dove Cottage he'd been a largely unknown poet of straitened means, but by 1813 he'd written several of his greatest works (though not all had yet been published) and was already being visited by literary acolytes. More importantly, he'd been appointed Westmorland's Distributor of Stamps, a salaried position that allowed him to take up the rent of a comfortable family house. Wordsworth, Mary, the three surviving children (John, aged 10; Dora, 9; and William, 3) and Dorothy arrived, plus his wife's sister Sara Hutchinson, by now living with the family. Later the household also contained a clerk, a couple of maids and a gardener. Dances and dinners were held, the widowed Queen Adelaide visited, and carriage-loads of friends and sightseers came to call – a far cry from the "plain living" back at Dove Cottage.

The house

Wordsworth only ever rented the property, but the house is now owned by descendants of the poet, who have opened it to visitors since 1970. It's a much less claustrophobic experience than visiting Dove Cottage and you're free to wander around what is still essentially a family home – summer concerts feature poetry readings by Wordsworth family members, and there are recent family pictures on the sideboard alongside more familiar portraits of the poet and his circle.

In the light-filled **drawing room** and **library** (two rooms in Wordsworth's day) you'll find the only known portrait of Dorothy, as an old lady of 62, and also Mary's favourite portrait of Wordsworth, completed in 1844 by the American portraitist Henry Inman. Memorabilia abound: Wordsworth's black-leather sofa, his inkstand and despatch box, a brooch of Dorothy's and, upstairs in the attic, their beloved brother John's sword (recovered from the shipwreck in which he drowned) and the poet's own encyclopedia and prayer book. **William and Mary's bedroom** has a lovely view, with Windermere a splash in the distance; in daughter **Dora's room** hangs a portrait of Edward Quillinan, her Irish dragoon, whom she married in 1841, much against Wordsworth's will. The couple spent their honeymoon at Rydal Mount, while the delicate Dora – often ill and eventually a victim of tuberculosis – later came home to die in the house in 1847.

The other bedroom was Dorothy's, to which she was virtually confined for the last two decades of her life, suffering greatly from what was thought to be a debilitating mental illness – an underactive thyroid is the current opinion. She died at Rydal Mount in 1855; Mary died there in 1859.

The garden

Many people's favourite part of Rydal Mount is the 4.5-acre **garden**, largely shaped by Wordsworth, who fancied himself as a gardener. He planted the flowering shrubs, put in the terraces (where he used to declaim his poetry) and erected a little rustic summerhouse (for jotting down lyrics), from which there are fine views of Rydal Water. Lining the lawns and surrounding the rock pools are rhododendrons and azaleas, maples, beeches and pines. If you're looking for an unusual souvenir, head for the Rydal Mount **tearoom and shop**, which sells fell-walking sticks fashioned from the wood found in the garden, and also has a little outdoor terrace in the corner of the garden.

Rydal and Rydal Water

Rydal sits at the foot of its own valley, whose beck empties into the River Rothay. As a hamlet, it's hardly any bigger than it was in Wordsworth's day; though, having seen the poet's house at Rydal Mount, you may as well wander back down the road for the other local sights – the village's **church** and **Rydal Hall** (which has a good tearoom), and the lake, **Rydal Water**. Less than a mile west is **Nab Cottage**, the former home of Hartley Coleridge.

St Mary's church

Rydal, LA22 9LX • Daily: March–Oct 9am–5pm; Nov–Feb 10am–3pm; Dora's Field always open • ⓦ rydal.org.uk • Buses #555 and #599 (between Windermere and Grasmere) stop on the A591 at the church

There was no local church in Rydal until **St Mary's** (at the foot of Rydal Mount on the main A591) was built; it opened on Christmas Day in 1824, and Wordsworth was churchwarden here for a year in the 1830s. A swing gate by the church entrance leads into **Dora's Field**, a plot of land bought by Wordsworth when he thought he might have to leave Rydal Mount because the owners, the Flemings, wanted it back. Wordsworth planned to build a house here instead, but when the Flemings changed their minds, he gave the land to his daughter. On Dora's death in 1847, the heartbroken Wordsworths planted the hillsides with daffodils.

Rydal Hall

Rydal, LA22 9LX • Gardens daily dawn to dusk • Free, though donation requested; free parking • ☎ 015394 32050, ⓦ rydalhall.org • Buses #555 and #599 (between Windermere and Grasmere) stop nearby on the A591 by the church

Across from St Mary's church, a driveway leads to **Rydal Hall**, erstwhile home of the Flemings, the local landed gentry who traced their ancestry back to the time of the Norman Conquest. The hall has a sixteenth-century kernel but was considerably renovated during Victorian times; it's now a residential conference centre owned by the Diocese of Carlisle. You're welcome to walk in to visit the wonderfully restored **gardens**, originally laid out on classical lines by celebrated landscape gardener and architect Thomas Mawson in 1911. There are captivating views of Rydal Water from the terrace, while the more informal woodland gardens include a restored, walled kitchen garden and orchard as well as summerhouse, ice house and game-larder. You could easily spend much of the day in the grounds – seeking out the waterfalls and ponds, and scrambling around on woodland walks or on the adventure playground – and don't miss the **tearoom** (see page 102).

2

Rydal Water

Around a 1hr footpath walk from Grasmere; or buses #555 and #599 (between Windermere and Grasmere) stop on the A591 near the church

Few people bother much with **Rydal Water**, one of the region's smallest lakes at under three-quarters of a mile long and just 50ft deep in parts. It's handsome enough – though it was considerably quieter before the A591 traced its northern shore – and there's a nice, easy walk along the southern shore, to or from Grasmere past Rydal Caves. For the best views of the water itself, follow the original upper route to Grasmere, along the so-called "**Coffin Trail**", which starts directly behind Rydal Mount and runs west under the craggy heights of **Nab Scar** (1450ft) and over **White Moss Common**. Medieval coffin-bearers en route to St Oswald's church in Grasmere would haul their melancholy load along this trail, stopping to rest at intervals on the convenient flat stones.

Nab Cottage

Rydal, LA22 9SD • ☎ 015394 35311, ⊕ rydalwater.com

Nab Cottage, less than a mile west of Rydal on the A591, overlooks Rydal Water. This was the family home of Margaret Simpson before she married Thomas De Quincey; and it was rented much later by the sometime journalist and poet Hartley Coleridge, a Wordsworth family favourite ("O blessed vision! happy child!") despite his trying ways. Abandoned by his father and effectively brought up in Robert Southey's Keswick household, Hartley was a frail, precocious child who took to the demon drink and failed to live up to his early promise. But Wordsworth always retained a soft spot for him, and when Hartley died in Nab Cottage in 1849 the poet picked out a plot for him in Grasmere churchyard. The cottage is now a language school, with B&B usually available outside the summer months (see below).

ACCOMMODATION   SEE MAP PAGE 88

Full Circle Yurts Rydal Hall, Rydal, LA22 9LX, 2 miles southeast of Grasmere on A591 ☎ 07975 671928, ⊕ lake-district-yurts.co.uk. Tucked into the lovely grounds of Rydal Hall are a variety of authentic Mongolian yurts close to tinkling stream, waterfalls, natural pools and rugged woodland. They sleep up to six, complete with proper beds, rug-strewn wooden floors, wood-burning stove and oven, gas hob and grill, with showers and toilets 100 yards away. Outside each is a raised-deck picnic area, barbecue and brazier, and children's playground nearby, and there's a tearoom at the hall and a decent pub a 5min walk away. The drawback? Only that the yurts are extremely popular, so book well in advance for summer (or consider an autumn/winter break, as the wood-burners keep them really warm). Pack sensibly because you can't drive to the yurt and it's a steep walk. Mon–Fri or Fri–Mon rental is £369–399, otherwise available by the week. Parking. Per week **£677**

Nab Cottage Rydal, LA22 9SD ☎ 015394 35311, ⊕ rydalwater.com. Both Thomas De Quincey and Hartley Coleridge lived in this gorgeous seventeenth-century oak-beamed farmhouse facing Rydal Water. It's now a treatment/ workshop venue and language school, but offers B&B in seven rooms (four en suite, £92) when space is available – usually *not* between July and Sept, but call to check. Light suppers and evening meals available on request (largely organic, and locally sourced or Fair Trade; £20), as are various forms of massage (£45/hr). Parking. **£84**

EATING   SEE MAP PAGE 88

Old School Room Tea Shop Rydal Hall, Rydal, LA22 9LX ☎ 015394 32050, ⊕ rydalhall.org. Around the back of Rydal Hall, the teashop has picnic tables from where you can watch Rydal Beck tumble under a moss-covered packhorse bridge. They make soup, scones and sandwiches here every day – their most expensive paninis cost just £5.50, and a cream tea is £4.50 – and if you come in winter you can warm up by the wood-burning stove. Cyclists receive a ten percent discount on drinks, as do those who bring their own mugs. Daily: March–Oct 10am–5pm; Nov–Feb 11am–3pm.

Skelwith Bridge and Little Langdale

Langdale ("long valley") is a byword for some of the region's most stunning peaks, views and hikes, and the route there starts at **Skelwith Bridge**, a cluster of buildings huddled by the bridge over the River Brathay, around three miles south of Grasmere and the same distance west of Ambleside. The main reasons to stop here are for the local **waterfall walks** and lunch at *Chesters By The River*, and you can always continue your walk the mile upriver to Elterwater and then take the bus back to Ambleside.

Skelwith Bridge and around

Slate has been quarried in the area since the nineteenth century and is still used for everything from kitchen work surfaces to tombstones. There's a slate workshop and showroom (next to *Chesters* café) at **Skelwith Bridge**, which you'll pass at the start of the signposted riverside stroll up to Elterwater, a mile away. The initial section of the path runs through moss-covered woodland, passing the tumbling waters of **Skelwith Force**, where there's a little viewing platform above the rocks. The waterfall really only gushes after heavy rain; for a finer waterfall altogether follow the hilly footpath west of Skelwith Bridge (it starts on the south side of the river) for the mile or so to **Colwith Force**, which is hidden in the woods off the minor road to Elterwater. A circuit taking in both falls and Elterwater won't take more than a couple of hours. There's also another short local walk from Skelwith, north through Neaum Woods to pretty **Loughrigg Tarn**, which sits under the crags of Loughrigg Fell.

Little Langdale

Heading west from Skelwith Bridge, a narrow minor road off the A593 twists into **Little Langdale**, a bucolic counterweight to the dramatics of Great Langdale to the north. For a good walk, cut north over **Lingmoor Fell** (1530ft) via Blea Tarn (where there's parking) into Great Langdale – the eight-mile circuit, returning via Elterwater to Little Langdale's *Three Shires Inn*, takes around four hours. The name of the inn, incidentally, is a reference to the fact that it stands near the meeting point of the old counties of Cumberland, Westmorland and Lancashire.

West from Little Langdale, the ever-narrower, ever-hairier road climbs to the dramatic **Wrynose Pass** (1270ft), before dropping down to Cockley Beck for the Duddon Valley or on to the Hardknott Pass.

PEOPLE AND PLACES: MOUNTAIN MAN

If anyone knows Langdale it's **Bill Birkett**, who conducts what he calls "a life-long love affair with the hills" through his climbing, walking, writing and photography. It's pretty much in his blood – born and bred in the valley, son of climbing legend Jim Birkett – but Bill also has developed a strong bond with both place and people, which pours from every page of his photographic essay, *A Year in the Life of the Langdale Valleys*. He's out in the mountains in any weather, with camera in hand, and has covered every Lake District hill and mountain more than 1000ft high in his encyclopedic **Complete Lakeland Fells**. This started out as a personal challenge, so it came as a bit of a surprise to find that people were buying the book and knocking off the 541 "Birketts", like they do with the more famous 214 Wainwrights. "I'm really pleased a lot of people are finding it inspiring and useful," says the man whose main motivation is communicating his passion for the hills to others. To this end, he'll take you with him on his walking-and-photography courses and show you what it is about the mountains that captivates him – from the wind on his face and the sun on his back to the pure buzz of the physical landscape.

For more about Bill Birkett, his photography, books and courses, go to ⓦ billbirkett.co.uk.

ARRIVAL AND DEPARTURE

By bus Bus #505 from Ambleside or Coniston stops at Skelwith Bridge, as does the #516 "Langdale Rambler"

SKELWITH BRIDGE AND LITTLE LANGDALE

between Ambleside and the *Old Dungeon Ghyll* in Great Langdale.

ACCOMMODATION AND EATING

★ Chesters By The River Skelwith Bridge, LA22 9NJ ☎ 015394 34711, ⊚ chestersbytheriver.co.uk. The word has long been out about *Chesters*, and on sunny days café and car park fill quickly, since there's nothing nicer than sitting outside on the riverside terrace with a glass of crisp white wine. The super-swish bakery-café turns out smashing cakes, scones, pastries and puds – all made daily – alongside superior breakfasts and lunches, from pancakes to soup, pizzas, salads and quiches (cakes from £3, dishes £5–10). Meanwhile, the adjacent shop is full of pretty, designer-ish homeware, crafts and gifts – always worth a look. Daily 9am–4pm.

Three Shires Inn Little Langdale, LA22 9NZ ☎ 015394

SEE MAP PAGE 88

37215, ⊚ threeshiresinn.co.uk. The nine bedrooms at the *Three Shires Inn*, about a mile west of Colwith Force, make the most of the valley views, and the inn is the traditional starting point for local rambles, notably the stroll down to the old packhorse crossing of Slater Bridge and to Little Langdale Tarn. They also rent out two attractive self-catering cottages in the area, sleeping five to seven people (£450–650/week). The bar is the place hereabouts for Cumbrian ales, and there are grand views from the garden. Food is at the fancier end of pub grub: Lancashire cheese soufflé to local lamb, with sandwiches and lunch dishes £6–12, dinner mains £14–19. Closed two weeks in Jan. Daily noon–11pm; kitchen noon–2pm & 6–8.45pm. **£116**

Elterwater and around

Elterwater village lies half a mile northwest of its water, named by the Norse for the swans that still glide upon its surface. It's one of the more idyllic lakeland beauty spots, with its riverside setting, aged inn, spreading maple tree and aimless sheep getting among the sunbathers on the pocket-sized green. Historically, the village made its living from farming, quarrying and lace-making, though these days it's almost entirely devoted to the passing tourist trade: only around a quarter of the houses here are lived in, the rest are used as holiday cottages. There are no sights, as such, just the quiet comings and goings of a country hamlet, albeit one inundated on fine summer days and bank holidays with vehicles disgorging hikers and bikers.

Chapel Stile

Numerous fell or riverside walks start straight from Elterwater, including the easy half-mile stroll northwest up the river – through the slate-quarry workings, still in use after more than 150 years – to **Chapel Stile**, where a simple quarrymen's chapel sits beneath the crags. There's a pub and café for those who need a target and, suitably refreshed, you can push on from Chapel Stile, either on the level walk alongside the beck into the lower reaches of Langdale or up through the crags to the north and across Silver Howe to Grasmere.

ARRIVAL AND INFORMATION

By car There's free parking on the common outside the village and more limited pay-and-display parking close to the bridge in the centre.
By bus The #516 "Langdale Rambler" bus from Ambleside (5–6 daily) stops by Elterwater village green (17min), then at Chapel Stile (20min), before heading on to the *Old Dungeon*

ELTERWATER AND AROUND

Ghyll in Langdale.
Services In Chapel Stile, the Langdale Co-operative (daily 9am–5.30pm; ☎ 015394 37260), in business since 1884, has everything a village store can provide – from cornflakes to hiking boots.

ACTIVITIES

Mountain activities Highpoint in Eltwerwater (Easter–Sept daily 10am–5pm; Oct–Easter by arrangement; ☎ 015394 437691 or ☎ 07789 642176, ⊚ mountainguides.co.uk) rents

out all types of outdoor kit and organizes guided walks, plus rock-climbing, canyoning and ghyll-scrambling courses (£35 for half a day) – you don't always need to book in advance.

2

AN EXILE IN LANGDALE

German abstract and performance artist **Kurt Schwitters** (1877–1948) was forced to flee Hitler's Germany in 1937 as his challenging, subversive collages were considered "degenerate" by the Nazis. He moved first to Norway and then to Britain in 1940 where, initially, he was interned as an enemy alien. He spent the later war years scratching a living in London before arriving in the Lake District in 1945 – impoverished, ill and largely unknown. Schwitters became a familiar figure in Ambleside, painting local portraits and landscapes, though it is his **Merzbauten** (Merz buildings) for which he's remembered. Schwitters had already produced earlier versions of this pioneering form of installation art, in Germany and Norway, and this final attempt – the only one to still survive – was begun in 1947 in an old stone barn just outside Elterwater. Constructed from discarded, salvaged and organic materials, the Lake District "Merzbarn" was an embodiment of Schwitters' long-standing "Merz" concept that art could spring from cast-off, found or otherwise useless objects. Schwitters died of pneumonia in 1948 – there's a memorial stone in Ambleside churchyard – and the unfinished Merzbarn was left abandoned, though the artwork on the end wall was removed to the Hatton Gallery at Newcastle University in the 1960s.

A major retrospective show at the Tate Britain in London in 2013 revived interest in this all-but-forgotten artist, and in 2016, the Littoral Arts Trust – which had for years been caretaking the Elterwater Merzbarn – received £45,000 in funding from various Cumbrian institutions and a Swiss gallery to help restore the building, which had been badly damaged by a storm. You can follow progress on ⓦ merzbarn.net, which also has details of public access to the Merzbarn and other events.

ACCOMMODATION   SEE MAP PAGE 88

Overnight **accommodation** is relatively thin on the ground, though there are plenty of **self-catering cottages** available by the week (sometimes less during winter); contact the *Langdale Estate* (see below) or Wheelwright's (ⓦ wheelwrights.com), who should be able to fix you up with something in the vicinity.

Britannia Inn Elterwater, LA22 9HP ☏ 015394 37210, ⓦ thebritanniainn.com. The hugely popular pub on Elterwater's green has nine cosy rooms – cosy being the operative word, since there's not a lot of space in a 500-year-old inn. But they are charming and quirky, fitted into every available nook, and do offer a fair bit more than basic comfort (weekend rates are typically £10 higher). Limited parking. **£125**

★ **Elterwater Hostel** Elterwater, LA22 9HX ☏ 015394 37245, ⓦ elterwaterhostel.co.uk. A converted farmhouse and barn, just across the bridge from the *Britannia*, provides simple hostel facilities sleeping up to thirty-eight people in two- to six-bed rooms. It's not at all fancy, but it's beautifully sited in great hiking and biking country. While you can unload here, you'll have to park overnight in the village car park. There's a decent self-catering kitchen, and evening meals are available (along with a beer or two), or the pub's just down the road. Bike storage, drying room and a small shop selling maps and the like. Closed Nov–Feb. Dorms **£21**

Langdale Estate Elterwater, LA22 9JD ☏ 015394 38014, ⓦ langdale.co.uk. Spreading up the valley, north of the village, this fancy hotel and spa resort blends in well with its surroundings. Set in the grounds of a former woollen mill and gunpowder works, it contains a variety of four-star-quality rooms in converted estate cottages, barns and buildings (£160–275/night; midweek stays the cheapest), plus self-catering Scandinavian-style lodges (from £500 for three nights), a glam indoor pool and spa, gym, games room, squash court, two restaurants and a café-bar – there's also an estate pub, *Wainwrights' Inn* (see below) within walking distance. It's pricey, though there are good last-minute website rates (down to £115 B&B). Parking. **£160**

EATING   SEE MAP PAGE 88

Brambles Langdale Co-operative, Chapel Stile, LA22 9JE ☏ 015394 37500, ⓦ langdalecooperative.co.uk. The store's upstairs café serves large breakfasts as well as sandwiches and lunches (£3.50–7), while hikers can buy a picnic pack and get their flasks filled with tea or coffee. There's free parking out front. Daily except Wed: Easter–Oct 9am–4.30pm; Nov–Easter 9.30am–4.30pm; closed one week in Jan.

★ **Britannia Inn** Elterwater, LA22 9HP ☏ 015394 37210, ⓦ thebritanniainn.com. The stone-flagged back-room bar is where the hikers congregate, while the merest hint of good weather fills the outdoor tables on the slate-covered terrace. There's a wide range of beers and loads of good value, home-made goodies such as chicken and leek pie, and wild and button mushroom stroganoff (most mains £13–15) served either in the dining room (booking advised) or cosy front bar. Daily 10.30am–11pm; kitchen noon–2pm & 6–9pm.

Wainwrights' Inn Chapel Stile, LA22 9JD ☏ 015394 38088, ⓦ langdale.co.uk/wainwrights-inn. Welcoming

slate-floored pub with local beers on tap and comforting bar meals like fish finger sandwiches with mushy peas, and steak, mushroom and ale pie (mains £11–18) – the terrace outside is a good spot to rest weary feet. Daily noon–11pm; kitchen noon–9.30pm.

Great Langdale

2

Beyond Chapel Stile you emerge into the wide curve of **Great Langdale**, flanked by some of the Lake District's most famous peaks – Crinkle Crags, Bowfell and the Langdale Pikes. It's a dramatic, yet sobering valley, one of the few in the Lakes where you get a real sense of scale from the lie of the land. It's also one of the oldest occupied parts of the region, the evidence in the shape of Stone Age axes found in "factory" sites in the upper valley.

You can drive up or take the bus for a quick look at Great Langdale's impressive scenery, but the valley really requires you to get out and put some mud on your boots. The **footpath from Elterwater** (signposted as the Cumbria Way) runs up the valley to its head – eight miles from Ambleside – from where there are popular hiking routes over the passes to Wasdale and Borrowdale. Alternatively, from the car park at **Stickle Ghyll**, where the Langdale Pikes and Pavey Ark form a dramatic backdrop, Stickle Ghyll itself provides a stiff hour's climb up to **Stickle Tarn**, following a wide stone-stepped path that's been put in place to prevent further erosion of the hillside.

Another obvious target is the dramatic 60ft waterfall of **Dungeon Ghyll**, around half an hour's climb from the Stickle Ghyll car park – the "dungeon" in question is a natural cave, and after rain the thundering fall itself is an impressive sight. The other car park, a mile further west up the road by the **Old Dungeon Ghyll Hotel**, is the starting point for a series of more hardcore hikes that are among the best in the Lakes.

ARRIVAL AND DEPARTURE
GREAT LANGDALE

By car Parking by the side of the B5343 road is discouraged, and drivers should make for either of the valley's (signposted) car parks, Stickle Ghyll or Old Dungeon Ghyll, depending on their target for the day.

By bus The #516 "Langdale Rambler" bus from Ambleside (5–6 daily) runs via Skelwith Bridge (10min), Elterwater

(17min) and Chapel Stile (20min) to the road's end at the Old Dungeon Ghyll (30min from Ambleside) at the head of the valley. The Central Lakes Day Rider ticket (buy from the driver; from £9, family £18) is valid, using any service from Bowness/Windermere.

ACCOMMODATION
SEE MAP PAGE 88

Make sure you've got the right **Dungeon Ghyll** hotel, since there are two in Langdale – the New Dungeon Ghyll, near the Stickle Ghyll car park, and the Old Dungeon Ghyll (the famous one), a mile further up at the head of the valley.

★ **Great Langdale Campsite** Great Langdale, LA22 9JU, campsite ☏ 015394 37668, bookings ☏ 015394 32733, ⓦ nationaltrust.org.uk/holidays/great-langdale-campsite-lake-district. The National Trust's stupendously sited Langdale campsite has always been popular, but it's gone stellar since fancy camping pods (£55), luxury yurts (minimum four days, from £365; ⓦ long-valley-yurts.co.uk) and Nordic tipis (from £50; ⓦ basecamptipi.co.uk) were added into the mix. The site's also got a separate family camping field, as well as laundry, drying room, well-stocked shop (with its own bread oven, for freshly baked bread

every morning) and kids' playground, while at night boozers decamp to the Old Dungeon Ghyll, a 5min walk away. It's immensely popular with climbers, hikers and cool campers alike, so you'll need to book ahead. Prices include one tent and a vehicle. Per person __£16__

Millbeck Farm Great Langdale, LA22 9JU ☏ 015394 37364, ⓦ millbeckfarm.co.uk. "What you see is what you get", says the owner – basically, three small, country-style rooms in the farmhouse (all sharing a bathroom and toilet), a big breakfast and glorious valley views. They also have two self-contained cottages near the head of the valley, sleeping three or six people (from £320). Also on offer are cuts of the farm's own Herdwick lamb and Angus beef, to take away. The farm is up the narrow lane by the bridge, just before the New Dungeon Ghyll. Parking. No credit cards. __£72__

2

WALKS IN GREAT LANGDALE

Walking in Great Langdale isn't necessarily an expeditionary undertaking, but you do need to be more aware than usual of time, weather conditions and your own ability before setting off on a hike. Once you leave the valley bottom there's nothing much that's simply a stroll – then again, of the classic routes picked out below, all save Jack's Rake are within the average walker's ability.

PAVEY ARK

Behind Stickle Tarn stands the fearsome cliff-face of **Pavey Ark** (2297ft), which can actually be climbed relatively easily if you approach it up the grassy path to its rear (north). Gung-ho walkers make the more dramatic climb up the cleft that is **Jack's Rake**, which ascends the face right to left and is the hardest commonly used route in the Lake District – in parts it's effectively rock-climbing and requires a head for heights and steady nerves. An alternative climb, up Easy Gully (it isn't), starts from near the base. However you get up, count on it taking an hour from Stickle Tarn.

THE LANGDALE PIKES

From the top of Pavey Ark it's a straightforward walk to the renowned "pikes" (from the dialect pronunciation of "peak"): first, **Harrison Stickle** (2414ft), then down to the stream forming the headwaters of Dungeon Ghyll and then slowly up to **Pike of Stickle** (2326ft). To make a long walk of it, aim then for **Stake Pass** to the northwest and return down the old Langdale packhorse route. Or you could walk the Pikes the other way round, starting with the approach up Dungeon Ghyll and finishing with a descent from Stickle Tarn. Either way, the walking is around seven miles and takes about five hours.

PIKE O'BLISCO

For a short(ish), sharp climb out of Langdale, **Pike o'Blisco** (2304ft) is a tempting target – you can see its summit cairn from the valley floor, and you'll be on the top in ninety minutes glorying in the views. The easiest route follows the path from the *Old Dungeon Ghyll* road-end, through Stool End farm, and then crosses Oxendale Beck to climb up via Brown Howe to Red Tarn (1hr) for the final push to the pike. Total walk is five miles, a three-hour round trip, but experienced hikers won't find it any problem to incorporate Pike o'Blisco in a full-day Crinkle Crags and Bowfell circuit.

CRINKLE CRAGS, BOWFELL AND ESK PIKE

The orthodox route up to the distinctive **Crinkle Crags** (2816ft) – the name, as you'll see, is deserved – is via Oxendale and Red Tarn. From the summit, an exciting ridge walk north along the "crinkles" drops down to Three Tarns (from where there's a possible descent down The Band to Langdale) or you continue north instead up to the rocky, conical summit of **Bowfell** (2960ft) – one of Wainwright's half-dozen favourite fells. From Bowfell, descend via Ore Gap to **Angle Tarn**, and then back to the *Old Dungeon Ghyll* down Rossett Gill and Mickleden Beck. This is a nine-mile (6hr) circuit, though determined peak-baggers will also want to add **Esk Pike** (2903ft) to the route, after Bowfell (total 11–12 miles; 7–8hr), before swinging back round and down to Angle Tarn.

New Dungeon Ghyll Great Langdale, LA22 9JX ☏ 015394 37213, ⦿ dungeon-ghyll.com. The Victorian-era hotel near Stickle Ghyll, beneath the Langdale Pikes, is a more modern experience than the "Old DG", a mile up the road, and though rooms – standard, superior and four-poster – are a touch pricier they've all got nice bathrooms and expansive views. Parking. **£134**

Old Dungeon Ghyll Great Langdale, LA22 9JY ☏ 015394 37272, ⦿ odg.co.uk. The en-suite rooms with elegant four-poster beds at this characterful old inn, which also serves great food and drink (see below) offer the best value; weekend and one-night-stay prices are £10 higher. Parking. **£125**

EATING

SEE MAP PAGE 88

For **groceries** and supplies of any kind you'll have to head back down to Elterwater or Ambleside.

New Dungeon Ghyll Great Langdale, LA22 9JX ☎ 015394 37213, ⓦ dungeon-ghyll.com. This Victorian hotel (see above) has a smart restaurant (three-course dinner £29.50) that's open to non-guests, and good bar meals (and breakfasts between 8am & noon) in the *Walker's Bar* or on the outdoor terrace (mains around £14). Bar meals daily noon–9pm, restaurant daily 6–8.30pm.

★ **Old Dungeon Ghyll** Great Langdale, LA22 9JY ☎ 015394 37272, ⓦ odg.co.uk. Langdale's most famous inn (see above) is decidedly old-school in character and appearance – well-worn oak, floral decor, vintage furniture and assorted dubious watercolours – but walkers have long appreciated its unrivalled location, while plump armchairs and an open fire in the lounge do much to soothe the day's aches and strains. Everyone is welcome for snacks and meals, whether coffee and flapjack for walkers (from 9am) or more substantial later in the day, whether eating outside on the terrace or in the barebones, stone-flagged *Hikers' Bar*, which has a range of real ales and hearty casseroles and chips-with-everything meals (from £12). Bar daily noon–11pm, kitchen noon–9pm.

Sticklebarn Tavern Great Langdale, LA22 9JU ☎ 015394 37356. Now run by the National Trust, the pub opposite the *New Dungeon Ghyll* has a sunny slate terrace outside the bar for drinks with the grandest of views. Sustainable, seasonal grub is the order of the day, with tempting plates such as slow roast pulled pork burger, and wild game casserole with blue cheese dumplings (mains around £14), alongside *glühwein* and hot chocolate for chilly days. Mon–Sat noon–11pm, Sun noon–10.30pm; kitchen daily noon–9pm.

2

Coniston Water, Hawkshead and the south

TARN HOWS

Coniston Water, Hawkshead and the south

Coniston Water is certainly not one of the most immediately imposing of the lakes, yet it's one of the oldest settled parts of the Lake District. For as long as there has been human habitation, there has been industry of sorts around Coniston, whether fishing in the lake by the monks of Furness Abbey, copper mining and slate quarrying in the valleys and fells, or coppicing and charcoal making in the forests. The lake's understated beauty attracted the Victorian art critic, essayist and moralist John Ruskin, and his lakeshore house, Brantwood, provides the most obvious target for a trip. Meanwhile, no one should miss a boat ride on the National Trust's elegant steam yacht, *Gondola*, or on the lake's wooden motor launches.

Those wanting to stay in the area usually look no further than the cute cottages and cobbled streets of **Hawkshead**, three miles east of Coniston Water, with its connections to the big two literary lakeland names of **William Wordsworth** (who went to school here) and **Beatrix Potter** (whose husband's former office has been turned into an art gallery). The one-time mining village of **Coniston** itself has to work hard to keep visitors in the face of such stiff competition, but it grows on some people after a while and is the usual base for an ascent of the **Old Man of Coniston**, the distinctive peak that backs the village. Wherever you stay, there are easy side-trips: to the renowned local beauty spot of **Tarn Hows**, the woodland paths, bike trails and sculptures of **Grizedale Forest**, or Beatrix Potter's former house of **Hill Top** – the last being one of the most visited attractions in the Lake District. Routes south towards the Furness peninsula take you through the pretty **Duddon Valley** – immortalized by Wordsworth in a series of sonnets – and to the quiet market town of **Broughton-in-Furness**, on the southern edge of the National Park.

Coniston

Its dimensions are nothing out of the ordinary – five miles long, half a mile across at its widest point – and its only village is the plainest in the Lakes, but the glassy surface of **Coniston Water** weaves a gentle spell on summer days. It's one of the best lakes to see by boat, with two separate services plying its waters, while the spreading Grizedale woodland on the east side and the limited road access mean it's easy to lose the worst of the crowds. The lake is also indelibly associated with two famous names. At the end of the nineteenth century, **Arthur Ransome** spent his childhood summer holidays near Nibthwaite at the southern end, and was always "half-drowned in tears" when it was time to leave. His vivid memories of messing about on the water, camping on the islets, befriending the local charcoal-burners and playing make-believe in the hills surfaced later in his children's classic, *Swallows and Amazons*, when Peel Island became the "Wild Cat Island" of the book. The sheltered Coniston waters also attracted speed-adventurer Sir Malcolm Campbell, who set the world water-speed record here (of 141mph) in 1939; his record-holding son, **Donald Campbell**, was to perish on the lake in 1967 in pursuit of an ever faster time, and the story rumbles on today with the ongoing restoration of his crashed powerboat *Bluebird*.

Highlights

❶ Ruskin Museum, Coniston The best of Coniston – its history, trades, pastimes and personalities – all under one roof. See page 117

❷ Steam Yacht Gondola The sumptuous way to cruise Coniston Water and reach Ruskin's Brantwood home is on the elegant nineteenth-century steam yacht. See page 118

❸ Climbing the Old Man of Coniston The finest single climb in the area for anyone who wants to say they've been up a classic Lake District mountain. See page 120

❹ Ospreys at Esthwaite Rent a rowing boat for the chance to see these rare birds on the water from the water. See page 128

❺ Drunken Duck Inn Boutique rooms and wonderful food in the gentle Hawkshead countryside. See page 129

❻ Hill Top, Near Sawrey No serious Beatrix Potter fan should miss touring the house she bought with the proceeds of her first book, *The Tale of Peter Rabbit*. See page 130

❼ Go Ape in Grizedale Forest The high-wire adventure course in the trees of Grizedale Forest brings out the Tarzan in visitors young and old. See page 133

❽ The Duddon Valley Drive – or better still, walk – the Duddon Valley, one of the region's best-kept secrets. See page 136

HIGHLIGHTS ARE MARKED ON THE MAP ON PAGE 114

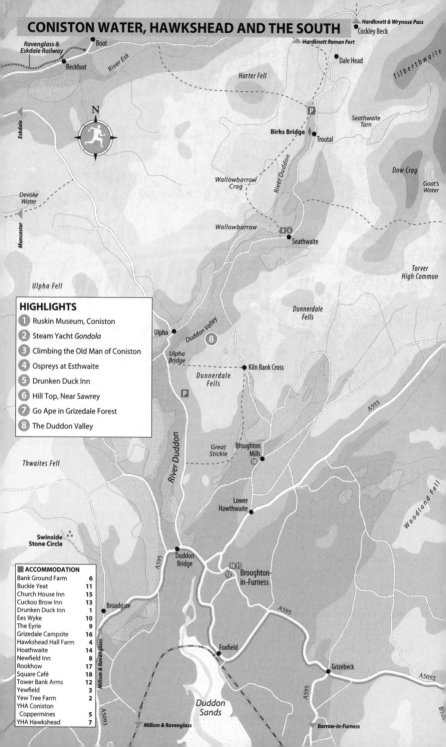

CONISTON WATER, HAWKSHEAD AND THE SOUTH

Hardknott & Wrynose Pass
Cockley Beck

Ravenglass & Eskdale Railway
Boot
Beckfoot
River Esk

Hardknott Roman Fort
Dale Head
Tilberthwaite

Harter Fell

Eskdale

Devoke Water

Muncaster

Birks Bridge
Troutal

Seathwaite Tarn

Dow Crag
Goat's Water

Wallowbarrow Crag

River Duddon

Ulpha Fell

Wallowbarrow
8 4
Seathwaite

Torver High Common

HIGHLIGHTS

1. Ruskin Museum, Coniston
2. Steam Yacht *Gondola*
3. Climbing the Old Man of Coniston
4. Ospreys at Esthwaite
5. Drunken Duck Inn
6. Hill Top, Near Sawrey
7. Go Ape in Grizedale Forest
8. The Duddon Valley

Ulpha
Duddon Valley
8

Ulpha Bridge

Dunnerdale Fells

Kiln Bank Cross

Dunnerdale Fells

River Duddon

Thwaites Fell

Great Stickle
Broughton Mills
10

Lower Hawthwaite

Woodland Fell

Swinside Stone Circle

ACCOMMODATION

Bank Ground Farm	6
Buckle Yeat	11
Church House Inn	15
Cuckoo Brow Inn	13
Drunken Duck Inn	1
Ees Wyke	10
The Eyrie	9
Grizedale Campsite	16
Hawkshead Hall Farm	4
Hoathwaite	14
Newfield Inn	8
Rookhow	17
Square Café	18
Tower Bank Arms	12
Yewfield	3
Yew Tree Farm	2
YHA Coniston Coppermines	5
YHA Hawkshead	7

Duddon Bridge
18 11
12
Broughton-in-Furness

Broadgate

Millom & Ravenglass

Foxfield

Grizebeck

A595

A5092

Duddon Sands

Millom & Ravenglass

Barrow-in-Furness

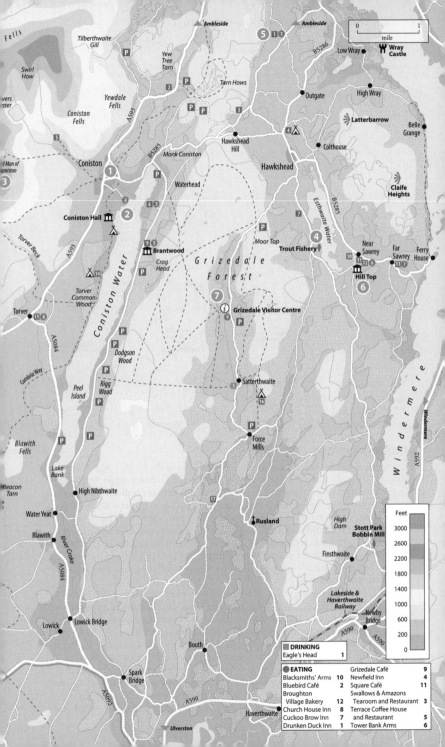

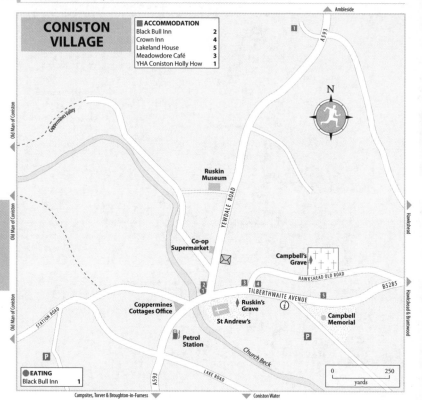

Coniston village

Copper has been taken from the Coniston fells since the Bronze Age, though the Romans were the first to mine it systematically. The industry again flourished in the seventeenth century, and by the nineteenth century hundreds of workers were employed in the local copper mines – producing ore used for the "copper-bottoming" of the wooden hulls of ships, which protected them from voracious, wood-devouring marine worms. Together with slate-quarriers – first recorded here in the seventeenth century – Coniston's industrious miners established themselves in the village of **Coniston** (a derivation of "King's Town"), hunkered under the craggy, mine-riddled bulk of the **Old Man of Coniston**, which looms to the northwest.

That Coniston was originally a mining village, pure and simple, is clear from the rather drab, utilitarian, rows of cottages and later Victorian shopfronts that make up the slate-grey-green settlement. By the late nineteenth century the copper-mining business was in terminal decline and the railway, built in 1859 to remove the mined ore and quarried slate, began to bring in tourists instead. The train to Coniston is long gone, but the seasonal influx of tourists continues to what is still just a smallish, functional kind of place – with a population of around eight hundred and just enough shops, pubs and cafés to kill an hour or two. Coniston keeps to itself to such an extent that some first-time visitors are surprised to find it even has a **lake** – the water is hidden out of sight, half a mile southeast of the village.

St Andrew's church

Hawkshead Rd, B5285, LA21 8EL • Daily 9am–5pm • ⓦ standrewsconiston.org.uk

At the heart of the village, by river and bridge, stands **St Andrew's church**, whose churchyard contains the **grave of John Ruskin**, beneath a beautifully worked Celtic cross. Ruskin – resident of nearby Brantwood, and pre-eminent authority on art and architecture in Victorian England– had a long association with Coniston. His handsome memorial was designed by Ruskin's longtime secretary and literary assistant W.G. Collingwood (who is also buried at St Andrew's) and, a year later, the first museum in Coniston was opened, also bearing Ruskin's name.

Ruskin Museum

Yewdale Rd, A593, LA21 8DU • Early March to mid-Nov daily 10am–5.30pm; mid-Nov to early March Wed–Sun 10.30am–3.30pm • £6.50, family ticket £16.50 • ☎ 015394 41164, ⓦ ruskinmuseum.com

Coniston's **Ruskin Museum** is the most thought-provoking in the Lakes. It's the first port of call for anyone interested in tracing John Ruskin's life and work, while – in relating his ideas and theories to local trades and pastimes – the museum also doubles as a highly effective record of Coniston's history through the ages.

The museum begins with a walk-through timeline, placing the village and Ruskin within the wider historical context. Stone and Bronze Age artefacts give way to an exposition of the local geology, essential for an understanding of why Coniston became an important mining and quarrying district. You'll learn about slate quarrying (the local slate flags the museum floors), dry-stone walling (there's a fine example outside the museum) and sheep farming, as well as about the traditional linen- and lace-making trades that Ruskin himself promoted as a means of sustaining local employment.

In the museum's separate **Ruskin Gallery** are found various personal artefacts (including a pair of his socks and his matriculation certificate from Oxford), alongside a mixed bag of letters, manuscripts, sketchbooks and a series of Ruskin's own watercolours. A side-gallery lets you view pages of Ruskin's sketchbooks at the click of a mouse. Meanwhile, in the **Bluebird** wing, you can track the latest developments in the reconstruction of Donald Campbell's powerboat *Bluebird*, whose wreckage was lifted from the bottom of Coniston Water in 2001 – keep up to speed with the latest news at ⓦ bluebirdproject.com.

3

FAMILY BUSINESS – THE COLLINGWOODS

Few families have had as sure a feel for the Lake District as the **Collingwoods**, whose home was at Lanehead at the northern end of Coniston Water. Local scholar, historian and artist William Gershorn **(W.G.) Collingwood** (1854–1932) was born in Liverpool, but visited the Lake District on holiday as a child and moved here as soon as was practicable. He became an expert on lakeland archeology, the Vikings and early Northumbrian crosses (his *Northumbrian Crosses of the Pre-Norman Age*, published in 1927, is a classic), writing his own guide to *The Lake Counties* (1902) and even a lakeland saga, *Thorstein of the Mere*, largely set around Coniston. While at Oxford University, Collingwood had studied under John Ruskin (who was Professor of Fine Art) and was immediately impressed by his mind and ideas; later, Collingwood became Ruskin's trusted secretary and literary assistant. It was W.G. who designed Ruskin's memorial cross and established the first Ruskin Museum in Coniston. The family befriended the young Arthur Ransome, who was of a similar age to W.G.'s son **Robin Collingwood** (1889–1943). Robin was later to become an Oxford professor of philosophy, influential historiographer and an authority on Roman Britain – he excavated the Galava site and fortifications at Waterhead near Ambleside. W.G.'s wife **Edith** and two daughters, **Barbara** and **Dora**, were also highly talented: Edith and Dora as painters, Barbara as a sculptor. Barbara's bust of the elderly Ruskin is on display in the Ambleside Museum. The family graves all lie, with Ruskin's, in Coniston's churchyard.

SPEED KING

It was an attempt too far for speed king **Donald Campbell** (1921–67) when he returned to Coniston Water at the beginning of 1967. Three years earlier, he'd set both land- (403mph) and water-speed (276mph) world records in Australia, and on January 4, 1967, his latest water-speed attempt on Coniston was looking promising. A first run had touched almost 300mph, but on the return his jet-powered *Bluebird K7* hit a patch of turbulence at an estimated 320mph. The craft went into a somersault and sank, and Campbell was killed immediately. His body and boat lay undisturbed on the lakebed until both were retrieved in 2001 by a team led by diver Bill Smith. Campbell's belated funeral was held at St Andrew's church, before the blue coffin (the colour of his boat) was carried by horse and carriage to the small church cemetery behind the *Crown Hotel*, where his **grave** lies today. There's also a **memorial plaque** dedicated to Campbell (and his chief mechanic, Leo Villa), which dominates the small green in the village centre, and a second plaque down near the piers by the lake.

The retrieval of *Bluebird* and the restoration of the craft have been controversial to say the least. But restoration work was finally completed in 2018 and *Bluebird* made its return to water in August on Loch Fad on the Isle of Bute in west Scotland. A proposed return to Coniston Water in 2019 was called off, though there are still plans to trial the vessel on the lake. There are photographs of Campbell, his funeral and the recovery of the craft on display in Coniston's Ruskin Museum (see page 117), along with related mementoes, like Campbell's crash helmet and overalls. Otherwise, the full story and the arguments are rehashed on the **Bluebird Project** website ⓦ bluebirdproject.com.

Coniston Water

It's a ten-minute walk down Lake Road from the village to **Coniston Water** and its piers. The pebble shoreline and grassy verges are very popular on sunny summer days, while the National Park's **Coniston Boating Centre** (see page 119) offers boat, kayak and dinghy rental – and there's a good lakeside café too, the *Bluebird*. Various **lake cruise services** operate around the lake, calling at Ruskin's house, Brantwood (on the opposite shore), as well as various other points – you can stop off at any pier en route.

Steam Yacht Gondola

Coniston Pier, Lake Rd, LA21 8AN • April–Oct all sailings daily: South Lake Cruise (1hr) 10.45am; North Lake Cruise (45min) noon & 1.30pm; Full Lake Cruise (1hr 45min) 2.30pm • South Lake Cruise £17, family ticket £38; North Lake Cruise £13, family ticket £29; Full Lake Cruise £23, family ticket £49 • ☎ 015394 32733, ⓦ nationaltrust.org.uk/steam-yacht-gondola

Boat speeds on Coniston Water are limited to 10mph, a graceful pace for the sumptuously upholstered and quilted **Steam Yacht Gondola**. This was first launched in 1859 and has now been fully restored by the National Trust – right down to the glorious golden sea serpent sitting on her prow – and even claims to be "green steam" as the boiler burns sustainable wood-waste logs. The boat leaves Coniston Pier for 45-minute circuits of the northern half of the lake, hourly circuits of the southern part of the lake, as well as longer cruises, which show you more of the lake and tell you a little about its history; all three cruises stop-off at Ruskin's Brantwood (ask for a discount voucher), while the North Lake and Full Lake cruises also stop at the jetty at Monk Coniston (from where you can walk to Tarn Hows).

Coniston Launch

Coniston Pier, Lake Rd, LA21 8AN • Easter–Oct hourly departures 10.45am–4.40pm; Nov–Easter up to 5 trips daily • Northern service (45min), £12, family ticket £27.50, or £17.85/£38.70 including Brantwood admission; Southern service (1hr 30min) £17.95, family ticket £35.50; unlimited use Seven-Day Explorer ticket £27, family £54 • ☎ 017687 75753, ⓦ conistonlaunch.co.uk

The eco-friendly **Coniston Launch** service is provided by solar-powered wooden vessels *Ruskin* and *Ransome*, which offer two routes around the lake, north and south. The southern route is longer, concentrating on sites associated with *Swallows and Amazons* or the speed-racing Campbells; both routes call at Brantwood but you only have time to look around the house and gardens there if you take the northern service. Walking information is available on board for anyone planning to stop off at one of the lakeside jetties.

ARRIVAL AND DEPARTURE   CONISTON

BY CAR

Drivers come in on either the A593 (Ambleside road) or the B5285 (from Hawkshead) – the latter runs through the village as Tilberthwaite Ave. The main car park is signposted; it's right in the centre (off Tilberthwaite Ave), next to the Coniston Information Centre (see below). Down by the lake, there's limited free parking by the *Bluebird Café*, and also a large pay-and-display car park.

BY BUS AND BOAT

Buses stop by the *Crown Inn*, on the main road (B5285) through the village. A Ruskin Explorer ticket (£20.60, family £43.60; buy on the bus) includes unrestricted bus travel, a return trip on the Coniston Launch to Brantwood and entry to Brantwood itself.

Bus #505 "Coniston Rambler" to: Hawkshead (18min); Ambleside (38min); Brockhole (47min); Windermere (54min). Service operates Easter–Oct roughly hourly; Nov–Easter roughly every two hours.

Bus #X12 to: Torver (7min); Ulverston (40min). Service operates Mon–Sat 6 daily.

Cross Lakes Experience (☎015394 48600, ⓦlake district.gov.uk/crosslakes) from Coniston *Waterhead Hotel* to: Hawkshead (18min), with connections on to Hill Top and Ferry House, Sawrey (for launch to Bowness), and also to Tarn Hows. Up to 9 daily April–Oct.

INFORMATION

Tourist office Coniston Information Centre, Ruskin Ave, next to the main car park (daily: Easter–Oct 9.30am–5pm; Nov–Easter 10am–4pm, though hours may vary; ☎015394 41533, ⓦconistontic.org).

ACTIVITIES

Bike rental Coniston Boating Centre (see below), at the lake, rents out bikes year-round; half-day £20, full day £25. They also have tag-alongs, trailers and electric fat tyre bikes available. Nearby Grizedale Forest has its own bike-rental outlet.

Outdoor activities Joint Adventures, Brocklebank Ground, Torver (☎015394 49003, ⓦjointadventures.co.uk) offers a full programme of activities such as abseiling, canyoning, archery, kayaking or hiking (half-day from £40), plus more involved skills courses.

Watersports Coniston Boating Centre (Feb half-term to mid-Nov daily 10am–5pm; mid-Nov to Feb half-term Wed–Sun 10am–3pm; ☎015394 41366, ⓦconiston boatingcentre.co.uk) at the lake has rowing boats (from £15/hr), electric motorboats (from £30/hr), paddleboards (£20/2hr), sit-on kayaks (£20 for 2hr) or Canadian canoes (£25 for 2hr). The centre also rents out sailing dinghies and offers lessons and weekend courses.

ACCOMMODATION   SEE MAPS PAGES 114 AND 116

Accommodation is plentiful and, for the most part, reasonably priced, and just outside Coniston are some fantastically appealing places, from farmhouse B&B to gourmet inn. There's one unique **self-catering** option – an apartment with a view in Ruskin's house, Brantwood (see page 123) – while other holiday **cottages** also linked with the area's heritage are available through *The Coppermines* (ⓦcoppermines.co.uk), namely a series of converted dwellings in the old sawmill in Coppermines Valley. Note that access to these, and to the Coppermines **youth hostel**, is up a steep and largely unsurfaced road. The nearest **campsite** to the village is busy *Coniston Hall*, a mile south by the lake, but it's nicer at the National Trust's shoreside *Hoathwaite*, 2 miles south near Torver.

CONISTON

★ **Black Bull Inn** Coppermines Rd, LA21 8DU, by the bridge ☎015394 41335, ⓦblackbullconiston.co.uk. The village's best pub (see page 122) has a variety of reasonably spacious B&B rooms (costing £20 more at weekends), either in the main building, in the renovated Old Man and Bluebird cottages or in the old coach house – the four rooms in the last share a pretty riverside patio, with grand views up to the fells. Parking. **£100**

Crown Inn Tilberthwaite Ave, LA21 8ED ☎015394 41243, ⓦcrowninnconiston.com. It's nothing fancy but the refurbished rooms at the *Crown* offer a fair amount of space for your money, and many have both baths and showers, a boon for aching walkers. There's a traditional bar downstairs (with meals, superbly gooey toffee pudding and a range of malt whiskies) and an outdoor terrace looking across the churchyard. Two- and five-night breaks (including dinner) are a bit of a bargain. Parking. **£110**

Lakeland House Tilberthwaite Ave, LA21 8ED ☎015394 41303, ⓦlakelandhouse.com. A good, centrally located budget option accustomed to walkers

3

WALKS FROM CONISTON

The classic walk from Coniston village is to the top of the Old Man of Coniston, which is tiring but not overly difficult – Wainwright's flippant reference to ascending crowds of "courting couples, troops of earnest Boy Scouts, babies and grandmothers" isn't that far wide of the mark. Other Coniston walks are similarly accessible to most abilities, ranging from lakeside strolls to ghyll scrambles.

OLD MAN OF CONISTON

Most walkers can reach the summit of the **Old Man of Coniston** (2635ft) – England's seventh-highest mountain, if you need an excuse – in under two hours from the village, following the signposted path from Church Beck and over the old Miner's Bridge, along what's known as **Coppermines Valley**. It's a steep and twisting route, passing though abandoned quarry works and their detritus, but there's a pause on the way up at Low Water tarn and the views from the top are tremendous – to the Cumbrian coast and Morecambe Bay, and across to Langdale and Windermere. It may sound an odd name, but "Man" is a common term hereabouts, signifying a peak or summit, while "Old" is merely a corruption of the Latin abbreviation "alt", or high.

OLD MAN CIRCULAR ROUTES

Hardier hikers combine the Old Man in a ridge-walk loop with **Swirl How** (2630ft) and **Wetherlam** (2502ft) to the north – a seven- or eight-mile walk (5–7hr). Wetherlam, too, is pitted with caves, mines and tunnels, requiring caution on the various descents to Coppermines Valley. Or instead of heading north you can loop around to the south, descending via **Goat's Hause** and Goat's Water tarn, under the fearsome **Dow Crag** (a famed lure for rock climbers). This eventually deposits you in Torver (see below), with the full circuit back to Coniston being something like eight miles (5hr).

LAKESIDE WALKS

From Coniston village the Cumbria Way footpath provides access to Coniston Water's west side. The route runs past sixteenth-century Coniston Old Hall (note its traditional circular chimneys) and through Torver Common Wood to **Torver**, where there's the excellent *Church House Inn* pub and the possibility of climbing up Torver Beck to see its waterfalls. There are also several park-and-walk spots on the lake's east side – nearest to the village is the northern pier of **Monk Coniston** at the head of the lake – with trails and picnic tables in the National Trust woodland. You can stroll up from here to the National Trust **gardens** of Monk Coniston Hall, known for their exotic conifers, and on to Tarn Hows.

TILBERTHWAITE GILL AND YEWDALE

North of Coniston the crags, beck and tarn of **Yewdale** offer a multitude of short walks. **Tilberthwaite Gill** is a quiet, narrow glen set among dramatic old quarry workings – there's free parking on a signposted lane off the Ambleside road (1.5 miles from Coniston), or you can walk here from Coppermines Valley via Hole Rake. **Yew Tree Tarn**, right on the Ambleside road (2 miles from Coniston), is another pretty spot – there's parking back down the road, and a footpath to Tarn Hows.

and cyclists – bike storage, drying facilities and packed lunches are all available. The ten doubles/twins have all been upgraded and many have decent views – there's most space to lounge about in the top-floor attic suite (£90–160). Breakfast is a hearty affair, but if you're in a rush they're happy to put something together to take away. £75
★ **Meadowdore Café** Hawkshead Old Rd, LA21 8ET ☎015394 41638, ⊛meadowdore.com. The B&B at the

café is of a high quality and excellent value. There are two en-suite rooms and one with a lovely private bathroom; all three are tastefully furnished, and two have great views. The café downstairs has a conservatory extension and slate patio, so summer mornings can start with an alfresco brekkie. Parking. £70
★ **YHA Coniston Holly How** Far End, LA21 8DD on A593 ☎0845 371 9511, ⊛yha.org.uk/hostel/coniston-

holly-how. The closest youth hostel to the village is in a big old slate house (with some four-bed family rooms) set in its own gardens just a few minutes' walk north of the centre on the Ambleside road. They've also got tipis (£99) and raised land pods (bedding, no heating) sleeping four (£79), while camping (£15) is also a possibility. It's popular with schools and families, and is accordingly well equipped (laundry, café, bar service, outdoor activities, plus unusually spacious dorms), and it gets good reviews for its food – there's even hand-pumped real ale! Eager-to-please staff can also book you on local adventure activities. Dorms £25, family rooms £78,

AROUND CONISTON

★ **Bank Ground Farm** Coniston Water, LA21 8AA, 2 miles southeast of Coniston ☎ 015394 41264, ⍟ bank ground.com. *Bank Ground Farm* is beautifully set on its own part of the shoreline, not far from Brantwood. There's atmosphere in abundance (low ceilings, exposed wood and open fires), and it was the original model for Holly Howe Farm in *Swallows and Amazons* and later used in the 1970s film. Six traditionally furnished rooms in the main house, five of them en suite, have oak beams, carved beds and heavy furniture, and many have sweeping views, especially Room 8, which has three windows overlooking lake and fells. They also rent out six adjoining self-catering cottages located halfway between Coniston and Hawkshead, sleeping two to seventeen people (from £450/week). Parking. £100

★ **Church House Inn** Torver, LA21 8AZ, 2 miles south of Coniston on A593 ☎ 015394 49159, ⍟ thechurch houseinn.com. Anyone after good food should drop by for a meal (see page 122), but there are also four comfortable, small and charming B&B rooms with a modern "country cottage" look, offering very good value plus two bunk rooms sleeping six (one double and two bunks in each), ideal for large families or groups (£30 per person); they've also got hook-ups for a few motorhomes out the back. Parking. £79

The Eyrie Brantwood, Coniston Water, LA21 8AD, 2.5 miles southeast of Coniston ☎ 015394 41396, ⍟ brantwood.org.uk. What a find for art-lovers and Ruskin enthusiasts – a very handsomely restored self-catering apartment for two on the upper floor of beautiful Brantwood, available for overnight stays or longer. There's a

double bedroom, kitchen-diner and a drawing room with the same lake views that used to inspire Ruskin himself. The gardens outside, and the Brantwood collections when open, are yours to explore. Parking. Minimum two-night stay £315

Hoathwaite Coniston Water, Torver LA21 8AX, off A593 ☎ 015394 63862/32733, ⍟ nationaltrust.org. uk/holidays/hoathwaite-campsite-lake-district. The National Trust's newest Lake District campsite has a terrific location, close to the lake with sweeping views; there are toilets and showers, but the site is otherwise fairly basic. Coniston and the shops are a couple of miles away, and the closest pub, happily, is the really good *Church House Inn* (see below) at Torver. Closed Oct–Easter. Prices include one tent and a vehicle. Per person £9

★ **Yew Tree Farm** Coniston, LA21 8DP, 2 miles north of Coniston on A593 ⍟ yewtree-farm.com, bookings ☎ 015394 32321, ⍟ heartofthelakes.co.uk. The best and classiest self-catering farmhouse in the Lakes – we're not just talking about the munching sheep in the garden but also the private outdoor hot tub for guests and not to mention the fully functioning fireplaces. Three hugely atmospheric rooms are tucked away amid the creaking floors and mind-your-head oak beams: it's period (1690) in feel – the solid doors have clunky wooden latches and there are handcrafted beds – but with a contemporary touch, including some bold paintwork and stylish green-slate-floor bathrooms. The farm sells its own meats, and there are walks straight from the gates (Tarn Hows is only 0.5 mile away). Parking. Minimum one week. £84

YHA Coniston Coppermines Coppermines Valley, LA21 8HP, 1.25 miles west of Coniston ☎ 0845 371 9630, ⍟ yha.org.uk/hostel/coniston-coppermines. The hikers' favourite is perfectly placed for ascents of the Old Man and Wetherlam – you're almost halfway up a mountain already by the time you get here. It's fairly basic, with 26 bunks in four-, six- and eight-bed rooms and few frills, but the dramatic setting can't be beaten, meals are served and you can buy a local beer or organic wine. It's a steepish hike from the village – follow the "Old Man" signs past the *Sun Hotel* or take the small road between the *Black Bull* and the Co-op; both routes lead to the hostel. Closed Nov–Feb. Dorms £15

3

CONISTON FESTIVALS

Annual festivals include the week-long **Coniston Water Festival** (beginning of July), a celebration of arts, sports, leisure, food and drink and the one-day **Coniston Country Fair** (third or fourth week of July; ⍟ conistoncountryfair.co.uk), when all manner of traditional country trades, crafts, contests and entertainment take place in the grounds of Coniston Hall. They both make really good family days out – the Country Fair especially puts on everything from bouncy castles and face-painting to archery and egg-throwing contests, while the showpiece fell race is nothing less than a run up a mountain (Coniston Old Man) and back.

PEOPLE AND PLACES: LIVING WITH MISS POTTER

You know how it is – working farm to run, B&B guests to look after, breakfasts to cook – so what's your reaction when you walk into your messy kitchen to discover Renée Zellweger? "I was horrified!" laughs Caroline Watson, who with husband Jon farms belted Galloway cattle and Herdwick sheep at **Yew Tree Farm** (see above), just outside Coniston. The Watsons have been at the farm since 2002 and are the current guardians of a most singular property, since **Beatrix Potter** herself owned and furnished the farm in the 1930s (it subsequently passed to the National Trust). This at least explains finding Bridget Jones in your kitchen – Yew Tree Farm doubled as Potter's house Hill Top in the lavish *Miss Potter* biopic (2006), yet the Watsons managed to live and work through the several weeks of pre-production and two days of filming. Renée may be gone, but Beatrix still makes her presence felt daily in the farm's parlour (now the breakfast room for B&B guests), which she established for the original tenants. Here, the furniture, paintings and ornaments are all Potter's, along with the Bible box and grandfather clock in the hall. But Caroline's favourite is the Cumberland dresser with the white plates that bear the motto "Persevere" – appropriate for a farm business she thinks, even one with the spirit of Miss Potter flitting through the kitchen.

3

EATING

SEE MAPS PAGES 114 AND 116

There are several **cafés and pubs** in the village – the outdoor tables at the *Black Bull* are perfect for a pint after a day on the fells – and you'll have no trouble finding somewhere to buy a sandwich or put together a picnic (there are basic supplies at the Co-op **supermarket** on Yewdale Rd). The best options, however, are a little further out.

Black Bull Inn Coppermines Rd, LA21 8DU, by the bridge ☏ 015394 41335, ⊛ blackbullconiston.co.uk. Hearty bar meals (£11–18) are very popular – there's always home-made soup and a veggie dish, with local lamb, sausage, steak and trout the mainstays. What really stands out, though, is the beer, brewed on the premises – their Bluebird bitter in particular is an award-winning ale that does wonders for tuckered walkers. Daily 10am–11pm; kitchen noon–9pm.

Bluebird Café Lake Rd, LA21 8AN ☏ 015394 41649, ⊛ thebluebirdcafe.co.uk. The big, covered outdoor terrace with lake views make this the perfect place to watch the comings and goings of the boats. On the menu are Cumberland sausage butties, soups and sandwiches, jacket potatoes and salads (£3.50–8), or it's good for a decent coffee and a cake. Daily: March, April & Oct 10am–5pm; May–Sept 9.30am–5.30pm; Nov–Feb 10am–4pm.

★ **Church House Inn** Torver, LA21 8AZ, 2 miles south of Coniston on A593 ☏ 015394 49159, ⊛ thechurch

houseinn.com. The single best local dining destination. You'll eat really well, either in the snug real-ale bar or dining room (reservations advised for both). At lunch, it's seasonal soups and superior sandwiches (£6.50); dinner is also locally sourced and strong on the classics (mussels, corned beef hash with duck egg, slow-cooked Herdwick lamb, steak and ale pie, fish pie; mains £12–20), while service and presentation are spot on. There's a generous Sunday roast too, served with classic Yorkshire pudding (£12.95). Daily 9am–midnight; kitchen noon–3pm & 6–9pm.

★ **Swallows & Amazons Tearoom and Restaurant** Bank Ground Farm, Coniston Water, LA21 8AA, 2 miles southeast of Coniston ☏ 015394 41264, ⊛ bankground. com. For a drive, cycle or walk with a café at the end of it, the *Swallows & Amazons Tearoom and Restaurant* is worth a special trip. Lunches, cakes and ice cream are served at the farmhouse associated with Arthur Ransome and his adventure stories; indeed, a walk here from Coniston, around the lake (which takes about 30min), more than justifies a sticky gingerbread dessert (£3). Scrumptious evening meals are also served, with mains (£12–18), such as beetroot- and gin-cured salmon, and pan-fried Coniston char with apple and fennel salad to whet the appetite. Easter–Oct Thurs–Mon 11am–5pm & 6–8pm; for days and times outside this period check website.

DIRECTORY

Banks There are ATMs in the petrol station and post office, though a fee is charged at both). Otherwise, the nearest banking facilities are in Ambleside.

Hospital The nearest hospital is in Kendal (Westmorland General Hospital, Burton Rd; ☏ 01539 732288, ⊛ uhmb. nhs.uk).

Pharmacy The nearest is in Hawkshead (Collins & Butterworth, Main St; ☏ 015394 36201).

Post office 6 Yewdale Rd (Mon–Fri 9am–12.30pm & 1.30–5.30pm, Sat 9am–noon).

Brantwood

Coniston Water, LA21 8AD • mid-March to mid-Nov daily 10.30am–5pm; mid-Nov to mid-March Wed–Sun 10.30am–4pm • £8.70,
gardens only £6.20; free with Ruskin Explorer bus ticket, 50p discount with Steam Yacht *Gondola*; combined Coniston Launch and
Brantwood ticket (£20.60, family £43.60) available on boat • ☎ 015394 41396, ⓦ brantwood.org.uk

If you come to Coniston, you shouldn't miss **Brantwood**, the magnificently sited
home of **John Ruskin** (1819–1900), which nestles among trees on a hillside above the
eastern shore of the lake. It's only two and a half miles by road from Coniston, off the
B5285, though the approach is greatly enhanced if you arrive by either the Steam Yacht
Gondola or Coniston Launch (see page 118).

Ruskin lived here from 1872 until his death: at first sight he was captivated though
by the stunning mountain and lake views and not by the house itself, which he
complained was "a mere shed". Indeed, the house today bears little resemblance to the
eighteenth-century cottage for which Ruskin splashed out £1500, as he spent the next
twenty years expanding it, adding another twelve rooms and laying out its gardens.
Thus adapted, Brantwood – "brant" is a Cumbrian dialect word meaning steep –
became Ruskin's lair, where the grand old *éminence grise* of Victorian art and letters
gardened, wrote, painted and pontificated.

Brantwood makes for a full day out, provided the weather is kind enough for a proper
tour of the gardens. There's a summer **theatre season** here, held in the grounds, and
various other lectures, recitals and **events** scheduled throughout the year, from drawing-

RUSKIN'S LIFE AND DEATH AT BRANTWOOD

John Ruskin was certainly looking for something other than mere bricks and mortar when
he acquired **Brantwood** in 1871. Following his father's death in 1864 he was independently
wealthy, lauded for his works and regarded as the country's foremost authority on art and
architecture – indeed, he had just been appointed Slade Professor of Fine Art at Oxford
University. But Ruskin's personal life was complicated by two singular relationships, which
perhaps led him to seek simplicity and harmony in the lakeland fells.

His **marriage** to Euphemia (Effie) Gray in 1848 – they honeymooned in the Lakes – had
been annulled in 1854, with the divorce a cause célèbre of the day, sensationally alleging
Ruskin's impotence. Euphemia eventually married the artist John Everett Millais, which – given
Ruskin's unflinching support of the Pre-Raphaelites – was a hard blow. Ruskin later formed
a long attachment with the young **Rose La Touche**, who was almost thirty years his junior.
Her parents disapproved (a proposal in 1866 came to nothing) and when Rose died in 1875,
Ruskin was affected badly. Retreating to his lakeland house, he suffered the first of a series of
mental breakdowns in 1878.

At Brantwood he was looked after by his married cousin Joan Severn and her husband
Arthur, whose family moved into the house in the early 1880s, supervising visits to Ruskin
from the Victorian great and good. **W.G. Collingwood**, for one, was always suspicious of the
Severns' influence and it's clear that they eventually restricted the number of Ruskin's visitors.
The Severns would argue it was to protect Ruskin's health and they had a point, since the last
years of his life were punctuated by bouts of depressive illness and mental breakdown. From
1885, he began to produce sections of his **autobiography**, *Praeterita*, and, eventually, it was
the only thing Ruskin would work on. Tellingly selective in content, it included no mention of
his former wife, Effie. Ruskin broke down again in 1889 and fell into silence, writing nothing
after this time, rarely receiving visitors or even speaking. He caught influenza and died at
Brantwood on January 20, 1900. **The Severns** inherited Brantwood, ignored Ruskin's wishes
that the house be open to the public for a set number of days each year and sold off many of
his paintings. Joan died in 1924, Arthur in 1931, following which the house and its remaining
contents were sold to **J.H. Whitehouse**, founder of the Birmingham Ruskin Society, who
began the task of restoration.

room concerts to craft fairs. Thursday is usually "activity day", always a good time to visit, when there might be children's craft sessions or lace-making demonstrations.

Brief history

The precocious only child of a wealthy wine merchant, Ruskin could afford to indulge his passion for art from an early age, **travelling** in Europe with his parents and maintaining diaries and sketchbooks. He went up to Oxford in 1836, publishing his first book, *The Poetry of Architecture*, a year later when he was just 18. He made his name as an **art critic** with the publication of the first part of his celebrated *Modern Painters* (1843), conceived as a defence of J.M.W. Turner, whose work he had admired (and collected) since his student days. Later a champion of the Pre-Raphaelites and a proponent of the supremacy of Gothic architecture, Ruskin came to insist upon the indivisibility of **ethics** and aesthetics. He was appalled by the conditions in which the captains of industry made their labourers work and live, while expecting him to applaud their patronage of the arts. "There is no wealth but life," he wrote in his study of capitalist economics, *Unto the Last* (1862), elaborating and with the observation: "That country is richest which nourishes the greatest number of noble and happy human beings."

Drawing a distinction between mere labour and craftsmanship, he promoted a revival of local woodcarving and linen- and lace-making, and ventures like this as well as his architectural theories did much to influence such disparate figures as Proust, Tolstoy, Frank Lloyd Wright and Gandhi. Nonetheless, not all Ruskin's **projects** were a success, partly because of his refusal to compromise his principles. A London teashop, established to provide employment for a former servant, failed since Ruskin refused to advertise; meanwhile, his street-cleaning and road-building schemes, designed to instil into his students (including Arnold Toynbee and Oscar Wilde) a respect for the dignity of manual labour, simply accrued ridicule. Perhaps more relevant today is the very Ruskinian notion of ecological **conservation** – some see him as the first "Green" – espoused in his opposition to the expansion of the railways and the creation of Thirlmere reservoir.

The house

The **house** has been kept very much as a home and you're free to wander around the various rooms, preserved as they were in Ruskin's day. His study (hung with handmade paper to his own design) and dining room boast superlative lake views; they are bettered only by those from the **Turret Room** where Ruskin used to sit in later life in his bath chair – itself on display downstairs, along with a mahogany desk and Blue John wine goblet, among other memorabilia. A twenty-minute film expands on the man's philosophy and whets the appetite for rooms full of his **watercolours**, as well as for the surviving Turners from Ruskin's collection that weren't sold off after his death. Other rooms and studios display Ruskin-related arts and crafts, and specially curated art exhibitions, while there's also a well-stocked **bookshop** for anyone interested in the Pre-Raphaelites or the Arts and Crafts Movement.

The gardens

April–Oct, free guided garden walks Wed, Fri & Sun at 2.15pm; also free garden activity trails available in school holidays for children

The 250-acre estate surrounding the house boasts a nature trail, while paths wind through the lakeside meadows and into eight distinct **gardens**, some based on Ruskin's own plans (like the curiously named "Zig-Zaggy") and others designed by his cousin Joan, notably the High Walk, with its wonderful lake views, and the lovely Harbour Walk, framed by sweet-smelling azaleas. You're welcome to potter about, as did Ruskin, among the native flowers, fruit, herbs, moorland shrubs and ferns – his slate seat is sited in the Professor's Garden – or climb the heights behind the house to Crag Head for some splendid views.

EATING   **SEE MAP PAGE 114**

Terrace Coffee House and Restaurant Brantwood, LA21 8AD ☎015394 49025. Set in the former stables, and with lake views from the outdoor terrace, this makes a good place to mull over Ruskin's world while indulging in soups, flans and open sandwiches (£4.50–8) followed by lovely home-baked cakes and cream teas. You can eat here without paying to go inside either house or gardens. Mid-March to mid-Nov daily 10.30am–5pm; mid-Nov to mid-March Wed–Sun 10.30am–4pm.

Hawkshead and around

Hawkshead, midway between Coniston and Ambleside, wears its beauty well, its half-dozen lanes of whitewashed cottages, cobbles, alleys and archways backed by woods and fells and barely affected by modern intrusions. This is partly due to the enlightened policy of banning traffic in the centre. Large car parks at the village edge take the strain, and when the crowds of day-trippers leave, Hawkshead regains its natural tranquillity. It's a busy stop on both the **Wordsworth** and **Beatrix Potter** trails, and a handy base for the big nearby draws of **Tarn Hows** and Beatrix Potter's house, Hill Top, while in the quiet country lanes just to the north are some of the finest boutique dining and lodging experiences in the whole region. Rural activities and entertainment are offered each August during the **Hawkshead Agricultural Show**.

Hawkshead Grammar School

Off Main St, LA22 0NT • April–Oct Mon–Sat 10am–1pm & 2–5pm, Sun 1–5pm, guided tours on the hour; • £2 • ☎ 015394 36735, ⓦ hawksheadgrammar.org.uk

In medieval times Hawkshead became an important wool market, the trade controlled by the monks of Furness Abbey, and this early wealth explains the otherwise puzzling presence of **Hawkshead Grammar School** in such a small community. This was founded in 1585 and – even by Wordsworth's day, when the wool trade had much declined

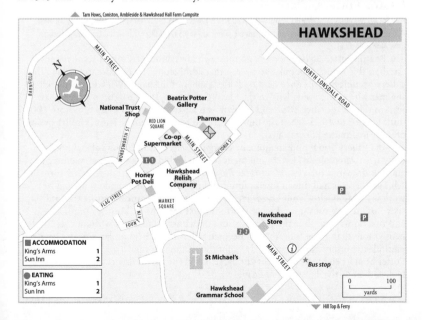

Tarn Hows, Coniston, Ambleside & Hawkshead Hall Farm Campsite

HAWKSHEAD

MAIN STREET

BARNSFIELD

NORTH LONSDALE ROAD

National Trust Shop

Beatrix Potter Gallery

RED LION SQUARE

Pharmacy

WORDSWORTH ST

Co-op Supermarket

MAIN STREET

VICTORIA ST

Honey Pot Deli

Hawkshead Relish Company

FLAG STREET

MARKET SQUARE

FOUNT

Hawkshead Store

P

P

ACCOMMODATION	
King's Arms	1
Sun Inn	2

EATING	
King's Arms	1
Sun Inn	2

St Michael's

MAIN STREET

ⓘ

★ **Bus stop**

0   100
yards

Hawkshead Grammar School

Hill Top & Ferry

3

– was considered to be among the finest schools in the country. Wordsworth and his brother Richard were sent here following the death of their mother in 1778 to acquire an expensively bought education; "grammar" of course being Latin grammar, knowledge of which was the mark of every gentleman. During term-times Wordsworth lodged with a local woman, **Ann Tyson** – someone he remembered kindly as "my old Dame" in *The Prelude*. Her Hawkshead cottage is now a guesthouse, though the Tyson family, and Wordsworth, actually lived for longer in another (unknown) house after 1783 when they moved half a mile east to Colthouse.

In the schoolroom the Wordsworth boys were taught geometry, algebra and the classics at timeworn wooden benches and desks (some date back to the school's foundation); you'll be shown the desk on which the rapscallion William carved his signature – a foolhardy stunt given the anecdote that miscreants were suspended from a pulley in the centre of the room to be birched. He also wrote his first surviving piece of poetry, a paean to the bicentenary of the school's foundation, before leaving in 1787 to go up to Cambridge. The only other things to see are the headmaster's study, an exhibition on English grammar schools and a few quills and nibs. The school closed in 1909.

St Michael's church

Hawkshead, LA22 0PQ • Daily: Easter–Sept 9am–5pm, often later in school hols; Oct–Easter 9am–4pm • ☎ 015394 36301, ⓦ hawksheadbenefice.co.uk

During his schooldays Wordsworth attended the fifteenth-century church of **St Michael's** sited above the school, which harks back to Norman and Romanesque designs in its rounded pillars and patterned arches. It's chiefly of interest for the 26 pithy psalms and biblical extracts illuminated with cherubs and flowers, painted on the walls during the seventeenth and eighteenth centuries. Outside, from its knoll, the churchyard gives a good view over the village's twin central squares.

Beatrix Potter Gallery

Main St, LA22 0NS • Daily mid-Feb to Oct 10.30am–4pm; timed-entry tickets • £6.80, family ticket £17, discount available for Hill Top visitors; buy tickets from the National Trust shop opposite the gallery; NT • ☎ 015394 36355, ⓦ nationaltrust.org.uk/beatrix-potter-gallery-and-hawkshead

The **Beatrix Potter Gallery** hoovers up most of Hawkshead's visitors at some point or another; this is such a popular attraction that admission is by timed-entry ticket. The gallery occupies rooms once used by Potter's solicitor husband, William Heelis, whom she met while purchasing land in the Hawkshead area. There had been a Heelis law firm in the village since 1861 and William was a partner in the family firm from 1900 until he died in 1945, when the building passed to the National Trust (Heelis's prewar office is maintained downstairs).

In the gallery you'll find an annually changing selection of Potter's sketchbooks, drawings, watercolours, letters and **manuscripts**, including the original manuscript and ink drawings for *The Tale of Peter Rabbit*, her first story. Although never formally schooled, Potter had drawn fossils, fungi and pet animals since childhood and her work is certainly closely observed. Her animals aren't caricatures, but neither are they "art" in any meaningful sense (Potter herself thought it "bosh" to think so), and to a non-Potterphile the paintings and drawings are pleasant without ever being more than mere fluff: the less devoted will find displays on her life as a keen naturalist, conservationist and early supporter of the National Trust more diverting. Potter bought eighteen fell farms and large parcels of Lake District land, which she bequeathed to the Trust on her death.

Tarn Hows

Tarn Hows, LA21 8DP, 1 mile off B5285; follow signposts • Always open • Free, though drivers have to pay to use the National Trust car park • ☎ 015394 41456, ⓦ nationaltrust.org.uk/tarn-hows-and-coniston • Seasonal buses sometimes run to the tarn; or take the Cross Lakes Experience bus (see page 128) to High Cross (top of Grizedale Forest) and follow the 0.75-mile footpath north past Wharton Tarn

A minor road off the Hawkshead–Coniston road (B5285) winds northwest to **Tarn Hows**, a beautiful body of water surrounded by spruce and pine, circled by paths and studded with grassy picnic spots. The land was donated to the National Trust by Beatrix Potter in 1930 – one of several such grants – since when the Trust has carefully maintained it. It takes an hour to walk around the tarn on its well-kept paths, during which you can ponder on the fact that this miniature idyll is in fact almost entirely artificial – the original owners enlarged two small tarns to make the one you see today, planted and landscaped the surroundings and dug the footpaths. It's now a Site of Special Scientific Interest – keep an eye out for some of the Lakes' (and England's) few surviving native **red squirrels**.

Tarn Hows is one of the Lake District's most popular beauty spots, and the best way to appreciate it is to **walk** there, so that its charms are gently unveiled as you approach. It's about two miles on paths and country lanes from Hawkshead; or it's the same distance from Coniston, and there's also a route to the tarn through the Monk Coniston gardens and grounds (from the north end of Coniston Water). It's nice to know that between Easter and October there's usually an ice cream van parked at the tarn.

ARRIVAL AND INFORMATION HAWKSHEAD AND AROUND

BY CAR
The B5285 between Coniston and Sawrey skirts the eastern side of Hawkshead; no traffic is allowed in the village itself, but everything lies within a 5min walk of the large car park.

BY BUS AND BOAT
The main bus service is the #505 "Coniston Rambler" between Windermere, Ambleside and Coniston, which stops by the car park. This is complemented by the Cross Lakes Experience (☎ 015394 48600, ⓦ lakedistrict.gov.uk/crosslakes), whose minibuses run from Hawkshead down to the Beatrix Potter house at Hill Top and on to Ferry House, Sawrey, for boat connections back to Bowness. There are also usually seasonal services to Tarn Hows and to Grizedale Forest, connecting with the Cross

Lakes Experience, though schedules sometimes change from year to year.
Bus #505 "Coniston Rambler" to: Coniston (15min); or to Ambleside (20min), Brockhole (30min) and Windermere (37min). Service operates Easter–Oct roughly hourly; Nov–Easter, roughly every two hours.
Cross Lakes Experience minibus to: Hill Top (7min) and Ferry House, Sawrey (15min, for boat connection to Bowness); also to Coniston *Waterhead Hotel* (14min, to connect with the Coniston Launch service to Brantwood and Coniston). Service operates up to 9 times dailyApril–Oct.

INFORMATION
Tourist office The locally run tourist information centre (Mon–Sat 9am–5pm, Sun 9am–4pm; ☎ 015394 36946, ⓦ hawksheadtouristinfo.org.uk) is by the main car park.

ESTHWAITE WATER: FISHING AND OSPREYS

Hawkshead's quiet lake, **Esthwaite Water**, isn't troubled by too many visitors, though Wordsworth, who rambled and splashed here as a boy, always remembered it fondly. Best view of the water is from the car-park access point on the far southwestern shore, two miles from Hawkshead, near which budding anglers can find **Esthwaite Water Trout Fishery** (ⓦ hawksheadtrout.com). You don't need any experience as there's tuition and tackle available, but best of all you can also rent rowing boats here for your own **osprey-spotting safaris**; up to four pairs nest in the vicinity between April and August, when there's a good chance of seeing them fishing.

ACCOMMODATION

SEE MAPS PAGES 114 AND 125

Reserve a long way ahead if you want to stay in and around Hawkshead during the peak summer season. For **cottages**, barn and farm conversions in Hawkshead and the surrounding area, contact Lakeland Hideaways Cottages near the National Trust office (⊛ lakelandhideaways.co.uk). The local **campsites** are always busy in summer – a nice alternative to the village is to stay a few miles down the road near Grizedale Forest where's there's an excellent site (see page 132).

HAWKSHEAD

King's Arms Market Square, LA22 0NZ ☎ 015394 36372, ⊛ kingsarmshawkshead.co.uk. The old pub in the main square has bags of character – there are eight B&B rooms altogether, retaining their oak beams and idiosyncratic proportions; bathrooms and furnishings, though, are reassuringly up to date. A permit is provided for parking. £110

★**Sun Inn** Main St, LA22 0NT ☎ 015394 36236, ⊛ suninn.co.uk. The boutique choice in the village is this revamped, family-run seventeenth-century inn near the car park. There's a contemporary sheen to the bare-wood bar, while upstairs are rooms that make the best of the building's antique feel – think exposed stone and original oak panelling combined with richly coloured designer fabrics and locally crafted furniture made from sustainably sourced wood. The four-poster room (£120) in particular is a really cosy bolthole. Free parking provided in the village. £100

AROUND HAWKSHEAD

★**Drunken Duck Inn** Barngates, LA22 0NG, 2 miles north of Hawkshead off the B5285 ☎ 015394 36347, ⊛ drunkenduckinn.co.uk. This 400-year-old inn – more a restaurant-with-rooms these days – is many people's favourite in the Lakes, and it's easy to see why. The thirteen bedrooms mix antiques and cool colours with bold contemporary design; standard rooms in the inn itself are on the small side, but there's more spacious superior accommodation across the courtyard, not to mention a sun-trap garden with private tarn and glorious valley views. Rooms and rates vary considerably – although midweek rates for the smallest, standard rooms in the inn start at

£125, weekend stays cost at least £155, and there's more deluxe accommodation too (up to £325 a night), including a sensational open-beamed Garden Room. Rates include afternoon tea. Parking. £155

Hawkshead Hall Farm Ambleside Rd, LA22 0NN, 0.5 mile north of Hawkshead ☎ 015394 36221, ⊛ hawks headhall-campsite.co.uk. You'll give yourself a chance of escaping the crowds and noise at this farm-field campsite, which is primarily for couples and families. It's on a big grassy site with hill and field views, and has a shower-block and campers' wash-up room; bus #505 passes the farm on the way into Hawkshead. Closed Jan & Feb. Tent, vehicle and two adults £22

★**Yewfield** Hawkshead Hill, LA22 0PR, 2 miles northwest of Hawkshead, off the B5285 ☎ 015394 36765, ⊛ yewfield.co.uk. Splendid vegetarian guesthouse set among organic vegetable gardens, orchards and wild-flower meadows. The house is a Victorian Gothic beauty, whose owners have filled it with Eastern artefacts, contemporary art and photography from their travels, and many of the rooms have been delightfully refurbished with Herdwick wool carpets and some lovely oak panelling and headboards from sustainable sources. Rooms (including a tower suite, £145) are split between the main house and the old coach house and stables. Breakfast is either a full cooked veggie blowout or wholefood continental buffet, and for other meals they'll point you down to nearby Ambleside and the owners' veggie restaurants Zeffirellis (see page 78) and Fellinis (see page 77). They do, though, host the occasional dinner and concert (classical (or contemporary) evening, as well as concerts at other times, which are open to all (donation requested). Parking. Closed Dec & Jan. £100

YHA Hawkshead Newby Bridge Rd, LA22 0QD, 1 mile south of Hawkshead ☎ 0845 371 9321, ⊛ yha.org.uk/ hostel/hawkshead. The local hostel is sited on Esthwaite Water's west side, housed in a Regency mansion that retains many of its original architectural features. There are more than one hundred beds and, with fourteen three- or four-bed rooms (four-bed from £69), and a family annexe, it's very popular with families and small groups. Tipis (£99), bell tents (£99), pods (£59) and an arctic cabin (£119) round off this impressive ensemble. Closed Nov to mid-Feb. Dorms £23

EATING

SEE MAPS PAGES 114 AND 125

Outside the gourmet destination that is the *Drunken Duck Inn*, Hawkshead's **pubs** provide the main eating options. There are a couple of **cafés** around the village square and a small **supermarket**, as well as the Honey Pot deli (for bread, sandwiches, preserves, biscuits, smoked meats and cheese; ⊛ honeypothawkshead.com) and the Hawkshead Relish Company (⊛ hawksheadrelish.com), where there are free tastings of their chutneys, relishes, mustards, pickles, preserves and dressings.

★**Drunken Duck Inn** Barngates, LA22 0NG, 2 miles north of Hawkshead, off B5285 ☎ 015394 36347, ⊛ drunkenduckinn.co.uk. Emphatically worth the journey up the hill from Hawkshead for lovely food in a lovely setting. The lunch (no bookings) and dinner (reservations recommended) menus are essentially the same, with starters (from £9) comprising the likes of Lancashire cheese and chive soufflé, or kipper scotch egg, and mains (£14–23) beef shin and stout pie or sea bass with tomato ragout and

3

tender stem broccoli. Everything is impeccably sourced, with local suppliers and producers much to the fore. All this, plus sharp but unstuffy service and award-winning beers from their own Barngates Brewery – many of the ales available in the bar are named after the inn's former dogs. Daily noon–11pm; kitchen noon–3.30pm & 6–8.45pm. **King's Arms** Market Square, Hawkshead, LA22 0NZ ☎015394 36372, ⓦkingsarmshawkshead.co.uk. There's a snug little bar with a fire and good-value meals, including sarnies, toasties and brunch baps (£5–8) as well as a wider-ranging dinner menu (£12–20) featuring the likes of Cumberland sausage with mustard mash, and braised minted

lamb shank. The beers are pretty good too, and when the sun shines there's no finer place in the village for an alfresco thirst-quencher. Daily noon–11pm; kitchen noon–2.30pm & 6–9.30pm. **Sun Inn** Main St, Hawkshead, LA22 0NT ☎015394 36236, ⓦsuninn.co.uk. All the meat served at the *Sun* is traditionally reared on Cumbrian farms – so, no qualms tucking into a tasty steak, rack of lamb, venison burger or Cumberland sausage (most mains £9–15). You can sit outside on a sunny day on the little front terrace, a good spot for a sundowner selected from their vast range of gin. Daily noon–11pm; kitchen noon–2.30pm & 6–9pm.

DIRECTORY

Banks There's no bank in Hawkshead, though there are ATMs inside the Co-op and the tourist information centre. Otherwise, the nearest banking facilities are in Ambleside.
Doctor Hawkshead Practice (Bragg Field ☎015394 36246, ⓦwww.centrallakesmedicalgroup.co.uk).

Hospital The nearest hospital is in Kendal (Westmorland General Hospital, Burton Rd; ☎01539 732288, ⓦuhmb. nhs.uk).
Pharmacy Collins & Butterworth, Main St (☎015394 36201).
Post office Main St (Mon–Sat 9am–5.30pm).

Hill Top and around

It's two miles down the eastern side of Esthwaite Water from Hawkshead to the twin hamlets of **Near and Far Sawrey**, overlooked by the woods and tarns of Claife Heights. Near Sawrey in particular – a cluster of flower-draped whitewashed cottages in a shallow vale – receives an inordinate number of visitors since it's the site of Beatrix Potter's beloved house, **Hill Top**. She might not be your cup of tea, but the house and garden make an interesting visit in any case, while the route here from Bowness in particular – across the lake and then up on foot or by minibus – makes for a fine day out in really pretty surroundings.

Hill Top

Near Sawrey, LA22 0NF · Feb half-term to May, Sept & Oct daily except Fri 10am–4.30pm; June–Aug daily 10am–5.30pm; shop and garden also open Fri & Nov & Dec Sat & Sun 10.30am–3.30pm · £11.80, family ticket £29.50; shop and garden free on Fri when house is closed; NT · ☎015394 36269, ⓦnationaltrust.org.uk/hill-top · There's very limited free parking at Hill Top; instead you're encouraged to use the Cross Lakes Experience bus-and-boat service (see page 128)

Hill Top, the small house where **Beatrix Potter** wrote many of her stories has always been a popular attraction, to say the least, so be prepared: you'll probably have to queue, entry in peak season is by timed ticket, and sell-outs are possible, especially in school holidays. One final word for anyone who's hoping to find the house as seen in the 2006 *Miss Potter* movie – that was actually Yew Tree Farm near Coniston (see page 121).

When you do get into Hill Top, you'll discover a modest house whose furnishings and contents have been kept as they were during Potter's occupancy – a condition of her will. The carved oak bedstead and sideboards, the small library of bound sets of Gibbons and Shakespeare, and the cottage garden are all typical of well-to-do, if unexceptional, Edwardian taste – though the few mementoes and curios do nothing to throw light on Potter's character. But if you love the books then Hill Top and the Sawrey neighbourhood will be familiar (many of the house fixtures and fittings, for instance, appear in scenes in the books, while the *Tower Bank Arms* next door is the inn in *The Tale of Jemima Puddle-Duck*). And where better to buy a Mrs

THE TALE OF BEATRIX POTTER

A Londoner by birth, **Beatrix Potter** (1866–1943) spent childhood holidays in the Lakes, first at Wray Castle on Windermere and later in houses with grand gardens, at Holehird (Troutbeck) and Lingholm (Derwent Water). Her landscape and animal sketching was encouraged by Canon Rawnsley, a family friend (and founder member of the National Trust), who inspired her to produce her first book, *The Tale of Peter Rabbit*. Potter had this privately printed in 1901 before it was taken up by Frederick Warne publishers. It was an instant success, and with the proceeds, Potter – remembering her happy holidays – bought the lakeland farmhouse at Hill Top in 1905.

There were to be 23 tales in all (or 24, after her *Kitty-in-Boots* was rediscovered and published in 2016), with half a dozen of the later books set in and around Hill Top, though Potter still lived for much of the year in London. Following her marriage to a local solicitor in 1913, when she was 47, Potter retained the house as her study but installed a manager at Hill Top to oversee the farm. Known locally as Mrs Heelis the farmer (rather than Beatrix Potter the author), she lived down the road in another house, Castle Cottage (not open to the public), but visited Hill Top most days, usually to work on business associated with her increasing portfolio of farms, which took up more and more of her time. She actually wrote very few books after her marriage, preferring to develop her interest in breeding the local Herdwick sheep, for which she won many prizes at local shows. When she died, her ashes were scattered locally by the Hill Top farm manager: the place has never been identified and there's no other memorial to her, save the house itself.

A **Miss Potter** biopic (2006), largely filmed in Cumbria, presented Renée Zellweger as Beatrix in "the most enchanting tale of all", namely her early love affair with her publisher Norman Warne (Ewan McGregor), which ended with his untimely death, after which Potter moved to Hill Top and married in later life. Fans can check out all the film location sites on the website ⓦ visitmisspotter.com.

Tiggy-Winkle salt-and-pepper shaker or a Peter Rabbit calendar than Hill Top's own souvenir-stuffed gift shop?

Near and Far Sawrey

The little hamlet of **Near Sawrey** regains its equilibrium once the Beatrix Potter house of Hill Top has closed for the day. It makes a lovely overnight stop if you can find a room (many places have Beatrix Potter connections), and if you can't, you can console yourself with a drink in the pub, the *Tower Bank Arms*, the very model of an English country inn.

A mile or so away, across the hay fields, lies **Far Sawrey**, an equally miniature hamlet, though this time with a church, shop and post office, and also with a pub, the *Cuckoo Brow Inn*, which has a welcome beer garden. From here, tracks fan out across **Claife Heights**, past its little tarns and down through the woods to the western shore of Windermere – the most direct route runs steeply downhill to Sawrey ferry pier, where you can catch the car-ferry or passenger launch across to Bowness. It must be the only route in England signposted in Japanese (the Japanese have a special fondness for Beatrix Potter).

ARRIVAL AND DEPARTURE   HILL TOP AND AROUND

By bus and boat Cross Lakes Experience bus-and-boat (April–Oct up to 9 daily; ☎015394 48600, ⓦ lakedistrict. gov.uk/crosslakes) runs directly here from Bowness or, on its way back, from Hawkshead: boat from Bowness connects with minibus from Ferry House, Sawrey, to Hill Top (7min) and Hawkshead (15min); or minibus runs from Hawkshead to Hill Top (8min) and Ferry House, Sawrey (15min, for boat connection to Bowness). **On foot** It takes about an hour to walk from the Sawrey ferry pier on Windermere up to Near Sawrey and Hill Top; going back downhill, slightly less.

Buckle Yeat Near Sawrey, LA22 0LF ☎015394 36446, ⓦbuckle-yeat.co.uk. Gorgeous seventeenth-century cottage close to the Potter house (and illustrated in Potter's *The Tale of Tom Kitten*), offering six cosy, country-style double or twin rooms with breakfast. There's always a colourful display of flowers and baskets outside the cottage; inside, the guest lounge has a slate-flagged floor, big armchairs and a log fire. Parking. **£90**

Cuckoo Brow Inn Far Sawrey, LA22 0LQ ☎015394 43425, ⓦcuckoobrow.co.uk. The old *Sawrey Hotel* has had a major facelift with fourteen refurbished rooms now offering a whole lot more style and comfort while retaining much of the inn's country character – "muddy boots, wet dogs and children welcome" pretty much sums up the ethos, with wood-burners and a games room to keep families warm and entertained. Bar meals are at the locally sourced, gastro end of the pub food scale and there's usually a tempting selection of pies of the day, such as rump of lamb with minted mash potato, or a catch of the day, such as pan-seared wild black bream fillet (mains £12–18); beers are mostly from the Coniston Brewery and breakfast is also available for non-guests if you give them a call first. Parking.

Daily 8am–11pm; kitchen noon–9pm. **£111**

Ees Wyke Near Sawrey, LA22 0JZ ☎015394 36393, ⓦeeswyke.co.uk. Georgian country house – Beatrix Potter stayed here on childhood holidays – most of whose nine elegant rooms have matchless views across the fields to Esthwaite Water. A three-course dinner (£37.95) – which might feature, say, wild mushrooms with parsley and tarragon, or grilled butterfly trout fillet – is accompanied by more lovely views from the dining room. Parking. **£120**

★ **Tower Bank Arms** Near Sawrey, LA22 0LF, next to Hill Top ☎015394 36334, ⓦtowerbankarms.co.uk. Hill Top's local pub, owned by the National Trust, looks the very part, with its oak beams, slate floors and cast-iron range. Upstairs are four simple but smart rooms, named Yan, Tan, Tethera and Methera (Cumbrian dialect for one, two, three, four); totter downstairs for an acclaimed array of beers and good food, from local lamb to Esthwaite trout (mains £10–14). And if you can't tell the Beatrix Potter joke in this pub (what do you call a lager-juggling female ceramicist…?), where on earth can you? Parking. Mon–Thurs & Sun 11.30am–10.30pm, Fri & Sat 11.30am–11pm; kitchen daily noon–2pm & 6–9pm. **£98**

Grizedale Forest

The green expanse on the map that separates Coniston Water from Windermere is **Grizedale Forest**, whose picnic spots, open-air sculptures, children's activities, cycle trails and high-wire adventure course make for a great day out away from the main lakes. There's always been thick forest here, though by the eighteenth century successive generations of charcoal making, coppicing and iron smelting had stripped the fells and dales virtually bare. Regeneration by the Forestry Commission has restored dense oak, spruce, larch and pine woodland to Grizedale and now red deer are seen occasionally, while the forest also provides a habitat for badgers and squirrels, grouse, woodcock and woodpeckers.

Exploring the forest

The best starting point, especially if it's your first time, is the **Grizedale Visitor Centre**, which has trail guides, information and advice about what to see and do in the forest. Grizedale, it's soon clear, is a whole lot more than just trees, starting with the outdoor **sculptures** for which the forest has become famous. There are around forty of them, located right across the forest, and it's quite something as you round a bend to find pinnacles rising from a tarn, sculpted wooden ferns, a 100ft-long wave of bent logs or a dry-stone wall slaloming through the conifers. They are all on or near the existing forest hiking trails which extend for between one and ten miles on undulating tracks – longest is the **Silurian Way**, which passes many of the sculptures en route and also climbs to Carron Crag, highest point in the forest, for some great views. Other walks are as little as a mile long and suitable for families with strollers or wheelchairs.

On a **bike**, you can see much of Grizedale in a day, and while there are climbs involved on every route you'll be rewarded by some excellent views. There are seven trails in all, the most challenging of which are the fourteen-mile Silurian Way, and the ten-mile **North Face Trail** on the west side of the forest, which gets rave reviews from serious mountain-bikers.

Go Ape

Grizedale Forest, LA22 0QJ • Sessions daily Feb half-term & Easter–Oct, otherwise weekends Nov to mid-Feb; advance booking essential, online or by phone • ☎ 01603 895500, ⓦ goape.co.uk

If there's shrieking from the skies above, that's the daredevils on the zip-wires of **Go Ape**, an aerial adventure course through the tree canopy, starting near the visitor centre. There are all manner of possibilities including a Treetop Challenge, which entails zipwires, high platforms and Tarzan swings (from £25; minimum age 10) and Treetop Adventure, a family-friendly high ropes course (from £23; minimum age 6); while, for true zip-wire fanatics, there's the Zip Trekking Adventure, which entails seven forest ziplines over a 3km course (from £55; minimum age 13).

ARTHUR RANSOME

Arthur Ransome (1884–1967) was born in Leeds and spent early childhood holidays with his brother and sisters at Nibthwaite by Coniston Water. His boyhood holiday pursuits were all put to use in his books, though it was the friendship he made with the outgoing Collingwood family as a young man of 20 which cemented his love affair with the Lakes – sailing with them on Coniston Water, picnicking on Peel Island, and visiting the local copper mines.

Ransome's first job was with a London publisher, though he was soon published in his own right, producing critical literary studies of Edgar Allan Poe and Oscar Wilde, and an account of London's bohemia. He met and **married** Ivy Constance Walker and they had one daughter, Tabitha, in 1910, but the marriage was never happy. In part this prompted a bold solo move to Russia in 1913, after which his marriage was effectively at an end. Ransome was keen to learn the language and had a special interest in Russian folklore – a well-received translation and adaptation of various fairy tales (*Old Peter's Russian Tales*) appeared in 1916.

During World War I, ill health prevented him joining up and he was hired as a **war correspondent** by the *Daily News*. Consequently, when the Russian Revolution broke out, he was well placed to report on events. Ransome clearly knew his Russian politics and was a sympathetic but critical observer of the Bolshevik revolution, producing two books of on-the-spot reportage. He interviewed Lenin and other leading figures, and was introduced to Trotsky's secretary, Eugenia, who – on the final break-up of his first marriage – became his second wife.

Ransome spent much of the following ten years in Russia and the Baltic States, latterly as special correspondent for the *Manchester Guardian*, for whom he travelled widely. In 1925 he bought his first lakeland house at **Low Ludderburn**, in the Winster Valley, and, having eventually abandoned journalism, it was here he wrote **Swallows and Amazons** (published in 1930). This was the first of twelve books he produced in the series (the last in 1947), most, but not all, set in the Lake District – spells in Norfolk and Suffolk provided the background for *We Didn't Mean To Go To Sea* and *Coot Club*.

Ransome was inspired to write for and about the five children of the **Altounyan family**, whose father, Ernest, brought them to the Lake District on holiday in 1928. Ernest Altounyan, married to Dora Collingwood, a longtime Ransome family friend, bought two boats (one called *Swallow*) and he and Ransome first taught the children to sail. That the Altounyan children were models for the "Swallows" is now accepted – the first edition of the book was dedicated to them – though when the relationship cooled in later years, Ransome denied this and withdrew the dedication. Other friends and local characters appeared in the books, while Coniston locations figured heavily – Peel Island as "Wild Cat Island", the Coniston fells and mines in *Pigeon Post* and the Old Man of Coniston as "Kanchenjunga". Ransome and Eugenia lived in Coniston itself between 1940 and 1945, but settled in retirement at a house called Hill Top in Haverthwaite. He died on June 3, 1967.

Eugenia donated various effects and mementoes of her husband's to **Abbot Hall** (see page 226) in Kendal, which maintains an Arthur Ransome exhibition and doubles as the HQ of The Arthur Ransome Society (TARS), whose zealous members keep his flame alive by means of literary events, publications and activities. For more information, contact the museum or visit the Arthur Ransome website: ⓦ arthur-ransome.org.uk.

Satterthwaite and Rusland

Two miles south down the road from the Grizedale Visitor Centre, the forestry hamlet of **Satterthwaite** has a good pub, the *Eagle's Head*, and a great campsite, while, hidden away in the narrow lanes a further two miles beyond, is rustic **Rusland church**. Surrounded by undulating grazing land, this is a serene setting for the simple graves of children's writer **Arthur Ransome** and his wife Eugenia.

ARRIVAL AND DEPARTURE

GRIZEDALE FOREST

By car Access to the forest is easiest from Hawkshead, which is just 2.5 miles northeast of the visitor centre. There's a big car park near the visitor centre; it costs around £7 to park for the whole day.

By bus Most years there's a seasonal bus (Easter–Oct daily),

which runs from Hawkshead via Moor Top, and connects with the Cross Lakes Experience service (☎ 015394 48600, ⓦ lakedistrict.gov.uk/crosslakes), so you can come direct from Bowness-on-Windermere and still have time for a decent day out. The bus stops by the visitor centre.

INFORMATION AND ACTIVITIES

Bike rental Follow the signs from the visitor centre to Grizedale Mountain Bikes (March–Oct 9am–5.30pm, last rental 3pm; Nov–Feb 9am–4.30pm, last rental 2pm; ☎ 01229 860335, ⓦ grizedalemountainbikes.co.uk), which has a wide variety of models available (from £25 for 4hr, full-day rental from £35), including "tag-alongs" and trailers for kids, as well as route maps and cycling gear.

Tourist information Grizedale Visitor Centre (daily; Easter–Oct 10am–5pm; Nov–Easter 10am–4pm; ☎ 0300 0674495, ⓦ forestryengland.uk/grizedale) is the forest's information and activity hub, where you can find out about anything from hiking conditions to entertainment programmes, including summer outdoor theatre.

ACCOMMODATION

SEE MAP PAGE 114

★ **Grizedale Campsite** Bowkerstead Farm, Satterthwaite, LA12 8LL ☎ 01229 860208, ⓦ grizedale-camping.co.uk. The best campsite in the region is this amiable hideaway on a working sheep farm, a couple of miles south of the Grizedale Visitor Centre. There's a family site on a large grassy pitch below the farmhouse, and a sustainably managed woodland site with space for smaller tents as well as six wooden camping pods (which sleep three adults or a family of four; £30), three yurts (sleeping up to eight; from £50) and a basic bunk cabin sleeping eight (£80). The pet goats roam at will, deer are regular visitors, and you're just half a mile from the pub. Woodland site open all year; field site closed Nov–Feb. Price includes tent and vehicle. Per person £7

Rookhow Rusland, LA12 8LA ☎ 07557 919879, ⓦ independenthostels.co.uk. For cheap backpacker accommodation see if there's space at *Rookhow*, which is mostly used by groups and families but is also available for individuals. Simple bunk rooms, and an open-plan self-catering kitchen and lounge with wood-burner are housed in the former stables of an adjacent Quaker chapel, which is still in use as a meeting place (ask to have a look). The chapel sits in twelve acres of magical private woodland gardens, where you're welcome to splash in the stream and toast marshmallows over a fire – you can sometimes camp here too (at half the price of a bed). You're 2 miles from Satterthwaite and the nearest pub, so you'll really need a car or bike to stay. Dorms £16

EATING

SEE MAP PAGE 114

Grizedale Café Grizedale Forest, LA22 0QJ ☎ 0300 0674495. Across the former farmhouse courtyard from the visitor centre, this bright café offers a big outdoor terrace overlooking an excellent children's playground. There's everything from sandwiches and toasties to

casseroles, quiches and pies (£5–8), plus a takeaway and ice-cream counter. March–Oct daily 10am–5pm; Nov–Feb 10am–4pm, closed Mon in Nov, and Mon & Tues in Dec & Jan.

DRINKING

SEE MAP PAGE 114

Eagle's Head Satterthwaite, LA12 8LN ☎ 01229 860237, ⓦ eagleshead.co.uk. The beer garden at the charming country pub in the southern reaches of the forest is a good target for a sunny day. Local ales help quench "hiker's throat" and a honey mustard and ham

toastie (£7) will help pad out the beer; while bar meals (£13–15) range from home-made pies to Bowkerstead pork belly with apple slaw. Daily noon–11pm; kitchen Mon–Thur noon–4pm & 5–8.30pm, Fri–Sun noon–8.30pm.

Broughton-in-Furness

Southwest of Coniston Water, a quiet triangle at the southern edge of the National Park is anchored by the small market town of **Broughton-In-Furness**. It dates back to medieval times, though its aspect is pure Georgian. Tall houses and tight lanes surround an attractive square, complete with spreading chestnut tree, commemorative obelisk, stone fish slabs and stocks, and a couple of old pubs. In the eighteenth century the market was a staging post for wool, wood and cattle, shipped out of the area from the nearby Duddon estuary. Follow Church Street to the edge of town and you'll reach the **church of St Mary Magdalene**, originally twelfth century, though now much restored. The town's only literary connection is a slight one: the scapegrace Brontë brother, Branwell, taught here briefly before terminally pickling himself in Haworth.

Swinside Stone Circle

Off A595; Broadgate turn-off, 1 mile southwest of Duddon Bridge • Always open • Free • Limited parking on a narrow lane

It's worth the short drive out of Broughton to investigate the **Swinside Stone Circle**, one of the Lake District's most alluring prehistoric sites. From the minor Broadgate turn-off (a mile past Duddon Bridge; keep an eye out, it's on the right), continue another mile up the narrow road and park by the verge at Cragg Hall. From here you can follow the rough Swinside Farm track another mile on foot (there's a bridleway sign, 20min walk) to the fifty-odd ancient stones, which stand in a natural amphitheatre surrounded by undulating fells. It's a magical spot, with the local name for the stones, Sunkenkirk, reflecting an old belief that the devil sunk the stones of an ancient church (kirk) into the ground. Hardy pagan souls troop up here for a winter solstice ceremony each year.

ARRIVAL AND INFORMATION   BROUGHTON-IN-FURNESS

By car Broughton is 10 miles from Coniston (along the A593, via Torver) and it's a handy stop en route to Ulverston or up the west coast towards Ravenglass.

By bus There is no useful bus service for visitors.

Tourist information The community-run Broughton

Information Centre is in the old town hall on The Square (April–Oct Mon–Sat 10am–12.30pm & 1.30–4pm, Sun 10am–2pm; Nov–March Thurs–Sat 10am–2pm; ☎01229 716115, ⓦlakedistrictinformation.com).

ACCOMMODATION AND EATING   SEE MAP PAGE 114

Blacksmiths' Arms Broughton Mills, LA20 6AX, 2 miles north of Broughton, off A593 ☎01229 716824, ⓦ blacksmithsarms.com. The best local country-pub choice is the venerable *Blacksmiths' Arms*, which has been a hostelry since at least the eighteenth century. It's a real old-school inn (with old-school hours), known hereabouts for having good food – there's a wider menu at dinner than at lunch, but expect posh fish and chips, fancy lamb dishes, belly pork confit, local sausage and black pudding, and the like (mains £12–18). July–Sept Mon 5–11pm, Tues–Sat noon–11pm, Sun noon–10.30pm; Oct–June Mon 5–11pm, Tues–Fri noon–2.30pm & 5–11pm, Sat noon–11pm, Sun noon–10.30pm; kitchen daily noon–2pm & 6–9pm.

★ **Broughton Village Bakery** Princes St, LA20 6HQ ☎01229 716284, ⓦbroughtonvillagebakery.com.

Down Princes St is a range of proper local shops, including butcher, greengrocer and a fantastic bakery-café, the *Broughton Village Bakery*, which uses organic flour and Fair Trade ingredients in a terrific range of breads, cakes, casseroles, soups and sandwiches (£5–8 for a sit-down meal). Mon–Sat 9am–5pm (café closes 1hr earlier); slightly reduced hours in winter.

Square Café Annan House, The Square, LA20 6JA ☎01229 716388, ⓦthesquarecafe.biz. The café on the handsome main square is always a good stop for home-made cake or a light lunch, while upstairs are three nice B&B rooms – the two cheapest share a bathroom, though there's also a double en-suite (£60). Owner, local artist Jane Rousseau, exhibits some of her work in the café. Daily 10.30am–4pm. **£50**

3

The Duddon Valley

A mile west of Broughton, a minor road leads from Duddon Bridge up the stunning **Duddon Valley**, twisting and turning its increasingly dramatic way northeast to the foot of the Wrynose and Hardknott passes. Wordsworth wrote a sequence of 34 sonnets about the valley (published as *The River Duddon* in 1820), his conclusion – "Still glides the Stream, and shall for ever glide" – a comment on the ephemeral nature of man. Lofty thoughts indeed as you navigate around the rocky outcrops and through the wandering sheep crowding the road.

Ulpha

On warm days cars line the verges at **Ulpha**, five miles north of Broughton, as picnics are spread on the riverbanks and kids plummet from the old stone bridge into the water. A small post office/shop a little way up from the bridge (near the Eskdale road junction) sells ice cream, while the local village hall – known as the **Browfoot Room** (ⓦmusicinulpha.org.uk) – is an inspiring little **music venue** for acoustic, folk and roots gigs by some acclaimed acts willing to bring their shows to small, rural concert rooms. There's a great weekend tearoom here too, right next to the hall.

Seathwaite and Birks Bridge

At **Seathwaite**, another three winding miles along the road, there's the excellent *Newfield Inn*, as well as a popular short walk to **Wallowbarrow Crag**, below which the river tumbles through a gorge. Beyond Seathwaite the road is ever more tortuous, though there's parking and picnic space a couple of miles further north close to **Birks Bridge**, an ancient crossing which spans a twenty-foot-deep chasm teeming with brown trout.

WALKS IN THE DUDDON VALLEY

Duddon Valley seems like a million miles from the main lakeland tourist spots, even though Coniston Water is within tramping distance away to the east. Consequently, **local walks** are likely to be enjoyed alone and the two classics below show you very different terrains and views.

HARTER FELL AND HARDKNOTT

If you just want to knock off a peak, you can climb from the car park at Birks Bridge through the forestry land to the west to ascend **Harter Fell** (2140ft), whose summit is a jumble of rocky outcrops with excellent views. It'll take a couple of hours, up and down. But a good, rugged circular walk (7 miles; 4hr) from Birks Bridge climbs first north to **Hardknott Pass** and then down to the Roman fort there, which is a good place for a picnic. Then you climb again to reach Harter Fell from around the back, followed by a final descent through the plantation land to the bridge and the river.

A DUNNERDALE ROUND

The rolling, rounded **Dunnerdale Fells**, east of Ulpha, have some fantastic views up into the central Lakes and south to the Duddon estuary and the glinting sea. An easy **Dunnerdale Round** (5 miles; 2hr 30min) starts from just south of Ulpha Bridge, up the signposted bridleway to Kiln Bank Cross. You walk east over towards the minor Kiln Bank Cross road and then climb up to **Stickle Pike** and across to **Great Stickle** for some wonderful views, before returning to the Ulpha Bridge road via Black Stones.

Dale Head and Cockley Beck

Shortly after Birks Bridge the head of the valley widens dramatically at Dale Head, whose "Big Sky" perspective is quite out of keeping with the confined Lakes – more New Zealand than Cumbria. The river is at its widest here, and at the bridge and junction of **Cockley Beck** you can debate the dubious pleasures of attempting your onward route: west over Hardknott Pass into Eskdale or east over Wrynose Pass to Little Langdale; both passes require careful driving or, in the case of out-of-condition cyclists, an oxygen tent. At *Cockley Beck Farm*, by the bridge, writer John Pepper spent several winters in a simple cottage, recounted in his classic "back to nature" book, *Cockley Beck*, marvelling at a place where "peaks rose into the stars like psalms" but enduring temperatures that "plummeted so dramatically, even dreams froze".

ARRIVAL AND INFORMATION   THE DUDDON VALLEY

By car You need your own transport to see much of the Duddon Valley – or be prepared to get out of the car and walk or cycle.

By bus There's a very slow early-morning postbus once a day (Mon–Sat) from Broughton-in-Furness to Cockley Beck, via Ulpha and Seathwaite; a quicker afternoon service (Mon–Fri) only goes as far as Seathwaite.

Tourist information There's plenty of information on ⓦ www.duddonvalley.co.uk, including links to lots of local B&Bs and holiday cottages.

ACCOMMODATION AND EATING   SEE MAP PAGE 114

★ **Newfield Inn** Seathwaite, LA20 6ED ☎ 01229 716208, ⓦ newfieldinn.co.uk. One of those classic lakeland country inns, with a dark, rustic interior, slate floors, local beers on tap and a garden that looks up onto the fells. Food is a hearty mix of traditional, locally sourced pub grub (with vegetarian and even vegan options); expect the likes of Cumberland sausage and mash, home-made Newfield burgers (a third gammon, two-thirds beef), and hand-cut chips (dishes £10–13). Two inexpensive self-catering flats are also available (two-night minimum stay, one sleeping up to four people, the other six). Parking. Daily 11am–11pm; kitchen noon–9pm. **£55**

3

Keswick, Derwent Water and the north

HIKING ABOVE DERWENT WATER

Keswick, Derwent Water and the north

Keswick – main town in the northern Lakes – stands on the shores of beautiful Derwent Water, backed by the imposing heights of Skiddaw and Blencathra. Most of Keswick's visitors are the type who like to rock-hop in the dramatic surroundings rather than clamber from tour-bus to gift shop and, consequently, there's slightly less of the themed lakeland packaging that afflicts the southern towns, and rather more of an outdoors air, with walkers steadily coming and going from the hills. The town also has solid literary connections – not with Wordsworth for a change, but with the other members of the poetical triumvirate, Samuel Taylor Coleridge and Robert Southey, who both settled in Keswick in the early years of the nineteenth century.

Derwent Water lies just a few minutes' walk from Keswick town centre, its launch service providing easy access to long-famed beauty spots like Ashness Bridge, Watendlath and the Lodore Falls. And even with just a day in town you should take in the charms of **Borrowdale**, the glorious meandering valley to the south of Derwent Water that's been a source of inspiration to artists and writers over the centuries. The Borrowdale settlements of Rosthwaite, Seatoller, Stonethwaite and Seathwaite are the jumping-off points for walking routes to the peaks around **Scafell Pike**, the Lake District's (and England's) highest mountain.

North of town lies **Bassenthwaite Lake**, from where minor roads and footpaths head northeast into the region known locally as **Back o' Skiddaw**, a little-visited neck of the Lakes hidden behind Skiddaw itself. This is as off the beaten track as it gets in the National Park, and handsome villages such as **Caldbeck** and the unsung heights of **Carrock Fell** make a trip worthwhile. East of Keswick, the old railway-line footpath makes a fine approach to the little village of **Threlkeld**, from where some are drawn south through bucolic **St John's in the Vale** to **Thirlmere**, the Lake District's largest reservoir.

Keswick

The modern centre of **Keswick**, a town of around five thousand people, sits south and east of the River Greta, though its origins lie around an early medieval church just over the river in Crosthwaite. Scattered farms probably provided its first local industry, if the town's name (*kes*, meaning cheese, and *wic*, meaning dairy farm) is anything to go by. Keswick became an important centre for trading wool and leather until around 1500, when these trades were supplanted by ore mining and, later, the discovery of local graphite, which formed the mainstay of the local economy until the late eighteenth century. The railway (long defunct) arrived in the 1860s, since when Keswick has turned its attention fully to the requirements of tourists. The recent spate of **winter flooding** throughout the Lake District hit Keswick hard in early 2016, when a tangle of river-borne trees, boulders and caravans dammed the town's bridges and saw the centre submerged under several feet of water. While a few businesses never resurfaced afterwards, plenty of accommodation and good cafés aimed at walkers survived, and bus routes radiate from the town, getting you to the start of even the most challenging

4

CASTLERIGG STONE CIRCLE

Highlights

❶ Castlerigg Stone Circle The mysterious standing stones above Keswick are a brooding presence. See page 147

❷ Climbing Cat Bells This celebrated climb and viewpoint above Derwent Water is a real family favourite. See page 154

❸ Evening cruise on Derwent Water Sit back and enjoy the sunset as the shadows fall across the lake. See page 156

❹ Via Ferrata, Honister Cumbria's most thrilling challenge is the fixed-rope high-mountain adventure climb from Honister Slate Mine. See page 163

❺ St John's in the Vale This hidden valley has some splendid walking and you can stop for ice cream at *Low Bridge End Farm*. See page 165

❻ Whinlatter Forest Park Bike, hike and Go Ape in England's only mountain forest. See page 165

❼ View the ospreys, Bassenthwaite Between April and August, you can usually see wild ospreys on Bassenthwaite Lake. See page 168

❽ Old Crown, Hesket Newmarket Enjoy a pint and a curry in Britain's first cooperatively owned pub. See page 173

HIGHLIGHTS ARE MARKED ON THE MAP ON PAGE 142

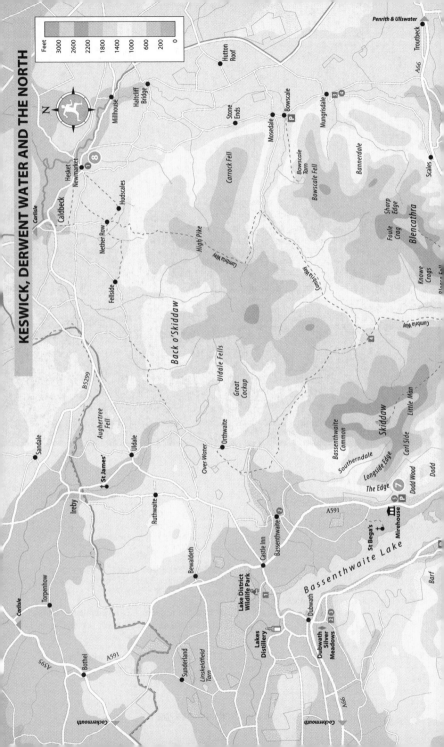

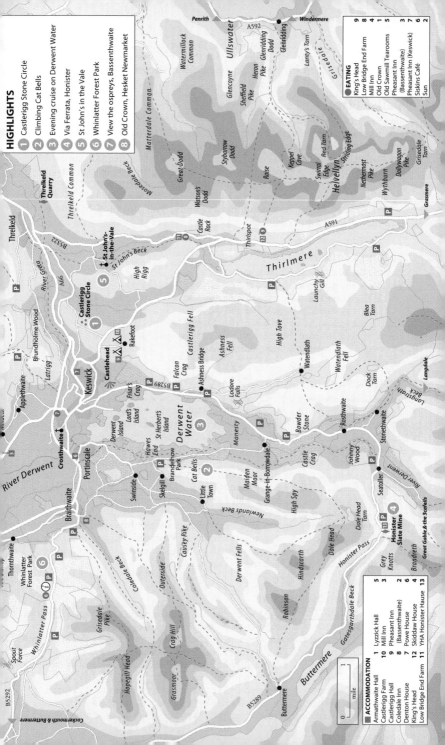

HIGHLIGHTS

1. Castlerigg Stone Circle
2. Climbing Cat Bells
3. Evening cruise on Derwent Water
4. Via Ferrata, Honister
5. St John's in the Vale
6. Whinlatter Forest Park
7. View the ospreys, Bassenthwaite
8. Old Crown, Hesket Newmarket

EATING

King's Head	9
Low Bridge End Farm	8
Mill Inn	4
Old Crown	1
Old Sawmill Tearooms	5
Pheasant Inn (Bassenthwaite)	3
Pheasant Inn (Keswick)	7
Siskins Café	6
Sun	2

ACCOMMODATION

Armathwaite Hall	
Castlerigg Farm	
Castlerigg Hall	
Coledale Inn	
Denton House	
King's Head	
Low Bridge End Farm	
Lyzzick Hall	5
Mill Inn	10
Pheasant Inn	3
Pheasant Inn (Bassenthwaite)	9
Powe House	8
Skiddaw House	7
YHA Honister Hause	6
Grey Knotts	2
Great Gable & the Scarfells	4
Braithéth	12
	13
	11

hikes. For those not up to a day on the fells, the town remains a popular place throughout the year, with its handsome **park**, interesting **museums** and old **pubs** – and you're only ever a short stroll away from the shores of **Derwent Water**.

Market Place

Market Place, CA12 5BJ • Markets Thurs & Sat 8.30am–4pm

Keswick was granted its market charter by Edward I in 1276, and the town is still definitely at its best on its traditional market day, Saturday, when the sloping, traffic-free **Market Place** fills with stalls and traders. You can buy fruit, veg and groceries, but it's just as much a stop for artisan cheese, Herdwick sheep fleeces, designer woolly jumpers and local crafts, and there are often some good takeaway food stalls too. A second weekly market on Thursdays is almost as busy. The **Moot Hall** (1813), marooned in the middle of Market Place, was formerly the town hall and prison, but now houses the National Park information office.

St John's church

St John St, CA12 4DD • Daily 8am–5pm • ⓦ keswickstjohn.org.uk

You'll spot the handsome spire of **St John's church** from all over town. Pretty stained glass aside, it's notable largely for the fact that the novelist Sir Hugh Walpole – who set his Herries novels in Borrowdale and the Back o' Skiddaw – is buried in the churchyard: follow the sign to where the "Man of Letters, Lover of Cumberland, Friend of his fellowmen" lies beneath a Celtic cross, looking towards the west side of Derwent Water, where his house still stands.

Keswick Museum and Art Gallery

Station Rd, CA12 4NF • Daily 10am–4pm • £5, family pass £12 • ☏ 017687 73263, ⓦ keswickmuseum.org.uk

Keswick's gloriously quirky **Museum and Art Gallery** is at the edge of the riverside **Fitz Park**. Founded in 1780, the museum is a classic of its kind, its elderly glass cases preserving anything from stuffed birds and a set of lion's teeth to antique climbing equipment and cockfighting spurs. The most famous exhibit is the massive set of xylophone-like "**musical stones**" – cordierite-impregnated slate known as hornfels – which sound in tune when you strike them. They were collected from the Skiddaw hillsides by musical stonemason Joseph Richardson in the 1830s, who painstakingly fashioned them into instruments, added percussion and bells and then toured Victorian England with his sons as the "Rock, Bell and Steel Band". The stones came to the museum in 1917, and sometimes now go out on tour (you can hear tunes played on them at ⓦ myspace.com/musicalstones). Meanwhile, under protective covers in the literary room sits a huge array of letters, manuscripts and poems by Southey, Wordsworth, De Quincey, Coleridge, Walpole and Ruskin.

Derwent Pencil Museum

Southey Works, Southey Lane, CA12 5NG • Daily 9.30am–5pm, last admission 4pm, hours extended in summer hols • £4.95, family ticket from £12.50 • ☏ 017687 73626, ⓦ derwentart.com • Visitors get a discount on pay-and-display parking at the museum

For the town's industrial history, you need to head for the entertaining **Derwent Pencil Museum**, by Greta Bridge. For centuries Borrowdale shepherds marked their sheep with a locally occurring substance they knew as wadd and, later, as plumbago or black lead. It was, of course, **graphite** (a pure carbon) from the Borrowdale fells, and after about 1500, when it was discovered that it could also be carved and cut to shape, graphite mining became commercially viable. In the early days, graphite was used in several ways – rubbed on firearms to prevent rusting, to make cannonball moulds

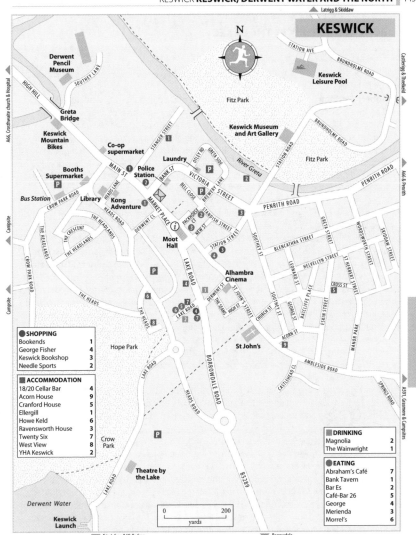

KESWICK

4

and as a medicinal cure for stomach disorders. With the idea of putting graphite into wooden holders (prototype pencils were used by Florentine artists), Keswick became an important pencil-making town – the mines and shipments were so valuable that they were put under armed guard to thwart smugglers. The town prospered until the late eighteenth century, when the French discovered how to make pencil graphite cheaply by binding the common amorphous graphite with clay. Keswick's monopoly was quickly broken, though its major pencil mills by the River Greta – first established in 1832 – continued to thrive.

All this, and more than you'll ever need to know about the pencil-producing business, is explained inside, where a mock-up of the long-defunct Borrowdale mine heralds multifarious examples of the finished product, including the world's longest (almost 26ft) pencil, duly acknowledged as such by the *Guinness Book of Records*. There are

ROBERT SOUTHEY IN THE LAKES

Few better or more blameless men have ever lived, than he; but he seems to lack colour, passion, warmth.
Nathaniel Hawthorne, *English Notebooks*, 1855

Robert Southey (1774–1843) – his surname, incidentally, pronounced "Sow-thee" and not "Suh-thee" – first visited the Lake District in 1801 at the request of his brother-in-law, Samuel Taylor Coleridge. The two poets already had a spiky relationship – a failed plan to form a Utopian society abroad dwindled into recriminations later as, having married Edith Fricker in 1795, Southey was accused of pushing Coleridge into an unhappy marriage with her sister, Sara. Moreover, Southey was already a published poet when Coleridge and Wordsworth produced their *Lyrical Ballads* (1798), which Southey reviewed, infamously, for the *Critical Review* (dismissing Coleridge's *Rime of the Ancient Mariner*, for example, as "a poem of little merit").

Reconciliation came with the deaths of Coleridge's and Sara's second son Berkeley, and Southey's and Edith's first child, Margaret Edith. Southey accepted an invitation to visit Coleridge, thinking it might alleviate Edith's grief. The Southeys arrived in September 1803 and later, when Coleridge suggested leaving for Malta for his health, Southey agreed to stay on and pay the rent. With Sara Coleridge now effectively a lodger in her own home, Edith's other sister (and widow), Mary Lovell, also arrived to stay – soon the family joke was that **Greta Hall** was the "Aunt Hill". Coleridge himself never returned to live there, but with Sara Coleridge's three children at Greta Hall, Mary Lovell's son, plus the Southeys' brood, there were now up to ten children in the house at any one time, whom Southey entertained with stories and poems, including his *Tale of Three Bears*.

Southey's poetry sold slowly and most of his income was derived from journalism and other works. A *History of Portugal* was planned on a huge scale, though only the volumes on Brazil (1810–19) were completed. This was the work Southey considered his best, though it was his *Life of Nelson* (1813) – only moderately successful during his life – that later became the work most associated with him.

Although never in financial difficulty, Southey felt compelled to accept the **Poet Laureateship** in 1813, which opened him up to attack from the likes of a young Shelley, who came to stay at Keswick and rather ungratefully belittled Southey as the "paid champion of every abuse and absurdity". At home, Edith was suffering bouts of depression, brought on by the steady loss of her children (four of the Southeys' eight children died), and she never really regained full mental health. She died in November 1837 and within a year Southey had married an author, Caroline Bowles, twelve years his junior, with whom he had corresponded for almost twenty years.

Caroline's arrival at Greta Hall upset everyone, especially the Southey girls, and when their father died on March 21, 1843 – a silent invalid for the last two years – the family was divided. Son Cuthbert was left in charge of the literary estate, which Wordsworth and others felt he wasn't up to – a point on which they felt vindicated following the poorly received publication of Southey's *Life and Correspondence*. And Southey's vast library – his pride and joy, catalogued by Sara Coleridge and his daughters – was broken up and sold.

plenty of opportunities for children to get busy drawing, as well as free **demonstration days** held throughout the year (check the website), when local artists lead hands-on sessions showcasing various drawing techniques. There's also a coffee shop at the museum, and you don't need to pay for entry to use this.

Crosthwaite church

Church Lane, CA12 5QG • Daily: April–Oct 9am–5pm; Nov–March 9am–2pm • ☎ 017687 71187, ⓦ crosthwaitechurchkeswick.co.uk

Keswick's other main church, **Crosthwaite church**, is on the western edge of town (over Greta Bridge, a 15min walk down High Hill and Church Lane), and is dedicated to St Kentigern (or Mungo), the Celtic missionary who founded several churches in Cumbria. Evidence suggests that Kentigern passed through in 553 AD and planted his cross in the clearing ("thwaite") here, though it's unlikely a permanent church was built on this site until the twelfth century, while the present structure dates from 1523.

That's all well and good, but the reason visitors make the trip out here is that the poet **Robert Southey** is buried in the churchyard, alongside his wife and children; his quasi-imperial marble effigy (inscribed by Wordsworth, who attended the funeral) stands inside the church, as does a plaque honouring Canon Hardwicke Drummond Rawnsley, one of the co-founders of the National Trust. Both men had strong links with Keswick. Rawnsley was the vicar at Crosthwaite between 1883 and 1917, while Southey moved into his brother-in-law Samuel Taylor Coleridge's house in the town in 1803 and, after Coleridge moved out, continued to live there for the next forty years. Southey was Poet Laureate from 1813 until his death in 1843 and his house, a Georgian pile known as **Greta Hall**, played its part in the Lakes' literary scene: it had a library stuffed with fourteen thousand books, which Southey delighted in showing to his visitors – Wordsworth (who tended not to hold with libraries) laments in his memorial inscription, "Loved books, no more shall Southey feed upon your precious lore." Greta Hall is now part of Keswick School (closed to the public), whose playing fields lie across from the church.

Castlerigg Stone Circle

Castle Lane, CA12 4XX • Always open • Free • Stone Circle is signposted off both the A66 and A591 on the way into Keswick

Keswick's most mysterious landmark, **Castlerigg Stone Circle**, can be reached by path along the disused railway line to Threlkeld (signposted by the *Keswick Country House Hotel*, at the end of Station Road) – after half a mile, look for the signposted turning to the right. The site is a mile further on atop a sweeping plateau, dwarfed by the encroaching fells. Thirty-eight hunks of Borrowdale volcanic stone, the largest almost 8ft tall, form a circle 100ft in diameter; another ten blocks delineate a rectangular enclosure within. The array probably had an astronomical or timekeeping function when it was erected four or five thousand years ago, but no one really knows. Whatever its origins, it's a magical spot – and particularly stunning in winter when frost and snow blanket the surrounding fells.

ARRIVAL AND DEPARTURE   **KESWICK**

BY CAR

Keswick is reached pretty quickly from most local destinations – Ambleside is 17 miles to the south (A591), while the town is on the A66, roughly midway between Penrith (18 miles east) and Cockermouth (14 miles northwest). Disc zones in town allow one or two hours' free parking, while large car parks down Lake Rd near the lake, and on either side of Market Place, soak up most of the visiting and shopping traffic. There are no restrictions in the streets off Southey St (where most of the B&Bs are) or on Brundholme Rd behind the park.

BY BUS

Buses use the terminal at The Headlands, in front of Booths supermarket, off Main St. The town is a major transport hub, with regular services in all directions.

Bus #77/77A "Honister Rambler" circular route to: Cat Bells (11min); Grange (20min); Seatoller (30min); Honister Slate Mine (40min); Buttermere (50min); Lorton (1hr 10min) and

Whinlatter Pass (1hr 20min); or to Whinlatter Pass (15min); Lorton (25min); Buttermere (45min); Honister Slate Mine (1hr); Seatoller (1hr 5min) and Grange (1hr 15min). Service operates 5–6 daily Easter–Oct.

Bus #78 "Borrowdale Rambler" to: Lodore (15min), Grange (20min), Rosthwaite (25min) and Seatoller (30min). Service operates every 30min–1hr.

Bus #208 to: Aira Force (28min); Glenridding (35min) and Patterdale (40min); or to Aira Force (28min) and Pooley Bridge (40min). Service operates 3–4 daily Sat, Sun & bank hols, plus Mon–Fri during school holidays.

Bus #554 to: Mirehouse (9min); *Castle Inn* for Wildlife Park (18min) and on to Carlisle (1hr 10min). Service operates 3–4 daily.

Bus #555 to: Thirlspot (13min); Grasmere (25min); Ambleside (50min); Windermere (1hr 5min) and Kendal (1hr 30min). Service operates every 30min–1hr.

Bus #555 to: Carlisle (1hr 10min; 3–4 daily).

Bus #X4/X5 to: Threlkeld (11min); Rheged (37min) and Penrith (50min); and also to Braithwaite (7min); Bassenthwaite (13min) and Cockermouth (35min). Service operates Mon–Sat hourly, Sun every 2hr.

BY TAXI

Davies Taxis (☎017687 72676, ⓦ daviestaxis.co.uk).

ACTIVITIES

Bike rental Keswick Mountain Bikes, 133 Main St (daily 9am–5pm; ☎017687 75202, ⓦ keswickbikes.co.uk). From £25/4hr, £30/day.

Guided walks Keswick Rambles sets off most days in season (Easter–Sept; £15; booking essential, ⓦ keswick rambles.blogspot.com). Walks – easy rambles to mountain climbs – depart from the Moot Hall, where a schedule is posted; don't forget a packed lunch.

Outdoor activities Contact Mick at *Denton House* backpackers (Penrith Rd ☎017687 75351, ⓦ dentonhouse-keswick.co.uk), for canoeing, ghyll-scrambling, crag-

INFORMATION

National Park Information Centre Moot Hall, Market Place (daily: April–Oct 9.30am–5.30pm; Nov–March 9.30am–4.30pm; ☎0845 901 0845, ⓦ lakedistrict.gov.uk). They sell a series of walk leaflets for popular routes (which you can download from the National Park website for free).
Websites ⓦ keswick.org.

climbing and abseiling (£30/half-day, £60/full day); you don't need to be staying at the hostel to book the activities. For climbing walls, try either Kong Adventure, in town on Heads Lane (☎017687 75907, ⓦ kongadventure.com; from £20), or the Climbing Wall and Activity Centre, about a mile east near Castelrigg Stones (☎017687 72000, ⓦ keswickclimbingwall.co.uk), which charges £20 for an hour's lesson (or £8 per day for competent climbers to use the wall), plus offers a range of activities from archery to canoeing and hiking.
Outdoor gear See "Shopping" (see page 152).

ACCOMMODATION   SEE MAPS PAGES 142 AND 145

Southey, Blencathra, Church and Eskin streets, in the grid off the A591 (Penrith road), abound in **B&Bs and guesthouses.** Smarter guesthouses and hotels line The Heads, overlooking Hope Park, a couple of minutes south of the centre on the way to the lake, and there's also a scattering of guesthouses and hotels in surrounding villages. If you're in the mood for an upmarket country-house-hotel experience, Keswick's rugged environs offer plenty of choice. The town's riverside **youth hostel** and out-of-town **backpackers** are open all year, but advance reservations in summer are a good idea. The same applies to the main **campsites**, which are all very popular. For self-catering **cottages** in the area, contact local specialists Keswick Cottages (ⓦ keswickcottages.co.uk) or Lakeland Cottages (ⓦ lakelandcottages.co.uk).

KESWICK

18/20 Cellar Bar 18–20 Lake Rd, CA12 5BX ☎0500 600725, ⓦ lakedistrictinns.co.uk. Four bright en-suite rooms (including two large twin/family rooms) located above a contemporary bar-brasserie. Furnishings are modern and comfortable, if plain, and it makes a useful town-centre base, with fell views from some windows, a good breakfast and the town's most spacious beer garden out back. Free parking permit provided. Add £20 for a weekend stay. £80
Acorn House Ambleside Rd, CA12 4DL ☎017687 72553, ⓦ acornhousehotel.co.uk. The handsome eighteenth-century house offers nine generously sized rooms with period furniture, including three with antique four-posters, while up top is an attic suite with views that can sleep up to four. Nice touches proliferate – bedside chocolates, and corkscrew and wine glasses provided – and it's a quiet,

friendly base, just 5min from the centre. Breakfasts are good too. Parking. £90
Cranford House 18 Eskin St, CA12 4DG ☎017687 71017, ⓦ cranfordhouse.co.uk. Classy townhouse B&B, whose appealing rooms feature large comfortable beds and decent linen and furnishings – you're guaranteed "freedom from flowery wallpaper and doilies". The six rooms include two singles (these share a bathroom), while the two rooms at the top have rooftop views and exposed beams. Breakfast (English, vegetarian or continental) is taken in front of the open fire, and walkers and cyclists can dry clothes, store bikes and browse the books and maps. £80
Denton House Penrith Rd, CA12 4JW ☎017687 75351, ⓦ dentonhouse-keswick.co.uk. Keswick's cheapest bed is at the independent backpackers and activity centre housed in a former stationmaster's house and cadet barracks, a 10min walk from the centre (by the railway bridge, just beyond the ambulance/fire station). Single-sex/mixed dorms range in size from four to twelve beds (62 in total), while plenty of showers, trim carpets and central heating; there are also kitchen, laundry, lockers and bike storage facilities. There's also a choice of a continental (£3.50) or cooked (£6) breakfast. Parking. Dorms £19
★ **Ellergill** 22 Stanger St, CA12 5JU ☎017687 73347, ⓦ ellergill.co.uk. A very friendly home from home, courtesy of owners Robin and Clare, who have grafted a chic European feel onto their restored Victorian house. Some magnificent Lakes photography brightens the breakfast room, while upstairs are four smartly furnished rooms with leather bedheads and chairs and a splash of deep colour.

None feels cramped, but "King Size" rooms (£15 extra) offer a bit more space. Street parking outside. £80

★ **Howe Keld** 5–7 The Heads, CA12 5ES ☎017687 72417, ⊚howekeld.co.uk. The Boujards' beautiful boutique guesthouse puts local crafts and materials centre-stage, with furniture and floors handcrafted from Lake District trees, plus smart green-slate bathrooms with walk-in showers and carpets of Herdwick wool. Soft browns, greens and creams create a very natural tone throughout – you're going to have no problem sleeping soundly in these designer quarters, which come as doubles or "Luxury Suites" (£140). The breakfast, too, served at handmade oak tables, has a signature style all its own, from crumpets and creamy porridge served with muscovado sugar to eggs Benedict. Parking. £120

Ravensworth House 29 Station St, CA12 5HH ☎017687 72476, ⊚ravensworthhouse.co.uk. Small, friendly, town-centre guesthouse that makes a real effort to please – it's hard not to like a place where organically grown lakeland lilies adorn the lounge. Just three smartly-turned out rooms, two of which have sleigh beds and spa baths, plus fell views. Breakfast is not offered here but there are plenty of decent cafés nearby, and they can whip up a packed lunch upon request; there are also maps and printed walks available, and a parking permit provided. £70

Twenty Six 26 Lake Rd, CA12 5DQ ☎017687 80863, ⊚cafebar26.co.uk. Four stylishly decorated rooms on the first floor above the café offer a chintz-free base right in the town centre. They're all nice and light, with pretty tiled shower rooms, and there's a car park just 100yds away. Note, though, that check-in is self-service and there's no breakfast. £80

West View The Heads, CA12 5ES ☎017687 73638, ⊚westviewkeswick.co.uk. The "west view" at Heather and Craig's restored Victorian guesthouse is across to the mountains, which is a good start. Downstairs it's all fairly traditional, though the rooms are much more modish, with oatmeal carpets and chic cream decor – three of the six are bigger, with king-sized beds and walk-in showers; these cost £40 extra. Guests are free to avail themselves of the first floor lounge, with its super views and extensive library of books, maps and guides. Street parking outside. £80

★ **YHA Keswick** Station Rd, CA12 5LH ☎0845 371 9746, ⊚yha.org.uk/hostel/keswick. Once a riverside woollen mill, Keswick's centrally located, well-equipped YHA is a big hit with families, walkers and travellers. Badly hit by the 2016 floods, the hostel has been superbly renovated, with rooms (some en suite) ranging in size from two to six beds (107 in total), and impressive ground floor social spaces including a café/bar, dining room and kitchen; other amenities include bike storage, drying room and laundry. The staff are extremely well informed on everything from local hiking trails to the best places to park your car long-term or find a strong coffee. Meanwhile, the

town park and play areas are right opposite. Street parking nearby. Dorms £35, doubles £78

AROUND KESWICK

Castlerigg Farm Rakefoot Lane, off A591, Castlerigg, CA12 4TE ☎017687 72479, ⊚castleriggfarm.com. A quiet, family campsite, just over a mile southeast of the centre – it's "silence" after 10.30pm, so it's not going to be suitable for everyone. It's mainly for tents, though there is space for motorhomes (£24). Facilities include a shop, laundry and the Hayloft Café. No advance reservations. Cars £4 extra. Per person £10

★ **Castlerigg Hall** Rakefoot Lane, off A591, Castlerigg, CA12 4TE ☎017687 74499, ⊚castlerigg.co.uk. Not near the lake, but with views to compensate, this award-winning tent-and-caravan site is the first one you reach up this road, just over a mile southeast of the centre. Tents and pods (including family- and "castle"-sized; from £53) are kept well away from the caravans and motorhomes. There's a shop, campers' kitchen, laundry, lounge and games room, plus a terrace-restaurant for cooked breakfasts, evening meals and weekly pizza nights. No advance bookings for camping. Closed Nov–Feb. Cars £4.90 extra. Per person £12.90

Coledale Inn Braithwaite, CA12 5TN, 3 miles west of Keswick off A66 ☎017687 78272, ⊚coledale-inn.co.uk. Cosy Victorian-era B&B on the hillside above Braithwaite, featuring twenty neat, reasonably spacious rooms, a sheltered garden and good-value lunchtime and evening meals, served in either the dining room or the Victorian or Georgian bars. There's some tremendous walking to be done from the village, and if you stay here rather than Keswick you can make an early start on the hills – they'll make you up a packed lunch and fill a flask for your day's hiking. Good discounts on longer stays. Parking. £105

Lyzzick Hall Under Skiddaw, CA12 4PY, 2 miles northwest of Keswick on A591 ☎017687 72277, ⊚lyzzickhall.co.uk. Set in its own extensive grounds with sweeping views, this is all a stone-built, lakeland country-house hotel should be. It's great for an intimate, indulgent weekend away at any time – lovely indoor pool and spa, a terrace for lazy-day drinks and lounges warmed by log fires. You don't need to go anywhere else to eat either, since D, B&B rates (from £226) are a good deal, with the highly rated restaurant serving a contemporary Cumbrian menu that combines local sourcing with Mediterranean flavours. Parking. £172

★ **Powe House** Portinscale, CA12 5RW, 2 miles west of Keswick off A66 ☎017687 73611, ⊚powehouse. com. For handsome, contemporary style on a budget, you can't beat this quiet, tidy B&B retreat near the head of the lake. Bold, bright, light rooms overlook the gardens of this detached country house, and while some are a bit bigger than others (no. 5 is the best), most have king-sized beds and all show a keen eye for design. Parking. £92

4

EATING

SEE MAPS PAGES 142 AND 145

Keswick is a real metropolis compared to anywhere else in the National Park, which means that there's no shortage of places to eat and drink, especially down Lake Road, Keswick's "food street". Daytime **cafés** are firmly aimed at the walking and shopping crowd – you won't want for a big bowl of soup or a cream tea – and there are some decent **restaurants** and lots of **pubs**, many also serving good food. The two **supermarkets**, Booths (the biggest and best, specializing in locally sourced produce) and the smaller Co-op, are near the bus station, off Main Street.

CAFÉS

★ **Abraham's Café** George Fisher, 2 Borrowdale Rd, CA12 5DA ☎017687 72178, ⓦgeorgefisher.co.uk. Just looking around the camping and hiking gear in Keswick's celebrated outdoors store soon works up an appetite, so all power to the top-floor tearoom – warming mugs of *glühwein*, home-made soups, big breakfasts with free-range eggs, rarebits, open sandwiches and other daily specials (dishes £5–9). Mon–Fri 10am–5pm, Sat 9.30am–5pm, Sun 10.30am–4.30pm.

Café-Bar 26 26 Lake Rd, CA12 5DQ ☎017687 80863, ⓦcafebar26.co.uk. Handily placed on the way to the lake, this bright and funky café-bar offers squishy sofas, decent coffee and good food, dishing up the likes of steak and chips or haddock fishcakes for lunch, with dinner more of a tapas and pizza affair (most dishes under £10). Tue–Sun 9.30am–11pm.

Merienda 10 Main St, close to the Moot Hall, CA12 5JD ☎017687 72024, ⓦmerienda.co.uk. This bright and cheerful café serves up everything from breakfasts of porridge with maple syrup (£3.45) or rare-breed bacon and eggs (£4.95), to lunchtime meze (£8.50) and dinners of baked trout or pulled pork tacos (around £14). As with their sister operation in Cockermouth, every detail – including the coffee – is just a cut above what you'd expect. The only quibble relates to the slightly cramped tables. Mon–Thurs 8am–9pm, Fri & Sat 8am–10pm, Sun 9am–9pm.

RESTAURANTS

Bar Es 1 New St, CA12 5BH ☎017687 75222, ⓦesbarltd.co.uk. Ditching the whole notion of courses in favour of "Mexican-inspired tapas", on the right night *Bar Es* can be a real buzz – have a drink in the downstairs bar, then move upstairs for sharing portions of chorizo stew and refried beans, ribs, breaded chillis, quesadillas or their superb, slow-cooked beef enchiladas (count on around £12 a head). Bookings only for groups of six or more. Mon 5–11pm, Tues–Fri 5pm–midnight, Sat 4pm–midnight, Sun 4pm–11pm, kitchen closes 9pm.

Morrel's 34 Lake Rd, CA12 5DQ ☎017687 72666, ⓦmorrels.co.uk. Keswick's top spot is a handsome-looking restaurant where Modern British and Mediterranean styles prevail – from lamb cannon with lemon couscous to swordfish loin on Spanish potatoes. While it's at the pricier end of Keswick dining (mains £15–22), there's a bargain three-course *table d'hôte* menu (£21.95; not Sun). It's also the closest restaurant to the Theatre by the Lake (see page 152) and opens early for pre-theatre meals. Tues–Sun 5.30–9pm.

PUBS

Bank Tavern 47 Main St, CA12 5DS ☎017687 72663, ⓦbanktavern.co.uk. Resolutely traditional pub that enjoys a local reputation for its classic bar meals – bangers and mash to rib-eye steak (£10–16) – which means that every table is often filled at meal times. The beer's good, too (usually half a dozen real ales available), while a terrace at the back looks towards Market Square. Daily 11am–11pm, Fri & Sat till 11.30pm; kitchen noon–9pm.

George St John St, CA12 5AZ ☎017687 72076, ⓦgeorgehotelkeswick.co.uk. Keswick's oldest inn has bags of character, with snug bars lined with portraits, pictures and curios, and wooden settles in front of the fire. There's a good bistro menu (mains £11–16), which you can eat in the restaurant or bar – slow-roast lamb to venison casserole, local trout to fish and chips, with hurrahs for anyone who finishes one of their two Gigantic Pies, namely the "cow pie", and the chicken and ham "farmhouse pie" (£20.95). Good-value Sunday roast too (£10.95). Mon–Thurs & Sun 11am–11pm, Fri & Sat till midnight; kitchen Mon–Fri noon–2.30pm & 5.30–9pm, Sat & Sun noon–4.30pm & 5.30–9.30pm.

Pheasant Inn Crosthwaite, CA12 5PP ☎017687 72219, ⓦthepheasantinnkeswick.co.uk. More for dining than drinking, this out-of-town Jennings pub has a classier menu than most, say beef pie with port and shallot gravy, posh fish pie (with salmon, prawns, mussels and smoked cod in a lemon-saffron sauce) or home-made beef Madras (mains £9–11). It's a 10min walk from town, through Fitz Park and just up from the hospital. Daily noon–11pm; kitchen noon–2pm & 6–9pm.

DRINKING

SEE MAP PAGE 145

Magnolia 33 Lake Rd, CA12 5DQ ☎017687 44343, ⓦmagnoliabarbistro.co.uk. You can certainly fill up on decent food at this popular Belgian beer bar and bistro – steamed mussels with garlic, fish pie, honey-roast duck breast with braised red cabbage (around £15) – but you're really here to work through the huge range of bottled Belgian beers (more than 45 varieties at last count, plus a few Austrian, American and Czech). The lively atmosphere is given further impetus courtesy of terrific Saturday night (9pm) music sessions. Daily 11.30am–midnight.

★ **The Wainwright** Lake Rd, CA12 5BZ ☎017687 44927, ⓦthewainwright.pub. Although the black-and-

WALKS FROM KESWICK

Keswick walks fall into two categories: **easy strolls** down by the lake or up to scenic viewpoints, and the considerably more energetic **peak-bagging** of Skiddaw and Blencathra. If you've got time to make only one local hike, there's a case for making it up Cat Bells (see page 154), which forms the distinctive backdrop to many a Keswick view.

AROUND THE LAKE

The **round-the-lake** route (8 miles; 5–6hr) is available on a leaflet at the National Park information office in Keswick, and it's an easy day out, past bays filled with waterfowl and lakeshore woodland. It passes some of the prettiest highlights (Lodore, Manesty Park, Brandlehow) and the real beauty of it is that you can bail out at any point and catch the launch back to Keswick.

LATRIGG

Latrigg (1203ft), north of town, gets the vote for a quick climb (45min) to a fine viewpoint – up Bassenthwaite Lake and across Derwent Water to Borrowdale and the high fells. Driving first to the Underscar car park gets you even closer, within twenty minutes of the summit, and the path from this point is fully accessible for wheelchairs and strollers. For a circular walk (4–6 miles; 2–3hr), follow the eastern ridge to Brundholme, returning through Brundholme wood or along the railway-line path.

FRIAR'S CRAG, WALLA CRAG AND CASTLEHEAD

South of town, the best half-day walk is to **Walla Crag** (1234ft) and back (5 miles; 4hr), approaching via the Derwent Water beauty spot of **Friar's Crag**. At Calf Close Bay you cross the Borrowdale road (B5329) and climb through Great Wood to the summit, which provides terrific views of the lake, St Herbert's Island and the fells beyond. The descent back to town is via Rakefoot, with a possible diversion to **Castlehead** (530ft) for more lake views, with Scafell Pike rising in the distance.

SKIDDAW

Easiest of the true mountain walks is the hike up the smooth mound of splintery slate that is **Skiddaw** (3053ft). From the Underscar car park it's a steady (and, it has to be said, boring) walk up a wide, eroded track, with a possible diversion up Skiddaw **Little Man** (2837ft), before reaching the High Man summit. Straight up and down is around five miles and takes about five hours, but there's a much better route back, descending to the southwest, along the ridge above Bassenthwaite formed by Longside Edge, **Ullock Pike** (2230ft) and The Edge, before dropping down into Dodd Wood (8 miles; 7hr). Either catch the bus along the A591 back to Keswick, or keep off the road on the signposted Keswick path from Dodd Wood.

BLENCATHRA

Blencathra (2847ft) – also known as Saddleback – could keep hikers occupied for a fortnight. Wainwright details twelve possible ascents of its summit and, though made of the same slate as Skiddaw, it's a far more aggressive proposition. Many use Threlkeld as the starting point: easiest route is via Blease Fell and Knowe Crags (an ascent that Wainwright pooh-poohs as too dull); the path starts from the car park by the Blencathra Centre. The more adventurous steer a course up any of the narrow ridges, whose names (Sharp Edge, Foule Crag) don't pull any punches – for most of these, the best starting point is the *White Horse* pub at Scales, another mile and a half up the A66 (towards Penrith) from Threlkeld.

---

white exterior fits the bill of a traditional Lakes pub, inside the *Wainwright* looks more like a café, with neatly polished wooden tables and rather anodyne decor (well, except for the Edwardian-era walk-in porcelain fittings in the gents'). But this is easily the best place in town for a real ale, of which there's usually at least eight local varieties to choose from on tap, and – predictably, given the name and photo-wall dedicated to Wainwright's life – it's pretty popular with fell-walkers. The food – pies, scampi, "build your own" burgers and the like – is of secondary importance, but still

nicely served (mains around £12). Daily noon–3pm & 5–9.15pm; kitchen noon–9pm.

ENTERTAINMENT

It's always worth checking to see what's on at the **Theatre by the Lake**, whose repertoire of performances, concerts and events makes Keswick something of a cultural centre for the Lake District. Otherwise, the biggest events in town are the **Jazz and Blues Festival** (w keswickjazzandbluesfestival.co.uk) and the Keswick **Mountain Festival** (w keswickmountainfestival.co.uk), both in May, the June **beer festival** (w keswickbeerfestival.co.uk), and the traditional **Keswick Agricultural Show** (w keswickshow) on August bank holiday), which is the place to learn more about sheep-shearing and other rural pursuits.
Alhambra St John's St, CA12 5AG ☏017687 72195, w keswickalhambra.co.uk. The town's enterprising cinema

shows all the mainstream releases, but there are foreign-language and indie screenings most Weds, while Keswick Film Club (w keswickfilmclub.org) puts on arthouse movies on Sun (Oct–March) and hosts an annual Film Festival at the end of Feb, featuring the best of world cinema.
Theatre by the Lake Lake Rd, CA12 5DJ ☏017687 74411, w theatrebythelake.com. England's loveliest theatre hosts a full programme of drama, concerts, exhibitions, readings and talks. "Words By The Water", a literature festival, takes place here in March, while the ground-floor Spotlight Café offers decent snacks, lunches and pre-performance drinks (daily 11am–4.30pm, till 7pm on performance days).

SHOPPING
SEE MAP PAGE 145

Bookends 66 Main St, CA12 5DX ☏017687 75277, w bookscumbria.com. A good selection of local-interest books and hiking guides, plus discounted books and novels. Mon–Fri 9.30am–6pm, Sat 9am–6pm, Sun 10am–6pm; July & Aug daily till 9pm.
George Fisher 2 Borrowdale Rd, CA12 5DA ☏017687 72178, w georgefisher.co.uk. The most celebrated outdoors store in the Lakes, with a big range of gear, guides and maps, plus boot rental, a daily weather information service and the Abraham's Café (see page 150). Mon, Tues & Thurs–Sat 9am–5.30pm, Wed 10am–5.30pm, Sun

10.30am–4.30pm.
Keswick Bookshop 4 Station St, CA12 5HT ☏017687 75535. Slightly eccentric secondhand and antiquarian bookshop, with a good number of out-of-print titles on the region. Wed–Sat 11am–5pm.
Needle Sports 56 Main St, CA12 5JS ☏017687 72227, w needlesports.com. The local climbing and mountaineering specialist, with a small but high-quality selection of everything from tents and shell jackets to crampons and flashlights. Daily 9am–5.30pm.

DIRECTORY

Hospital Keswick Community Hospital (Crosthwaite Rd; ☏01768 245678) has a 24hr minor injuries unit.
Laundry Victoria St (Mon–Fri 8am–7pm, Sat & Sun 9am–6pm).
Pharmacies Boots, 31 Main St (Mon–Sat 9am–6pm, Sun 10am–5pm; ☏017687 72383); Murray's, 15–17 Station St (Mon–Fri 9am–5.30pm, Sat 9am–1pm; ☏017687 72049).

Police station 8 Bank St (☏101, w cumbria.police.uk). Enquiry desk closed Thurs & Sun.
Post office 48 Main St (Mon–Sat 9am–5.30pm).
Swimming pool Keswick Leisure Pool, Station Rd (Mon–Fri 8am–10pm, Sat & Sun 10am–7pm; winter hours may vary; ☏017687 72760, w better.org.uk), has a wave machine, waterslide, fitness centre and poolside café.

Derwent Water

Derwent Water may not be that big – three miles long and, at most, a mile wide – but it's a really pretty spot, only five minutes' walk south of the centre of Keswick (down Lake Road and through the pedestrian underpass). Of all the major lakes it's the easiest to get to know quickly, since you can either walk around the entire perimeter or catch the useful launch service that circles the lake at regular intervals. In fact, if you're planning on doing any of the famous walks, like Cat Bells, or visiting the local beauty spots, it's far better to take the boat to the nearest pier since parking is restricted to prevent congestion on the narrow lanes. Otherwise, spread out a picnic on the grassy banks of **Crow Park**, on the northern shore closest to Keswick, and look down the lake to its crags and islets – you might even catch sight of the mysterious floating island, which appears only after sustained periods of dry weather.

Friar's Crag

The most popular short walk by the lake – no more than ten minutes from the Keswick launch piers – is to **Friar's Crag**, a wooded peninsula on the northeastern shore. From here, medieval pilgrims once took a skiff over to **St Herbert's Island**, in the middle of the lake, which was thought to be the site of the seventh-century hermitage of St Herbert, disciple and friend of St Cuthbert of Lindisfarne. The Friar's Crag land was

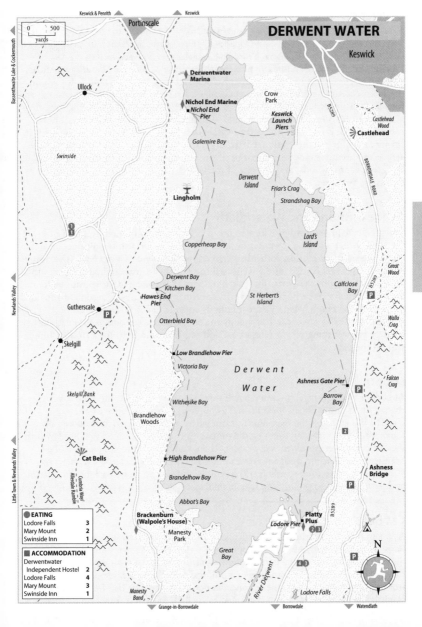

DERWENT WATER

Keswick & Penrith   Keswick

0   500
yards

Portinscale

Keswick

Derwentwater
Marina

Crow
Park

Nichol End Marine
Nichol End
Pier

Keswick
Launch
Piers

Castlehead
Wood

Castlehead

Galemire Bay

Swinside

Derwent
Island

Friar's Crag

Lingholm

Strandshag Bay

Copperheap Bay

Lord's
Island

Great
Wood

Derwent Bay

Kitchen Bay

Hawes End
Pier

St Herbert's
Island

Calfclose
Bay

Otterbield Bay

Gutherscale

Walla
Crag

Skelgill

Low Brandlehow Pier

Victoria Bay

Derwent

Water

Ashness Gate Pier

Falcon
Crag

Skelgill Bank

Barrow
Bay

Withesike Bay

Brandlehow
Woods

Cat Bells

High Brandlehow Pier

Ashness
Bridge

Brandlehow Bay

Abbot's Bay

EATING
Lodore Falls   3
Mary Mount   2
Swinside Inn   1

Brackenburn
(Walpole's House)

Manesty
Park

Platty
Plus

Lodore Pier

ACCOMMODATION
Derwentwater
  Independent Hostel 2
Lodore Falls   4
Mary Mount   3
Swinside Inn   1

Great
Bay

Manesty
Band

River Derwent

Lodore Falls

N

Grange-in-Borrowdale   Borrowdale   Watenlath

Bassenthwaite Lake & Cockermouth

Newlands Valley

Little Town & Newlands Valley

Cumbria Way/
Allerdale Ramble

Ullock

4

acquired by the National Trust in 1922, and is held in memory of its founder Canon Rawnsley, though it's long been a beauty spot. Ruskin's childhood visit to Friar's Crag famously inspired "intense joy, mingled with awe", which is a bit over the top, but the grass banks and little rocky coves are very attractive and you'll get some good photos on a sunny day.

Derwent Island

Tours usually on five selected days annually, April–Aug; departures from Derwent Water lakeshore every 45min, 10am–3.15pm • £14.25, family £28.50; bookings at the National Trust shop on the lakeshore, but not until three days before each date (announced on website); NT • ☎ 017687 73780, ⓦ nationaltrust.org.uk/borrowdale-and-derwent-water/features/derwent-island-and-house

During the eighteenth and early nineteenth centuries, Derwent Water saw regular regattas, orchestrated initially by Joseph Pocklington, a wealthy banker, for whom the word eccentric seems woefully inadequate. He built himself a house, church and fortress on **Derwent Island** (the house is still there, owned by the National Trust) and appointed himself "Governor and Commander-in-Chief", blasting off brass cannons at the boats. The house is privately occupied, but for five days each year in spring and summer the National Trust organizes trips to the island. Visitors canoe across and are given a 45-minute tour of the house; they are then free to explore the gardens and woods, and the rest of the island, for another hour or so before returning by canoe.

4 Ashness Bridge and Watendlath

The pier at **Ashness Gate** provides access to a narrow road branching south off the B5289 that climbs a steep half-mile to the photogenic **Ashness Bridge**, an old dry-stone packhorse bridge providing marvellous Derwent Water views. The minor road past Ashness Bridge (and a well-used footpath) ends two miles further south at **Watendlath** – from the Norse for "lake-end barn" – an isolated farmstead, tearoom and tarn which can be hopelessly overrun at times in summer. Watendlath provided the setting for Hugh Walpole's most famous episode of his Herries Chronicles, *Judith Paris* (1931); you can buy a copy in the tearoom and lounge about for an hour or two on the grass, or rent a boat and rod from the farm for a trout-fishing trip on the tarn.

Lodore

At **Lodore** landing stage, three and a half miles south of Keswick, there are kayaks, rowing boats and sailboats for rent, and a couple of hotels for lunch or afternoon tea. The bus stops on the road nearby, from where a path heads to the **Lodore Falls**, much visited in Victorian times by the romantically inclined though only really worth the diversion after sustained wet weather. Then, you'll be able to appreciate Robert Southey's magnificent, assonant evocation of the falls in *The Cataract of Lodore*: "Collecting, projecting, receding and speeding, and shocking and rocking, and darting and parting", and so on, for line after memorable line.

Cat Bells

Asked to pick a favourite Lake District walk and climb, many would plump for **Cat Bells** (1481ft), a renowned vantage point above the lake's western shore. It's not difficult (possible for all the family), the views from the top are stupendous, and it's easy to combine with the launch to or from Keswick. The name, incidentally, derives from the age-old belief that the fell once harboured a wild cat's den (*bield*, the Old English word for den, was later corrupted to "bells"). Since it featured on the BBC's

CANON RAWNSLEY AND THE NATIONAL TRUST

Hardwicke Drummond Rawnsley (1851–1920) was ordained in 1875, gained his first living in the Lakes (at Wray, near Ambleside) two years later, and was appointed vicar at Crosthwaite, Keswick, in 1883. It was a period of rapid industrial development and the conservation-minded Canon Rawnsley found himself opposing the proposed Braithewaite & Buttermere Railway, fighting footpath disputes and lining up with Ruskin (an old Oxford college friend) against the creation of Thirlmere reservoir – though Rawnsley later accepted the needs of the northern cities for water and even attended Thirlmere's official opening. His time served on the County Council and the newly formed Lake District Defence Society convinced him of the need for a preservation society with money and teeth. In 1893, together with Octavia Hill and Sir Robert Hunter, and the backing of the Duke of Westminster, he established the **National Trust**. This received its first piece of donated land (in Wales) the following year: the first parcel of land purchased in the Lake District was that of **Brandlehow woods and park** in 1902, and the Trust went on to acquire much of Derwent Water and Borrowdale by 1908. It's now easily the largest landowner in the Lake District.

Rawnsley remained an active part of the Trust while continuing to preach and write – he produced many collections of lakeland sonnets, poems, histories and guides, including an entertaining book of "reminiscences" of Wordsworth by the local peasantry (none of whom thought the Poet Laureate's poetry was any good). After Rawnsley's wife died in 1916 he retired to Wordsworth's old house at Allan Bank in Grasmere. He married again in 1918, but died just two years later on May 28, 1920.

4

"Wainwright Walks" series, the Cat Bells walk has become so popular that parking near the foot is now extremely restricted and you're encouraged to come by "boat, bus or boot". Most people use the path from **Hawes End** launch pier, though the longer haul up from Manesty to the south (High Brandlehow launch) has its merits. Return to either launch pier along the lakeside path through Manesty Park and **Brandlehow** woods and park, allowing, say, two and a half hours for the entire walk. Walpole fans should note that Sir Hugh lived and worked for many years in the lee of Cat Bells, at the house he called **Brackenburn**, by Manesty Park.

The *Swinside Inn* in Newlands Valley is only a mile from Hawes End – a welcome stop for a post-Cat Bells pint – while a signposted path from Hawes End pier runs all the way back to Keswick, which is only a couple of miles away through the woods and round the top of the lake.

Lingholm and Portinscale

Less than a mile north of Hawes End, the path to Keswick passes the entrance to the private estate of **Lingholm**, whose octagonal, red-brick walled garden (daily 9am–5pm) is well worth a visit. Within the garden walls is an outdoor gallery dedicated to the work of Beatrix Potter, who spent many childhood holidays at Lingholm's grand house (closed to the public) and, hardly surprisingly, the surroundings here and in the lovely Newlands Valley to the southwest appeared in several of her later stories. The garden's substantial vegetable plot, meanwhile, sustains the on-site *Lingholm Kitchen*. Just beyond, there are refreshments at hand at the lakeside café at **Nichol End**, a marine store and boat-rental place. The name is a corruption of "St Nicholas' Ending", as the site was once an embarkation point for medieval pilgrims crossing to St Herbert's Island (St Nicholas being the patron saint of sailors).

After Nichol End, the path joins the main road as it snakes through the village of **Portinscale**, a satellite of Keswick, where you can relax with a drink in the conservatory-bar and lakeside gardens of the *Derwentwater* hotel, before striking off over the River Derwent and through the fields to emerge by Greta Bridge in town.

Newlands Valley

A valley for connoisseurs unfolds along Newlands Beck, to the west of Cat Bells and Derwent Water. Save for the very minor road over Newlands Hause to Buttermere, there's little in the isolated farms and sparse hamlets of the **Newlands Valley** to lure touring drivers. But hikers have the choice of two fine circuits, one following the pastoral valley lowlands, the other tracing the encircling ridges and peaks. Either walk can be done from Keswick, via the launch to Hawes End, and should culminate in a visit to the valley's only **pub**, the excellent *Swinside Inn*.

The **valley walk** (5 miles; 3hr) follows a path from Hawes End pier to **Little Town** – the main valley hamlet, with an isolated chapel – beyond which can be made out the old Goldscope lead mines. These have been long abandoned, but were a hive of activity as far back as the sixteenth century when German miners were brought here to work the seams.

Better, if you (and the weather) are up to it, is the exhilarating **Newlands Horseshoe** (11 miles; 6–7hr), which begins with the ascent of Cat Bells and then links Maiden Moor (1887ft), High Spy (2143ft), Dale Head (2473ft) and Hindscarth (2385ft) in a terrific circular walk above and around the valley. The views, needless to say, are magnificent.

ARRIVAL AND ACTIVITIES   DERWENT WATER

By car There are small pay-and-display car parks dotted around the lake, but bus and boat from Keswick are just as convenient for seeing Derwent Water.

By boat The Keswick Launch piers (see box) are just a few minutes' walk from Keswick town centre and departures are frequent enough to combine a cruise with a walk and a picnic.

By bus The year-round #78 "Borrowdale Rambler" runs down the east side of the lake (B5289) from Keswick, via Lodore, or there's the seasonal #77/77A "Honister Rambler",

which runs along the western shore via Portinscale, Cat Bells (for Newlands Valley) and Grange. Day Rider tickets (buy on the bus) cost £8.50.

Watersports Derwentwater Marina (☏017687 72912, ⊛derwentwatermarina.co.uk) rents rowing boats, canoes, kayaks, paddleboards and windsurfers (from £10/hr); as do outlets at Lingholm, Portinscale (Nichol End Marine; ☏017687 73082, ⊛nicholend.co.uk) or Lodore (Platty +; ☏016973 71069, ⊛plattyplus.co.uk).

ACCOMMODATION AND EATING   SEE MAP PAGE 153

★ **Derwentwater Independent Hostel** Barrow House, CA12 5UR, 2 miles south of Keswick on B5289 (Borrowdale) road ☏017687 77246, ⊛derwentwater. org. Much-loved 200-year-old shoreside mansion now serving as a not-for-profit outward-bound-style hostel. The best bits include a fine original interior and 17 acres of grounds (plus own waterfall), while the accommodation runs to 88 beds spread across eleven basic but serviceable bunk-bed rooms. Family rooms can sleep four to six, with prices from £60 to £108; there's a self-catering kitchen while meals

are also served. It's a bit far to walk in and out for the shops and pubs, but bus #78 runs past, and the Keswick Launch stops at nearby Ashness Gate pier. Parking. Dorms £26

Lodore Falls Lodore, CA12 5UX, 3.5 miles south of Keswick on B5289 (Borrowdale) road ☏0800 840 1246, ⊛lakedistricthotels.net. The most prominent accommodation at the bottom end of Derwent Water, the three-star *Lodore Falls* is a slick, family-oriented operation with extensive lakeshore and woodland gardens, plus leisure centre, tennis court and two pools (one indoor,

KESWICK LAUNCH

Keswick Launch (☏017687 72263, ⊛keswick-launch.co.uk) runs services around the lake calling at six points en route (single-stage journey £2.35, round trip £11, family £27.50). Between mid-March and mid-November services run every 30min from 10am until 5pm, either clockwise or anticlockwise around the lake. From mid-November until mid-March services depart on Saturdays and Sundays only (though daily during school hols), three times daily in each direction. There's also an enjoyable one-hour **evening cruise** in school summer holidays (6.30pm & 7.30pm; £9.95, family £23.50), with anecdotal commentary and a glass of wine or soft drink included; buy a ticket earlier in the day to ensure a place.

one outdoor). There are great views from most rooms, a major selling point here – though if you want to see the lake, rather than the fells, expect to pay another £30 a night. Daytime dining is in the lounge-bar, while a fancier dinner, featuring seasonal local produce (£44), is served in the Lakeview restaurant. Kitchen daily noon–5pm & 6.30–9.15pm. **£220**

Mary Mount Lodore, CA12 5UU, 3.5 miles south of Keswick on B5289 (Borrowdale) road ☏017687 77223, ⓦmarymounthotel.co.uk. Nestling under the crags in four acres of lakeside and woodland garden, this intimate family-run hotel is just a few yards from the Lodore piers. The twenty rooms are either in the main house, cottage or annexe, with those in the latter manifesting a more contemporary style – weekend stays cost another £20. There's a nice oak-panelled bar serving lunch (hot sandwiches and mains £10–14) – which you can eat outside on the terrace in good weather – as well as a moderately priced restaurant serving more bistro-style fare (mains £15–18) and with picture windows giving you a grandstand lake view. They'll also pack you a picnic lunch and fill a flask if you ask. Kitchen Mon–Thurs noon–2pm & 6–9pm, Fri–Sun noon–4pm & 6–9pm. **£132**

Swinside Inn Newlands Valley, CA12 5UE, 3 miles south of Keswick ☏017687 78253, ⓦswinsideinn.com. An old inn whose beer garden is its best feature – with dramatic views up to the encroaching fells. Six smallish B&B rooms offer straightforward en-suite accommodation – including dog-friendly and family rooms – while downstairs you can content yourself with real ales, bar meals and log fires in winter. Daily 11am–11pm; kitchen Mon–Fri noon–2pm & 6–9pm, Sat noon–9pm, Sun noon–8pm. **£75**

Borrowdale

Beautiful **Borrowdale** stretches beyond the foot of Derwent Water, south of Keswick, and it's difficult to overstate the attraction of its river flats, forested crags, oak woods and yew trees. Early visiting writers and poets, including Thomas Gray who marvelled at the prospect in 1769, saw it as an embodiment of their Romantic fancy; Turner and Constable came to paint it; and Wordsworth praised its yews, "those fraternal Four of Borrowdale, joined in one solemn and capacious grove". It's easy to see Borrowdale's pretty hamlets and natural attractions – the bus from Keswick down the B5289 is one of the Lake District's most scenic rides, and it's only half an hour from town to the head of the valley at Seatoller. On good days, and especially in summer, there's a fairly steady stream of hiker traffic intent on conquering the peaks of Scafell and Scafell Pike (the two highest in the Lakes) and Great Gable, the latter one of the finest-looking mountains in England.

Grange-in-Borrowdale and around

The riverside hamlet of **Grange-in-Borrowdale**, four miles south of Keswick, sits back from an old twin-arched packhorse bridge, under which the River Derwent tumbles from the narrower

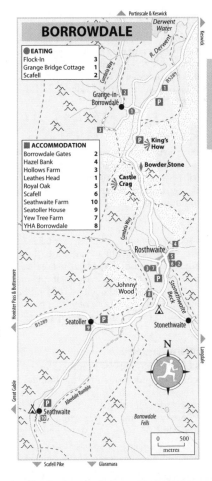

BORROWDALE

● EATING
Flock-In	3
Grange Bridge Cottage	1
Scafell	2

■ ACCOMMODATION
Borrowdale Gates	2
Hazel Bank	4
Hollows Farm	3
Leathes Head	1
Royal Oak	5
Scafell	6
Seathwaite Farm	10
Seatoller House	9
Yew Tree Farm	7
YHA Borrowdale	8

4

confines of Borrowdale and runs across the flood plain to the lake. And flood it does on occasion, which is why the raised wooden walkways snake across the flats between here, Lodore and Manesty. The hamlet name, incidentally, goes back to medieval times – in the thirteenth century the monks of Furness Abbey were farming the valley here from their "grainge" (an outlying farmhouse), both grazing sheep and smelting iron ore along the becks.

Jaws of Borrowdale

Around a mile south of Grange, the valley narrows at a crag-lined gorge known as the **Jaws of Borrowdale**. Until the eighteenth century, the route beyond was considered wild and uncertain, and there was no permanent road through until the mid-nineteenth century, when travellers other than locals first began to venture into the valley. The views are famed from **Castle Crag** (985ft), possibly the site of an ancient fort and one of the western "teeth" of the Jaws, which you can reach on paths from either Grange or – the next hamlet on – Rosthwaite.

Bowder Stone

Always open • Free • Pay-and-display car park on the B5289

Reached from the road, around a mile from Grange, stands the 1870-tonne **Bowder Stone**, a house-sized lump of rock scaled by a wooden ladder and worn to a shine on top by thousands of pairs of feet. Controversy surrounds the origin of this rock, pitched precariously on its edge. Some say it came from the fells above, others contend it was brought by glacier movement during the last Ice Age. Either way, most people can't resist a clamber. The crag behind the Bowder Stone, **King's How**, is named in memory of Edward VII. It's a fair climb to the top, but the views are worth it.

Rosthwaite

Both riverside path and B5289 run through the straggling hamlet of **Rosthwaite**, two miles south of Grange. Its whitewashed stone buildings, backed by the encroaching fells, sustain the most concentrated batch of accommodation in the valley, while at the Rosthwaite **village shop** (open daily) – the only one in the valley – you'll be able to put together a basic picnic and buy a map or a postcard. Both hotels on the road, the *Royal Oak* and the *Scafell*, offer drinks, meals and teas to non-guests, while the *Scafell* is also the starting point of the annual **Borrowdale Fell Race** (first Sat in Aug), a seventeen-mile gut-buster that takes in the peaks of Scafell Pike and Great Gable. The winners clock in at well under three hours, their names immortalized on an honours board displayed in the hotel's *Riverside Bar*. Tortoises can reflect on these hare-like exploits while seated on the memorial bench in the hotel grounds dedicated to Walter ("W.A.") Poucher (1891–1988), author, fell-walker and photographer, whose classic *Lakeland Peaks*, first published in 1960, is the only serious rival in scope and breadth to the Wainwright guides.

Stonethwaite

Stonethwaite, a place of some antiquity just to the southeast of Rosthwaite and half a mile up a side road, is the trailhead for those aiming to walk into Langdale via Langstrath and the watershed of Stake Pass. There's more foot traffic than you might expect, since it's on the route of both the Cumbria Way and the Coast-to-Coast walk. Whitewashed stone cottages huddle around the sixteenth-century *Langstrath Country Inn*, while the bleak Langstrath Valley beyond makes for a tough day's outing.

RED SQUIRREL, WHINLATTER FOREST PARK

Seatoller

End of the ride on the Borrowdale bus is the old farming and quarrying settlement of **Seatoller**, a mile from Rosthwaite and eight from Keswick. There's a National Trust car park, from where a path leads into **Johnny Wood**, on a two-mile nature trail past its moss-covered boulders and lichen-draped trees. Borrowdale's indigenous oak woods once effectively formed part of a temperate rainforest – the surviving fragments are still known for their mosses, ferns, liverworts and lichens, and provide cover for a wide range of berries and birds, including warblers and flycatchers.

Seatoller itself has a few slate-roofed houses clustering around the *Yew Tree* café, which was fashioned from seventeenth-century stone-flagged quarrymen's cottages. **Seatoller House**, a B&B next door, is owned by the family of the historian G.M. Trevelyan, who first visited a century ago as a Cambridge undergraduate and later organized "hare and hound" hunts on the fells above – pursuing people rather than animals – which are still held here each year.

Seathwaite

A minor road south from Seatoller runs to **Seathwaite**, twenty minutes' walk away, where there's limited parking and a farmhouse campsite and camping barn. Seathwaite is a major departure point for **walks** up the likes of Great Gable and Scafell Pike, but prospective campers might like to know that it is always accused – unfairly according to locals – of being the wettest inhabited place in England, since it once recorded over 140 inches of rain in a single year.

ARRIVAL AND DEPARTURE   BORROWDALE

By car You're not allowed to park anywhere down the narrow Borrowdale road (B5289) outside the designated pay-and-display car parks. Scafell and Gable hikers can park by the road at Seathwaite, but you'll need to get there early.
By bus Public transport access is either by bus #77A (down the minor road on the west side of Derwent Water) or the highly scenic #78 "Borrowdale Rambler" (down the east side, the B5289). Both start in Keswick and stop at Grange and Seatoller, and other points on the way, with the #77A continuing up to Honister and across to Buttermere. A Honister and Borrowdale Day Rider ticket (buy from the driver, £8.50) gives a day's unlimited travel on both routes.
By boat Take Keswick Launch to Lodore or High Brandlehow for paths to Grange and Borrowdale.

ACCOMMODATION   SEE MAP PAGE 157

GRANGE-IN-BORROWDALE

Borrowdale Gates Grange, CA12 5UQ ☎017687 77204, ⓦborrowdale-gates.com. The traditional choice hereabouts is this superbly sited country-house hotel in two acres of wooded gardens (it's 200 yards up the western shore road, past the church). Panoramic views are a given, while some rooms have patio doors leading out onto the lawns, and others balconies. It also has a deserved reputation for its food – dinner is accompanied by more fine views from the restaurant. Parking. Closed three weeks Jan. **£220**

★ **Hollows Farm** Grange, CA12 5UQ ☎017687 77298, ⓦhollowsfarm.co.uk. Three B&B rooms set on a working National Trust hill farm, half a mile from Grange – breakfast is from the kitchen Aga. There's also a fantastic farm-field campsite with amazing views (and free hot showers at the farm), though pods are in the planning. B&B closed Dec & Jan, campsite closed Nov–Easter. Parking. Camping/person (including vehicle) **£7**, doubles **£72**

Leathes Head 1 mile north of Grange, CA12 5UY ☎017687 77247, ⓦleatheshead.co.uk. Welcoming family-run hotel with eleven spacious rooms, all with fell views – two in particular have windows on two sides, letting the light flood in. The elegant, polished Edwardian house has three interlinked lounges, including a conservatory with telescope, while the three-course dinner (£42.95) is the main event every night – this rate is slightly discounted if booked as part of a D, B&B package. Closed Dec–Jan. Parking. **£180**

ROSTHWAITE

Hazel Bank Rosthwaite, CA12 5XB, 200 yards from the road, over the bridge ☎017687 77248, ⓦhazelbank hotel.co.uk. Victorian-era country house set in its own serene gardens, with magnificent fell views to all sides. There are seven elegant rooms, often full, since guests return year after year, drawn by the seclusion, the intimate atmosphere and the well-regarded food – a daily-changing

SCAFELL PIKE AND GREAT GABLE

In good weather the minor road to Seathwaite is lined with cars by 9am as hikers take to the paths for the rugged climbs up some of the Lake District's major peaks, including Scafell Pike, England's highest mountain. Technically, they're not too difficult; as always, though, you should be well prepared and reasonably fit.

SCAFELL PIKE

For England's highest peak, **Scafell Pike** (3210ft), the approach from Seathwaite is through the farmyard and up to **Styhead Tarn** via Stockley Bridge. This is as far as many get, and on those all-too-rare glorious summer days the tarn is a fine place for a picnic. From the tarn the classic ascent is up the thrilling **Corridor Route**, then descending via Esk Hause – a fairly arduous eight-mile (6hr) loop walk in all from Seathwaite.

GREAT AND GREEN GABLES

A direct but very steep approach to **Great Gable** (2949ft) is possible from Styhead Tarn, though most people start out from Seathwaite campsite, climb up Sourmilk Ghyll and approach the peak via **Green Gable** (2628ft), also an eight-mile (6hr) return walk. However, the easiest Great Gable climb is actually from Honister Pass, following a six-mile (4hr) route past Grey Knotts and Brandreth to Green Gable, before rounding Great Gable and returning along an almost parallel path to the west.

four-course candlelit dinner (£45/person, or £39 for residents), with coffee and chocolates served afterwards in the cosy lounge. Closed Jan. Parking. £210

★ **Royal Oak** Rosthwaite, CA12 5XB ☎ 017687 77214, ⓦ royaloakhotel.co.uk. Right on the main village road, this traditional inn is the hikers' favourite – an expanded eighteenth-century farmhouse with converted barn annexe that they invite you to think of as "alpine pension" rather than boutique hotel. A hearty lakeland dinner (no choice, but vegetarian alternative available; included in the price) is served promptly at 7.30pm, a bacon-and-eggs breakfast at 8am. Weather conditions are posted daily, packed lunches and filled flasks supplied, but if the rain comes down you may prefer to repair to the firelit sitting room for tea and scones, or to the age-old stone-flagged bar. Parking. £150

Scafell Rosthwaite, CA12 5XB ☎ 017687 77208, ⓦ scafell.co.uk. Rosthwaite's grandest choice is an old country mansion set back from a trimmed lawn, with rooms in the main building (including a designer suite named after Barnes "Bouncing Bomb" Wallis, once a regular visitor) and some slightly less spacious ones in the annexe. Prices vary according to season, but special deals can bring the price down to as low as £60/person D, B&B. Despite the formalities, this is a relaxed, friendly place to stay, with an on-site restaurant and bar (see page 162). Parking. £180

Yew Tree Farm Rosthwaite, CA12 5XB, 200 yards up the narrow road opposite the shop ☎ 017687 77675, ⓦ borrowdaleyewtreefarm.co.uk. The Blands' traditional farmhouse B&B has the unofficial royal seal of approval, since Prince Charles has stayed here occasionally on incognito walking trips. You get a choice of three homely en-suite rooms (two doubles, one twin), and there's also a nice tearoom (see page 162). B&B closed Dec–Jan. No credit cards. Parking. £95

★ **YHA Borrowdale** Longthwaite, CA12 5XE, 1 mile south of Rosthwaite ☎ 0845 371 9624, ⓦ yha.org.uk/ hostel/borrowdale. Alpine-style lodge in a quiet riverside clearing (right on the footpath to Seatoller) that offers a really good budget base for hikers. It's a cosy set-up all round, from open fire in the lounge to home-cooked meals, and there are eight two-person bunk-rooms available, as well as larger dorm rooms for families and groups; there are also three, two-person pods (£59) as well as possibilities to pitch your tent. It's a peaceful place to stay, with riverside picnic tables in the grounds, but tends to get busy so it's best to book. Closed Jan & first two weeks in Feb. Dorms £30, two-person bunk-rooms £69, camping £15

SEATOLLER

★ **Seatoller House** Seatoller, CA12 5XN ☎ 017687 77218, ⓦ seatollerhouse.co.uk. Stay the night in a beautifully preserved seventeenth-century Borrowdale farmhouse, which boasts plenty of original panelling, plus library, parlour and roaring fire. The ten cottage-style rooms (four of which are en suite) are named after the wildlife hereabouts (Rabbit, Otter, Badger, Eagle etc), and in the beam-and-slate "Tea Bar" you can help yourself to drinks and cake. Breakfast, as well as communal four-course dinners (Wed–Mon 7pm) using local produce, are served at two oak tables in the former kitchen – it's an informality that many love, and return to experience year after year. Closed Nov–Feb. £150

SEATHWAITE

★ **Seathwaite Farm** Seathwaite ☎017687 77394, ⓦseathwaitefarmcamping.co.uk. The hardcore hikers' favourite, at the end of the Seathwaite road and last stop before the high fells. It has a very popular campsite (with shower block, toilets, and hot and cold water) as well as a barn (£7) sleeping ten (with bunk beds, kitchen and lounge with pot-bellied stove; there are gas cookers, but you'll need your own utensils, pots and pans), and a tipi (no bedding but there is a wood-burning stove) sleeping seven. Individuals are welcome, though it may be full at weekends with groups. No credit cards. Closed Nov–Easter. Camping/ person (includes vehicle) **£5**

EATING

SEE MAP PAGE 157

GRANGE-IN-BORROWDALE

Grange Bridge Cottage Grange, CA12 5UQ ☎017687 77201. After a splash about in the river, it's always nice to stop for a drink or an ice cream at the tearoom by the bridge. Feb half-term to mid-Nov daily 10am–5pm.

ROSTHWAITE

Flock-In Yew Tree Farm, Rosthwaite, CA12 5XB, 200 yards up the narrow road opposite the shop ☎017687 77675, ⓦborrowdaleyewtreefarm.co.uk. Sit in the garden over a tea or coffee (available in pints for thirsty walkers) at this tearoom, part of a very good farmhouse B&B (see page 161), and gaze across the valley fields

– some of the farm's Herdwicks end up in the tearoom's pasties, stews, sausages and burgers (meals £4–7). No credit cards. Feb–Dec Thurs–Tues 10am–5pm.

Scafell Rosthwaite, CA12 5XB ☎017687 77208, ⓦscafell.co.uk. The silver-service restaurant at Rosthwaite's grandest hotel (see page 161) offers traditional country-house "fayre"; dinner £32, Sun lunch £16. If you're after something less formal, head for the attached *Riverside Bar* – the only local pub – where you can eat cheaper bar meals (£6–14), including things like slow-cooked lamb. Restaurant Mon–Sat 6.30–9pm, Sun noon–2pm & 6.30–9pm; bar daily noon–11pm, kitchen noon–2.30pm & 6–9pm.

Honister Pass and Honister Slate Mine

Near the head of Borrowdale at Seatoller, the B5289 road cuts west, snaking up and over the dramatic **Honister Pass**, en route to Buttermere, on one of those unforgettable lakeland drives. At the top of the pass, below the craggy heights of **Fleetwith Pike** (2126ft), lie the unassuming buildings of **Honister Slate Mine** – an unexpectedly great place for daredevil adventurers with its deep mine tours and mountain activities. Come suitably clothed – it's either wet or windy up here at the best of times. The pass is also the starting point for climbs up Great Gable and back (6 miles; 4hr), and it's a day out you can do by bus, on the circular routes out of Keswick.

Honister Slate Mine

Honister Pass, CA12 5XN • Visitor centre, shop & café daily 9am–5pm • Mine tour £17.50, child £9.50, Day pass, including mine tour and Via Ferrata £55, child £47; individual attractions priced separately • Parking £5, refunded on mine tours or shop purchases • ☎017687 77230, ⓦhonister.com

Slate has been quarried from around Honister Pass since Elizabethan times, and by the eighteenth century the local green roofing slate was much sought after. Miners – living in wooden huts on the mountainside and working by candlelight – hand-dug eleven miles of tunnels and caverns within the bulk of Fleetwith Pike, leaving vicious scars, slate waste piles and old workings that are visible even today. Until well into the nineteenth century, the finished slate was either carried down the severe inclines in baskets on men's backs, or guided on heavy hand-pulled wooden sledges, since pit ponies couldn't get a foothold on the scree.

All this and more you can learn at England's last working slate mine, **Honister Slate Mine**, rescued by local entrepreneurs in 1996 and now in full operation again as a sustainable, commercial enterprise, complete with mine tours and adventure experiences. You'll need to book in advance if you want to join one of these, but it's free to look around the visitor centre, factory trail, slate stone garden and shop, and

PEOPLE AND PLACES: THAT'S MINE

Reviving Honister Slate Mine was the personal vision of local businessman **Mark Weir**, who died (aged 45) in a helicopter accident in 2011. Despite never having worked in the industry, Mark had bought the disused 300-year-old slate mine in the 1990s and turned it into a thriving commercial business – partly as a nod to his grandfather, who once worked at the mine, but also "to create real jobs for local people". Born and bred in Borrowdale, Mark had been conscious of the mine's demise – "like the right arm of the valley being missing", he said – and was proud that the old skills had been revived and that Westmorland green slate was once again being extracted in significant volumes.

The other challenge was to give visitors an experience they wouldn't forget, and there's certainly no chance of that on the high-adrenaline tours of mine and mountain. Mark's family continues to run the mine – you might find a family member leading a tour – and they are heavily involved in the legacy project that Mark was working on at the time of his death (subject of a BBC documentary, *Tales of a National Park*). His grand idea was to run a **zip-wire** from Fleetwith Pike all the way down to the visitor centre, a plan that – until its approval by the Lake District Park Authority in 2019 – had met with some resistance from planning and other organizations. It is expected to be completed by 2021.

see some of the revived skills in action, like the "docking, riving and dressing" of the slate. All-in **day-pass tickets** are a good option if you want to do a mine tour and the Via Ferrata.

Mine tours

Daily 10.30am, 12.30pm, 2pm & 3.30pm • £17.50, child £9.50, reservations essential

The best way to get an idea of what working life was really like in past centuries is by donning a hard hat and lamp and joining one of the hugely entertaining ninety-minute **guided mine tours**, which lead you through narrow tunnels into illuminated, echoing, dripping caverns. A more extreme version of the standard "Kimberley" tour takes you around "The Edge", a high-level shortcut into one of the most extensive mine workings. Tours run in all weathers (in fact, it's one of the best wet-weather attractions around), but make sure you wrap up warm.

Via Ferrata

Tours daily, various times; children have to be over 10 and over 130cm (4ft 3in) tall; reservations essential • Via Ferrata Classic £40; Via Ferrata Xtreme £45; Infinity Bridge by arrangement only • ☎ 017687 77714, ⊕ honister.com

The **Via Ferrata** ("Iron Way") uses a system pioneered in the Italian Dolomites as a way to get troops and equipment over unforgiving mountain terrain. By means of a permanently fixed cableway and clip-on harness, you follow the miners' old route up the exposed face of the mountain, clambering up and along iron rungs, ladders and supports to reach the top of Fleetwith Pike, before walking back down to the visitor centre. The whole thing takes two to three hours to complete, and it's a truly exhilarating experience – but to see what you're in for you should definitely check out the photos and videos first on the website.

There are two options – as well as the introductory **Classic** route, there's also the far more challenging Via Ferrata **Xtreme**, which basically decides that you haven't been scared silly enough and throws in more vertical climbs, cliff-face ladders, an Indiana Jones-style "Infinity Bridge" across a yawning 2000ft chasm and a giant scramble net.

ARRIVAL AND DEPARTURE HONISTER PASS AND HONISTER SLATE MINE

By car There are sporadic side-of-the-road parking places up on Honister Pass, though there's also a "walker's car park" at Honister Slate Mine (£5/day).

By bus The #77/77A runs up to Honister from Keswick on a circular route, coming either via Borrowdale (40min) or via Whinlatter and Buttermere (1hr).

YHA Honister Hause Honister Pass, CA12 5XN ☎ 0845 371 9522, ⓦ yha.org.uk/hostel/honister-hause. At the top of Honister Pass (near the slate mine) stands this isolated, low-slung youth hostel, superbly sited for mountain walking. It's only small, with 26 beds in rooms sleeping either two or four people, and you'll need to be pretty self-sufficient as, other than the café at the slate mine, there are no other local facilities up here (the nearest pub is a winding drive back down in Borrowdale). But there's a full meal service, breakfast to dinner, and a self-catering kitchen. Closed mid-Nov to Easter; also closed Tues & Wed Easter–May, Sept & Oct. Dorms **£21.50**

Threlkeld to Thirlmere

The A591 between Keswick and Grasmere runs directly past **Thirlmere**, and this is the way the buses go. But if you're in no particular hurry, it's more pleasant to detour east to **Threlkeld** first and then turn south along the minor road through **St John's in the Vale**. You can come this way entirely on foot too – it's an extremely attractive route (7 miles; 4hr) – and take the bus back up the A591 to complete the circuit back to Keswick.

Threlkeld

Keswick's disused railway path (signposted by the *Keswick Country House* hotel on Station Road) runs straight to **Threlkeld** ("Thrall's Spring"), three miles east of Keswick. The riverside walk's a delight, enhanced by the promise of a drink in one of Threlkeld's charming old pubs at the end, either the *Horse & Farrier* or the *Salutation* (aka *The Sally Inn*). Threlkeld is also the starting point for many of the strenuous hikes up Blencathra and there's parking at a couple of places up the signposted road to the Blencathra Centre.

Threlkeld Quarry

Easter to mid-Oct daily 10am–5pm • Museum and site £3; mine tour £5; railway £3 • ☎ 017687 79747, ⓦ threlkeldquarryandminingmuseum.co.uk • From the A66 near Threlkeld, take the B5322 (St John's in the Vale road) and follow the signs through the old quarry works

A century ago Threlkeld was a busy, dirty industrial centre, with lead and copper mined in the valley and granite quarried from the hillsides for road- and railway-making. At **Threlkeld Quarry**, volunteers help run a fascinating open-air industrial history museum which covers all facets of the local mining industry. There's a comprehensive indoor collection of mining artefacts and minerals, but you're also welcome to roam around the site and have a look inside the locomotive shed and machine shop, where restoration work is being carried out on the impressive vintage excavators and quarry machinery. There are 45-minute guided tours down a re-created lead and copper mine – children will enjoy the underground experience and gritty anecdotes – while the re-laid narrow-gauge mineral railway provides rides up into the inner quarry and back.

St John's in the Vale

A bucolic walk from Threlkeld cuts south from the railway path, across Threlkeld Bridge and through the fields into **St John's in the Vale**; the B5322 shadows the same route. The old chapel of St John's and views of the Blencathra ridges behind are the draws, with the southward path hugging the base of **High Rigg** (1163ft) and eventually following the river to *Low Bridge End Farm* (see page 165), where there's a rustic tea garden and roaming hens, plus a woodland trail and craft workshop. From the farm the A591 is less than a mile away – on the way, keep an eye out for climbers scaling **Castle Rock** across the river, Walter Scott's model for the fairy castle in his poem *The Bridal of Triermain*.

Thirlmere

Thirlmere, a five-mile-long reservoir at the southern end of St John's in the Vale, was created from two smaller lakes at the end of the nineteenth century when Manchester's booming population and industry required water. More than a hundred miles of gravity-drawn tunnels and pipes still supply the city with water from here. In an ultimately unsuccessful campaign – but one that foreshadowed the founding of the National Trust – the fight against the creation of Thirlmere was led by John Ruskin and other proto-environmentalists, outraged at a high-handed raising of the water level, which drowned the hamlet of Armboth and various small farms. No one was best pleased either by the subsequent regimental planting of thousands of conifers around the edge (to help prevent erosion), which dramatically changed the local landscape. The century since the creation of the reservoir has softened the scene – these are among the oldest planted trees in the National Park – and you'd be hard pushed now to tell that Thirlmere was man-made.

The eastern shore

The only side of Thirlmere served by public transport is the **eastern** one, from where some visitors choose to make the climb up Helvellyn and back – in which case, you'll be pleased at the thought of a pint afterwards in the roadside *King's Head* at **Thirlspot**.

The western shore

For Thirlmere's waterside paths, forest trails and viewpoints, you need to be on the minor road that hugs the **western shore**. There are several small car parks, with trails leading off from each, for instance at **Launchy Gill**, an oak and birch woodland Site of Special Scientific Interest. Alternatively, the #555 bus can drop you at the foot of the reservoir for the six-mile walk up the western side and around to Thirlspot.

ARRIVAL AND DEPARTURE   THRELKELD TO THIRLMERE

By bus It's a quick ride on bus #X4/X5 or #73A from Keswick to Threlkeld. For Thirlmere, take any bus along the A591 between Grasmere and Keswick to reach the eastern side – there are stops at Wythburn and at the *King's Head*, Thirlspot.

ACCOMMODATION AND EATING   SEE MAP PAGE 142

King's Head Thirlspot, CA12 4TN, on A595 ☎017687 72393, ⌨lakedistrictinns.co.uk. Even without the gorgeous location, this old coaching inn at the foot of Helvellyn would be handy for a pint and a bite to eat – there's a bar and beer garden as well as a more formal restaurant. The rooms are bright (the "Superior" comes with a four-poster bed), and breakfast is included. Parking. Daily noon–11pm; bar meals noon–9.30pm, restaurant 7–9pm. **£80**

★ **Low Bridge End Farm** St John's in the Vale, CA12 4TS ☎017687 79242, ⌨campingbarn.com. A peaceful hideaway with a couple of overnight accommodation options – a self-catering apartment in the old stable and hayloft (sleeps four; £295–405/week) or overnight on a mattress in the camping barn (sleeps up to eight, breakfast and packed lunches available). Walkers can stroll right through, calling in at the tea garden for home-made cakes and local ice cream – it's always open, with a kettle, tea, coffee, cakes and an honesty box left out when the owners aren't around. Parking. Camping barn/person **£9.50**

Whinlatter Forest Park

On the heights to the west of Keswick lie the extensive woodland plantations of **Whinlatter Forest Park**, England's only true mountain forest. It's easy to spend a day here doing all sorts of outdoor activities and the excellent visitor centre can put you on track – in particular, the park has the Lake District's two longest purpose-built mountain-bike trails, including the challenging twelve-mile **Altura Trail**. Bikes and trail guides are available at the park's bike centre – hardcore show-offs can even rent a helmet-cam. There are also nine waymarked hiking trails (30min–3hr), including a couple specifically for children and families, while **Go Ape** puts gung-ho visitors 40ft up in the trees on a high-ropes and zip-wire adventure course.

WALKS FROM WHINLATTER AND BRAITHWAITE

There are plenty of signposted **walks and trails** within Whinlatter Forest Park, all detailed on the park's website – or ask at the visitor centre. Some start from the main car park, and others from the forest car parks at Revelin Moss and Noble Knott. For great views on a good day, Grisedale Pike is the best local climb, which can be incorporated into a much longer circular, or "horseshoe", walk. It's one of the Lakes' best one-day hikes, and dedicated Wainwright peak-baggers can knock off up to ten summits on the one circuit. You can access the hike from various points in the forest, though the traditional starting place is the village of **Braithwaite**, just below Whinlatter.

GRISEDALE PIKE

From the small quarry car park on the Whinlatter road, just above Braithwaite village, it's 90min to the top of **Grisedale Pike** (2593ft), along a very well worn route. Moving on to **Hopegill Head** (2525ft) – from where the Isle of Man can be seen on the best days – you then drop to the head of the valley at Coledale Hause for the straightforward valley return to the village (total trip 5 miles; 3hr).

COLEDALE HORSESHOE

Unless you're pushed for time, on a clear day you'd be mad not to complete the circuit since, having gained the height at Grisedale Pike and Hopegill Head, there's a relatively small amount of extra climbing involved to return to Braithwaite via **Sail** (2530ft), **Outerside** (1863ft) and **Barrow** (1494ft) – with a possible diversion to **Grasmoor** (2791ft; superb Crummock Water views) en route, and an alternative return via **Scar Crags** (2205ft) and **Causey Pike** (2035ft; Newlands Valley views). It's a hugely satisfying circuit, with changing panoramas all the way round. Depending on your peak choices, it's nine to twelve miles – six to eight hours – on clearly defined paths and ridges, with just the odd bit of scrambling.

Inside the centre, seasonal exhibitions concentrate on the area's wildlife, most notably Bassenthwaite's wild **ospreys** (see page 168), which can usually be seen on the visitor centre's live video nest-cam link (Easter–Aug only). The forest is also a national red squirrel reserve, while roe deer, badgers, foxes and buzzards all live in the park too.

ARRIVAL AND DEPARTURE   WHINLATTER FOREST PARK

By car From Keswick, take the A66 (west), then turn off on the B5292, which climbs west past Braithwaite, en route to Buttermere or Cockermouth – it's 3 miles to the visitor centre car park, where all-day parking costs around £8.

By bus The regular bus service to Whinlatter is the #77/#77A from Keswick, a 15min ride.

INFORMATION AND ACTIVITIES

Bike rental Cyclewise bike centre (daily 10am–5pm; ☎017687 78711, ⓦcyclewise.co.uk) rents out mountain bikes from £21/3hrs, £29/day.

Go Ape Sessions daily during Feb half-term and Easter–Oct, otherwise weekends only in Feb, March and Nov; closed Tues in term-time and from Dec to mid-Feb; advance booking essential, online or by phone (£33; ☎0845 643 9215, ⓦgoape.co.uk). It takes a good two hours to get around – there's a minimum age of 10 and a minimum height of 4ft 7in, but apart from that anyone can do it.

Tourist office Whinlatter Visitor Centre (Jan Sat & Sun 10am–4pm; Feb, March & Oct–Dec daily 10am–4pm; April–Sept daily 10am–5pm; ☎017687 78469, ⓦforestryengland.uk/whinlatter); they've also got an exhibition here on the ospreys at Bassenthwaite, with a live cam trained on the nest (see page 168).

EATING   SEE MAP PAGE 142

Siskins Café Whinlatter Visitor Centre, Whinlatter Forest Park, CA12 5TW ☎017687 78410. The visitor centre's alpine-style café serves good food (meals £3–8) and proper coffee, and has an outdoor terrace (with bird feeder) that looks over the plantations and down the valley. Daily Easter–Oct 10am–5pm, Nov–Easter 10am–4.30pm; closed two weeks in Jan.

Bassenthwaite Lake

Pub-quiz fans love **Bassenthwaite Lake** as it's the only "lake" in the Lake District (all the others are known as waters or meres). It's also the northernmost of the major patches of water, but it doesn't receive much attention otherwise, partly because of the difficulty in actually reaching its shores. Although just three miles from Keswick, and linked by the River Derwent which flows across the broad agricultural plain between the two, most of the shoreline is privately owned with restrictions in place to preserve the lake's rich variety of plants and animals. The shoreline habitat, for example, is the best preserved in the National Park, where more than seventy species of bird and wildfowl (including **osprey**) winter and breed, while Bassenthwaite is one of the few places in Britain where the vendace, a nine-inch fish related to other Arctic species, is found. However, the habitats are currently under threat from increased silting and pollution, and invasion by alien plants and other species, all factors that have prompted a long-term lake restoration programme to improve the water quality at Bassenthwaite.

Dubwath Silver Meadows

Always open • Free • ⓦ dubwathsilvermeadows.org.uk • Drive up A66 from Keswick, ignore the first left signposted turn to the *Pheasant* and take the second left turn instead (opposite the Dubwath turn); the site is just on your right, through a gate by a bus stop, with the inn a bit further along

One of the newest nature reserves in Cumbria has been established in the water meadows of Dubwath, just west of Bassenthwaite. At **Dubwath Silver Meadows**, a 1.5-mile-long circular boardwalk runs through waist-high wild flowers and meadow plants, with some very rustic wattle, daub and thatch hides provided at various points so that you can spy on the resident roe deer, butterflies and visiting birds. It's an enjoyable walk, despite the ever-present traffic noise from the A66, and the only current problem is finding the site – the entrance is about two hundred yards north of the *Pheasant Inn.*

4

Lakes Distillery

Setmurthy, CA13 9SJ • Sun–Wed 10am–6pm, Thurs–Sat 10am–7pm; last tour 1hr before closing • £12.50 • ☎ 01768 788850, ⓦ lakesdistillery.com • About 10 miles northwest of Keswick via the A66 and B5291; there is parking on site

There's been a long history of moonshine production in the Lakes, but it took until 2014 for this, Cumbria's first commercial distillery, to set up shop inside the attractive stone shell of a nineteenth-century model farm. With water drawn from the River Derwent, the **Lakes Distillery** currently produces a single malt and a couple of blended whiskies, as well as vodka (unambiguously branded as The Lakes Vodka) and gin (The Lakes Gin). Highlight of the hour-long tour – which also takes in the copper distilling vats and heady fumes inside the bonded warehouse, full of wooden barrels – is an amazing, vertigo-inducing video following the Derwent from the fell tops to the sea, all filmed in one continuous shot. The tour rounds off with a tasting session, after which you might want to stock up with a bottle or two from the shop.

Lake District Wildlife Park

Bassenthwaite, at the head of Bassenthwaite Lake CA12 4RD • Daily: March–Oct 10am–5pm, Nov–Feb 10am–4pm; last entry 1hr before closing • £9.95, family ticket £34 • ☎ 017687 76239, ⓦ lakedistrictwildlifepark.co.uk • Follow signs from A591 or A66; it's around the back of *Armathwaite Hall* hotel; or bus #554 from Keswick to *Castle Inn*

Lake District Wildlife Park is well worth an extended visit, since what started life as a simple animal farm is now a highly individual wildlife-conservation project, presenting domestic, endangered and exotic animals within an educational framework. A re-created early medieval roundhouse is used to demonstrate sustainable crafts, while in

LINSKELDFIELD TARN

Sheltered in farmland just north of Bassenthwaite, **Linskeldfield Tarn** (open access; free; ☎01900 822136, ⓦ linskeldfield.co.uk) is a real hidden gem – a farm **wildlife reserve**, set in six acres of peat and wetland, and home to otters, red squirrels and all manner of wildfowl. There's a wooden birdwatching hide (spotting charts provided), and though the viewing is best in winter or spring there's always something to see. Even if you don't know your widgeon from your pintail, you're going to like the farm's grazing ostriches – and you can hardly miss the eighteen thousand free-range hens. To find the sanctuary, turn off the A591 at Bewaldeth, just north of the *Castle Inn* junction, and then keep an eye out for signs for Sunderland and the farm.

the surrounding enclosures you'll come across a lively troop of gibbons, plus lemurs, meerkats, marmosets, tapirs, red pandas and Eurasian lynx, among many other species. Handling the animals is encouraged (even the snakes) during feeding programmes, demonstrations and other activities – in spring children can help feed a newborn lamb. There are daily flying displays with the hawks, vultures and owls, plus children's play areas, tractor and pony rides, a tearoom and picnic sites. There's always something going on, though school holidays tend to offer the pick of the child-oriented events, like the popular candlelit tours in December.

Dodd Wood

Three miles north of Keswick on A591 • Always open • Free, though parking fee charged; park here too for Bassenthwaite wild ospreys and Mirehouse (see below) • ⓦ forestryengland.uk/dodd-wood • Bus #73/73A or #554 from Keswick

The only permitted parking places close to the east shore are at the heavily planted Forestry Commission land of **Dodd Wood**. Starting from the car park at the *Old Sawmill Tearooms* (see page 169), there are four marked trails of varying length. Some of the crowded pines, planted in the 1920s, are now 120ft high, which makes the climb (3 miles; 3hr return) to the heights of **Dodd** itself (1612ft) a rather disorienting experience. But native trees – including oak, ash, hawthorn and hazel – are being replanted in the wood to prevent hillside soil erosion, while roe deer and some of the Lakes' few surviving red squirrels are occasionally seen around here. Dodd Wood is also the best place to see Bassenthwaite's famous **wild ospreys**.

The Bassenthwaite wild ospreys

Viewpoints April–Aug daily 10am–5pm • ⓦ ospreywatch.co.uk

Wild ospreys recolonized Bassenthwaite in 2001 and, although there's no guarantee, they have returned every year since to nest and breed on the lakeshore, below the woods. The ospreys usually arrive at the beginning of April; the eggs hatch in June, and then both adults and youngsters head back to Africa in August or September.

A quarter-mile path (15min uphill climb) from the *Old Sawmill Tearooms* leads to the lower viewpoint, with an upper viewpoint another thirty-minute climb beyond. High-powered telescopes are provided, or bring your own binoculars (visibility is best in the mornings) – on most days during the osprey season, you'll be able to see them fishing and feeding, hovering over the lake, then plunging feet first to catch roach, perch, pike and trout. For an up-close-and-personal look, don't miss the live, online video feed from the nests.

Mirehouse

Bassenthwaite Lake, CA12 4QE • House Easter–Oct Wed, Thurs & Sun 1.30–4.30pm; gardens Easter–Oct daily 10am–5pm • Gardens only £4; house and gardens £8.50, family £23 • ☎017687 72287, ⓦ mirehouse.co.uk • Pay-and-display parking at Dodd Wodd, 3 miles north of Keswick, on A591; bus #73 or #554 from Keswick

Mirehouse (built 1666) has been the manor-house home of the Spedding family since 1802 and is still lived in today, which explains the restricted opening days but also lends it a welcoming, informal air that's quite delightful. A pianist plays in the Music Room as you wind through the other rooms and corridors, while the claim that "little has been thrown away over the years" is demonstrably true – gentlemen's clay pipes, a Victorian knife-cleaner and an unexploded World War I grenade-turned-paperweight are just a few of the items displayed. Mirehouse has notable literary connections: Sir James Spedding (1808–81) was a respected biographer of Francis Bacon, and a friend of Tennyson (who is supposed to have sought inspiration for his *Morte d'Arthur* here) and Thomas Carlyle among others, and the varied portraits, drawings, manuscripts, letters and books on show reveal the close relationships that many had with Carlyle's "dear hospitable Spedding".

Outside are **gardens**, lawns, mixed woodland (with children's adventure playgrounds) and wildflower meadows, all connected by a lovely lakeside walk that takes around an hour to complete.

St Bega's church
Daily 9am–5pm; services first and third Sun of the month

A short diversion from the Mirehouse grounds runs down through the fields and past two-hundred-year-old oak trees to **St Bega's church** on the shores of Bassenthwaite. Originally Norman, and heavily restored, it's completely serene and protected by the looming flanks of Skiddaw; authors from Tennyson (again) to Melvyn Bragg (who set his Anglo-Celtic epic *Credo* here) have been drawn to the landscape. There's a public right of way from the road as well, so you don't need to pay for Mirehouse to visit the church.

ARRIVAL AND DEPARTURE   BASSENTHWAITE LAKE

By car The west shore as far as Dubwath and its wetland nature reserve is paralleled by the busy A66, but the main attractions are on the east shore of the lake, reached on the narrow A591 from Keswick.

By bus Main bus routes are the #554 and #73, which stop at Mirehouse, Dodd Wood (for the ospreys), Bassenthwaite village and *Castle Inn* (for the Wildlife Park).

ACCOMMODATION   SEE MAP PAGE 142

★ **Armathwaite Hall** Bassenthwaite, CA12 4RE, on B5291 at northern end of the lake ☎017687 76551, ⓦarmathwaite-hall.com. Live the noble life at one of the Lake District's most glamorous country-house hotels, a restored sixteenth-century hall set in 400 acres of deer park and woodland, with terraces overlooking rabbit-filled lawns and the lake beyond. There are obligingly attentive staff at every turn, and the oak-panelled lounges, leaded windows, soaring stonework and oil paintings are just what you'd expect, while rooms, though traditional in style, are perfectly appointed in eight different categories with varying outlooks (up to £500 for a studio suite). There's also a very fancy spa, plus infinity pool and outdoor hot tub,

and all sorts of country pursuits available. The *Courtyard Bar and Brasserie* (mains £14–19) has a contemporary menu (including pizza and tapas), or there's fine dining in the more formal *Lake View* restaurant (lunch from £19.95, dinner £46.95). Parking. Bar/brasserie daily 10am–9.30pm, kitchen noon–9.30pm; restaurant daily noon–2.30pm & 7–9pm. **£220**

Pheasant Inn Bassenthwaite, CA13 9YE, off A66, just before Dubwath ☎017687 76234, ⓦthe-pheasant.co.uk. This coaching inn offers upmarket dining (see page 169); why not round off the experience by booking into one of the fifteen characterful rooms (two are in the Garden Lodge, while three superior rooms offer a bit more space)? Parking. **£160**

EATING   SEE MAP PAGE 142

In addition to fine dining in the swanky surrounds of *Armathwaite Hall* (see above) there are a number of good options for more relaxed **eating**.

★ **Old Sawmill Tearooms** Mirehouse, CA12 4QE ☎017687 74317, ⓦtheoldsawmill.co.uk. Best place locally for a snack or a daytime meal is the seasonal café opposite Mirehouse, housed in what was a working sawmill until 1970 – you'll park right by it if you come to see the

ospreys. There's always a veggie soup of the day, while alongside the usual sandwiches, home-made cakes and puddings, are house specials like Cumberland sausage in a warm roll with apple sauce or a Welsh rarebit muffin (dishes £3–8). Easter–Oct daily 10am–4.30pm.

Pheasant Inn Bassenthwaite, CA13 9YE, off A66, just before Dubwath ☎017687 76234, ⓦthe-pheasant.co.uk. An old, very upmarket coaching inn (see page 169), set just

4

back from the main road in its own lay-by, that still looks the part, especially in the carefully preserved period bar and comfortable lounges filled with flowers. There's a bistro for classic bar meals (mains £14–18), served at lunch and dinner – you can have lunch in the garden, weather permitting – while evenings in the polished *Fell* restaurant (mains £14–21) are more formal affairs. Parking. Bistro daily noon–2.30pm & 6–9pm; restaurant Tues–Thurs 6.30–9pm.

Sun Bassenthwaite, CA12 4QP ❶ 017687 76439, ⓦ sun innbassenthwaite.co.uk. At the heart of the pretty village, the *Sun* retains its seventeenth-century air – oak beams, open fires – and serves traditional bar meals (mains £11–14), which you can eat outside on a warm day. The views are lovely too, up to the fells and Skiddaw in particular. Mon–Sat 4–11pm, Sun noon–10.30pm; kitchen Mon–Sat 5–8.30pm, Sun noon–2.30pm & 5–8pm.

Back o' Skiddaw

People often complain that the Lake District is too crowded, that tourists have overwhelmed the infrastructure and transformed the villages – none of which, happily, is true of the **Back o' Skiddaw**, the local name for the arc of fells and valleys that stretches around the back of Skiddaw mountain, tucked into the northernmost section of the National Park. For the most part it's countryside that really does deserve the epithet "rolling", with farmland tumbling down from Skiddaw's gentle humps to encircle small hamlets and villages that see little tourist traffic. And if you really want to get away from it all, consider the hike into the middle of nowhere – there's no road – for a night's stay at England's highest and most remote hostel, the incomparable *Skiddaw House*.

Uldale and Ireby

From the *Castle Inn* junction, half a mile from the northern edge of Bassenthwaite Lake, the sweeping road into Uldale ends three miles further on at **Uldale** village where the cow dung on the road announces its farming credentials. Farming in the Lakes is a precarious business at the best of times: what it must have been like in the past in "wolf's dale" doesn't bear thinking about. Walpole used the quiet village and moorland surroundings as the backdrop in the middle two Herries novels, *Judith Paris* and *The Fortress*, with the fictional Fell House as the Herries family lair. Fortified by a drink from the *Snooty Fox* pub, you can press on to tiny **Over Water**, one and a half miles south – it's the northernmost splash of water in the Lake District, with the farms of Orthwaite beyond. Only bad things await, surely, on the heights of **Great Cockup** (1720ft), an easy two-mile walk east from Orthwaite.

In the other direction, Uldale's **St James' church** lies a full mile from the village on the Ireby road, a pretty building with some interesting old gravestones and uninterrupted fell views. Another mile beyond is sleepy **Ireby**, with its lion's-head drinking trough and a beer garden (and great bar food) at the venerable *Black Lion*.

Caldbeck

Prosperity came easily to **Caldbeck**, six miles east of Ireby and just twelve from Carlisle, and it remains one of the Lakes' most appealing villages. The fast-flowing "cold stream" from which it takes its name provided the power for the rapid expansion in the number of mills here in the seventeenth and eighteenth centuries. Corn, wool and wooden bobbins flowed out, lead and copper from the fells was carted in; and the many surviving contemporary buildings and pastel-coloured cottages (look for the dates carved on the lintels above the doors) attest to its wealth. A signposted quarter-mile walk from the car park up to the limestone gorge known as **The Howk** shows you the river in all its rushing glory, as well as the restored ruins of one of the old bobbin mills.

St Kentigern's church
Caldbeck, CA7 8EW

The village is anchored by **St Kentigern's church**, dedicated to the sixth-century saint better known as Mungo, who journeyed from Scotland through Cumberland to Wales to preach the gospel to the heathen Saxons and Celts. The well he is supposed to have used for baptism lies by the packhorse bridge, next to the churchyard. The first stone church here was built in the twelfth century, and although a medieval tombstone survives in the chancel, today's church bears the brunt of heavy nineteenth-century restoration. No matter, since all the interest is outside in the **churchyard**, where you'll easily find the ornate marble tombstone of **John Peel** of Ruthwaite (d. 1854) – the fox hunter of *D'ye ken John Peel* fame, not the famous DJ – emblazoned with reliefs of hunting horns and his faithful hound. Peel was just one of several hardened and hard-drinking nineteenth-century hunting men of local repute; his fame today derives squarely from the song, written after his death by one of his friends. Eighteen paces from his grave, walking away from the church, is the tombstone of the Harrisons of Todcrofts: Richard was a simple farmer; it's his wife Mary (d. 1837) who is better known – as Mary, the Maid of Buttermere, the most celebrated beauty of her day (see page 198). These days, Caldbeck's most famous resident is mountaineer and writer Chris Bonington.

Priest's Mill
Caldbeck, CA7 8DR • Shops Feb–Dec daily 11am–4pm • Free • ☎ 016974 78267, ⊛ priestsmillcaldbeck.co.uk

Priest's Mill, at the back of the church, was a corn mill for more than two hundred years, but was restored in 1986 and has been turned into a little arts and business centre, with a café, goldsmith and jeweller, and cooperative wool-shop among the outlets. It's always worth a browse, and on a sunny day you can sit outside on the terrace of the old mill with a coffee and cake (see page 173). A riverside path runs from the mill back to the village green.

High Pike
For a stretch of the legs, Caldbeck's most favoured local walk is the climb up **High Pike** (2157ft), the fell to the south, mined for its minerals in the nineteenth century. The most obvious route is from Nether Row, a mile south of Caldbeck – count on five miles, three

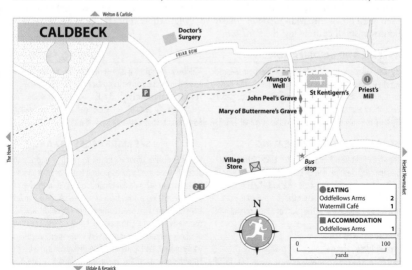

hours, there and back. Views from the cairn and bench at the summit sweep from the Solway Firth to the Yorkshire hills, with Blencathra and Bowscale Fell in the foreground.

Hesket Newmarket

There's a path from Caldbeck one and a half miles southeast through the fields to the small eighteenth-century village of **Hesket Newmarket**, which straddles a long village green. Markets were long held here, though the last was a century ago, and the prosperous village once supported half a dozen inns; the *Old Crown* by the green is the only survivor. Incidentally, if Caldbeck can boast John Peel and Chris Bonington as local famous names, Hesket Newmarket is not to be outdone – road-haulage king and spotter's cult hero Eddie Stobart started out here in the family firm.

Carrock Fell

The road south from Caldbeck and Hesket Newmarket winds the eight miles back to the A66, effectively down the eastern boundary of the Lake District. Away to the east lie fields not fells, and beyond is the Eden Valley and Yorkshire. The bulk looming to the west, behind Blencathra and Bannerdale, is **Carrock Fell** (2174ft), best climbed from Stone Ends Farm – you can park by the road – three miles from Hesket Newmarket.

The fell is riddled with abandoned mines (keep back – exploration is dangerous), while a huge tangle of fallen rocks litters the hillside: Charles Dickens and Wilkie Collins had a particularly disastrous time climbing Carrock Fell in mist, described in Dickens' *The Lazy Tours of Two Idle Apprentices* (1857).

Mosedale and Mungrisdale

The broad valley of **Mosedale** has a minor road running up to meet the Cumbria Way at the valley's head. Day-walkers usually head instead for **Bowscale Tarn**, 1600ft up, scooped dramatically out of Bowscale Fell and ringed by crags. It's an easy walk (1hr) from the roadside parking at nearby Bowscale, following a clear bridleway for much of the route.

The summit of **Bowscale Fell** (2306ft) itself is reached from the tarn by a further, gut-busting, 45-minute climb, and to make a circular walk of it (5 miles; 4hr) you can then drop down into **Mungrisdale**, a narrower valley whose foot embraces a few stone houses, a small church and the *Mill Inn*.

ARRIVAL AND INFORMATION BACK O' SKIDDAW

By car Caldbeck is a good 30min drive from Keswick, whichever way round you go – take care on the narrow roads, which can be slippery in winter. There's free parking in Caldbeck near the river.

By bus The only public transport is the seasonal #73/73A

"Caldbeck Rambler" bus, which runs to all the places covered in this section on a circular route from Keswick.

Tourist information Check local information at ⓦ caldbeckvillage.co.uk – it's especially good for finding B&Bs and other accommodation in the area.

ACCOMMODATION AND EATING SEE MAPS PAGES 142 AND 171

The area might be off-radar for many Lake District visitors, but that just results in nice surprises for those who do venture this way, not least some excellent places to stay and – in the *Crown* at Hesket Newmarket – a terrific example of a thriving village pub at the heart of a local community.

BACK O'SKIDDAW

★ **Skiddaw House** Back o' Skiddaw, CA12 4QX ☎ 07747 174293, ⓦ skiddawhouse.co.uk. At 1550ft,

this is England's toughest hostel to reach – and it's an absolute beauty, a former shooting lodge and shepherds' shelter set in magnificent mountain terrain in the lee of Skiddaw. It takes a good hour or so to walk the 3.5 miles from the nearest car park (Latrigg, above Keswick), and it's completely off-grid – no mains electricity, central heating or phone reception, and only very basic shop provisions (carry in fresh food for dinner, though you can buy a beer). Furnishings and facilities are on the rudimentary side, but hikers and outdoor types love its well-worn rustic ways and it makes a wonderful base for some stupendous walks right off the doorstep. Reservations are pretty much essential (there are only 22 beds, in eight, four-/five-bed dorms), and check directions (on the website) and weather conditions before setting out. Closed Nov–Feb. Dorms **£20**

CALDBECK

Oddfellows Arms Caldbeck, CA7 8EA ☎ 016974 78227, ⓦ oddfellows-caldbeck.co.uk. There's old-school B&B (shampoo in sachets, UHT milk pots) at the village pub – most of the rooms are in a converted mill at the back. It's better for home-cooked bar meals, Cumberland sausage to slow-roast lamb (most mains £10–15), which are really popular, especially at weekends when the place is often packed. Parking. Daily 11am–11pm; kitchen Mon–Sat noon–9pm, Sun noon–8pm. **£80**

Watermill Café Priest's Mill, Caldbeck, CA7 8DR ☎ 016974 78267. A nice place for snacks, meals, and Fair Trade drinks, especially when the weather's good enough to sit outside on the riverside terrace. It's not completely veggie, but there are always specials of broccoli bakes and the like (meals £4.50–9), while changing exhibitions showcase the work of local artists and photographers. Feb–Oct daily 9am–5pm.

HESKET NEWMARKET

★ **Old Crown** Hesket Newmarket, CA7 8JG ☎ 016974 78288, ⓦ theoldcrownpub.co.uk. A cosy local of great charm, owned by a local cooperative (the first such in Britain), and brewing half-a-dozen tremendous ales out the back in the Hesket Newmarket Brewery. It's a traditional place with an antique bar and a ceiling full of hanging tankards. The food is very popular, too – from local gammon and lamb to the speciality curries (mains £10–15) – and you're advised to book for dinner. Mon–Thurs 5.30–11pm, Fri & Sat noon–11pm, Sun noon–10.30pm; kitchen Tues–Thurs 6–8pm, Fri–Sun noon–2pm & 6.30–8.30pm.

MUNGRISDALE

Mill Inn Mungrisdale, CA11 0XR ☎ 017687 79632, ⓦ robinsonsbrewery.com. A stone millwheel props up the bar, while outside is a riverside beer garden. The half-dozen rooms have been nicely refurbished and the inn serves local, seasonal produce (mains £9–14), including lots of fresh fish (and a memorable steak and ale pie). Parking. Daily noon–11pm; kitchen noon–8pm. **£75**

4

The western fells and valleys

BLACK COMBE FELL AND SILECROFT BEACH

The western fells and valleys

The western fells and valleys contain some of the National Park's most dramatic scenery, from stunning lakeland vistas and isolated hamlets to deep forests and a little-visited coastline. "No part of the country is more distinguished by sublimity", claimed Wordsworth, and he had a point. Today, the region is hardly unknown, but it doesn't have anything like the visitor density of the north or south Lakes, in part because it's more difficult to reach. Public transport is limited and both the main road (A595) and railway stick to the coastal plain, meaning long circular journeys from the central tourist hotspots or painstaking climbs over the dramatic Hardknott and Honister passes into the western valleys.

Emphatically, though, the western Lake District (ⓦ western-lakedistrict.co.uk) is worth the journey, whether it's for a stroll around lovely **Buttermere** or the rattling journey into **Eskdale** on the tremendous **Ravenglass & Eskdale Railway**. It's a toss-up whether **Wast Water** (England's deepest lake) or **Ennerdale Water** is the better-looking lake, though Ennerdale is, if anything, even more remote, while tiny **Loweswater** and unsung **Crummock Water** each have their fair share of stunning scenery, great hikes and hidden corners.

Above all, however, it's the **mountains** that dominate in the west, sporting names (Pillar, Great Gable, the Scafells) that are among the most resonant in the region. Certainly, there's enough great walking here to keep you occupied for weeks. The other point of interest is the **Cumbrian coast**, though this is rather less celebrated, since only a short protected section lies within the National Park boundary. It's been more brutally shaped instead by the old industrial towns between **Millom** and Workington, and if there's a symbol of where economic priorities lie it's the sprawling Sellafield nuclear reprocessing plant, a major local employer that lurks on the coast just north of Ravenglass.

Millom and around

The small, plain town of **Millom** lies just outside the National Park boundary, flanked to the south and east by the shifting sands of the Duddon Channel. As a product of the nineteenth-century mining industry, the town isn't an obvious target for most Lakes tourists, but Millom's excellent **museum** (at the town's train station) is worth the short detour, while the local beach and **nature reserve** are great for a stretch of the legs.

Millom Discovery Centre

Old Station Building, Millom Railway Station, Station Rd, LA18 5AA • Mon–Sat 10.30am–3.30pm • Free • ☎ 01229 772555, ⓦ millomdiscoverycentre.co.uk

The **Millom Discovery Centre** tells a graphic story of boom and bust, as the local discovery of high-grade iron ore led to the establishment of mining and ore-processing operations on the neighbouring Hodbarrow peninsula, now a nature reserve. In its day, it was a massive operation, with millions of tonnes of iron ore extracted by thousands of workers housed in drab, company-built streets. Their employment came to an end in 1968 when the mine finally closed, and the museum recalls their working and living conditions, alongside a re-creation of an old mine (using original items from the last pit to close), and many other fascinating finds, photographs and relics.

Highlights

❶ Silecroft beach The only stretch of beach within the National Park extends for miles, providing wholesome walks and a habitat for wildlife. See page 180

❷ Ravenglass & Eskdale Railway The finest approach to quiet Eskdale is in the toy-town carriages of the Ravenglass & Eskdale Railway. See page 182

❸ Muncaster A great family day out – gardens, ghosts and owls. See page 182

❹ Boot Beer Festival Cumbria's best and friendliest beer fest lights up Eskdale each June. See page 187

❺ Viking cross, Gosforth This intricately carved stone cross is the finest reminder of the Norse influence on the Lakes. See page 189

❻ Wasdale Head Inn Relive the old days in the atmospheric rural inn, where walkers and climbers congregate over drinks and dinner. See page 193

❼ Ennerdale For dark skies, glorious walks and remote lodgings, visit one of the region's best-kept secrets – a lake and valley for nature-lovers. See page 193

❽ Haystacks The favourite peak of avid fell-walker Alfred Wainwright, whose ashes are scattered here. See page 199

HIGHLIGHTS ARE MARKED ON THE MAP ON PAGE 178

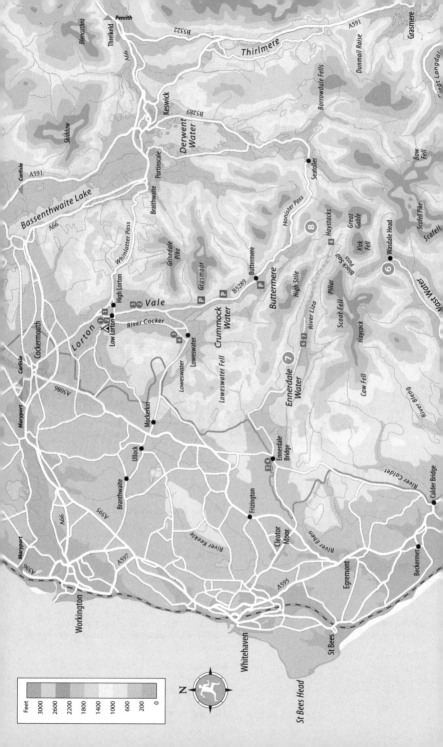

IRISH SEA

HIGHLIGHTS

1 Silecroft beach
2 Ravenglass & Eskdale Railway
3 Muncaster
4 Boot Beer Festival
5 Viking cross, Gosforth
6 Wasdale Head Inn
7 Ennerdale
8 Haystacks

THE WESTERN FELLS AND VALLEYS

0   2
|————————|
miles

5

NORMAN NICHOLSON, MILLOM'S LOCAL POET

Millom's most famous son is the poet **Norman Nicholson** (1914–87), who spent almost his entire life in the town. An only child, he contracted TB at 16 and spent two years in a Hampshire sanatorium before returning to Millom. His wide reading in convalescent isolation was one of the main factors, he considered, that made him a reflective poet; that, and his deep attachment to his Cumberland roots, whose industry, landscape, people and history informed all his work. There's more about his life and work in the Millom Discovery Centre, while his house, at **14 St George's Terrace**, just off the small market square, two minutes from the train station, is marked by a blue plaque. In **St George's church**, up the drive opposite the square, a beautiful contemporary stained-glass window celebrates Nicholson's life and work, while he is buried with his wife in the new part of St George's churchyard. The grave lies beyond the church and down to the right, in front of a wooden bench by a wooden fence, and is inscribed with a moving line from his last published work, *Sea to the West*: "Let our eyes at the last be blinded/Not by the dark/But by dazzle."

Hodbarrow RSPB Reserve

Two miles from Millom, near Haverigg • Always open • Free • ⓦ rspb.org.uk

A mile south of Millom, the local beach at **Haverigg** is a lengthy, duned stretch that leads a quiet existence, even in summer, despite the children's playground and beach café. The nearby **Hodbarrow RSPB Reserve** (signposted from the town centre), sited around a freshwater lagoon formed from flooded mine workings, is a better place for a stroll. From the parking area, a path runs all the way around the lagoon, and from either the stone beacon or the ruined windmill there are sweeping views in all directions. The lagoon is of national importance for wintering waterfowl such as wigeon, goldeneye, red-breasted merganser and pintail, while in summer three species of tern can be viewed from the hide on the sea wall. The number and variety of **orchids** at Hodbarrow also catch the eye in summer – not just the plentiful marsh, spotted and pyramidal orchids but the largest colony of bee orchids in Cumbria. Seals are also regularly seen from the sea wall at low tide.

ARRIVAL AND DEPARTURE   MILLOM

By train Trains on the Cumbrian Coast line from Barrow-in-Furness (connections from Lancaster/Ulverston) stop here (hourly; 30min), with onward services to Ravenglass (15min) and Whitehaven (45min).

The National Park coast

A short twenty-mile section of the west Cumbrian coast – between Silecroft and Ravenglass – falls within the National Park. It's not that appealing, unless you simply fancy a stroll on the sands, but it does have one unique feature – the bulky fell of **Black Combe**, the only Lake District mountain to fall straight to the sea.

Silecroft

After the dunes of Haverigg, the next decent sweep of beach is at **Silecroft**, four miles northwest of Millom; there's a train halt on the coastal line, a mile from the beach, and a useful pub near the station. Silecroft is a place for wildlife enthusiasts, since the coastal scrub here is a habitat for the natterjack toad, while (as elsewhere along the Cumbrian coast) terns, oystercatchers and ringed plovers nest and breed, scraping the shingle over their camouflaged eggs.

CLIMBING BLACK COMBE

The A595 makes a V-shape around the distinctive **Black Combe** massif, with the angle at the hamlet of Whicham, near Silecroft, where there's a path up to the summit (1857ft) that starts from the minor Kirkbank road, behind the church. It's not a particularly demanding climb (Wainwright reckoned you could do it in carpet slippers) and, in fine weather at least, you can certainly discount William Wordsworth's dire warnings ("Dread name derived from clouds and storms!"). It's around three miles there and back (2hr 30min), and the views from the top are fantastic, stretching out to sea to the Isle of Man, up the coast to St Bees Head and south to Morecambe Bay. Indeed, it's traditionally claimed that you can see up to fourteen English and Scottish counties from here, plus Snowdon and even the Irish coast, but that would require one of those all-too-rare crystal-clear days and Clark Kent-like vision.

Bootle and Eskmeals

At **Bootle**, five miles up the A595 from Silecroft, the sandstone-faced church is split from its cemetery by the road. Bootle's nearest beach is three miles to the northwest, at **Eskmeals**, which has a stony foreshore, though when the tide is out a large expanse of sand is exposed, from which you can admire the views as far north as St Bees Head. North of here, as far as Ravenglass, the coastline itself is off limits – red flags fly over an experimental firing range – while beyond lie the hard-to-miss towers and buildings of Sellafield (see page 182). Whether you'd choose to swim anywhere in the vicinity of a nuclear reprocessing plant is, of course, entirely a matter for you.

ARRIVAL AND DEPARTURE

THE NATIONAL PARK COAST

By car You're going to need a car either to get to the starting point of the Black Combe walk or to easily visit any of the coastal destinations covered in this section.

By train Silecroft station at least is reasonably close to the beach, about a mile's walk from station to sea. It's a request stop on the train service from either Millom (5min) or Whitehaven (40min), and there's a handy pub near the station.

Ravenglass and around

The one big attraction on the coast is at **Ravenglass**, a sleepy village at the estuary of three syllabically challenged rivers, the Esk, Mite and Irt. The village is the starting point for the wonderful narrow-gauge **Ravenglass & Eskdale Railway**, but it merits a closer look anyway before you take the train or visit the other main local attraction, nearby **Muncaster Castle**.

The single main street in Ravenglass preserves a row of characterful nineteenth-century cottages – one with a huge profusion of tumbling flowers and shrubs, another fronted by an ancient "National" petrol pump with the pre-decimal price still showing. The cottages back onto estuarine mud flats and dunes that are accessible when the tide's out – the northern section, across the Esk, is a **nature reserve** where black-headed gulls and terns are often seen (get there by crossing over the main-line railway footbridge).

Roman bathhouse

Walls Drive, Ravenglass, CA18 1SR • Always open • Free

The Romans first used the estuary as a harbour, and established a supply post at Ravenglass in the first century AD for the northern legions manning Hadrian's Wall. Nothing remains of what the Romans knew as Glannaventa save the remarkably complete red-stone cobble buildings of their **bathhouse**, part of a fort that survived in Ravenglass until the fourth century. Access to the remains is from the road out of the village, just past the station – walk 500 yards up the (signposted) single-track lane, past the caravan site.

5

Ravenglass & Eskdale Railway

Ravenglass station, CA18 1SW • Easter–Oct, at least 6 daily departures (up to 12 in school summer hols), plus trains most winter weekends, and Christmas, New Year and Feb half-term hols • £15.50, family ticket £44.95 for one day's unlimited travel • ☎ 01229 717171, ⓦ ravenglass-railway.co.uk

You'd have to have a heart of stone not to enjoy the ride on the fabulous **Ravenglass & Eskdale Railway** (known locally as "La'al Ratty"), a narrow-gauge steam trip from the Esk estuary to the foot of the western fells. It originally opened in 1875 to carry iron ore from the Eskdale mines to the coast at Ravenglass, but now pays its way by transporting gleeful passengers on a seven-mile, forty-minute ride up two of the Lake District's prettiest valleys – first along Miterdale under Muncaster Fell and then into the valley of the River Esk, where the train terminates at Dalegarth station, near Boot. The ticket allows you to get off and walk from one of the half-dozen stations en route; the full return trip, assuming you don't get off along the way and including waiting time at the far end, takes an hour and forty minutes.

There's also a small **railway museum** at Ravenglass station (Feb half-term to Oct half-term daily 10am–5pm, plus winter when trains are running; ⓦ ravenglassrailwaymuseum.co.uk), a short film showing you the route, a café on the platform, and a shop where budding engine-drivers can buy that all-important driver's cap. Special days out, involving Thomas the Tank Engine and the like, are held throughout the year.

Muncaster Castle

Ravenglass, CA18 1RQ, on A595 • Easter–Oct: castle Sun–Fri noon–4pm; grounds, gardens & hawk and owl centre daily 10.30am–5pm; Nov to Christmas & mid-Feb to Easter: castle Sat & Sun 11.30am–2.30pm; grounds, gardens & hawk and owl centre Sat & Sun 11am–4pm • Castle, grounds, gardens & hawk and owl centre £15.50; £12.50 without castle • ☎ 01229 717614, ⓦ muncaster.co.uk

A mile east of Ravenglass spreads the estate of **Muncaster Castle** whose house, grounds and attractions are one of the region's best family days out. The castle aside, there's plenty to do and see – including **flying owl displays** and some wonderful **gardens**, with a café – and you can even stay the night (see page 183) if you fancied waking up to some rather grand surroundings.

The castle

The **castle** itself was built around a medieval pele tower, and has been home to the Pennington family since the thirteenth century; family members still live here today, as photographs throughout and contemporary portraits in the Drawing Room attest.

NO MORE NUKES? THE SELLAFIELD STORY

The main blot on the Cumbrian coast is **Sellafield nuclear reprocessing plant**, midway between Ravenglass and Whitehaven. It's changed its name twice, from Calder Hall to Windscale and then to Sellafield, in what might seem, to a cynic, an attempt to hide its manifest dangers. It's always been controversial, since the site was first developed in the 1950s to produce plutonium for Britain's early nuclear-weapons programme. Today, Sellafield contains more than two hundred separate nuclear facilities, including redundant defence work (ie, weapons) sites and Calder Hall, the world's first fully commercial nuclear power station (1956–2003). The problem is that Sellafield was developed quickly at a time when little thought was given to nuclear waste treatment, with the result that there is now a massive clean-up and decommissioning project under way at what is, in anyone's view, a dangerous industrial site. Unfortunately, returning Sellafield to a "safe, passive state" will cost billions of pounds and won't be complete until 2150 – none of which will help the government sell its current policy of promoting a new generation of "clean" British nuclear-power stations, in an attempt to combat rising carbon emissions.

A NIGHT WITH THE MUNCASTER SPOOKS

Muncaster Castle claims to be one of the most haunted houses in Britain, with tales told of spooks like the jester Tom Fool or the Muncaster Boggle. Evidence? Nothing tangible so far, though an electromagnetic "spectre-detector" has been set up to probe for poltergeists, while the castle's reputation is sufficient to attract ghost researchers and paranormal conferences. Sceptics and others can even test their nerve with an occasional **Ghost Sit** (see ⓦ muncaster. co.uk for details), when you get to sit the night out in the most haunted castle rooms, with breakfast included for bleary-eyed survivors. There are also special **ghost tours** each Halloween week, which always sell out quickly.

An audiotour points out the family treasures (a Gainsborough here, a Reynolds there) and leads you through various rooms, notably the impressive octagonal library and the Tapestry Room, with its Flemish wall-hangings and mighty Elizabethan fireplace.

The grounds and gardens

The seventy-acre **grounds and gardens** are at their best in spring and autumn, but lovely to walk in at any time, with a stupendous view straight up Eskdale from the Terrace Walk, and half a dozen other marked trails, including one winding through a hilly Sino-Himalayan Garden. The plants here, all grown from seeds from Bhutan, Vietnam, and Yunnan and Sichuan provinces in China, thrive in conditions apparently similar to those 11,000 feet up a Far Eastern mountain – which doesn't say a lot for Cumbrian weather patterns. Children, meanwhile, are steered towards the **meadowvole maze**, a light-hearted look at mole-sized life in the wild-flower meadows, where escaping being eaten by an owl is the challenge for younger visitors.

Hawk & Owl Centre

Owl displays Easter–Oct daily 11.30am & 2pm; winter daily 1.30pm

Run in association with the Hawk Conservancy Trust, the excellent **Hawk & Owl Centre** in the castle grounds acts as a breeding centre for some twenty different species (including diminutive burrowing owls, giant steppe eagles and even hooded vultures). You can see some of them put through their paces daily on the castle lawns at the entertaining "Sky Hunters" display, or learn more about raptors at a Falconer's Talk and Tour (both included in the Muncaster entrance fee). There's also a heronry in the grounds with **wild herons** fed daily at 4pm (3pm in winter).

ARRIVAL AND DEPARTURE

By car Ravenglass is just 0.5 mile off the A595. There's free parking at Muncaster Castle, and plenty of parking at Ravenglass station.

By train Ravenglass is on the Cumbrian Coast train line, with regular services from Barrow-in-Furness (hourly; 45min) or Whitehaven (hourly; 30min). The Ravenglass & Eskdale

RAVENGLASS AND AROUND

Railway station is adjacent to the mainline station, and there are discounted through-tickets available if you arrive by train.

On foot It's an easy walk from Ravenglass to Muncaster Castle, either following the main road (there's a pavement; 20min) or the signposted path (30min) up past the Roman bathhouse, across the fields and down through the grounds.

ACCOMMODATION

SEE MAP PAGE 178

Ravenglass makes a quiet night's stopover – as well as the places we review here, there are a couple of other local B&Bs, a small shop, and public bars at the two hotels.

★ **Coachman's Quarters** Muncaster Castle, CA18 1RQ ☎ 01229 717614, ⓦ muncaster.co.uk. Live like a lord – or at least like a lord's servant – in Muncaster's bright-as-a-button B&B rooms in the former coachman's quarters, which have direct access to the castle grounds. A couple of

family rooms (including the Granary Suite; £110) offer a fair amount of extra living space and, while breakfast is served in the castle café, guests also have the use of a lounge and large, fully equipped kitchen (under the exposed stone and original beams of the old haylofts). It's only a mile's walk down the path to Ravenglass, for meals at the *Ratty Arms* pub or the bar-restaurant at the castle's own hotel, the *Pennington* (see below) – or stick a bottle of bubbly in the

5

TRAIN UP, BIKE DOWN ON THE ESKDALE TRAIL

There's a great return **bike route** from Dalegarth station to Ravenglass (8.5 miles), which only takes around two hours, though with lunch and a visit to Muncaster en route it's also a fine day out. You'll whizz along sun-dappled wooded tracks and across open farmland, following markers all the way. For the most part it's fairly easy, either flat or downhill – aside from the hellishly steep twenty-minute push uphill onto Muncaster Fell. From Dalegarth it's around fifty minutes to the start of the hill – once you've slogged to the top be sure to see Muncaster Tarn and its huge water lilies. Descending from here, there are wonderful sea and estuary views as you freewheel down to Muncaster Castle and to the Roman bathhouse just outside Ravenglass.

A route guide to the **Eskdale Trail** is available from Ravenglass or Dalegarth stations. You'll need to call the Ravenglass & Eskdale Railway a day in advance to book your cycle on the train; you leave your car at Ravenglass and then buy a one-way ticket to Dalegarth (£11.50, including bike carriage).

fridge and toast yourself on the Muncaster lawns. Guests also get free access to the gardens and Hawk & Owl Centre, and a discount on the Ravenglass & Eskdale Railway, so it's a bit of a bargain all round. Parking. **£90**

The Pennington Main St, Ravenglass, CA18 1SQ ☎01229 717222, ⓦmuncaster.co.uk. The owners of Muncaster Castle also run this restored three-star estuary-facing hotel, with fine rooms in a contemporary style (bold colours, iPod docks, fancy bathrooms, big thick towels)

set within what was once an old coaching inn. There's a restaurant, too (see below). Parking. **£110**

Rosegarth Main St, Ravenglass, CA18 1SQ ☎01229 717275, ⓦrose-garth.co.uk. Hike- and bike-friendly B&B in the old doctor's house, facing the estuary. Rooms are neat and tidy, most have views of the water and bobbing boats and there's a spacious suite sleeping four (£165) in the attic. Breakfasts are huge ("never knowingly underfed"). Parking. **£78**

EATING
SEE MAP PAGE 178

There's a good **café** at Muncaster Castle, and there are also cafés at Ravenglass and Dalegarth stations – ie, either end of the Ravenglass & Eskdale Railway line. If you're relying on them for lunch in winter, though, a call first wouldn't go amiss.

The Pennington Main St, Ravenglass, CA18 1SQ

☎01229 717222, ⓦmuncaster.co.uk. The airy, fresh feel of the hotel rooms (see above) continues in the fashionable bar and restaurant, with a locally sourced menu (bar meals £9–19) including sausages from down the road, fell-bred lamb, and herbs and veg from Muncaster's kitchen gardens. Daily noon–8.45pm.

DRINKING
SEE MAP PAGE 178

Ratty Arms Ravenglass station, CA18 1SN ☎01229 717676. The main-line station house has been a popular local pub for many years – the bar is actually the old booking hall and ticket office. Real ales are on tap, and there are reasonably priced bar meals (£8–10), including specials like

crab salad, lamb chops and a huge mixed grill. Easter–Oct Mon–Sat 11am–11pm, Sun noon–10.30pm, kitchen daily noon–9pm; Nov–Easter Mon–Fri 11.30am–2.30pm & 5.30–11pm, Sat 11am–11pm, Sun noon–10.30pm, kitchen daily noon–2pm & 6–9pm.

Eskdale

Eskdale, accessed most easily from the Cumbrian coast, is just twelve miles long from start to finish, but what a finish it provides – in the dramatic high-fell surroundings of Hardknott Pass. The best ride in is on the Ravenglass & Eskdale Railway, though there are also minor approach roads (from Ulpha in the Duddon Valley, from Wasdale or along the River Esk itself) all meeting at the elongated hamlet of **Eskdale Green**, on a rise above the valley. From Eskdale Green, the valley road continues east, passing **Dalegarth station** (terminus of the Ravenglass & Eskdale Railway), which lies just a short walk from the valley's isolated church and from Eskdale's other hamlet, **Boot**. Here there's an old mill to explore and several more local hikes, not to mention the walk or drive up and out of the valley to the superbly sited **Hardknott Roman Fort**.

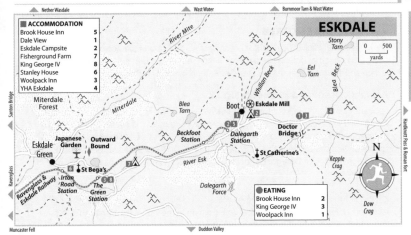

There's plenty of rustic, hideaway **accommodation** in Eskdale, including a great selection of old inns – if you're looking for an off-the-beaten-track stay in the rural western Lakes, with walks off the doorstep, you won't find better.

Eskdale Green

First village stop on the Ravenglass & Eskdale Railway is **Eskdale Green**, where you can access short walks into nearby Miterdale Forest and up to the valley head, or even plan on hiking back along the spine of Muncaster Fell to Ravenglass. This is around four miles and shouldn't take more than a couple of hours. It's a pretty sleepy village all round, only lurching into life during the annual country bash, the **Eskdale Show** (last Saturday in September), one of the biggest of the traditional rural meets in Cumbria (see page 34), which is held on the field by the *King George IV* pub. Aside from the local pubs, the only other facilities are a small but useful village shop, complete with post office counter.

Japanese Garden

Entrance across from St Bega's church • Always open • Free • From the green sign by the parking area ("Forest Enterprise, Giggle Alley"), walk a few yards up a driveway (past the parking bay) to a second, smaller sign on your left ("Giggle Alley, Japanese Garden")

A meandering path through the curiously named Giggle Alley Wood climbs up to Eskdale Green's even more curious **Japanese Garden**, originally laid out in 1913 by landscape artist Thomas Mawson as a private garden for the country-house estate of what is now the Outward Bound Centre. After the estate was sold in 1949 the garden was lost to the undergrowth, but it's being slowly restored by the Forestry Commission and is a magical place for a wander, through the larch groves, rhododendrons, magnolia, maples and stands of bamboo. The little pools, crossed by wooden bridges, fill after rain, and the encompassing shrub- and boulder-strewn woodland is a great place for a family stroll.

ARRIVAL AND INFORMATION
ESKDALE GREEN

By car There's a small parking area across from St Bega's church, by the entrance to Giggle Alley.

By train Eskdale Green has two stations on the Ravenglass & Eskdale Railway: Irton Road for the western end of the village and The Green for the eastern end.

Tourist information The village church of St Bega (in between the two stations) doubles as an unstaffed visitor

centre, with some display boards in the entrance covering the local sights and history.

Services Directly opposite the church, the village post office and store (Mon–Fri 8am–5.30pm, Sat 8.30am–5pm, Sun 9am–noon; ☎019467 23229) sells essential maps, outdoor gear and groceries.

5

WALKS FROM ESKDALE

Eskdale is a great choice for a **walk** at any time of year: you'll rarely come across many other people on the routes outlined below, even on the shorter strolls. There's parking at Dalegarth station and in Boot, and as the train runs year-round the valley makes a fine off-season day out.

DALEGARTH FORCE AND THE RIVER ESK

Footpaths along both sides of the **River Esk** between Eskdale's St Catherine's church and Doctor Bridge (near the *Woolpack Inn*) allow an easy two-mile (1hr) riverside walk – in low water you can cross the river below the church by stepping stones, or there's a bridge further up. You can combine this with the steep climb up the wooded ravine that holds the impressive 60ft falls of **Dalegarth Force** (also known as Stanley Ghyll Force), in full spate for much of the year.

HARDKNOTT AND THE ESK FALLS

It's harder going east of Doctor Bridge, where a path to the foot of the **Hardknott Pass** keeps to the south side of the River Esk beneath Birker Fell, before cutting up, via the farm at Brotherikeld, to the Roman fort. Keeping to the Esk, you can hike on up the narrow valley between overhanging crags to **Lingcove Bridge**, beyond which tumble the **Esk Falls** – an eight-mile (5hr) round trip that requires fine weather and good visibility, otherwise you risk getting bogged down and lost.

THE WOOLPACK WALK

The most strenuous hike from Eskdale – and one of the most extreme in the Lakes – is the **Woolpack Walk** (18 miles; 11–12hr), a tough high-level circuit topping the two highest mountains in England (the Scafells) and several others (Bowfell, Crinkle Crags, Harter Fell) that aren't much lower. It is not easy going and a certain amount of scrambling is required, but the views and the varied terrain make this one of the finest lakeland walks. Traditional starting and finishing point is the *Woolpack Inn*, where full route details and advice are available (*Woolpack* residents who complete the walk in under 9hr even get a free pint).

ACCOMMODATION   SEE MAP PAGE 185

Fisherground Farm Eskdale Green, CA19 1TF, 400 yards up the Boot road ☎01946 723723, ⓦfisherground campsite.co.uk. Camp at the peaceful, family-friendly *Fisherground* and you can arrive by train, as it has its own station on the Ravenglass & Eskdale Railway. It's great for kids (there's an adventure playground, and splashing in the nearby river), and you're only a few minutes from the *King George IV* pub. Closed Nov–Feb. Vehicles £2.50 extra. Per person __£8__

King George IV Eskdale Green, CA19 1TS ☎019467 23470, ⓦkinggeorge-eskdale.co.uk. The nearest pub to The Green station (200 yards away to the right, by the turn-off to Boot), this traditional hostelry (see page 186) has a couple of flouncy B&B rooms (you can stay for as little as £60 if you forgo breakfast). Parking. __£80__

★ **Stanley House** Eskdale Green, CA19 1TF ☎019467 23230, ⓦstanleyghyll-eskdale.co.uk. Promises "more than just B&B" and delivers, with its home-from-home, house-party feel and contemporary air. Accommodation is in a dozen light and spacious rooms, including a couple of two-room family suites (£130). Downstairs is a huge open-plan kitchen-diner with views over the riverside gardens, plus lounge with wood-burner. Although accommodation is on a room only basis, there is the option of a basic "Help Yourself Breakfast" for £5, which includes use of the well-equipped kitchen. The genial owners – who also run the *Woolpack Inn* up the valley (see page 188) – can arrange for their pub pizzas to be delivered to the door or a lift to the *Woolpack* for the night. __£75__

EATING   SEE MAP PAGE 185

King George IV Eskdale Green, CA19 1TS ☎019467 23470, ⓦkinggeorge-eskdale.co.uk. A traditional inn, handy for The Green station, and offering an impressive collection of real ales and malt whiskies. The grub's not bad either, with mains such as home-made beef lasagne and smoked haddock fishcakes going for around £11. Mon–Thurs & Sun noon–midnight, Fri & Sat till 1am; kitchen daily noon–8.45pm.

Boot and around

The train terminus for the Ravenglass & Eskdale Railway is **Dalegarth station**, two miles east of Eskdale Green, where passengers pour out in summer for local walks, including that to Dalegarth Force (see page 186). The local village, the dead-end hamlet of **Boot**, is another 350 yards up the valley road from the station. The mines near Boot that supplied ore for the railway to Ravenglass never really paid their way and closed in 1913. Now there are just a few stone cottages and a pub, cowering beneath the fells, which mark the last remnant of civilization before the road up and over Hardknott Pass turns serious.

St Catherine's church

A track opposite Dalegarth station leads in a couple of hundred yards to Eskdale's **St Catherine's church**. Its riverside location is handsome in the extreme, and in the small cemetery you can't miss the distinctive gravestone of Thomas Dobson (d. 1910), former hunt master of the Eskdale and Ennerdale Hounds whose likeness grins from the top of the stone, above a carved fox and hound. Dobson actually died in the *Three Shires Inn* in Little Langdale, which involved his coffin being carted to Eskdale over the gruelling Wrynose and Hardknott passes. If he hadn't already been dead the bearers would probably have killed him for his thoughtlessness.

Eskdale Mill

April–Sept Wed–Sun 10.30am–4.30pm; winter some weekends, check website • £4, family £10 • ☎ 019467 23335, ⓦ eskdalemill.co.uk

There's been industry of sorts in the valley for centuries, since the Furness Abbey monks first introduced a corn mill into Eskdale. Over the packhorse bridge at the back of the hamlet, the sixteenth-century **Eskdale Mill** preserves its wooden machinery – the resident miller will show you around – and you can picnic near the waterfalls that power the wheels. For a stretch of the legs, follow the signposted path up the heights to **Eel Tarn**, a mile away.

ARRIVAL AND INFORMATION   BOOT AND AROUND

By car There's parking at Dalegarth station and at a couple of other designated areas in Eskdale, but the valley road is very narrow and roadside parking is well-nigh impossible. Come by train if you can for a hassle-free day out, or leave your car at your accommodation and walk or cycle.

By train There are year-round services on the Ravenglass & Eskdale Railway (see page 182), terminating at Dalegarth station, a short walk from Boot and around 1.5 miles from the *Woolpack Inn* and *YHA*.

Tourist information ⓦ eskdale.info.

Outdoor activities West Lake Adventures (☎ 019467 23753, ⓦ westlakesadventure.co.uk), next to the *Woolpack Inn*, organizes bike rental and all manner of activities, from archery and abseiling to kayaking and ghyll-scrambling.

Services A small general store/post office in Boot sells lakeland ice cream and even rents out hiking boots. The *Woolpack Inn* also has a great shop, selling everything from locally sourced deli foods and wines from their cellar to rainy-day toys and games.

HERE FOR THE BEER… AND THE WINE

The best booziest day out each year is during the **Boot Beer Festival** (ⓦ bootbeer.co.uk), held over a June weekend, which splits its festivities between the three local pubs, the *Brook House Inn*, the *Boot Inn* in the village, and the *Woolpack Inn* further up the valley road. Well over a hundred ales are on offer – each pub chooses its own favourites – with an emphasis on Cumbrian and northern brews, and it makes for a really good family-oriented trip, especially if you come up on the La'al Ratty train from Ravenglass. The *Woolpack* also runs the Eskdale **wine festival** (Nov), with tastings, speakers, music and wine dinners; accommodation packages are available at both the *Woolpack* and its sister B&B *Stanley House* (see page 186).

ACCOMMODATION

SEE MAP PAGE 185

Boot is the obvious base for an extended stay in the valley, with a range of **accommodation**, from quiet rooms in old inns to dorm beds and family rooms in the youth hostel.

★ **Brook House Inn** CA19 1TG, 350 yards east of Dalegarth station, at the Boot road junction ☏ 019467 23288, ⊛ brookhouseinn.co.uk. Cheery, family-run hotel and pub/restaurant (see below) with eight refurbished rooms – two of which are family rooms (one with a bunk) – all with lovely rustic views. Parking. **£95**

Dale View The Post Office, Boot, CA19 1TG ☏ 019467 23706, ⊛ booteskdale.co.uk. The post office offers B&B in a double, a twin and a single, all sharing a bathroom, and can pack you a lunch for a day's walking – the village pub is right over the road for meals. Advance reservations recommended in winter, when B&B is not always available. No credit cards. **£75**

Eskdale Campsite Hardknott Pass road, CA19 1TF, 200 yards east of Boot ☏ 019467 23253, ⊛ nationaltrust. org.uk/holidays/eskdale-campsite-lake-district. Small campsite, beautifully sited in the Esk Valley, just a short walk from the railway and the valley's pubs. They also have ten heated "pods" (£45). It's definitely a family-friendly place, with zero tolerance for noise, music and large groups. Closed Jan & Feb. Per person **£12**

Woolpack Inn Hardknott Pass road, CA19 1TH, 1 mile east of Boot ☏ 019467 23230, ⊛ woolpack.co.uk. Seven smart, cheerful but unflashy rooms – one of which has a double Jacuzzi bath – offer a peaceful night's sleep above this excellent bar/restaurant (see below). Closed three weeks in Dec. Parking. **£80**

YHA Eskdale Hardknott Pass road, CA19 1TH, 200 yards east of Woolpack Inn ☏ 0845 371 9317, ⊛ yha. org.uk. There's an eco feel to this secluded hostel nestling beneath Eskdale Fell, which has its own environmentally friendly heating system, plus wildlife garden, a nature trail for bird- and red-squirrel-spotting, and 15 acres of its own grounds. It's a firm family favourite, but in a great location for walkers too, and although you're only a 5min walk from the *Woolpack Inn*, the two-course dinners here get good reviews (£9.95 plus beer and wine available). Closed Nov to mid-March. Dorms **£25**

EATING

SEE MAP PAGE 185

In addition to the pubs, there's a **café** at Dalegarth station (open when the trains are running).

★ **Brook House Inn** CA19 1TG, 350 yards east of Dalegarth station, at the Boot road junction ☏ 019467 23288, ⊛ brookhouseinn.co.uk. The bar's a bit heavy on the stuffed animals, but it's a good place for beer buffs and the food's a step up from ordinary pub meals – for example grilled seabass in a sweet chilli jam, or chicken Ballantine in a whiskey and mustard sauce, and some unusually varied veggie options. Mains £11–17. Daily noon–2pm & 5.30–8.30pm.

★ **Woolpack Inn** Hardknott Pass road, CA19 1TH, 1 mile east of Boot ☏ 019467 23230, ⊛ woolpack.co.uk. The terrific public bar sports a cool, contemporary look with stripped-back wooden floors, leather sofas and fancy wood-burner. It's a great place simply for a pint of real ale in the garden after an exhausting hike, but other refreshments are a cut above. A terrific daytime café menu featuring the likes of warm home-made flatbread (with, for example, shredded duck) is complemented by excellent value bar meals like home-made pies and proper chips, hot-smoked salmon fishcakes and Herdwick lamb tattie pot (mains £12–16), plus tapas and pizza from their wood-burning beehive oven. Bar meals daily noon–9pm, pizza Thurs–Sat 4–10pm, Sun noon–10pm; café menu daily 10am–5pm.

Hardknott Roman Fort

Hardknott Pass Rd, CA19 1TH • Always open • Free; EH • ⊛ english-heritage.org.uk/visit/places/hardknott-roman-fort • Parking available by the side of the road

Three miles beyond Boot and 250 yards up the twisting road, the remains of **Hardknott Roman Fort** – known as Mediobogdum to the Romans – command a strategic and panoramic position just below Hardknott Pass. If ever proof were needed of how serious the Romans were about keeping what they had conquered, then Hardknott proves the point. This full-scale fortification was built during the reign of Hadrian by a cohort of Dalmatian (Croatian) troops, who gave it walls 12ft thick and a double-towered gateway, and endowed it with granaries, bathhouses and a plush, stone-built *praetorium* or commandant's quarters. The troops had to endure the discomforts of timber barracks, though since the *praetorium* was built along Roman lines – rooms ranged around an open courtyard – the commandant probably cursed his luck at his assignment every time the wind blew (about every ten seconds up here). Much of the lower part of the defensive wall is original Roman work; elsewhere, the foundations of the granaries and various other buildings have been re-erected to indicate their scale.

It's worth a brief stop at least for a tramp around in the heather and bracken and, needless to say, the views back down into Eskdale and up to the Scafells are stunning.

Hardknott and Wrynose passes

Beyond the Roman fort, the dramatic, narrow switchback road climbs to **Hardknott Pass** (1289ft) – often cited as the steepest road in England and an undeniably challenging drive, as you have to negotiate some very tight corners in a very low gear. The views are – naturally – magnificent, with the fells of Hard Knott (1803ft) to one side and Harter Fell (2140ft) to the other, but if you've got any sense at all only your passengers will be able to admire them. The pass road then drops to Cockley Beck (for the Duddon Valley), before making the equally alarming ascent of **Wrynose Pass** (look for the upright "Three Shire Stone" here, marking where the counties of Lancashire, Cumberland and Westmorland once met), gateway to Little Langdale and, ultimately, Ambleside.

Wasdale

Glorious **Wasdale** is all about the mountains, despite the presence of three-mile-long **Wast Water**, England's deepest lake. Awesome 1700ft screes plunge to its eastern shore, separating Wast Water from Eskdale to the south, while the highest peaks in England – Great Gable and the Scafells – frame **Wasdale Head**, the tiny settlement at the head of the lake. As every local business and website will undoubtedly tell you, it's officially "Britain's favourite view", following a TV show public vote; and you'll have seen the panorama up the lake to Great Gable, unwittingly, countless times already since the National Park Authority uses the outline as its logo on every publication, signpost and notice board.

Apart from a few farms and cottages, and a single inn, the valley head is a remote yet starkly beautiful environment – mountain hikers know all about it, and can access some of the toughest, most rewarding lakeland peaks and circuits from here. But Wasdale has its softer side too, starting in the approach village of **Gosforth**, with its ancient cross, just off the A595. Beyond here, through forestry plantations and farmland, lie the Wasdale hamlets of **Santon Bridge** and **Nether Wasdale**, with the foot of the lake just a mile and a half east of Nether Wasdale. The drive in is a treat – bracken-covered walls hide the fields from view, while the roads cross little stone bridges and pass farm shops selling jars of bramble jelly or bags of new potatoes. Beyond Nether Wasdale the road is single-track for the most part and hugs Wast Water's western shore, with occasional parking spots by bosky groves, stony coves and little promontories.

Gosforth and around

At the Wasdale turn-off from the A595, **Gosforth** ("ford of geese") – a large if unremarkable village – has one extraordinary attraction: the tall, carved **stone cross** in the churchyard of St Mary's on the eastern edge of town. Signposted as the "Viking" cross, it's a rare example in Cumbria of the meeting of pagan and Christian cultures, with the four faces of the slender shaft carved with figures from Norse mythology, which are surmounted by a Christian cross. There's been a church on this site since at least the tenth century, though it's been rebuilt many times since: nineteenth-century restoration revealed the church's other treasures, the two Viking "hogback" **tombstones**, found buried in the foundations.

If your imagination is captured by the Gosforth cross, you should really drive the three miles south back down the A595, through Holmrook, and take the left turn signposted to **Santon Bridge**, a rustic hamlet by the River Irt. A mile up the ruler-straight road, a signposted track – accessible with care for cars – leads to isolated **St Paul's**, Irton, which has another worn tenth-century stone cross in its churchyard.

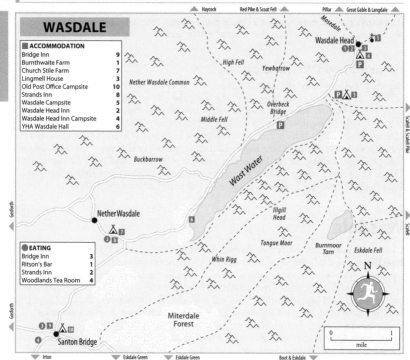

WASDALE

■ ACCOMMODATION
Bridge Inn	9
Burnthwaite Farm	1
Church Stile Farm	7
Lingmell House	3
Old Post Office Campsite	10
Strands Inn	8
Wasdale Campsite	5
Wasdale Head Inn	2
Wasdale Head Inn Campsite	4
YHA Wasdale Hall	6

● EATING
Bridge Inn	3
Ritson's Bar	1
Strands Inn	2
Woodlands Tea Room	4

ARRIVAL AND DEPARTURE

By car Take the Wasdale turn off the A595 for Gosforth; there's a free car park just off the main through road in the village.

By train The nearest station to Gosforth is 2.5 miles west on the coast at Seascale, a stop on the main Preston–Carlisle line via Ulverston, Millom, Silecroft, Bootle, Ravenglass and Whitehaven.

GOSFORTH AND AROUND

ACCOMMODATION AND EATING

SEE MAPS PAGES 176 AND 190

There is village **accommodation** in Gosforth, but it's nicer to stay in the sticks and closer to the lake, either in **Nether Wasdale** (which is basically a group of inns near the green, plus a local hostel) or two miles southwest of here in or around **Santon Bridge**. However, it's Gosforth that has all the local facilities, including two or three pubs, village shop and café, bakery, and farm grocery shop (plus post office, petrol station and ATM).

GOSFORTH

★ **Gosforth Bakery** Meadow View, CA20 1AS ☎019467 25525. We'd drive a long way for home-made pies, pasties and quiches from Gosforth Bakery – and so would others, judging by the queues out of the door at lunchtimes. You can make up a great meal here for a waterside picnic at Wast Water; you'll find the bakery on the main through road, near the car park. Tues–Fri 6am–3pm.

Rainors Farm Wasdale Rd, CA20 1ER, 1.5 miles east of Gosforth ☎019467 25934, ⊕rainorsfarm.co.uk. Overnighters can choose one of two B&B rooms in the very picturesque farmhouse, and the owners promise fab views without leaving your bed. Otherwise, there's a charming two-bedroom cottage suite annexe (from £350/three nights, no breakfast) and two cosily furnished yurts (sleep up to five, from £385/three nights, £585/seven), one in the paddock, the other by the stream, the latter available all year round; breakfast is available Fri–Sun for an extra £12. Packed lunches upon request too. Parking. No credit cards. **£80**

AROUND GOSFORTH

★ **Bridge Inn** Santon Bridge, CA19 1UX ☎019467 26221, ⊕santonbridgeinn.com. Bump over the little humpback bridge that crosses the River Irt to find this modest country pub, a handy Wasdale halt for rooms and food. There's great excitement and tall tales once a year (see box), but otherwise it's a peaceful overnight stop offering handsome rooms and honest-to-goodness food – with big walkers' breakfasts (£9.20, best to book) as well as very popular bistro meals in the bar (mains £13–17). Mon–Sat 7am–11pm, Sun 8am–11pm; kitchen daily noon–9pm, hours slightly reduced Oct–Easter. **£90**

Church Stile Farm Wasdale, CA20 1ET, 1.5 miles east of Nether Wasdale ☎019467 26252, ⓦchurchstile. com. Well-thought-out campsite, fringed by oak woods, with a small on-site café and store, showers, laundry, picnic tables and children's play area. It's a decent size, able to accommodate around seventy tents on a flat lawn, with holiday caravans sleeping up to six (from £360/week), custom-built wooden shepherd's huts for two (from £160/3 nights), and camping pods (without any furnishings at all) sleeping four (£50/night). Oh yes, and you're just across the road from the *Strands Inn* (see below). Tents £3–7 each, and cars £2 extra. Per person **£6**

Irton Hall Irton, CA19 1TA, 1 mile south of Santon Bridge ☎019467 26025, ⓦirtonhall.co.uk. Once the seat of the local gentry, who traced their ancestry right back to the Norman Conquest, now a rather gracious B&B set in sprawling parkland in a quiet Wasdale backwater. The sixteen rooms are all fashionably decorated in muted earth tones and with sparkling bathrooms – some have bigger beds and a bit more space (up to £120). There's a very accomplished a la carte menu (mains £14–18) in the restaurant as well as bar meals, though you're less than a mile's walk from the *Bridge Inn* at Santon Bridge (a nice stroll in summer). Parking. Bar daily 4–11pm; kitchen Mon–Thurs & Sun noon–9pm, Fri & Sat noon–9.30pm. **£100**

Old Post Office Campsite Santon Bridge, CA19 1UY ☎019467 26286, ⓦtheoldpostofficecampsite.co.uk. A small, bucolic family site with babbling river on one side and *Bridge Inn* just over the bridge – the pub can even supply Jennings' beer takeaways to happy campers, and there's a handy farm shop nearby. It's always busy in school holidays, so reservations are best. Closed Oct–Feb. Two adults, tent and vehicle **£22**

★ **Strands Inn** Nether Wasdale, CA20 1ET ☎019467 26237, ⓦstrands-brewery.co.uk. The pick of the inns on the green has some nicely turned-out country-style rooms above a restaurant where you can dine well on locally sourced produce, including Cumbrian air-dried ham, fell-bred lamb and Wasdale goat's cheese (most mains £13–16). The bar's a cosy place to hunker down in wet weather; there's a beer garden out back; they've even got their own microbrewery, with a beer called "Errmmm" (they couldn't decide on a name). Parking. Mon–Sat noon–11pm, Sun noon–10.30pm; kitchen Mon–Sat noon–2.15pm & 5.30–9pm, Sun noon–8pm. **£100**

Woodlands Tea Room Santon Bridge, CA19 1UY ☎019467 26281, ⓦsantonbridge.co.uk. A few hundred yards away from the bridge (on the Irton road, towards the A595), with breakfasts (served until 11.30am), lunches (try their terrific seasonal wild garlic and mushroom soup) and cakes available at the café attached to a country crafts and gift shop. Daily 9.30am–5pm.

YHA Wasdale Hall Wasdale Hall Wasdale, CA20 1ET, 1.5 miles east of Nether Wasdale ☎0345 371 9350, ⓦyha.org.uk/hostel/yha-wasdale-hall. Stay in a country mansion at budget rates at Wast Water's impressive YHA hostel (owned by the National Trust). It's a baronial beauty, with a half-timbered facade and wood-panelled restaurant, and there are dramatic lake views from some of the rooms. Families love this place (four-bed rooms £75) as the grounds reach to the shore, while nearby Low Wood has one of the Lakes' finest displays of spring bluebells. Food's good, too, with a nightly supper club offering tasty two-course meals for £9.95. Advance reservations essential. Closed Nov to mid-March. Parking. Dorms **£25**

DON'T BELIEVE A WORD OF IT

The *Bridge Inn* at Santon Bridge (see above) is best known for hosting the annual **World's Biggest Liar** competition every November, a tradition started in the late nineteenth century by publican **Will Ritson** (1808–90) of nearby Wasdale Head, who told famously tall tales of country life to his gullible guests. The Victorian gentleman fell-walkers and pioneer mountaineers – mostly professional men and academics from the cities – were, for example, given to believe that Wasdale turnips grew so large that farmers quarried them for food and then used the hollowed-out husks for sheep sheds. The annual contest is open to all-comers (though, for obvious reasons, lawyers and politicians are barred from entering), who have five minutes to tell the biggest lie they can. The winner gets a cup and £25, and entrants have to convince a sceptical local crowd that their tall tales of lakeland life just might have something in them, whether it's Cumbrian mermaid farms, dogs with false teeth being pursued by foxes or flatulent sheep causing the hole in the ozone layer.

5

Wasdale Head

The Wast Water road ends a mile beyond the lake at **Wasdale Head**, a Shangri-La-like clearing between the mountain ranges, where you'll find the **Wasdale Head Inn**, one of the most celebrated of all lakeland inns. British mountain-climbing was born here in the days when the inn's landlord – and champion liar (see page 191) – was the famous Will Ritson: black-and-white photographs pinned to the panelled rooms inside show Victorian gents in hobnailed boots and flat caps scaling dreadful precipices with nonchalant ease. The inn's gone a bit upmarket since those days, but still attracts a genuine walking and climbing crowd, not bothered in the slightest by the general lack of TV or mobile phone reception in the valley.

For a true measure of your own insignificance, take a walk down to **Wast Water** and along the eastern lakeshore path, approaching the unnerving, implacable screes. Thomas Wilkinson, an overawed eighteenth-century Quaker, fancied that he was gazing upon "the Pyramids of the world, built by the Architect of the Universe".

St Olaf's church

What's reputed to be England's smallest church, **St Olaf's**, lies a couple of hundred yards from the *Wasdale Head Inn*, encircled by evergreens and dwarfed by the surrounding fells. The small cemetery contains graves and memorials to several of those killed while climbing them. There's been a church at Wasdale since medieval times and though no one knows quite how old this plain chapel is, its current appearance – moss-grown slate roof and all – dates from a complete overhaul in 1892. The path over Eskdale Moor, via **Burnmoor Tarn**, was the former "corpse road" along which the dead were carried for burying in Eskdale church, since St Olaf's had no consecrated churchyard until 1901.

WALKS FROM WASDALE HEAD

Wasdale Head is at the heart of some serious walking and climbing country, offering popular climbs up to Scoat Fell, Pillar, the Scafells and Great Gable, among others, and classic routes over the passes into Ennerdale or Borrowdale. It's not really beginners' country, though walks down to the lake, a scramble along its eastern shore or the hike over moorland to Burnmoor Tarn and Eskdale should be within most capabilities.

A MOSEDALE HORSESHOE

Mosedale – the valley to the northwest of Wasdale Head – is crowned by an impressive ring of high peaks and crags. A terrific horseshoe circuit starts from the **Overbeck Bridge** car park (2 miles from Wasdale Head, down the lake road) and then climbs and scrambles up via Yewbarrow (2060ft), Red Pike (1710ft) and Scoat Fell (2760ft) to **Pillar** (2927ft). The walk then continues along the ridge via Looking Stead to the top of **Black Sail Pass**, from where you descend down the old Mosedale packhorse trail right to the door of the *Wasdale Head Inn* for a welcome drink. The whole route is around twelve miles, or six to seven hours' fairly tough walking.

SCAFELL

Scafell (3163ft) is England's second-highest mountain, though it's actually more prominent seen from many directions than the superior Scafell Pike. The two peaks are connected by the col known as **Mickledore**, though the Broad Stand rock face – the most direct approach – presents an impassable obstacle to walkers. Meanwhile, the classic ascent of Scafell from Wasdale via **Lord's Rake** is generally off-limits because of dangerous rock falls. Instead, walkers from Wasdale will need to make the long-winded ascent via **Foxes Tarn**. The easier route from Wasdale to the summit of Scafell (3hr) is the circuitous one taken since Victorian times, from Burnmoor Tarn and the old corpse road – either route starts at Brackenclose car park, at the head of Wast Water.

ARRIVAL AND DEPARTURE

WASDALE HEAD

By car There's a public car park near the head of the lake and another close to the *Wasdale Head Inn*, but the spaces fill quickly with hikers, even on the grottiest of days. There are other parking places down the side of the lake.

By bus Regular services have rarely stuck, and there was no bus to Wasdale at the time of writing. Contact local accommodation for current information.

INFORMATION AND ACTIVITIES

Tourist information ⓦ wasdale.com.

Outdoor gear and supplies The Barn Door Shop next to the inn (daily: Easter–Oct 9am–5pm; Nov–Easter 9am–4pm; ☎ 019467 26384, ✉ barndoorshop@yahoo.co.uk) is the only store for miles, and has a full range of outdoor clothes, equipment, camping gear, maps and guides – and the staff give great local walking advice. They also sell basic foodstuffs, including those crucial slabs of Kendal Mint Cake to get you up any mountain.

ACCOMMODATION

SEE MAP PAGE 190

★**Burnthwaite Farm** Wasdale Head, CA20 1EX ☎ 019467 26242, ⓦ burnthwaite.co.uk. The last building in the valley – up a driveable track from the parking area near the inn – is a handsome old working sheep farm on National Trust land, with seven traditional B&B rooms available inside the white-painted farmhouse. Two rooms are en suite (£80), otherwise you share a bathroom, while all rooms have up-close-and-personal views of Lingmell, the adjacent mountain. There is also a self-catering cottage (sleeps four, from £395/week, or £65 a night when available). A big farmhouse breakfast sets you up for the day; the pub's half a mile away, back down the track. Parking. No credit cards. **£75**

Lingmell House Wasdale Head, CA20 1EX ☎ 019467 26229, ⓦ lingmellhouse.co.uk. This weatherbeaten guesthouse (by the parking area) was once the vicarage and now has three agreeable rooms sharing a couple of bathrooms, all glorying in stunning fell views. Tim, the owner, can point you in the right direction for a hike and pack you a lunch. Parking. **£78**

Wasdale Campsite Wasdale Head, CA20 1EX ☎ 015394 32733, reservations on ☎ 015394 63862, ⓦ nationaltrust.org.uk/holidays/wasdale-campsite-lake-district. The National Trust's Wasdale site is a mile from the pub, but you pitch your tent under the glowering mountains at the head of the lake. There's a shop, showers and a laundry room beneath the trees, and camping pods for softies (with heating, lighting and mattresses, sleeping between three and five people; from £35). Open all year. Vehicles included in price. Per person **£13.50**

Wasdale Head Inn Wasdale Head, CA20 1EX ☎ 019467 26229, ⓦ wasdale.com. In addition to the excellent bar (see below) there are nine compact guest rooms in the main building of this famous inn; three "superior rooms" (£130) in the adjacent cottage conversion offer more space with a lounge area and full bathroom. There are also six self-catering apartments in a converted barn (sleeping two to five, £490–560/week, short breaks and winter discounts available). Parking. **£118**

Wasdale Head Inn Campsite Wasdale Head, CA20 1EX ☎ 019467 26229, ⓦ wasdale.com. The hardiest hikers of all stay at the basic field campsite across from the inn (and operated by them). Campers' toilets, hot showers (£1) and wash-up area are at the back of the inn. There's no vehicle access (though you can park nearby), and no reservations; pay on arrival at the hotel. Space is always available, except if there's an event on (such as the Lakes Challenge in Sept) – check website for dates. Open all year. Breakfast available to purchase. Per person **£5**

EATING

SEE MAP PAGE 190

Ritson's Bar Wasdale Head Inn, Wasdale Head, CA20 1EX ☎ 019467 26229, ⓦ wasdale.com. There's no finer sight at the end of a day's hiking than the famous *Wasdale Head Inn* (see above) at the head of the valley. *Ritson's Bar* is the nerve centre of the place, a rugged walkers' haunt of wooden booths and benches, serving things like steak and ale pie, hunter's chicken and lamb shank (mains £12–17); a separate, more distinguished, dinner menu (£29.95 for three courses) is available in the hotel dining room. Bar Mon–Sat 11am–11pm, Sun noon–10.30pm; kitchen daily noon–8.30pm.

Ennerdale

Ennerdale is about as far off the beaten track as you can get in the western fells and valleys. There's only one very small village, limited public transport and no road at all around **Ennerdale Water**, which makes it one of the most inaccessible of the lakes – or one of the best for walkers, depending on how you look at it. Having made the effort, you'll find that Ennerdale Water is among the most alluring of the lakes, its quiet

5

two-and-a-half-mile length (fiddle-shaped, according to Coleridge) ringed by crags and dominated at the head by the dramatic heights of Pillar. If you haven't seen this peak before, you won't recognize it from the name alone – the bulky fell takes its name instead from one of its northern crags, the devilish **Pillar Rock**, the proving ground of British mountaineers for over a century. The whole valley, meanwhile, is real "dark sky" country – with no light pollution, and so few inhabitants, an increasing number of visitors are making their way up Ennerdale for star-gazing events, with the Milky Way easily visible on clear nights.

Ennerdale Bridge

While the valley undergoes a gradual, natural transformation (see box), the village, **Ennerdale Bridge**, seems barely changed since Wordsworth's day, especially in the peaceful shaded churchyard; still "girt round with a bare ring of mossy wall", as the poet described it at the beginning of *The Brothers*. Straddling the River Ehen, and encircled by a bowl of rounded fells, the village is only ten miles from Cockermouth and seven from the coast, but seems much further from anywhere. A couple of pubs provide what few facilities there are, though the village sees a fair amount of foot traffic as it's the first overnight stop on the Coast-to-Coast walk from St Bees.

Ennerdale Water

Ennerdale Water is a mile and a half to the west of Ennerdale Bridge, where you'll find car parks for walkers and a couple of lakeside picnic areas. The standard **circuit of the lake** (8 miles; 4hr) is an enjoyable low-level walk, with the option of a scramble up **Angler's Crag** on the southwestern promontory. Sterner tests are provided by any of the peaks on the valley's southern side, though unless you're staying at either of the Ennerdale youth hostels you've got to add the valley walk-in and return to Bowness Knott car park to your day's hike. For that reason, you won't see too many others en route (most choose to climb Pillar, say, from Wasdale), which is a recommendation

---

WILD ENNERDALE

Ennerdale was the valley most affected by the mass imposition of conifer plantations by the Forestry Commission in the 1930s. There was nothing new about planting trees for profit in the Lakes – Wordsworth was already complaining about it in his *Guide to the Lakes* (a "vegetable manufactory" he called it) – but the sheer scale in Ennerdale was unprecedented. Before 1930 the upper part of the valley was a desolate, rocky wilderness, devoid of trees. Afterwards, thousands of acres lay under a thick blanket of uniform conifer plantations – only local resistance prevented Eskdale, Wast Water and Buttermere going the same way. In England's mild climate, the rigid blocks of larch, spruce and pine grew quickly, blocking out the light and carpeting the valley floors with slow-decomposing acidic needles. Wild plants (and therefore animals) were quickly forced out of their natural habitat. More enlightened planting policies (mixing in broad-leaved trees and following the contours instead of straight lines) softened the scenery over the years, but it wasn't until the **Wild Ennerdale** (🌐 wildennerdale.co.uk) initiative that a new, holistic approach was taken. It's still a major timber provider, but Ennerdale's three main landowners (Forestry Commission, National Trust and water company United Utilities) have undertaken to "allow the evolution of Ennerdale as a wild valley" – in essence, thinning and clearing conifers, re-establishing native trees and heather and allowing the River Liza to find its own course. Free-grazing Galloway cattle have been introduced (don't be surprised to come across some while hiking), and red deer, red squirrels and otters have returned to the valley. If you've steered clear of Ennerdale's brutal man-made forest swathes in the past, now's the time to come back for a look at a land reclaiming itself.

5

in itself: an **Ennerdale peaks circuit** (12 miles; 7hr) from Bowness Knott, taking in Haycock (2618ft), Scoat Fell (2760ft), Steeple (2687ft) and Pillar (2927ft), is one of the most exhilarating fell walks in the region.

ARRIVAL AND INFORMATION   ENNERDALE

By car There are car parks at Ennerdale Water – two at the western end of the lake, near the village, and a third at Bowness Knott, midway along the northern shore. Cars aren't allowed any further than Bowness Knott, though there is a track for vehicle access to Low Gillerthwaite and the *YHA Ennerdale* hostel.

By bus Jansen Travel (☎ 01946 862091, ⓦ jansentravel. com) runs a Whitehaven–Frizington service, which can get you to within about 4 miles of the lake.

On foot Shortest walk to *YHA Black Sail* hostel is the 2.5-

mile high-level route from Honister Pass, which has the great advantage of a bus service to the trailhead (#77/77A from Keswick). From *Black Sail* it's a reasonably gentle downhill miles to the lake at Ennerdale and another couple of miles to the village of Ennerdale Bridge.

Tourist information The Gather Café and Shop in Ennerdale Bridge (Mon–Fri & Sun 10am–4pm, Sat 9am–4pm; ☎ 01946 862453; ⓦ thegatherennerdale.com) is a fabulous community-run centre with stacks of local info; ⓦ wild ennerdale.co.uk is another useful source of information.

ACCOMMODATION AND EATING   SEE MAP PAGE 178

★ **Fox & Hounds** Ennerdale Bridge, CA23 3AR ☎ 01946 861373, ⓦ foxandhoundsinn.org. If you want a decent pub you really have to buy your own – which was what the local community did, turning the *Fox & Hounds* into both a local social centre and a welcome stop for Coast-to-Coasters, who rock up here most nights in season. There are three decent B&B rooms, and camping too (£8 campers' breakfasts available), while the bar serves up good food (dishes £9–13; dinner reservations advisable) and scrumptious beers from the local Ennerdale Brewery. Parking. Mon–Sat 11am–11pm, Sun noon–11pm; kitchen daily noon–11pm. Camping/tent **£5**, doubles **£90**

Low Gillerthwaite Field Centre Ennerdale, CA23 3AX, 2.5 miles east of Bowness Knott ☎ 01946 861229, ⓦ lgfc.org.uk. Seventeenth-century Low Gillerthwaite farmhouse has been refitted as an outdoor activity centre, used by small groups but available for individual overnight stays for hikers – call in advance to check. It's bunkhouse style (bring your own sleeping bag), and there's a decent self-catering kitchen, lounge with open fire and drying room. Even if the house is full, walk-in or bike-in campers can usually pitch a tent outside. Parking. Camping/person **£10**, dorms **£18**

★ **YHA Black Sail** Ennerdale, CA23 3AX, 6 miles east of Bowness Knott ☎ 0845 371 9680, ⓦ yha.org.uk/hostel/ yha-black-sail. The Lakes' most isolated and basic hostel (no

vehicle access – only foot visitors) is a stone former shepherd's bothy with just sixteen beds (advance reservations essential), but it's stunningly set at the head of Ennerdale and the walking around here is sensational. It's not a complete back-to-basics experience – true, there's no TV, phone reception or electric sockets, and whatever the weather, you have to go outside to use the shower and loo, but there's a fire-warmed lounge where a nightly supper club offers wholesome grub (£9.95 for two courses). The hostel is also usually open all day for hikers to call in for a cuppa. Longest walk in (and easiest parking) is from Bowness Knott on Ennerdale Water, but the shorter high-level route from Honister Pass gets you there quicker and can be done car-free. Closed Nov to two weeks before Easter. No credit cards. Dorms **£21.50**

YHA Ennerdale Cleator, CA23 3AX, 2.5 miles east of Bowness Knott ☎ 0845 371 9116, ⓦ yha.org.uk/hostel/ yha-ennerdale. Ennerdale's main YHA hostel is a fully refurbished eco-retreat converted from two old forestry cottages, providing 24 beds in both private and dorm rooms, as well as a spillover barn with sleeping areas over two floors. It has its own hydroelectric power, and there's a wood-burner in the cosy lounge-diner, while good-value meals (two courses £9.95) use locally sourced, organic and Fair Trade ingredients – and you can buy a Cumbrian ale or a bottle of organic wine. No mobile phone coverage or wi-fi. Closed Nov–Easter. Parking for up to three cars. Dorms **£21.50**

Loweswater and around

The western fells – and Buttermere – might be beckoning, but a diversion to **Loweswater**, six miles from Cockermouth, provides an opportunity to see one of the region's smallest, shallowest and least-known lakes. The water only averages a depth of 60ft, and the reeds and lily pads that cling to the shores are a habitat for many species of insects and birds. You'll never be bothered by crowds here. There's no village to speak of, rather a collection of houses, a church and a telephone box, with a couple of signs pointing you towards the excellent local pub, the *Kirkstile Inn*.

5

Around the lake

Loweswater itself is a mile beyond the *Kirkstile Inn* and really the only thing to do is to walk around it, on a gentle low-level route (4 miles; 1hr 30min) that stays under a woodland canopy for much of the duration. A detour in Holme Wood up to **Holme Force** adds a bit of interest after sustained rain; while the best views of the water are from Waterend, at the northern end of the lake.

Melbreak

The distinctive volcano-shaped peak that towers above the southern end of Loweswater is **Melbreak** (1676ft). The view of the fell from the beer garden of the *Kirkstile Inn* is impressive, but it's fairly easily climbed too – follow the road over the small bridge from the pub, then the obvious track up through the screes to the top (1hr). Descending, you can return to the inn either along the old drover's track along the Mosedale Valley bottom, or along the Crummock Water shore path (either route 6 miles; 3hr return).

Lorton

The scattered settlement of **Lorton** – divided into **Low Lorton** and **High Lorton** – has a twelfth-century church, St Cuthbert's, of minor interest; but there's also a pub and post office/general store, and some gentle walking in the fields near the River Cocker. The fiery Quaker George Fox preached to a seventeenth-century Lorton crowd under a spreading yew tree, which Wordsworth later commemorated ("pride of Lorton Vale") in his poem *Yew-trees* (1803).

ARRIVAL AND DEPARTURE   LOWESWATER AND AROUND

By car It's a 15- or 20min drive to Loweswater from Cockermouth via Lorton (B5292, then B5289); longer if you come over either pass (Whinlattter via Lorton or Honister via Buttermere) from Keswick. There's also a back-country route on minor lanes from Ennerdale. Waterend, at the northwestern end of Loweswater, has a couple of small parking places, and there's a National Trust car park (unmarked on most maps) near Watergate Farm at the southern end.

By bus For Lorton and the Whinlatter Pass, the service is the #77A from Buttermere, which runs up the B5289 before turning east along the B5292 towards Keswick.

ACCOMMODATION AND EATING   SEE MAP PAGE 178

LOWESWATER

★ **Kirkstile Inn** Loweswater, CA13 0RU ☎ 01900 85219, ⓦ kirkstile.com. Rooms at this welcoming sixteenth-century riverside inn retain their beams and country furniture but also have smart bathrooms, crisp linen and very comfortable beds. There are seven in the main inn and two self-contained family suites (£169) in the adjoining buildings, one of which can accommodate up to four adults (£224) – one also has a kitchen and lounge. On-the-ball staff deliver quality bar meals (duck and orange sausage, slow-cooked lamb shoulder, fell-bred steak; mains £13–17), and you can take in the sunsets in the beer garden while downing one of their own award-winning beers. Parking. Mon–Sat 10am–11pm, Sun noon–10.30pm; kitchen noon–2pm & 6–9pm. __£119__

LORTON

★ **New House Farm** Lorton, CA13 9UU, on B5289, 1 mile south of Low Lorton ☎ 0784 1159 818, ⓦ newhouse-farm.com. This is a gem of a place with five hugely attractive rooms, either in the meticulously restored seventeenth-century farmhouse or its period outbuildings – the Old Dairy room (the largest), for example, has an extraordinary carved four-poster bed and a stunning bathroom with free-standing bath and hanging tapestry; guests receive a rather yummy cream tea upon arrival. Outside, 15 acres include mown grass walkways, ponds, gardens and an outdoor hot tub (champagne under the stars anyone?), while the barn tearoom provides all-day meals, such as smoked salmon salad or Cumberland ham with eggs and chips, as well as coffee, cakes and afternoon cream teas. Parking. Tearoom mid-March to Oct Sun–Fri 10.30am–5pm. __£180__

Old Vicarage Church Lane, Low Lorton, CA13 9UN ☎ 01900 85656, ⓦ oldvicarage.co.uk. Wooded grounds surround this impressive Victorian B&B, where a mahogany staircase ascends to the rooms. Some are rated superior (with bigger beds and good views) and there are also two separate rooms in an old coach house which are handy for families. They provide packed lunches for a day out (£8), and the pub is only 5min walk away for dinner (they'll lend you a torch for evening visits). Parking. **£110**

Wheatsheaf Inn Low Lorton, CA13 9UW ☎01900 85199, ⓦwheatsheafinnlorton.co.uk. Lorton's local

pub has a pleasant beer garden, substantial bar meals (mains £13–18) – with fresh fish on Thurs and Fri nights – and Jennings ales. Out the back, there's a camping and caravan site (closed Dec–Feb) with shower, toilet block and drying facilities. Mon–Wed 6–11pm, Thurs–Sun 11am–11pm; kitchen Mon–Thurs 6–8.30pm, Fri & Sat noon–3pm & 6–8.30pm, Sun noon–8.30pm. Camping/person **£7.50**

Crummock Water and Buttermere

A simple glance at the map shows that **Crummock Water** and **Buttermere** – separated by just a half-mile of slightly elevated flood-prone farmland – were once joined as a single lake. In the main, they're visited as one, with nearly all the day-traffic concentrated in and around **Buttermere village**, a small settlement in the middle of the two lakes with an outlying church, two inns, and the rest of the local facilities.

The two lakes, however, have entirely different aspects: small Buttermere ("Boethar's lake") is ringed by crags and peaks, culminating in the desolate heights of Gatesgarthdale; more expansive Crummock Water ("crooked lake") is almost twice as long (at two and a half miles) and half as deep again, yet peters out in the gentle flat lands of Lorton Vale. It's a contrasting beauty that brought back that most obsessive of fell-walkers, Alfred Wainwright, again and again. A plaque in the small parish **church of St James**, on a hillock above Buttermere village, asks you to pause and remember him and then lift your eyes to Haystacks, his favourite peak, where his ashes are scattered. In *Fellwanderer*, his account of the writing of his famous *Pictorial Guides*, he's typically and playfully brusque: "If, dear reader, you should get a bit of grit in your boot as you are crossing **Haystacks** in the years to come, please treat it with respect. It might be me."

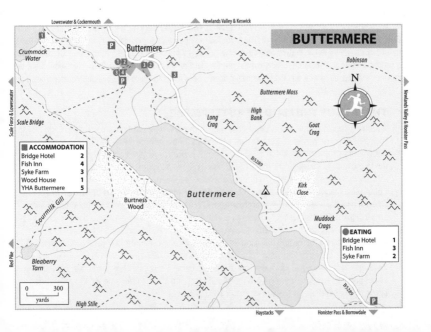

5

ARRIVAL AND DEPARTURE

CRUMMOCK WATER AND BUTTERMERE

By car There's an official pay-and-display car park behind the *Fish Inn* and another 300 yards up the road to Crummock Water. Alternatively, free parking places can be found on the Crummock Water lakeshore road or up the minor Newlands Valley road, past the church, though it gets very busy everywhere in holidays and good weather.

By bus The direct bus service is the #77, which runs on a circular route from Keswick, via Whinlatter Pass (15min) and Lorton (25min) to Buttermere (45min), and then back via Honister Pass and Borrowdale; the #77A comes the other way round, through Borrowdale first, to Buttermere (50min) and then back via Lorton and Whinlatter Pass. Service operates April–Oct 4 daily, and with a Honister and Borrowdale Day Rider ticket (from £8.50) from the driver, you can use both services all day.

ACCOMMODATION AND EATING

SEE MAP PAGE 197

Buttermere village has no shops, but it does have two **hotels**, the *Bridge* and the *Fish*, plus a youth hostel and various local farms and houses offering B&B and camping. Both hotels have bar meals and beer gardens, or you can get sandwiches and put together a picnic at *Croft House Farm Café* or the *Syke Farm* tearoom – the latter sells great ice cream, made with milk from their own Ayrshire cows.

BUTTERMERE

Bridge Hotel Buttermere, CA13 9UZ ⓣ017687 70252, ⓦbridge-hotel.com. The best rooms in the big Victorian hotel are the cheerfully decorated superior ones with large bathrooms, some with balconies; and there are also south-facing, self-catering apartments available across the beck (sleep two to four, £784–959/week). On Fridays and Saturdays the only rate available is for dinner and B&B (£190) – the fancy restaurant menu aside (reservations essential), you can chomp on breakfasts, sandwiches and filling Cumbrian specials (£8–15) in the oak-beamed *Walkers' Bar*. Parking. Closed Jan. Daily 8am–11pm; bar kitchen 9.30am–9.30pm; restaurant 6–8.30pm. £120

Fish Inn Buttermere, CA13 9XA ⓣ017687 70253, ⓦfishinnbuttermere.co.uk. Buttermere's other hotel is a smaller, simpler place than the *Bridge*, but has history, romance and price on its side, and the better beer garden – with views straight up to the Red Pike ridge. It's all-round traditional in character, with no real surprises from either rooms or bar meals (mains £8–12), but it's a terrific place to wake up in the morning, with the lake just a few minutes' walk away. Parking. April–Oct daily 10.30am–10.30pm; Nov–March Thurs–Mon 10.30am–3pm & 6–10.30pm; kitchen noon–2pm & 6–8.30pm. £115

★**Syke Farm** Buttermere, CA13 9XA ⓣ017687 70222, ⓦsykefarmcampsite.com. The farm offers simple camping near the lake (toilet and shower block provided) – simple, that is, save for the amazing mountain views – as well as two well-furnished yurts sleeping four people (£359/3 nights, £539/week). There are no campsite reservations, so best get there early in summer and on bank holidays – walkers and cyclists (rather than drivers) tend to get preference since parking is limited. The on-site tearoom offers camper's breakfasts (£5) as well as snacks and the Lakes' best ice cream, direct (well, almost) from cow to customer. No credit cards. Tearoom Feb half-term to Nov daily 10am–5pm. Per person £8

YHA Buttermere Buttermere, CA13 9XA, 0.25 mile southeast of Buttermere village ⓣ0845 371 9508, ⓦyha.org.uk/hostel/yha-buttermere. Overlooks the lake on the road to Honister Pass – not surprisingly, the views from this sturdy slate-built hostel (once a hotel) are

THE TALE OF THE MAID OF BUTTERMERE

With the Lakes in vogue among travelling men in the late eighteenth century, many made their way over the passes to Buttermere, which was then a remote hamlet with a reputation for good fishing in the twin lakes. A certain Captain Budworth – resident at the *Fish Inn*, the only inn in those days – waxed lyrical about the beauty of the landlord's daughter in his bestseller, *A Fortnight's Ramble in the Lakes*. Within a couple of years, curious sightseers – Wordsworth and Coleridge included – were turning up to view **Mary Robinson, the Maid of Buttermere**. One such visitor was Colonel Alexander Augustus Hope, Member of Parliament and brother to an earl. Flush with money and manners, he wooed and married Mary – only to be revealed as the bigamous impostor John Hatfield, whose whole life had been one of deception and fraud. Arrested and tried for forgery (franking letters as an MP without authority was a capital offence), Hatfield was hanged at Carlisle in 1802 – the entire scandal recorded for the *Morning Post* by Coleridge in investigative journalist mode. Mary became a cause célèbre, the subject of ballads, books and plays, before retiring from the public gaze at the *Fish* to become wife to a Caldbeck farmer. She died there, as Mary Harrison, in 1837 (see page 171).

5

WALKS FROM CRUMMOCK WATER AND BUTTERMERE

Many hikers have their fondest memories of the fells around Buttermere and Crummock Water, and one – Haystacks – is the final resting place of the greatest walker of them all, **Alfred Wainwright**. It's easy to gain height quickly around here for some terrific views, though the low-level circuits of the two lakes are also very rewarding.

CRUMMOCK WATER AND SCALE FORCE

Any circuit of **Crummock Water** should include the diversion to the 170ft drop of **Scale Force**, among the most spectacular of Lake District waterfalls. You can then either regain the western shore and stick close to the lake for the rest of the circuit (8 miles; 4hr), or climb past the falls and follow the Mosedale Valley path to Loweswater (where there's a pub, the *Kirkstile Inn*) before completing the circuit (10 miles; 5–6hr).

AROUND BUTTERMERE

The four-mile stroll circling **Buttermere** shouldn't take more than a couple of hours – in wet weather, the waters tumbling 1000ft down Sour Milk Ghyll are amazing. And you can always detour up **Scarth Gap** to Haystacks (see below) if you want more of a climb and some views. It's worth knowing that, in summer, there's usually an ice-cream van parked by Gatesgarth Farm at the southern end of the lake.

RED PIKE TO HAYSTACKS

The classic Buttermere circuit (8 miles; 6hr 30min) climbs from the village up **Red Pike** (2479ft) and then runs along the ridge, via **High Stile** (2644ft), **High Crag** (2443ft) and **Haystacks** (1900ft), before descending to the lake – either by backtracking and heading down Scarth Gap or by picking your way down off Haystacks, rounding Inominate Tarn and descending via **Warnscale Bottom**. For a fuller experience, add another hour to the beginning of the hike by first climbing up Scale Force from Buttermere and working your way across to Red Pike from there.

ROBINSON

The quickest ascent from Buttermere (2.5 miles; 1hr 30min) for some top-drawer views is the climb up **Robinson** (2417ft) – the path is signposted a little way up the Newlands Valley road, past the church. You'll get a bit wet at any time of year crossing the wide marsh of Buttermere Moss (the only way water can escape from here, opines Wainwright, is by being carried away in the boots of pedestrians), but then it's up to the rocky plateau summit for majestic mountain views.

---

supreme, which makes it one of the more popular ones in the Lakes. There are twin rooms and four-bed family rooms (£75) available as well as wooden platforms for camping (£15). The pubs are close by, but the hostel also has a bar of its own and good-value evening meals (£9.95 for two courses). Dorms £23.50, twin rooms £57

CRUMMOCK WATER

Wood House Crummock Water ☎017687 70208, ⓦwdhse.co.uk. Quite the nicest local choice is this

attractive house in a serene setting on Crummock Water, just a few hundred yards from Buttermere village. Three elegant bedrooms and the drawing room enjoy marvellous views, while the gardens and surrounding woodland harbour red squirrels and woodpeckers. A two-course dinner (£24) is offered on Tuesday, Thursday and Saturday, albeit only for groups of four or more, while packed lunches can be made up too. They've also got mountain bikes and canoes for hire, and can also arrange guided walking services. Closed Nov–March. Parking. No credit cards. £132

Ullswater

STRIDING EDGE, HELVELLYN

Ullswater

Wordsworth declared Ullswater "the happiest combination of beauty and grandeur, which any of the Lakes affords", a judgement that still holds good. At almost eight miles, it's the second longest lake in the National Park, with a dramatic serpentine shape that's overlooked by soaring fells, none higher than the challenging reaches of Helvellyn (one of the Lakes' celebrated three-thousand-footers). The shores meanwhile are stippled with woods of native oak, birch and hazel – one of the best surviving examples of pre-plantation lakeland scenery. Ullswater has been a tourist magnet for a couple of centuries, and steamer services around the lake – which started as far back as 1859 – are a major draw at any time of the year.

Twin lakeside settlements, **Patterdale** and **Glenridding**, less than a mile apart at the southern tip of Ullswater, soak up most of the visitors intent upon the local attractions: namely **cruises** from Glenridding, the tumbling waterfalls of **Aira Force** and the Wordsworthian daffodils of **Gowbarrow Park**. From Glenridding, boats run across to **Howtown** on the eastern side, where walking routes run up glorious hidden valleys such as Fusedale and Martindale and along the High Street range. Last stop is at **Pooley Bridge** at the head of Ullswater, where you're close to the historic house at **Dalemain** and the attractive village of **Askham**, gateway to the rolling **Lowther** parklands.

The northeastern lakes finish with a flourish in the crinkled valleys between the southern foot of Ullswater and the desolate Shap Fells at the eastern edge of the National Park. The A592, heading south from Ullswater for the Kirkstone Pass and Ambleside, passes **Brothers Water**. Otherwise the only roads are the minor lanes south from Askham and west of Shap, which meet at **Haweswater**, easternmost and very possibly the least visited of all the lakes (and, with Thirlmere, the Lake District's other main reservoir).

Glenridding and around

A fast-flowing beck, flanked by stone buildings and cottages, tumbles through the centre of **Glenridding**, which was formerly a mining village and is now the busiest of Ullswater's lakeside settlements. It was this beck that led to Glenridding bearing the brunt of the devastating floods of 2015–16, and it's only recently that many businesses have returned to anything like normality. Although the village itself consists of little more than a couple of rows of cottages set back from the lake, there's also a huge car park, two or three tearooms, a general store and a fair amount of accommodation – not to mention rowing boats to rent and plenty of places to sit on the grass banks or wade into the water from the stony shore. While that may sound too popular for comfort, it isn't particularly – many visitors just park up for a day's walking or lake-cruising and by early evening the lakeshore regains much of its peace and quiet. There are several local rambles to make, though the main target for nearly all visitors is the **Aira Force** waterfall, a little way north of Glenridding.

Glenridding Beck and Lanty's Tarn

If you're not here to climb Helvellyn, you can at least stretch your legs in the local valley and follow **Glenridding Beck** half a mile west as far as **Rattlebeck Bridge**. It's another mile from here up to the *Helvellyn* youth hostel, which sits amid old lead **mine**

Highlights

❶ **Aira Force** Visit the romantic lakeland waterfall whose daffodil-strewn surroundings inspired Wordsworth to pen one of his most famous poems. See page 206

❷ **A steamer ride on Ullswater** Disembark for some marvellous local walks or stay aboard for the round-the-lake cruise. See page 207

❸ **Striding Edge** There's no more exciting mountain walk than inching your way along Striding Edge, en route to the summit of Helvellyn. See page 208

❹ **Pooley Bridge** Ullswater's prettiest village has a popular farmers' market and some excellent accommodation and cafés nearby. See page 212

❺ **Dalemain** Successive generations of the same family have lived in this handsome stately home since 1679. See page 212

❻ **Lowther Castle and Gardens** Explore the magnificent "lost gardens" and castle ruins – open to the public after decades of neglect. See page 216

❼ **George and Dragon, Clifton** The Lowther Estate's gastropub showcase shines a light on the best local produce – and offers some lovely rooms. See page 217

❽ **Haweswater** Get right off the beaten track on the trail of Withnail and Uncle Monty. See page 217

HIGHLIGHTS ARE MARKED ON THE MAP ON PAGE 204

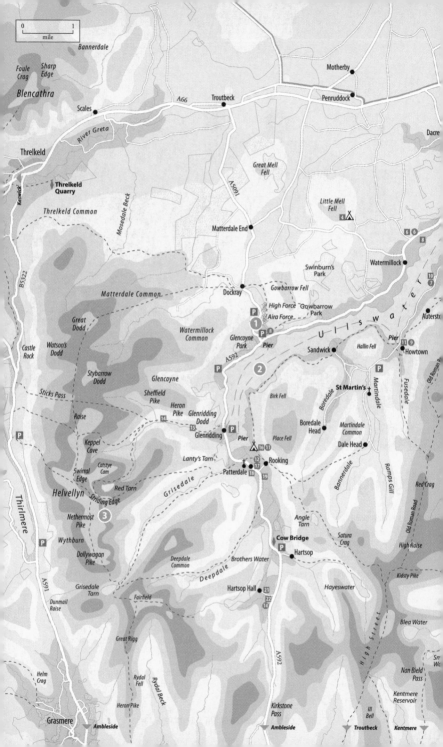

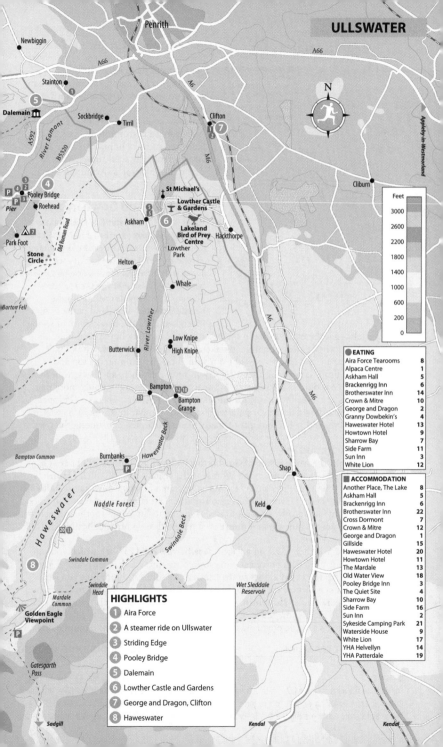

6

▲ Aira Force, Pooley Bridge & Penrith

GLENRIDDING

■ ACCOMMODATION	
Beech House	4
Glenridding Hotel	2
Inn on the Lake	1
Mosscrag	3

● EATING	
Fellbites	1

Helvellyn & YHA

GREENSIDE ROAD   A592

Glenridding Beck

General Store (ATM)

Ullswater Steamers jetty, Howtown & Pooley Bridge

N

0   100
yards

A592

St Patrick's Boat Landing

St Patrick's Well

Lanty's Tarn, Helvellyn & Campsite

▼ Patterdale, Troutbeck & Windermere

workings, which were first exploited in the seventeenth century and only ceased operation in the 1960s. The other way from the bridge, south and east, you can wind up to pretty little **Lanty's Tarn**, set in a grove of trees and with views from a nearby knoll over Ullswater. The name is probably a corruption of "Lancelot", bestowed more in hope than accuracy on any romantically sited stretch of water that might conceal an Arthurian sword.

Aira Force and Gowbarrow

Aira Force, CA11 0JS, 3 miles north of Glenridding, along A592 • Always open • Free, though parking fee charged • Buses #508 from Glenridding/Penrith and #208 from Glenridding/Keswick stop nearby (it's not advised to walk from Glenridding along the busy A592) – there are also ferries from Glenridding to Aira Force Pier (June–Aug 8 daily, rest of year 3–6 daily; £6.40 single, £9.80 return; 20min)

To avoid the crowds trailing up the needle-carpeted woodland paths to **Aira Force** – and for the best chance of seeing red squirrels – get there first thing in the morning or last thing in the evening. This is one of the prettiest, most romantic, of lakeland "forces" – a 70ft waterfall that's spectacular in spate and can be viewed from stone bridges spanning the top and bottom of the drop. It's only a thirty- to forty-minute walk there and back from the car park – keep an eye out for red squirrels in the woods on the way – though note that the steep paths aren't really suitable for families with pushchairs. There's a National Trust information board at the car park (and stewards present in summer), as well as a seasonal **tearoom**, and you'll find lots of shady places for a picnic in among the trees.

Gowbarrow Park and Fell

Aira Force flanks the western side of **Gowbarrow Park**, whose hillside still blazes green and gold in spring, as it did when the Wordsworths visited in April 1802. Dorothy's sprightly recollections of the visit in her journal inspired William to write his **Daffodils** poem, though it was not until two years later that he first composed the famous lines (borrowing many of Dorothy's exact phrases). Despite its fame now, nothing much was thought of the poem at the time; it didn't even have a title on first publication in 1807 (in *Poems in Two Volumes*).

The walking is tougher going on adjacent **Gowbarrow Fell** (1579ft), which you can climb in an hour from Aira Force car park. The route runs via the viewpoint of Yew Crag and then up the boggy slopes to the cairn at the summit. From here you can descend to Dockray (where there's a pub) or, more directly, over the top to Green Hill and thence to Aira Force (2hr return). The National Park Authority is trying to cut the number of sheep grazing the fell in an attempt to lure back some of the wildlife, while every spring there's a battle of wits with visitors intent on picking the famous daffs.

ARRIVAL AND DEPARTURE   **GLENRIDDING AND AROUND**

BY CAR

The road to Ullswater is the A592, which runs through Patterdale and Glenridding en route to Aira Force, Pooley Bridge and Penrith. Parking along the lake is sometimes difficult, especially in summer, but it's easy to park in Glenridding and use bus or boat to visit local attractions. There's limited short-time free parking in Glenridding itself – you're best off using the large car park by the visitor centre, where it costs £4 for all-day parking. Glenridding is small, and everything is just a few minutes' walk from the car park.

BY BOAT
Pier House and the steamer pier are just a 5min walk from the main road in Glenridding, or there's pay-and-display parking by the pier. Steamer services operate year-round (see box) to Howtown, across the lake from Glenridding, and to Pooley Bridge at the head of the lake. There's also a ferry to Aira Force Pier (see page 207).

BY BUS
Buses (from Penrith, Pooley Bridge, Windermere and Keswick) all stop on the main road in Glenridding. An Ullswater Bus & Boat ticket (from £16, buy on the bus) is available for return bus travel and a steamer trip, using the #508 (between Windermere and Pooley Bridge).

Bus #208 (2 daily) to: Aira Force (7min); Keswick (35min). Service operates Easter–Oct; daily during school holidays, otherwise Sat & Sun only.

Bus #508, "Kirkstone Rambler" to: Patterdale (5min), Brothers Water (12min), Kirkstone Pass (27min), Troutbeck *Queen's Head* (40min), Windermere (52min) and Bowness (1hr 5min). Service operates 5 daily from late July to early Sept, otherwise on Sat, Sun & bank hols from Easter to late July, Sept & Oct.

6

INFORMATION AND ACTIVITIES

Tourist office The National Park Information Centre (April–Oct daily 9.30am–5.30pm; Nov–March Sat & Sun 9.30am–3.30pm; ☎ 07769 956144/0845 901 0845, ⓦ lake district.gov.uk), on the edge of Glenridding car park, posts a daily weather report for walkers and has a route map and advice for tackling Helvellyn.

Website There's useful local information on ⓦ ullswater.com.

Bike and boat rental There's bike and boat rental at St Patrick's Boat Landing (March–Oct daily 9.30am–5pm, weather depending; ☎ 017684 82393, ⓦ stpatricksboat landings.co.uk), a few minutes' walk south of Glenridding village (car park is free for customers). Bikes £15/half-day, £25/day; rowing boats from £16/hr (for two people); motorboats from £26/hr (for two people).

ACCOMMODATION

SEE MAPS PAGES 204 AND 206

Two big traditional slate **hotels** dominate Glenridding village, the *Inn on the Lake* and the *Glenridding Hotel*, and there are several cheaper **B&Bs**. Hikers meanwhile make a beeline for the out-of-village youth hostel, campsite and bunkhouse, all lying en route to the area's major peak, Helvellyn. The alternative to Glenridding is to stay a mile down the road in Patterdale (see page 209), where there's some reasonable B&B accommodation as well as a second local youth hostel.

Beech House Glenridding, CA11 0PA, on A592 ☎ 017684 82037, ⓦ beechhouse.com. The end-of-terrace slate house (by the steamers' turn-off) is a spick-and-span B&B base for local walks and excursions. Seven rooms, though small, are prettily furnished, and a couple sport lake inlet and fell views. The water's edge is just a minute or two's stroll away across the grassy common. Parking. £98

★ **Gillside** Glenridding, CA11 0QQ ☎ 017684 82346, ⓦ gillsidecaravanandcampingsite.co.uk. Campsite in a beautiful spot, en route to Helvellyn, 0.25 mile up the valley behind the village – follow the path along the beck (and note there are no camping reservations: it's first come,

---

ULLSWATER STEAMERS

Five vintage **Ullswater Steamers** (❶ 017684 82229, ⓦ ullswater-steamers.co.uk) operate a year-round service on the lake – one, *Lady of the Lake*, launched in 1877, is claimed to be the oldest working passenger vessel in the world. Services run from Glenridding to Howtown (45min; £7.30 single, £11.65 return) and on to Pooley Bridge (1hr 5min; £10.20 each way), and back again, and there's also a service between Glenridding and the National Trust Aira Force Pier (20min; £6.40 single, £9.80 return). The one-day hop-on, hop-off Cruise All Piers Pass (from £13.50, family £39) also nets you a fifty percent discount on the Ravenglass & Eskdale Railway (see page 182); there are good savings to be had on all these tickets if purchased online, otherwise you can buy tickets at the piers. Bikes, incidentally, can be taken aboard for £1.50.

In school and summer holidays there are up to nine **daily departures** from Glenridding (basically an hourly service), down to between three and six a day at other times of the year – only Christmas Eve and Christmas Day have no sailings. There are also special cruises and activity weekends (like Halloween's "Ghostly Galleons", and Santa Specials), with current details posted on the website.

There's a bar on board the steamers, and parking, a café and picnic area at Glenridding's Pier House. At Pooley Bridge, a café operates during the summer season.

6

HELVELLYN WALKS

The climb to the summit of **Helvellyn** (3114ft) is among the region's most challenging. You are unlikely to be alone on the yard-wide approaches – on summer weekends and bank holidays the car parks below and paths above are full by 9am – but the variety of routes up and down at least offers a chance of escaping the crowds. The most direct route from Glenridding, via Striding Edge, returning via Swirral Edge and Red Tarn, is a good seven-mile (5–6hr) walk, while for any of the other variations you can count on being out all day. Note that if it's just the summit you're after, there's a far less demanding walk (3hr return) up the western approach from the A591 at Thirlmere, between Grasmere and Keswick.

STRIDING EDGE

The most frequently chosen route to the summit is via the infamous **Striding Edge**. Purists negotiate the undulating ridge top of Striding Edge; slightly safer, but no less precipitous tracks follow the line of the ridge, just off the crest. However you get across (and some refuse to go any further when push comes to shove), there's a final, sheer, hands-and-feet scramble to the flat **summit** (2hr 30min from Glenridding). Every year people get into serious trouble on Striding Edge and have to be stretchered off the mountain: a point emphasized by the occasionally hovering rescue helicopters.

SWIRRAL EDGE AND RED TARN

The classic return from the summit is via the less demanding **Swirral Edge**, from where a straightforward route leads down to stunning **Red Tarn** – the highest Lake District tarn – then follows the beck down to Glenridding past the Helvellyn youth hostel. This is the best route *up* Helvellyn if you don't fancy Striding Edge, as Swirral Edge is far less exposed an approach (though there is still some hands-and-feet climbing). If you come up this way, then you can make your return circuit to the north instead (see next walk).

RAISE AND STICKS PASS

North from the Helvellyn summit there's an obvious cairned route heading towards **Raise** (2897ft), with stupendous views away to the east over Red Tarn and down the valleys. The path then drops down to **Sticks Pass** for an interesting descent alongside Sticks Gill and through the scars of the old mine workings. The route runs right past *YHA Helvellyn* for the final mile into Glenridding. Depending on the time and weather conditions, peak-baggers might make the decision at Sticks Pass first to tick off **Stybarrow Dodd** (2766ft), an easy twenty-minute diversion, and even **Watson's Dodd** (2589ft) beyond.

GRISEDALE

South from the Helvellyn summit, you can follow the flat ridge past **Nethermost Pike** (2920ft) and **Dollywagon Pike** (2810ft), after which there's a long scree scramble down to **Grisedale Tarn** and then the gentlest of descents down **Grisedale** Valley, alongside the beck, emerging on the Patterdale–Glenridding road. This really is a fantastic walk, with a fine mix of terrain, a good six hours all told for the entire circuit.

first served). There are also caravans for rent (from £380/ week), and a bunkhouse with two rooms sleeping seven and thirteen, and a modern kitchen, though you need your own sleeping and cooking equipment. Milk and eggs are available from the family farm, and breakfast supplies at weekends. No credit cards. Closed mid-Nov to Feb. £2/tent and £1/vehicle extra. Camping/person __£9__, bunkhouse __£15__
Glenridding Hotel Glenridding, CA11 0PB, on A592 ☎017684 82228, ⓦtheglenriddinghotel.com.

Following the 2015 floods, this venerable three-star hotel was totally refurbished with a new bistro, bar and coffee shop. Contemporary rooms come in a range of categories, including standard and lakeview rooms (£30 supplement) plus family rooms and suites. You also get an impressive indoor pool and sauna for your money, as well as a snooker table and table tennis in the Campbell library. Parking. __£110__
★ **Inn on the Lake** Glenridding, CA11 0PE, Ullswater lakeside ☎017684 82444, ⓦlakedistricthotels.net/

innonthelake. If you're going to shell out in Glenridding, you might as well go for a lakeview room (from £310) at this classy four-star hotel set in 15 acres of gardens stretching down to Ullswater. The whole place is pretty nicely turned out, with sophisticated lounge bar and water-view restaurant, plus gym, sauna, jacuzzi, croquet lawn and tennis court – families will like the sense of space, as well as the fact that the kids can play in the grounds while you enjoy afternoon tea on the lawns. The hotel also has its own pub, the separate *Ramblers' Bar* in the grounds. Parking. **£210**

Mosscrag Glenridding, CA11 0PA, south side of the beck near the shops ☎ 017684 82500, ⓦ mosscrag.co.uk. A genial village-centre B&B with six cottage-style rooms, four of which are en suite (£96), including a superior four-poster room (£100). You're guaranteed a quiet night, and while the

pubs and hotels are all an easy walk away. Parking. **£80**

YHA Helvellyn Greenside, CA11 0QR ☎ 0845 371 9742, ⓦ yha.org.uk/hostel/yha-helvellyn. Walkers wanting an early start on Helvellyn (see page 208) stay at this dramatically sited hostel, 900ft and 1.5 miles up the valley road from Glenridding (the last half unmetalled, but suitable for vehicles if taken with care). You can be out of the door first thing in the morning, and beat the crowds on the well-trodden path up the mountain, which runs right past the hostel. There are lots of beds (and private rooms available for families, from £53 for three people, £65 for four), camping space for five (£9/person), plus a full meals service (£9.95 for two courses) and alcohol licence. The nearest pub, the *Travellers Rest*, is only a mile away. The hostel is closed on occasional nights, and advance bookings are advised. Dorms **£25**

EATING

SEE MAPS PAGES 204 AND 206

Local facilities in Glenridding include a general store on the main road, and two or three other shops selling walking gear and supplies – you'll be able to put together a **picnic** easily enough. There are **restaurants** in both main hotels (best at *Inn on the Lake*), and both also have attached pubs, though the best **pub** by far hereabouts is Patterdale's *White Lion*.

Aira Force Tearooms Aira Force, CA11 0JS, 3 miles north of Glenridding on A592 ☎ 017684 82881. The tearoom by the car park at Aira Force is ideally sited to catch visitors who have trudged up to the falls and back – it's a fairly back-to-basics experience (soup, sandwiches and home-made cakes £2–5) but there is an outdoor terrace

with Ullswater glimpsed through the trees. Theoretically, you're supposed to pay the car-park fee, so it's best to combine the tearoom with a waterfall visit, otherwise it's a pricey drinks stop. Daily 10.30am–4.30pm.

Fellbites Glenridding, CA11 0PD ☎ 017684 82781, ⓦ fellbitescafe.co.uk. Next to the beck and car park, cheery *Fellbites* dishes up sandwiches, melts, burgers and other light bites in its hiker-friendly daytime café (£3.50–11), with more substantial pub-style roast of the day, steaks, cod and chips and the like on offer in the evening (£12–20). A few outdoor tables catch the sun in summer. Mid-Feb to Sept Thurs–Tues 9am–8.30pm, Wed 9am–5pm.

Patterdale and around

Less than a mile south of Glenridding down the A592 (a path avoids the road for much of the way), and off the lake (though not that far from the water), **Patterdale** is the other local southern Ullswater settlement. St Patrick is supposed to have preached here (Patterdale is "Patrick's Dale") and the water in St Patrick's Well, on the road between Glenridding and Patterdale, was once thought to have miraculous powers. The saint's church, at the northern end of the village, is a nineteenth-century replacement of the medieval original, known for the locally made embroidered tapestries that hang inside.

Patterdale lies at the foot of **Grisedale**, which provides access to a stunning valley hike up to Grisedale Tarn and back (see page 208). There are also several other great places for local strolls, accessed from the car park at **Cow Bridge**, two miles south of Patterdale. The village is also an overnight stop on the Coast-to-Coast footpath, so a steady stream of hikers wends its way here from Grasmere, en route to Haweswater.

Brothers Water

From the car park at Cow Bridge, off the southwern end of Ullswater, it's just a short walk along a quiet stretch of Goldrill Beck to **Brothers Water**. The water itself (possibly taking its name from a corruption of the Norse name "Brothir") is a mere liquid scoop, but the path along the western shore takes you under the canopy of some of

6

the Lakes' oldest oak woodlands. This was the way Dorothy Wordsworth came on Good Friday in April 1802, after her daffodil-spotting excursion of the previous day, and it's easy to trace her exact route from her journal: "I left William sitting on the bridge, and went along the path on the right side of the lake through the wood. I was delighted with what I saw. The water under the boughs of the bare old trees, the simplicity of the mountains, and the exquisite beauty of the path." When she got back to Cow Bridge, William was busy writing a poem, which he later entitled (mistakenly) *Written in March*.

The path alongside Brothers Water runs a mile or so up to the 500-year-old **Hartsop Hall Farm**, standing on land that experts reckon has been farmed since the Bronze Age. You can press further on if you're in the mood for a decent hike – there are routes up Dovedale, for Dove Crag, Hart Crag and Fairfield – while the *Brotherswater Inn* is a handy halt for a drink.

Hartsop and Hayeswater

At the Cow Bridge car park, you cross the main road for the tiny hamlet of **Hartsop**, from where it's a mile-and-a-bit walk east up the valley to **Hayeswater**, a limpid little lake sitting under the High Street range. It's hard to believe now, but Hartsop was once a thriving mining and quarrying centre, the biggest in the region, and the track up to Hayeswater sits beneath crags riddled with old workings.

ACCOMMODATION AND EATING   **SEE MAP PAGE 204**

PATTERDALE

Old Water View Patterdale, CA11 0NW ☎017684 82175, ⓦ oldwaterview.co.uk. South, past the pub, on the bend in the road, *Old Water View* is an attractive B&B with half a dozen rustic rooms, a fabulous bar as well as an ace beer garden with terrace bar. They're used to walkers – even Alfred Wainwright stayed here on occasion. Parking. **£115**

Side Farm Patterdale, CA11 0NL ☎017684 82337, ⓦ lakedistrictcamping.co.uk/campsite_side_farm. The track to the farm is across from Patterdale's church, with the campsite set on the eastern shore of the lake, overlooked by Place Fell. It's small and quiet, and great for hikers, bikers and kayakers, with the pub only 0.25 mile or so away. Closed Nov–Easter. No advance bookings. Per person (plus £2 for vehicle) **£9**

White Lion Patterdale, CA11 0NW ☎017684 82214, ⓦ whitelionpatterdale.com. Patterdale's pub fills its seven straightforward guest rooms (five en suite) with passing Coast-to-Coast hikers and tourers, while many more make their way here for late breakfasts (served until 4pm; £9.25) and classic bar meals (£10–12), from sizzling steak platters to Whitby scampi. Parking. Daily 11am–11pm; kitchen noon–9pm. **£74**

YHA Patterdale Patterdale, CA11 0NW ☎0845 371 9337, ⓦ yha.org.uk/hostel/yha-patterdale. Patterdale's quirky youth hostel vaguely resembles a 1970s ski lodge – "retro and full of character" is what the YHA says, which means a bit old-fashioned in terms of decor but you don't need to worry about your kids spoiling the furniture. It's a pretty popular spot – and no wonder, when you can often get a room for a family of four from £54 – with the steamers and watersports on Ullswater just a mile or so away. There's space, too, for around fifteen tents (£15 per person). Two-course meals (£9.95) are prepared each evening. Parking. Restricted opening Nov–March. Dorms **£21.50**

BROTHERS WATER

Brotherswater Inn Brothers Water, CA11 0NZ, 3 miles south of Patterdale on A592 ☎017684 82239, ⓦ sykeside.co.uk. The outdoor terrace and big picture windows at the inn let you soak up the wonderful mountain backdrop. Inside are seven straightforward B&B rooms, plus rib-sticking full English breakfasts available daily, and a traditional bar menu (mains £11–15) that includes Cumberland sausage, braised lamb, home-made pies and pasta. Parking. Daily 8am–11pm; kitchen 8–9.30am, noon–2pm (3pm at weekends) & 6–9pm. **£96**

Sykeside Camping Park Brothers Water, CA11 0NZ, 3 miles south of Patterdale on A592 ☎017684 82239, ⓦ sykeside.co.uk. The campsite and bunkhouse attached to the *Brotherswater Inn* enjoys the same fine location, and facilities are good, from the centrally heated bunk-rooms and indoor cooking area to the campsite shop and *Barn End* bar (though you can also drink and eat at the inn itself). Camping (including one adult and vehicle) **£20.40**, bunkhouse **£19.50**

Pooley Bridge and around

Pooley Bridge, at the head of Ullswater, has a boulder-speckled shore with wonderful views south down the lake. Barely two streets grouped about the old village square, this was nonetheless a substantial settlement in past times, with a market charter granted by King John in the twelfth century – the modern equivalent being the thriving **farmers' market** (April–Sept, last Sun of the month 10.30am–2.30pm), which attracts up to twenty local farmers, growers and producers to one of the region's most enjoyable foodie events. Sadly, the old **stone bridge** itself, spanning the usually placid River Eamont, was washed away by **floods** in 2016, though work has begun to replace this with a stainless steel bridge, believed to be the first of its kind in the country. Pooley Bridge is a cute little place, rendered less so once the car parks are full, but it's still not a bad lunch or overnight stop, with a couple of tearooms, three pubs and some excellent nearby country cafés. It's also a convenient halt for anyone bound for the grand stately home of **Dalemain**, a couple of miles to the north.

Dalemain

Dalemain, CA11 0HB, 2 miles north of Pooley Bridge on A592 • April–Oct Mon–Thurs & Sun: house 10.30am–3.30pm; gardens & tearoom 10am–4pm; see website for opening hours through rest of the year • House and gardens £12.50; gardens only £9.50 • ☎ 017684 86450, ⓦ dalemain.com

Set back from the road amid close-cropped lawns, **Dalemain** has – remarkably – been residence to the same family since 1679. It started life in the twelfth century as a fortified tower, but has subsequently been added to by every generation, culminating with a Georgian facade grafted onto a largely Elizabethan house. There's enough to keep you here all day, especially if you take a long walk in the grounds, and the **Medieval Hall** provides drinks, lunches and afternoon teas – you don't need a ticket to visit this. Meanwhile every March the house hosts the "world's original" **Marmalade Festival**, a great day out with competitions, tastings, garden visits and children's games (and, naturally, Paddington Bear in attendance).

The house

Visitors are given the run of the **public rooms**, which the Hasell family still uses – hence the photographs and contemporary portraits alongside those of the ancestors. The house is heavy with oak, hewn from the estate's plantations, though lightened by unusual touches such as the eighteenth-century hand-painted wallpaper in the Chinese Room. The servants' corridors and pantries offer a glimpse of life "below stairs", commanded from the Housekeeper's Room – at the rear of which was discovered a priest's hole.

Outside, the medieval **courtyard** and Elizabethan **great barn** doubled as the schoolroom and dormitory of Lowood School in a TV adaptation of Charlotte Brontë's *Jane Eyre*. There's an agricultural and countryside collection in the great barn, and plenty of other displays and exhibits throughout the house, from dolls' houses and old toys to Gillows and Chippendale furniture and the family glassware.

Gardens and grounds

The Dalemain **grounds** are gorgeous – pristine terraces, radiant roses and Tudor gardens provide the main interest, best in late May and June – while the estate stretches west to encompass the fourteenth-century keep of Dacre Castle (no public access), which you can reach on a mile-long footpath from the house (there's also a nice old pub in Dacre village).

ARRIVAL AND INFORMATION	POOLEY BRIDGE AND AROUND

By car Pooley Bridge is just off the A592, 8 miles northeast of Glenridding and 6 miles southwest of Penrith. There are pay-and-display car parks either side of the bridge, and limited free parking in the village itself.

By boat The steamer jetty is a couple of hundred yards from the bridge and village; you can buy tickets at the jetty, at the information centre (see below) or on the boat. Steamer services operate year-round (see page 207).

By bus The #508 (4–5 daily) runs to Pooley Bridge, either from Penrith (18min) or from Patterdale/Glenridding (26min/

21min). For Dalemain, you'll need to drive or go by bike.

Tourist information The Ullswater Steamers shop and information centre (Easter–Oct daily 9.15am–5pm; Nov–Easter Sat & Sun 9am–5pm; closes over Christmas and New Year; ☎01768 486135), in the village square, sells steamer tickets and has walk brochures and other local information.

ACCOMMODATION

SEE MAP PAGE 204

As well as the places reviewed here, a few local **B&Bs** advertise vacancies. However, the most genteel places to stay are the various lakeside **country-house hotels** outside the village, doyen of which is the incomparable *Sharrow Bay*. Plenty of **campsites** on both sides of the lake make the Pooley Bridge area popular with families looking for a quiet place to stay.

POOLEY BRIDGE

Pooley Bridge Inn Pooley Bridge, CA10 2NN ☎017684 86215, ⊛pooleybridgeinn.co.uk. Just by the village square, this alpine-style hotel seems to have been plucked out of a *Heidi* story. Breakfast in the wicker chairs on your own balcony is tempting, while the old stable courtyard has been turned into a sunny beer garden. Parking. **£95**

Sun Inn Pooley Bridge, CA10 2NN ☎017684 86205, ⊛suninnpooleybridge.co.uk. Nine decent rooms – plainly furnished but of a good size, and with modern bathrooms – in this terrific village inn (see page 214), a whitewashed lakeland building which dates back at least to the eighteenth century. Parking. **£105**

AROUND POOLEY BRIDGE

Another Place, The Lake Watermillock, CA11 0LP, on A592, 2 miles southwest of Pooley Bridge ☎017684 86442, ⊛another.place. Part of the Another Place suite of hotels, this grand Georgian house offers a magnificent lakeside location on the western shore with gardens running right down to the water's edge, and a terrace with sweeping views. The forty rooms are divided into easily definable categories (Standard, Better and Best), though all are thoroughly modern and beautifully appointed, while there are also family suites available in a newer wing. Eating possibilities extend to the Rampsbeck restaurant (three-course dinner £40) or the more informal Living Space, where you can chow down on juicy burgers, stone-baked sourdough pizza and the like. Parking. **£170**

★ **Brackenrigg Inn** Watermillock, CA11 0LP, on A592, 2 miles southwest of Pooley Bridge ☎017684 86206, ⊛brackenrigginn.co.uk. Best place for a lake view without spending a fortune is this traditional roadside inn, with water views both from the nicest rooms at the front and from the outside terrace. Good for families, too, as some rooms can be linked together. The food's great, too (see page 214). Parking. **£90**

Cross Dormont Howtown, CA10 2NA, on the Howtown road ☎017684 86537, ⊛crossdormont.co.uk. Simple family-run camping and caravan site situated on a working farm (raising alpacas and sheep), with a fabulous children's play area complete with trampoline and rope swings. You can launch dinghies and kayaks from the lakeside fields, or walk right off the farm onto the fells. Price includes two adults and a vehicle. Per tent **£16**

★ **The Quiet Site** Watermillock, CA11 0LS ☎07768 727016, ⊛thequietsite.co.uk. The eco-friendly choice for cool campers is this hilltop site with sweeping views, sited on a former farmstead 1.5 miles up past the *Brackenrigg Inn*. It's largely for caravans and RVs, though grassy camping pitches are kept separate and there are a dozen cosy camping pods sleeping two adults and two (small) children (from £40). It's thoughtfully designed, from the family bathrooms and adventure playground to a great bar-in-a-barn that's open most summer evenings. Direct bus service (#208) from Penrith train station, Glenridding and Keswick. Price covers two adults. Per tent **£15**

★ **Sharrow Bay** 2 miles south of Pooley Bridge, Sharrow Bay, CA10 2LZ, on the Howtown road ☎017684 86301, ⊛sharrowbay.co.uk. The special-occasion place *par excellence*, England's first country-house hotel (in business since 1948) offers a breathtaking setting, personal service and refined food (see below). Needless to say, prices are high, but there are few places in England that compare. You can choose from a variety of lovely, antique-filled rooms in the main Victorian house, a garden annexe, the Edwardian gatehouse or in a converted Elizabethan farmhouse a mile away. Lake and fell views abound, there are acres of gardens and woods to wander in, and you'll find books and games in the rooms to pass the time when it pours. Parking. **£220**

Waterside House Howtown, CA10 2NA, on the Howtown road ☎017684 86332, ⊛watersidefarm-campsite.co.uk. Right on the water just a mile from Pooley Bridge, on a working farm, this is a tent- and motorhome-only site, with pods (from £55/night), tipis and bell tents available too (from £70/night). It has a separate family field and is pretty well equipped, with canoes, kayaks, rowing boats and bikes for rent – currently the only place to rent these things at this end of the lake – plus laundry, shop and children's playground. Closed Nov–Feb. Price is for two adults. Per tent **£18**

6

EATING

POOLEY BRIDGE

Granny Dowbekin's Pooley Bridge, CA10 2NP ☎017684 86453, ⊛grannydowbekins.co.uk. Charming, terraced riverside tea garden, by the bridge, serving home-made cakes and gingerbread inspired by the recipes of the owner's great-great Lancastrian granny. There are locally sourced meats and free-range eggs in the all-day brekkies, and mains (£5–9) from veggie pie to Cumbrian lamb casserole – and muddy boots and dogs are welcome. Daily Feb–Oct 10am–5pm; Nov–Jan 10am–4pm.

Sun Inn Pooley Bridge, CA10 2NN ☎017684 86205, ⊛suninnpooleybridge.co.uk. The best of the village pubs (100 yards up the road from the square) is the eighteenth-century *Sun*, with a carved, panelled bar and a beer garden to catch the rays; a very creditable menu is available in the shape of burgers and other grilled meats, platters (£9–12) and tasty mains like creamy fish pie and *tartiflette* (mains £12–16). Mon–Sat 11.30am–11pm, Sun 11.30am–10.30pm; kitchen daily noon–9pm.

AROUND POOLEY BRIDGE

Alpaca Centre Snuff Mill Lane, Stainton, CA11 0HA ☎01768 891440, ⊛thealpacaclothingco.co.uk. For drinks and cakes with a difference, head to this small tearoom on a working alpaca farm a couple of miles north of Pooley Bridge (signposted just past Dalemain). You can

see the alpacas from the paddock, and there's a craft shop and gallery selling clothes made from alpaca fibre, South American artefacts and jewellery, and handcrafted furniture and ornamental wood. Mon–Sat 10am–5pm.

★ **Brackenrigg Inn** Watermillock, CA11 0LP, on A592 2 miles southwest of Pooley Bridge ☎017684 86206, ⊛brackenrigginn.co.uk. The food at this roadside inn (see page 213) is a high point, emphasizing locally sourced produce, fish and seafood, from lamb hotpot to lake char (mains £13–18), and it's very easy-going – you can eat from the same menu in the bar, the family dining area, the more formal dining room, or even outside. Better still, their ace micro brewery, occupying the old stables out back, now conjures up a handful of delicious real ales. Daily 8am–11.30pm; kitchen noon–9pm.

★ **Sharrow Bay** 2 miles south of Pooley Bridge, Sharrow Bay, CA10 2LZ, on the Howtown road ☎017684 86301, ⊛sharrowbay.co.uk. The dining room at this fancy country-house hotel is open to non-residents (reservations essential); afternoon tea (£27.50) is famous, while lunch (three-courses for £29.50) and dinner (gourmet menu £70, eight-course tasting menu £90) are classy, formal affairs – desserts are renowned, notably the "icky sticky toffee pudding", which the hotel claims as its own invention. Lunch noon–1.30pm, afternoon tea 3.30pm, dinner 6.30pm–9pm.

Howtown and around

Howtown is tucked behind a little indented harbour halfway down the lake and four miles south of Pooley Bridge. It's a popular spot for a summer day out, with one isolated gem of a hotel and bar, plenty of nearby picnic places, some sparkling lake views and several fine walks. Many people in fact cross to Howtown by boat from Glenridding or Pooley Bridge and then walk back, and on a blue-sky summer's day it's hard to think of a better way to spend your time.

Martindale

The minor road from Pooley Bridge runs south through Howtown and climbs up in switchbacks to a car park at the foot of **Martindale**. The road, in fact, continues another couple of miles up to Dale Head, but it's best to abandon the car and walk the ten minutes along to **St Martin's**, the most beautifully sited of all the Lake District's isolated churches. An Elizabethan stone chapel of great simplicity, with just a stone-flagged floor, a seventeenth-century altar table and lectern, and rows of plain wooden benches, it has barely changed in centuries. Outside, the feeling of time immemorial is emphasized by the vast, spreading yew tree, thought to be 1000 years old, whose gnarled branches shroud the tomb of Martindale's nineteenth-century curate George Woodley.

ARRIVAL AND DEPARTURE

HOWTOWN

By car Howtown is a 4-mile drive down the minor road from Pooley Bridge.

By boat The most atmospheric way to arrive is on one of the regular steamer services from Glenridding (see page 207).

WALKS FROM HOWTOWN

For some of the nicest but least-vaunted walking in the Lake District, cross Ullswater on the steamer from Glenridding. Various routes radiate from Howtown, including the following.

TO PATTERDALE

The most commonly taken route from Howtown is also the easiest (6 miles; 3hr), following the shore of Ullswater around Hallin Fell to **Sandwick** and then through the woods and around the bottom of the lake to Patterdale.

FUSEDALE

A more strenuous route (8 miles; 4–5hr) cuts past the *Howtown Hotel* and heads up lovely **Fusedale**, at the head of which there's an unrelenting climb up to the **High Street**, a broad-backed ridge that was once a Roman road. The path is clearly visible for miles and following the ridge south you meet the highest point, **High Raise** (2632ft) – two hours from Howtown – where there's a cairn and glorious views. The route then runs south and west, via the stone outcrops of **Satura Crag**, past **Angle Tarn** and finally down to the A592, just shy of Patterdale's pub and post office.

TO POOLEY BRIDGE

Time the steamer services from Glenridding right and you can cross to Howtown, walk to Pooley Bridge and catch the boat back. The most direct route (5 miles; 3hr) leaves Howtown pier and runs northeast under Auterstone Crag before cutting up to the **Stone Circle** on the Roman road, south of Roehead, a couple of miles from Pooley Bridge. But for the best views and most exhilarating walk climb up to High Street from Fusedale (see above) and then charge straight along the ridge to the Stone Circle (7 miles; 3–4hr).

ACCOMMODATION AND EATING SEE MAP PAGE 204

★**Howtown Hotel** Howtown, CA10 2ND ☎017684 86514, ⊕howtown-hotel.com. There are only a few houses in Howtown, huddled around the resolutely old-fashioned and rather wonderful *Howtown Hotel*, which has been owned and run by the same family for more than a century. There's a cosy wood-panelled and stained-glass snug bar around the back where hikers can revive themselves with a beer or a cup of tea. A three-course lunch menu (Tues–Sun at 1pm; £22) is complemented by a four-course evening menu (£37) served daily at 7.30pm featuring the likes of chateaubriand with fondant potato and red wine sauce. Parking. Closed Nov–March. No credit cards. Lunch daily noon–2pm. **£198**

Askham and Lowther Park

The serene little village of **Askham** – three miles east of Pooley Bridge and five miles south of Penrith – is a pretty little spot. It lies across the River Lowther from the rolling lands of **Lowther Park**, seat of the eighteenth-century coal-mining and shipping magnates, the Lowthers, creators of the Georgian port of Whitehaven. The most notorious family member, Sir James, employed William Wordsworth's father as his agent but, when John Wordsworth died, refused to pay his back-salary to the Wordsworth children. Not that there was any shortage of Lowther money in those days, as attested by an extravagantly built Gothic Revival castle in the estate grounds, though eventually its ruinous upkeep was too much, even for the Lowthers, and it was allowed to fall into disrepair.

Both **castle** and **gardens** remained in ruins and closed for more than seventy years, until a new generation of Lowthers started an ambitious restoration project that will take up to twenty years to complete – it's judged to be the largest such restoration ever undertaken in Britain. The estate, meanwhile, is the centrepiece of a thriving farm, forestry, events and recreation business that dominates the area – in particular,

Lowther is a major local food producer, showcasing its products at the annual **Game and Country Fair** (every August) and at its own restaurant-with-rooms operation at nearby Clifton.

Lowther Castle and Gardens

Lowther Castle, CA10 2HH, 1.5 miles east of Askham • Daily: April–Oct 10am–5pm; Nov–March 10am–4pm • £11 • ☎ 01931 712192, ⓦ lowthercastle.org • Free parking at the castle

After decades of neglect, visitors are once again welcomed to **Lowther Castle and Gardens**, but you need to bear in mind that the scheme is a work in progress – and that the overall idea is not to restore things to a pristine state but rather to preserve the hugely romantic nature of the ruins and grounds. Consequently, while some of the long-lost themed gardens at the castle will be restored, others won't, allowing visitors to explore abandoned structures, stone follies, old summer-houses and historic buildings that lie within the park. A walk through the ruined castle walls and roofless rooms is an extraordinary experience, while out in the grounds are some grandstand views of the River Lowther and the distant fells. Ultimately there will be 140 acres of estate parkland to explore and another 360 acres of woodland, but even now some of the formal gardens are beginning to take shape, while there are surprises at every turn, from hidden, reed-fringed ponds to panoramic terraces. A visitor centre, and a museum and sculpture gallery in the stable courtyard, fill you in on the background, notably the lives of the Lowthers and their renowned fine-art collection. There's also a fabulous timber-hewn adventure playground called The Lost Castle with zipwires, walkways and slides – and then once you're done with it all, a rather nice courtyard café.

St Michael's church

Lowther, CA10 2HH, 1 mile east of Askham • Erratic opening hours • There's limited parking by the church, or you can walk here through the park from the castle

There's a glimpse of the Lowther heritage at **St Michael's church**, just outside Askham, on a ridge above the river. The site is old – Saxon burial stones have been unearthed here – though the current building dates from 1686. Effectively the family chapel, this

---

PEOPLE AND PLACES: FROM ESTATE TO PLATE

The French call it "terroir", a sense of place that influences **local produce**, and Charles Lowther – youngest son of the late seventh Earl of Lonsdale – knows a thing or two about it. His family, the Lowthers, have lived on their estate near Penrith since at least the eleventh century and have a long history of food production. Lowther Park itself has been a working farm since 1283 and the same principles of local, sustainable production underpin the venture today. "We have a real affinity with what comes off our land", says Charles, who runs the farm, including three thousand acres that are currently farmed organically. That means fish from estate rivers, free-range beef, pork, lamb and chicken, game from the Lowther woods and moors and seasonal vegetables from a traditional kitchen garden. All of this finds its way onto the menu at the estate's inn, the **George and Dragon** (see page 217), which Charles also oversees. Food miles, accordingly, are kept to a minimum (most produce is from only two or three miles away), while more local skills and crafts were drawn upon to help with the inn's meticulous restoration, from stone-wallers and joiners to artists and photographers. If you want to know exactly what's on your plate and where it came from, then it's hard to resist the Lowther lure in this part of the Lake District – "Basically, our family home for the last thousand years," says Charles. "We hope everyone else loves it as much as we do."

is filled with memorials to one Lowther or another – whose scions took the title Earl of Lonsdale – including a fine brass portraying a splendidly bewhiskered Henry Lowther. A later Lowther, the fifth Earl, Sir Hugh, was a keen sportsman, whose title at least is remembered in boxing's Lonsdale Belt.

Lakeland Bird of Prey Centre

Lowther, CA10 2HH, 500 yards from Lowther Castle entrance, 1 mile east of Askham • April–Oct daily noon–5pm • £9, family £25 • ☏ 01931 712746, ⊚ thelbpc.co.uk

You'll drive through rolling Lowther Estate land – which includes two small villages, various farms and plantations and a deer park – en route to the **Lakeland Bird of Prey Centre**. Here eagles, hawks, falcons and owls are put through their paces daily from 2pm onwards, though they are also all on show in the aviaries set in the Victorian walled garden. There's a tearoom here, too (you don't have to pay for entrance), which is particularly proud of its cream teas.

6

ACCOMMODATION AND EATING   **SEE MAP PAGE 204**

Askham itself has a couple of pubs, a handful of local B&Bs and two village shops at the top of the sloping village green, but the best place to stop hereabouts for your money – even just for a coffee – is the *George and Dragon* on the Lowther Estate.

Askham Hall Askham, CA10 2PF, ☏ 01931 712350, ⊚ askhamhall.co.uk. Fifteen bedrooms in a manorial stone pile, parts of which date back to the sixteenth century. Standard rooms are smart but straightforward and overlook the old stables, while others have increasingly lavish decor and views, peaking with the Pele Tower Master rooms (from £200), complete with elegant four-posters, antique claw-foot baths and views of the gardens, river and fells. The Grade II-listed gardens are a delight (open to non-guests; £4), while residents also get access to a spa and outdoor pool. Evening meals in the elegant restaurant feature guinea fowl, turbot or stewed belly pork (bookings essential; three courses £55,

five-course tasting menu £70). Restaurant Tues–Sat 7–9.30pm. Closed Jan. **£170**

★ **George and Dragon** Clifton, CA10 2ER, on A6 3 miles northeast of Askham ☏ 01768 865381, ⊚ george anddragonclifton.co.uk. This revamped eighteenth-century inn is a truly class act. Country-chic rooms feature woollen carpets, Roman blinds, big beds with brocade headboards and slate-floor bathrooms with claw-foot baths – some rooms are rated superior or deluxe and run up to £155. Downstairs, the bar and restaurant (mains £12–19) take local sourcing to a new level. Pretty much everything is from the adjacent Lowther Estate, whether it's organic meat, farmhouse cheese, kitchen-garden veg and herbs or wild fish – seasonally changing dishes from the open kitchen might include char-grilled vegetables or shorthorn beef burger; the twice-baked cheese soufflé is a signature dish. Parking. Daily 11am–11pm; kitchen noon–2.30pm & 6–9pm. **£100**

Haweswater

With the example of Thirlmere already set, there was less opposition when **Haweswater** was dammed in the 1930s to provide more water for the industrial northwest. The Lake District's easternmost lake became almost twice as long as a result (now 4 miles in length), while the water level rose by 100ft, completely drowning the village of Mardale. (It was visible in the hot summers of 1976, 1984 and 1995, when its deluged buildings emerged briefly from the depleted reservoir.) Such brutal dealings seem a long way off nowadays: the water company manages the valley and lake as a nature reserve, where woodpeckers and sparrowhawks inhabit **Naddle Forest**, and buzzards and peregrine falcons patrol the fells.

Walks around Haweswater

You can park at **Burnbanks**, at the northern end, near the dam wall, which is the best place to start the moderately strenuous **round-the-lake walk** (10 miles; 5hr), perhaps the best lakeside walk in the entire region – you'll usually be completely on your own on the way round. The path meanders above the water and through the woods on both sides of the lake, and if you walk anticlockwise you can reward yourself near the end with a drink at the *Haweswater Hotel*.

The road ends at the southern foot of the lake where there's an official car park at **Mardale Head**: from here, walkers can climb south over the passes to Kentmere (Nan Bield Pass) and Longsleddale (Gatesgarth Pass) or west up to High Street for Troutbeck, Patterdale or Howtown. The traditional **circular day-walk** from Mardale Head (7 miles; 5hr) is up via Kidsty Pike to High Street (2719ft) and then south and east along the ridge to Mardale Ill Bell (2496ft) and Harter Fell (2539ft) before dropping down Gatescarth Pass back to the car park. On a clear day – and get them you do, occasionally – the views for most of the way around are magnificent.

Bampton and Bampton Grange

Apart from the *Haweswater Hotel* on the reservoir, the only other local facilities are in the small village of **Bampton** (a couple of miles before the water) and neighbouring **Bampton Grange**, less than a mile beyond and approached over a sandstone bridge; both are very cute and each has a really good pub. There's also a bend-over-backwards-to-be-helpful village shop in Bampton, not to mention a yesteryear cottage garage with retro petrol pumps.

ARRIVAL AND DEPARTURE   HAWESWATER

By car From Ullswater, Penrith or the M6/A6, the route to Haweswater is via Bampton Grange and Bampton; there are car parks at either end of the reservoir.

On foot The Coast-to-Coast footpath has one of its hardest days, and crosses its highest point, on the 16-mile section

from Patterdale via Haweswater to Bampton and then up to Shap. Many choose to stay the night in Bampton, instead of Shap, shortening the day, so you can expect a fair amount of foot traffic in these otherwise backwater parts of the Lakes.

ACCOMMODATION AND EATING   SEE MAP PAGE 204

★**Crown & Mitre** Bampton Grange, CA10 2QR ☎01931 713225, ⓦcrownandmitre.com. The local B&B inn has eight lovely rooms with curvy, comfy beds, moody Lake District photography and modern bathrooms with

deep roll-top baths – the best, or "superior" (at £100) are worth the extra for the increased space. Good food is served downstairs in a cosy spot that's more lounge-bar than pub – lamb shank, steak pie, sea bass and stir-fries cost

---

WITHNAIL AND I: A LOCATION GUIDE

"We've gone on holiday by mistake," bleats Withnail (Richard E. Grant) in cult film classic *Withnail and I* (1987), about two booze-and-pill-ridden unemployed actors who leave London for a trip to the country. The holiday in question is a disastrous stay in a bleak, freezing, rain-sodden cottage belonging to Withnail's lecherous Uncle Monty. While the location – "No, I'm not in London, Penrith!" – is only briefly mentioned, such as during Withnail's classic rant to his agent from inside a rural phone box (still standing in **Bampton** village, near Haweswater), the "country" parts of the film are indeed largely set on the eastern fringes of the Lake District between Shap and Haweswater. Uncle Monty's cottage was, in fact, the delapidated **Sleddale Hall** overlooking **Wet Sleddale Reservoir**, two miles south of Shap, off the A6 (and 12 miles south of Penrith). In the past you could park at the reservoir and walk up to see the building – for a few years there were even annual screenings of the film here – though things may change now that it's in private hands. If all else fails, fans can still track down some of the other locations. The lake shown in the film isn't the Wet Sleddale reservoir but the far larger **Haweswater** to the west. Sadly, the **Penrith Tearooms** – scene of a desperate search for alcohol ("We want the finest wines available to humanity") – doesn't exist, or at least, not in Penrith: this and the Penrith pub scene were actually filmed in Stony Stratford, near Milton Keynes.

from around £10 and (with a nod to the hiker and cyclist crowd) portions are immense. Parking. Daily 11am–11pm; kitchen noon–2pm & 6–9pm. £85

Haweswater Hotel Haweswater, CA10 2RP ☎01931 713235, ⓦhaweswaterhotel.com. This extremely peaceful old hotel, built in 1937 to replace the inn at Mardale, lost when the valley was drowned, is the only place to stay by the water. The views from all sides are magnificent, while the rooms have a style that harks back to the 1930s. There's a mix of standard and lakeview rooms on two floors, and five first-floor suites (up to £149) with whirlpool baths – some of the front-facing rooms have their own balconies. The walker-friendly bar is open for home-made cakes, drinks and bistro-style lunches (mains £12–15); otherwise, for dinner there's a contemporary Cumbrian menu (mains £13–18) served in Le Mardale restaurant (you have to love that "Le", out here in deepest Cumbria). Parking. Bar Mon–Sat 11am–11pm, Sun noon–10.30pm, bar kitchen daily noon–4pm; dinner daily 6–8.30pm. £99

★**The Mardale** Bampton, CA10 2RQ ☎01931 713244, ⓦmardaleinn.co.uk. Lovely eighteenth-century inn sympathetically refurbished as a country guesthouse, with handcrafted tables, stripped-back ancient beams, slate floors, underfloor heating and a peaceful green interior. There are four comfortable, rustic-chic rooms upstairs, three of which are en suite, while groups of up to six can opt to use the self-contained, stripped-down comforts of the Bothy (£150/night). It's all self-catering, with access to a modern kitchen and appliances, though take the place for a week and they're willing to order in a keg of your favourite ale. £80

6

Out of the National Park

THE COURTYARD CAFE AT HOLKER HALL

Out of the National Park

When the Lake District National Park boundary was drawn around the lakes and fells, it excluded several peripheral Cumbrian towns, as well as nearly all of the west Cumbrian coast and the southern Furness peninsulas. A subsequent boundary extension, in 2016, did little to change that. Most visitors to the Lakes will pass through at least one of these areas – indeed, the usual approaches to the Lake District make it hard to avoid Kendal or Penrith. And there's a case for aiming to see several other destinations not strictly within the National Park on any trip to the region. The distances help: it's not much more than thirty miles between Penrith and Cockermouth, and about the same around the west coast, making it easy to nip from lakeland valley to outlying town.

7

En route to Windermere, **Kendal**, in the southeast, was once the county town of Westmorland and is still an enjoyable market town, with a fine riverside location and plenty of local attractions. **Penrith**, to the north, is also an ancient commercial centre and, like Kendal, retains the ruins of the castle that defended it during the turbulent medieval border wars. It's not far from Ullswater and the northern Lakes, and many combine a visit with nearby **Rheged**, the Cumbrian visitor centre and 3D film experience. Religious foundations established in the south at **Cartmel** and **Furness Abbey** had a lasting regional significance; the enterprising Furness monks could be said to have made early Cumbria an economic powerhouse well before the Industrial Revolution. Of the busy Cumbrian ports and towns of the eighteenth and nineteenth centuries, **Ulverston** still thrives as a market town (and claims comedian Stan Laurel as its best-known son), while **Whitehaven**, on the west Cumbrian coast, has been rejuvenated by investment in its fine harbour and quayside. Here, and at nearby **Cockermouth** – yet another handsome market town – well-to-do Georgians (including the young Wordsworth family) lived out their comfortable lives.

Kendal and around

The self-billed "Gateway to the Lakes" (though nearly 10 miles from Windermere), limestone-grey **Kendal** is the largest of the southern Cumbrian towns, with a population of around 28,000. Sited on the banks of the fast-flowing River Kent, it thrived as a medieval market town and became renowned for the dexterity of its archers – who fought at Crécy and Poitiers in the Hundred Years War with France – and for the quality of its cloth, particularly the "Kendal green" (plant-dyed wool), which earned the town a mention in Shakespeare's *Henry IV*. No wonder that the town motto became the no-nonsense "Cloth is my bread". There are still plenty of reminders of Kendal's market and manufacturing history, not least the singular layout of the long **main street** (Stricklandgate and Highgate), with houses and shops to the fore, stables and workshops to the rear in the numerous "yards" and "ginnels". Strolling along here will eventually take you down to the riverside, past restored almshouses, mullioned shopfronts and old trade signs mounted up on the walls, among them the curious pipe-smoking Turk outside the snuff factory on Lowther Street.

Around Kendal are many easily accessible sites, including the nearest lake at Windermere, and Cartmel and the "peninsulas" area, each around twenty minutes'

WORDSWORTH HOUSE

Highlights

❶ Kendal Museum A good introduction to all things Kendal, especially former clerk Alfred Wainwright. See page 225

❷ Cartmel A cutting-edge gastronomic retreat in one of the region's prettiest medieval villages. See page 232

❸ Holker Hall The gardens and grounds of this stately pile make a fine family day out. See page 233

❹ Laurel and Hardy Museum, Ulverston Picking over the life of Ulverston's finest son, Stan Laurel, provides a happy diversion from the lakes and fells. See page 235

❺ Whitehaven West Cumbria's most captivating town has a Georgian centre and revitalized harbour. See page 240

❻ Wordsworth House, Cockermouth Wordsworth's childhood home has been enterprisingly restored as a working Georgian household. See page 245

❼ Market day in Penrith See this busy market town at its best every Tuesday when the centre bustles with stalls. See page 250

❽ Shepherd's Hut, Crake Trees Manor Experience a romantic night under the stars at Crake Trees Manor's boutique version of a rustic shepherd's hut. See page 253

HIGHLIGHTS ARE MARKED ON THE MAP ON PAGE 224

drive away. But the two main local out-of-town attractions – the stately homes of **Sizergh** and **Levens Hall** – have enough to occupy you for a good half-day each, more if you plan on a picnic and a walk in the grounds. And though they're on the increase elsewhere in the Lakes too, ospreys now nest on the marshlands of **Foulshaw Moss**, easily accessed off the main road between Kendal and Cartmel – though you'll be lucky to see them without good binoculars.

HIGHLIGHTS

1. Kendal Museum
2. Cartmel
3. Holker Hall
4. Laurel and Hardy Museum, Ulverston
5. Whitehaven
6. Wordsworth House, Cockermouth
7. Market day in Penrith
8. Shepherd's Hut, Crake Trees Manor

● EATING

Bay Horse	5
La Casa Verde	3
Courtyard Café	7
Low Sizergh Barn	4
The Plough	6
UpFront Gallery & Coffee Shop	1
Wellington Farm Café	2

■ ACCOMMODATION

Askham Hall	2
Bay Horse	6
Castle Green Hotel	5
Crake Trees Manor	4
Moresby Hall	3
Old Homestead	1
The Plough	7

■ DRINKING

Royal Yew	1

OUT OF THE NATIONAL PARK

Market Place

Market Place, LA9 4TN • Markets Wed & Sat 8am–4.30pm; farmers' market last Fri of month 9am–3.15pm

Kendal's old **Market Place** has long since succumbed to development, with the market hall now converted to the Westmorland Shopping Centre (off Stricklandgate), but traditional stalls still do business outside every Wednesday and Saturday, and there's a well-established farmers' market on the last Friday of the month.

Kendal Castle

Castle Hill, LA9 7BL • Always open • Free • Cross the footbridge just north of the parish church and follow the footpath from the end of Parr St

First erected in the early thirteenth century, **Kendal Castle** is claimed as the birthplace of Catherine Parr, Henry VIII's sixth wife, but the story is apocryphal – she was born in 1512, at which time the building was already in an advanced state of decay and has remained so ever since. But it's well worth the brief climb for the view down over the town from the ruined walls – this is a good picnic spot on sunny days and there's plenty of space for children to run around in.

7

Kendal Museum

Station Rd, LA9 6BT • Thurs–Sat 9.30am–4.45pm • £5 • ☎ 01539 815597, ⓦ kendalmuseum.org.uk

The **Kendal Museum** contains the district's natural history and archeological finds. Founded as early as 1796, what was essentially a gentleman's private collection was later given to the town and moved into an old wool warehouse in 1913, where it's been stationed ever since. It's highly entertaining, since as well as the usual flints, stuffed birds and Roman and Viking finds, there are plenty of well-presented displays relating to the town's history and many unclassifiable curiosities – from the original key to the town castle to a stuffed grizzly bear, shot by the Earl of Lonsdale.

There are exhibitions, events and family crafts and activities, especially in school holidays, while the museum also makes a big fuss of famous fell-walker **Alfred Wainwright**, which is fair enough seeing as he was honorary clerk at the museum between 1945 and 1974. There's a reconstruction of his office here, together with various original pen-and-ink drawings and some of his personal effects (including his socks and pipe) – many of the museum artefact labels are also written in Wainwright's distinctive hand.

Quaker Tapestry

Friends Meeting House, Stramongate, LA9 4BH • March & Nov Mon–Thurs 10am–4pm; April–Oct Mon–Sat 10am–5pm • £7.50 • ☎ 01539 722975, ⓦ quaker-tapestry.co.uk

Just off the river, between New Road and Stramongate, one of Britain's largest Quaker meeting houses (built 1816) contains the 77 beautifully embroidered panels of the **Quaker Tapestry**. This area of the southern Lakes was a hotbed of early Quakerism, beginning with the travelling ministry of George Fox (1652), a seeker

---

ON TOP OF THE WORLD

No rundown of Kendal's historic accomplishments would be complete without mention of **Kendal Mint Cake**, a brutal peppermint confection first produced in the town in 1869 – and, as legend has it, invented by accident during the process of combining sugar and peppermint oil for clear mint sweets. It was quickly apparent that the grainy, energy-giving "mint cake" would go far in a region where you often needed a quick boost if you were to scale the local fells and crags. Romney's of Kendal, established 1919, is still the biggest producer, famous since Sir Edmund Hillary carried their mint cake up to the top of Everest in 1953. Stick some in your backpack and there's not a Lake District peak you can't knock off before breakfast.

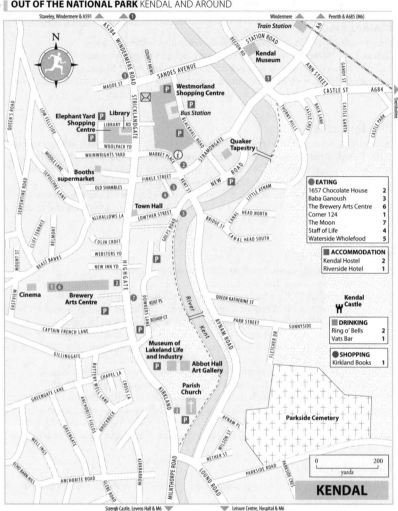

KENDAL

EATING

1657 Chocolate House	2
Baba Ganoush	3
The Brewery Arts Centre	6
Corner 124	1
The Moon	7
Staff of Life	4
Waterside Wholefood	5

ACCOMMODATION

| Kendal Hostel | 2 |
| Riverside Hotel | 1 |

DRINKING

| Ring o' Bells | 2 |
| Vats Bar | 1 |

SHOPPING

| Kirkland Books | 1 |

after truth, whose followers were dubbed Quakers "because we bid them tremble at the Word of the Lord". The tapestry – produced by almost four thousand people gathered in embroidery groups between 1981 and 1996 – forms a narrative history of Quaker experience through the ages, with the delicately worked panels portraying historical subjects such as Elizabeth Fry's work in Newgate prison and the antislavery "underground railroad" in the USA, as well as contemporary Quaker campaigns for peace, relief work and reconciliation. Embroidery workshops and demonstrations are also held throughout the year.

Abbot Hall Art Gallery

Abbot Hall, LA9 5AL • Closed until 2022 • ☎ 01539 722464, ⓦ abbothall.org.uk • Pay-and-display parking available

Kendal's main cultural attractions are based at the Georgian **Abbot Hall**, by the river near the parish church. Painstakingly restored to its 1760s townhouse origins, it's the

FELL-WALKER EXTRAORDINAIRE – ALFRED WAINWRIGHT

If ever a person has changed the way others look at the Lake District hills it's **Alfred Wainwright** (1907–91), whose famous handwritten walking guides are studied with the intensity normally reserved for religious texts. Wainwright was born in Blackburn in Lancashire, left school at 13 and worked his way up through the Borough Treasurer's office, qualifying as an accountant in 1933. After a first visit to the Lake District in 1930 he became a keen walker and returned to the Lakes at every possible opportunity. So taken was he with the fells that he engineered a move to Kendal in 1941; he was Borough Treasurer from 1948 until his retirement in 1967.

Wainwright was nothing if not obsessional, setting off alone at the crack of dawn every weekend to tackle distant lakeland fells and valleys. In 1952, dissatisfied with the accuracy of existing maps, he started work on a series of seven walking guides, each painstakingly handwritten with mapped routes and delicately drawn views. These **Pictorial Guides** to the Lake District were a remarkable undertaking, especially since the original idea was only for his own amusement. The first book, *The Eastern Fells*, was published in 1955 and was an unexpected success; six others followed by 1966, thus completing the task he had set himself of recording in detail 214 separate lakeland fells. The seven volumes have subsequently sold over two million copies. Many other titles followed: a *Pennine Way Companion* (1968), the *Coast-to-Coast* route he devised from St Bees to Robin Hood's Bay (1973), endless sketchbooks and guides to the Lake District, Scotland, Wales, the Yorkshire Dales and the Lancashire hills; fifty-odd books in all. His first wife, Ruth, left him in 1966, and in 1970 Wainwright married Betty McNally, with whom he'd corresponded (and secretly met on his walking trips) for years. He died in 1991, having given away most of his considerable earnings to animal rescue charities, and his **ashes were scattered** on Haystacks in Buttermere.

The effect his books have had is plain to see. People who don't normally consider themselves walkers are happy to tick off the routes and peaks in his guides, though others point to the problems this has caused in terms of visitor numbers to certain areas. The BBC's "Wainwright Walks" and "Coast to Coast" series have also had a significant effect on traffic at popular targets like Cat Bells. It's tempting but wrong to treat Wainwright as gospel, as many do in their attempts to "bag" his 214 recorded fells. The number was an entirely arbitrary figure – most of the Wainwright fells are more than 1400ft high, but there are plenty of other crags and fells lower than that but just as spectacular, not to mention the lakes, tarns and valleys which he covered only in passing.

Wainwright allowed no revision of the *Pictorial Guides* to be made during his lifetime, but with the agreement of the Wainwright Estate, revised editions of all seven guides have now been completed by cartographer and Wainwright disciple Chris Jesty. Up-to-date news and views about this and other related subjects are observed by the **Wainwright Society** (ⓦwainwright.org.uk), dedicated to the "Master Fell-walker" and his works.

site of the town's splendid, long-running **Art Gallery** – one of the best in the north. However, in 2020 the museum closed for a lengthy period in order to undergo major refurbishment, and will not reopen until 2022 at the earliest. Generally speaking though, there are changing exhibitions throughout the year, though the lower-floor galleries are more locally focused, concentrating on the works of the eighteenth-century "Kendal School" of portrait painters, notably Daniel Gardner and, most famously, **George Romney**. Born in Dalton-in-Furness (and buried there), Romney set himself up as a portrait painter in Kendal in 1757, where he stayed for five years before moving to London to further his career. His society portraits are the pick of the gallery's collection, though you'll also find changing displays of works by those who came to the Lakes to paint, such as Constable, Ruskin and Turner, and a growing collection of contemporary British art. In addition, eighteenth-century chairs, writing desks and games tables designed and built by famed furniture-makers Gillows of Lancaster have all survived in Abbot Hall in excellent condition.

There's a good café at the gallery (with outdoor seating on the riverside lawn in summer), while the former stables across the lawn house the Museum of Lakeland Life and Industry (see below).

Museum of Lakeland Life and Industry

Abbot Hall, LA9 5AL • Closed until 2022 • ☎ 01539 722464, ⊛ lakelandmuseum.org.uk

The best place to explore Cumbria's social history and traditional heritage is at Abbot Hall's excellent **Museum of Lakeland Life and Industry**, but which, like the gallery, will also be closed until 2022 pending a major revamp. Expect, though, to see reconstructed house interiors from the seventeenth, eighteenth and nineteenth centuries alongside artisans' workshops to create a vivid presentation of rural trades and crafts, from mining, spinning and weaving to shoe-making and tanning. You will be able to trace Cumbrian fashion through the ages, or investigate the Arts and Crafts movement, while the museum will also contain a room devoted to the life and work of the children's writer Arthur Ransome, whose widow donated his pipes, typewriter and other memorabilia to the collection after his death.

Sizergh Castle

Sizergh, LA8 8DZ, off A591, 3 miles south of Kendal • **House** late March to Oct Tues–Sun noon–4pm, guided tours noon–1pm • £12.50 (includes gardens), family ticket £31.25; NT • **Gardens** Daily: late March to Oct 10am–5pm; Nov to late March 10am–4pm • £4.90; NT • **Café** Easter–Oct daily 11am–5pm • ☎ 015395 60951, ⊛ nationaltrust.org.uk/sizergh • Bus #555 from Kendal

Although an extension of the park boundaries in 2016 nudged **Sizergh Castle** into the National Park, it remains a natural side-trip from Kendal. Home to the Strickland family for eight centuries, it owes its "castle" epithet to the fourteenth-century pele tower at its core – one of the best examples of these towers, which were built as safe havens during the region's protracted medieval border raids. The Great Hall underwent significant changes in Elizabethan times, when most of its rooms were panelled in oak with their ceilings layered in elaborate plasterwork. There are guided tours between

---

WALKS FROM KENDAL

Although Kendal isn't the most obvious **hiking** centre, you can in fact walk straight out of town and on to the nearby hills. There are no particularly dramatic heights to gain, but it's pretty countryside. The two moderate walks below offer a variety of scenery, while you're also only a short drive or train ride away from Staveley, the access point for Kentmere and its walks.

THE RIVER KENT TO STAVELEY

Follow the path along the **River Kent** north out of Kendal (or jump on the train for one stop) to Burneside – the *Jolly Anglers* (⊛ thejollyanglersinn.com) is a good pub – where you cut northeast up minor roads and farm tracks before climbing to **Gurnal Dubs** and **Potter Tarn**, two prettily located tarns. The path skirts both before descending to Staveley (and its Mill Yard craft shops and cafés), where you pick up the signposted Dales Way, which then meanders back down the River Kent through pastoral country to Burneside. From Burneside, this is a longish (7.5 miles; 4hr) circular walk; if you walk in and out of Kendal you can add another three miles (1hr) to this.

SCOUT SCAR

The high limestone ridge known as **Scout Scar** is three miles southwest of Kendal and, on a clear day, provides some scintillating views. Again, you can walk out of Kendal if you want to make a day of it, though it's more usually climbed from either the Underbarrow road (north) or from Brigsteer (south) – there's parking at both places and a pub in Brigsteer.

noon and 1pm, but space is limited so advance reservations are recommended; thereafter you can wander around the house at will, though a timed-ticket system may be in operation at busy times. If you're making a day of it you can take a picnic into the grounds or eat at the castle **café**, but it's worth noting the excellent nearby farm shop and café at Low Sizergh Barn (see page 230).

Levens Hall

Levens Hall, LA8 0PD, off A6, 6 miles south of Kendal • Easter to Sept Mon–Thurs & Sun: house noon–4pm; gardens 10am–5pm • House and gardens £14.50, family ticket £36; gardens only £10, family £26; free admission to tearoom, shop and plant centre • ☏ 015395 60321, Ⓦ levenshall.co.uk • Bus #555 from Kendal stops outside

Like Sizergh, a couple of miles away, **Levens Hall** was also built around a medieval tower (1250–1300), though the atmosphere here is very different since the bulk of the house was built or refurbished in classic Elizabethan style between 1570 and 1640. House stewards are on hand to answer any questions and point out the oddities and curios – for example, the dining room is panelled not with oak but with goat's leather, printed with a deep-green floral design. Upstairs, the bedrooms offer glimpses of the beautifully trimmed topiary **gardens**, where yews in the shape of pyramids, peacocks, top hats, spirals and crowns stand adjacent to blooming bedding plants and apple orchards. The oldest ha-ha (sunken ditch and wall) in England allows views across the fields beyond, while on Sundays and bank holiday Mondays a showman's steam engine is put to work.

Foulshaw Moss

Off A590, 4 miles southwest of Sizergh near Witherslack • Open access • Free • ☏ 01539 816300, Ⓦ cumbriawildlifetrust.org.uk • Small parking area

A spread of lowland peat bog, grassland and reedbeds draining into the River Kent estuary, **Foulshaw Moss** is one of the easiest places in the Lakes region to see **ospreys**, with the current single pair of nesting adults usually in residence between April and August. Most of the reserve is inaccessible, but a half-mile of level boardwalks leads to a small viewing platform, from which a telescope or good set of binoculars will allow you to spot the ospreys in their distant tree – though don't be surprised if all you can see is a white head poking up over the rim of the nest. For better views, of course, you could cheat and spy on them via the website's live nest-cam link. Keep eyes peeled for sedge warblers and adders too, and don't stray off marked paths into the swamp, even if you are wearing wellies.

ARRIVAL AND INFORMATION

By car Driving in from the M6, take junction 38 (north) or 36 (south). There are signposted car parks all over town, including one at the Westmorland Shopping Centre (Blackhall Rd) and several off Highgate, plus free unlimited parking on New Rd by the river (though this is always busy). For Sizergh and Levens Hall, follow signs from town for "M6, South, Lancaster".

By train Trains leave the West Coast main line at Oxenholme, north of Lancaster, for the hourly branch line service to Kendal (5min) and on to Windermere (19min).

KENDAL AND AROUND

Kendal's train station is a 10min walk from the town centre.

By bus The bus station is on Blackhall Rd (off Stramongate), with main routes including the #599 (to Windermere, Bowness, Ambleside and Grasmere) and #555 (towards Keswick, or to Lancaster).

By taxi Blue Star Taxis (☏ 01539 723670, Ⓦ bluestartaxis. net).

Tourist information Fantastic Kendal, 26–28 Finkle St (Mon–Sat 9.30am–4pm, Sun 10am–3pm; ☏ 01539 725139).

ACTIVITIES

Lakes Outdoor Experience ☏ 01539 737332 Ⓦ lakes outdoorexperience.co.uk. Individually tailored rock-climbing, caving and watersports packages around the

National Park and beyond. They can cope with any grades, from providing guides for hill-walking to offering courses in solo mountaineering.

7

ACCOMMODATION

SEE MAPS PAGES 224 AND 226

Kendal makes a reasonable overnight stop on the way to or from the Lakes, and can be a useful base for the southern region – though walkers should note that the central fells and valleys are all a good drive or bus ride away. Most of the local **B&Bs** lie along Windermere Road, north of the centre, and on Milnthorpe Road, to the south.

Castle Green Hotel Castle Green Lane, LA9 6RG ☎01539 734000, ⍟castlegreen.co.uk. Kendal's biggest hotel is a large, efficiently run resort-style development with spa, health club and restaurant, a mile or so out of the centre. There's plenty of space in the modern rooms, and a touch more style in the executive ones, and families find it particularly handy – there are dedicated family rooms available, separate children's swimming times in the pool and there's even a Little One's afternoon tea. The hotel's dining options extend to a restaurant, bar and, best of all, its own pub (*Alexander's*) occupying the old stables block. Parking. **£125**

Kendal Hostel 118 Highgate ☎01539 724066, ⍟kendalhostel.co.uk. Kendal's independent hostel sits right in front of the Brewery Arts Centre, so the location can't be beaten. It sleeps up to 52 in eleven bunk-rooms of various configurations – a couple of rooms sleep two, while two others have a double bed as well as bunks, so families and small groups will get a good deal. It's self-catering only, but you're right on the high street for neighbouring cafés, bars and restaurants. Weekend prices are £2/person higher, while there are discounts for under-16s. Closed Christmas

week. Dorms **£20**, doubles **£40**

★ **The Plough** Cow Brow, Lupton, LA6 1PJ, 9 miles south of Kendal on A65, Kirkby Lonsdale road ☎015395 67700, ⍟theploughatlupton.co.uk. Sister to the *Punch Bowl* at Crosthwaite, the chic and very cheerful *Plough* at Lupton repeats the boutique trick in a handsome roadside inn that's well placed for the south Lakes and just 2min off the M6. There are just six guest rooms (all named after historic local landowners) and a personal welcome, so you feel special from the start – fashionable earth tones and French country rusticity predominate and the huge underfloor-heated bathrooms, especially, are sensational, with deep roll-top baths sitting beneath wood-slat blinds. Each room is individually priced, with the two largest suites, Torsin and Bellingham, costing up to £225. There's fresh tea and coffee on demand, delivered to your room, with destination dining downstairs (see page 231) in the fabulously relaxed bar and restaurant. Parking. **£155**

★ **Riverside Hotel** Stramongate Bridge, LA9 6EL ☎01539 734861, ⍟riversidekendal.co.uk. One of Kendal's old stone-built riverside tanneries has proved to be a perfect location for a hotel restoration. The long rows of riverside windows let light into the spacious rooms, while a decent restaurant makes the most of the riverside setting – ingredients are sourced from the hotel group's own kitchen garden and farm. There's also a leisure club on site with heated pool, spa, sauna and gym. Parking. **£125**

EATING

SEE MAPS PAGES 224 AND 226

Kendal has the best selection of places to **eat and drink** in the south Lakes, so if you're moving on to the fells you'll want to get your cappuccinos, artisan breads and veggie specials while you can. There are sandwich bars, cafés and delis down Finkle Street especially, as well as a huge Booths **supermarket** in Wainwrights Yard.

CAFÉS AND DELIS

1657 Chocolate House 54 Branthwaite Brow, Finkle St, LA9 4TX ☎01539 740702, ⍟chocolatehouse1657.co.uk. Olde-worlde spot that sells divine hot chocolate in dozens of guises (£2.50), plus a belt-threatening selection of home-made gateaux (£3.25) and a fabulous ice cream parlour (cone £1.80). Up in the Chocolate Loft you can find out how the stuff is made, and don't miss a browse in the lovely handmade-choccie shop. Shop Mon–Sat 9.30am–5pm; café Mon–Sat 10am–4.30pm.

★ **Baba Ganoush** 3 & 4 Berry's Yard, Finkle St, LA9 4AB, food shop ☎01539 731072, canteen ☎01539 738210. Two outlets in the same yard off Finkle St, great foodie stops for grazers, diners and the local pick-something-up-for-later crowd. The original Food Shop is a handsomely stocked sandwich/salad bar and deli, specializing in amazing soups

plus home-made pâtés, terrines and the like; there's more space for a sit-down in the *Canteen*, where Med-tinged gastro offerings range from a scrambled eggs and chorizo breakfast to a veggie meze platter (dishes £4–10). Food Shop Mon–Sat 7.30am–4pm; Canteen Tues–Sat 9.30am–4pm.

★ **Low Sizergh Barn** Sizergh, LA8 8AE, 4 miles south of Kendal on A591, follow signs from town for M6/South/Lancaster ☎015395 60426, ⍟lowsizerghbarn.co.uk. A cracking farm shop, tearoom and craft gallery housed in a seventeenth-century barn, full of pretty things under gnarled oak beams and with a wide range of farm produce, from home-grown organic veg to local cheese. The tearoom is a great stop for big breakfasts (£7.95), rustic sandwiches, ploughman's lunches, rarebit or pies (most dishes around £8) – and best of all, it has a viewing window onto the dairy herd's milking parlour, into which the cows shuffle every afternoon at around 3.30pm. Their generous farmhouse afternoon tea (2.30–4.30pm; £12.95) will probably see you through to breakfast the next day. Shop daily 9am–5.30pm; café daily 9am–5pm.

Staff of Life 2 Berry's Yard, Finkle St, LA9 4AB ☎01539 738606. Kendal's original artisan bakery is worth tracking down (hidden up an alley off Finkle St) for its marvellous handmade continental-style bread, plus acclaimed gingerbread, flapjacks and chocolate brownies, all great stuff for picnics. They also run bread-making courses. Mon–Sat 8.30am–4pm.

Waterside Wholefood Kents View, LA9 4DZ ☎ 01539 729743. Long-running veggie and vegan café with a terrific range of salads, bakes and cakes (dishes £3.50–8) forming the mainstay of the menu, while stuffed tortillas, wraps and other specials (buckwheat burgers to lentil pie) provide a bit of daily variation. Mon–Sat 8.30am–4.30pm.

RESTAURANTS AND GASTROPUBS

★ **The Brewery Arts Centre** 122 Highgate, LA9 4HE ☎ 01539 725133, ⓦ breweryarts.co.uk. Everyone likes the easy-going Arts Centre *Vats Bar*, which has a street food based menu, hence the likes of Alabama chicken wings, sweet potato *taquitos* and spiced broth noodles, all going for between £5–10. Gourmet pizzas are big news here (£8–9.50), and are also available to takeaway. If you just want a coffee, or are hanging out until lunch, the Arts Centre also has the family-friendly *Intro Café*. (Mon–Fri 10am–4.30pm). Vats Bar Mon–Fri 4.30–11pm, Sat 10am–11.30pm, Sun noon–10.30pm; food served Tues–Fri 4.30–9pm, Sat noon–9.30pm.

Corner 124 124 Stricklandgate, LA9 4QG ☎ 01539 724843, ⓦ corner124.com. This colourful, contemporary outfit serves up classic bistro dishes (pan-roasted Iberico pork with Padron peppers, mushroom and walnut croquettes, Moroccan-spiced vegetable millefeuille at pretty

unbeatable prices – including a three-course menu for £15. A reliable, laidback place to dine on a budget. Mon–Fri & Sun 5.30–10pm, Sat noon–2pm & 5.30–10pm.

The Moon 129 Highgate, LA9 4EN ☎ 01539 729254, ⓦ themoonhighgate.com. Contemporary bistro with a seasonally changing menu that leans towards the Mediterranean. Lunch sticks to things like panini, tagines, pastas and salads (around £10), but at dinner (most mains £13–17) there's a modish take on locally sourced ingredients, like a date-stuffed roast loin of pork or a spring dish of grilled salmon with char-grilled asparagus. There's always a good choice for fish-eaters and vegetarians too. Tues–Fri 11.30am–2pm & 5.30–9pm, Sat 11.30am–2pm & 6–9.30pm.

★ **The Plough** Cow Brow, Lupton, LA6 1PJ, 9 miles south of Kendal on A65, Kirkby Lonsdale road ☎ 015395 67700, ⓦ theploughatlupton.co.uk. The out-of-town treat is a meal at the thoroughly lovely *Plough*, a sweeping, open-plan pub featuring adjoining eating areas under majestic oak beams – so you can choose comfy sofas around the wood-burners, conservatory window seats, a romantic corner for two or big family dining tables. It's a very modern menu of small starters (wildflower sourdough cob, black pepper squid, whole baked Camembert) and larger mains (rack of Cumbrian lamb, damson and duck sausages, wild mushroom ravioli), and the eminently reasonable prices (starters around £7, mains £12–22) extend to the wine list, with a celebratory Prosecco under a fiver. Between meals you can always pop in for an excellent pint. Daily 11am–11pm; kitchen noon–9pm.

DRINKING SEE MAP PAGE 226

Many of the town-centre **pubs** have had unsympathetic makeovers, but there are still one or two traditional boozers left, plus a few more stylish bars – and coffee houses – ranged up and down the main street.

Ring o' Bells 37 Kirkland, LA9 5AF ☎ 01539 720326, ⓦ ringobellskendal.webs.com. This pub, uniquely, stands on consecrated ground by the parish church, making it the bell-ringers' local. Does its holy location make the beer taste better? You decide. Mon–Wed & Sun noon–11pm, Thurs

5–11pm, Fri & Sat noon–midnight.

★ **Vats Bar** Brewery Arts Centre, 122 Highgate, LA9 4HE ☎ 01539 725133, ⓦ breweryarts.co.uk. Best bar in town is the Arts Centre hangout – the huge "vats" provide circular booth seating and there's a great summer terrace that turns into a real social hub. There's terrific food on offer too (see above) alongside comedy nights, quiz nights and the like. Mon–Fri 4.30–11pm, Sat 10am–11.30pm, Sun noon–10.30pm.

ENTERTAINMENT

Apart from the regular programme at the **Brewery Arts Centre**, the town plays host to several fabulous festivals, including the **Torchlight Carnival** and **Westmorland County Show** (both September) and the **Kendal Mountain Festival** (November), which presents climbing- and mountain-related films, events and speakers from around the world.

Brewery Arts Centre 122 Highgate, LA9 4HE box office ☎ 01539 725133, ⓦ breweryarts.co.uk. Hub of everything that's happening in Kendal and the south Lakes, there's a cinema, theatre, galleries and concert hall here, in addition to a bar/restaurant and café. Showcase gigs and stand-up comedy nights are held here throughout the year, and there are live outdoor concerts on summer Sundays.

DIRECTORY

Hospital Westmorland General Hospital, Burton Rd (☎ 01539 732288, ⓦ uhmb.nhs.uk).

Pharmacies Boots, 10 Elephant Yard (☎ 01539 740072); Highgate Pharmacy, 41 Highgate (☎ 01539 720461);

7

Lloyds, Station Yard (☏ 01539 723988).

Police station Busher Walk (Mon–Fri 8am–6pm, Sat 8am–noon; ☏ 101, ⓦ cumbria.police.uk).

Post office 75 Stricklandgate (Mon & Tues 9.30am–5.30pm, Wed–Fri 9am–5.30pm, Sat 9am–12.30pm).

Swimming pool Lakes Leisure, Burton Rd (☏ 01539 729777, ⓦ better.org.uk), has a 82ft-long swimming pool. Public admission usually lunchtime and evenings only during school termtime, otherwise all day, but call or check the website for specific times; there's also a sauna, gym and squash court.

Cartmel and around

The pretty village of **Cartmel** is something of an **upmarket** getaway, with its famed Michelin-starred restaurant (*L'Enclume*), artisan food stores, handsome priory, winding country lanes and cobbled market square brimming with inns and antique shops. You're in luck if you're looking to buy a handmade dolls' house or antique embroidered footstool, and in the Cartmel Village Shop they sell the finest sticky toffee pudding known to humanity. The local stately home, **Holker Hall**, is just down the road, while in keeping with this rather genteel air is the village's delightful **Cartmel Racecourse** (ⓦ cartmel-racecourse.co.uk), home of fashionable race days for the county set each May and August bank holiday weekend.

Cartmel Priory

Cartmel Priory, LA11 6PU • Easter–Oct Mon–Sat 9am–5.30pm, Sun 9am–4.30pm; Nov–Easter daily 9am–3.30pm; tours Easter–Oct Wed 11am & 2pm • Church free; tours £2.50 • ⓦ cartmelpriory.org.uk

Quite what the original monks would have made of Cartmel's current incarnation is anyone's guess – the village grew up around its twelfth-century Augustinian **priory** and is still dominated by the proud priory **church of St Mary and St Michael**. It's one of the finest churches in the northwest, agree both Nikolaus Pevsner and Simon Jenkins, with the fine interior illuminated by a 45ft-high east window and featuring immaculate misericords, carved with entwined branches, bunches of grapes, tools, leaves and crosses. A patron of the church, one Rowland Briggs, paid for a shelf on a pier near the north door and for a supply of bread to be distributed from it every Sunday in perpetuity "to the most indigent housekeepers of this Parish".

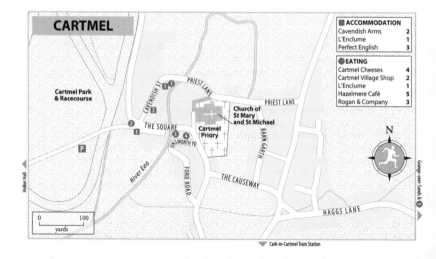

CARTMEL

◼ ACCOMMODATION	
Cavendish Arms	2
L'Enclume	1
Perfect English	3

● EATING	
Cartmel Cheeses	4
Cartmel Village Shop	2
L'Enclume	1
Hazelmere Café	5
Rogan & Company	3

Cartmel Park & Racecourse

CAVENDISH ST

PRIEST LANE

PRIEST LANE

Church of St Mary and St Michael

Cartmel Priory

THE SQUARE

AYNSWORTH YD

BARN GARTH

P

River Eea

FORD ROAD

THE CAUSEWAY

HAGGS LANE

Holker Hall

Grange-over-Sands

N

0   100
yards

Cark-in-Cartmel Train Station

7

TIME, TIDE AND GUIDE

It's only three miles by road from Cartmel to the coast at **Grange-over-Sands**, whose grand yesteryear hotels and floral gardens are fronted by a mile-long esplanade with fine views of the sands and salt marsh of **Morecambe Bay**. It may look benign, but the sands of Britain's second largest bay are treacherous and many lives have been lost here over the centuries (including, notoriously, 23 Chinese cockle-pickers caught by the racing tide in 2004). Monks from Cartmel who knew the slip sands and hidden channels once led intrepid travellers safely across the bay, but from the sixteenth century onwards the route was considered so dangerous that an official guide was appointed by royal command. The tradition continues today with cross-bay walks in the company of the Queen's Guide, Michael Wilson, who takes groups out at least weekly (conditions permitting) between May and September. Many of the walks are charity ventures, though anyone is welcome (as are donations). You have to book in advance by calling the Guide Over Sands Trust (☎015395 58555, ⓦguideoversands.co.uk), which is also where you can check the walk schedule; alternatively contact the Grange-over-Sands tourist office (☎015395 34026, ⓦgrange-over-sands.com).

Holker Hall

Cark-in-Cartmel, LA11 7PL • late March to early Nov Wed–Sun: house 11am–4pm; gardens 10.30am–5pm • £13; gardens only £9; hall only £9 • ☎015395 58328, ⓦholker.co.uk • Cark-in-Cartmel train station is less than a mile to the southeast

A couple of miles west of Cartmel, **Holker Hall** is one of Cumbria's finest stately homes, still in use by the Cavendish family, who have owned it since the late seventeenth century. The impressive 25-acre **gardens** are the highlight, featuring sweeping views from the surrounding meadows to the fells and estuary beyond. There's plenty to seek out – sunken garden, grotto, stone labyrinth and massive slate sundial – while a water cascade tumbles from a seventeenth-century marble Neptune down through the rhododendrons and oak trees. There's also a **spring fair** here in May, the hugely popular **Chilli Fest** in September, and a three-day winter **market** in early November. You don't have to pay for entrance to visit the **food hall and café** (see page 234).

Yew Tree Barn

Low Newton, LA11 6JP, 3 miles northeast of Cartmel • Mon–Sat 9am–5pm, Sun 10am–4pm • ☎015395 31498, ⓦyewtreebarn.co.uk • Free parking outside

You never know when you might be in the market for an old church pulpit or a traditional Cumbrian willow basket, and there's all that and more at **Yew Tree Barn**, a vast nineteenth-century barn that doubles as craft gallery and art studio, with an architectural reclamation business on the side. Artists and crafters are usually around to talk to – from sculptors to ceramicists – and there's a huge range of work for sale under the soaring oak beams, not to mention a decent **café**.

ARRIVAL AND INFORMATION

By car Cartmel lies a few miles inland of Morecambe Bay and just 5 miles south of Lakeside, the southern tip of Windermere; the turn-off from the M6 is junction 36. There's limited free parking in and around the village square, but it's much easier to park in the pay-and-display car park, off the top of the square by the racecourse.

By train and bus Realistically, you're visiting Cartmel by car, certainly if you're hoping to nip down from the

CARTMEL AND AROUND

Lakes for a day out. There are trains to Cark-in-Cartmel, 2 miles southwest of the village (the station is a mile from Holker Hall), while local bus #530 stops in Cartmel on its run between Kendal and the coast at Grange-over-Sands (which also has a train station).

Tourist information The local website ⓦcartmelvillage. com is useful, and includes a village map.

ACCOMMODATION

SEE MAP PAGE 232

Save for race meeting weekends (when prices are also at their highest), **accommodation** in Cartmel is generally easy to find, either in several local B&Bs or in one of the old pubs around and about the main square. It's usually a pretty quiet place to spend the night, which is one of its charms.

Cavendish Arms Cavendish St, LA11 6QA ☎015395 36240, ⓦthecavendisharms.co.uk. The oldest of Cartmel's inns – on the road through the gatehouse – retains many of its original sixteenth-century features (oak beams, wobbly floors) and has an open fire in the public bar; the guest rooms are traditionally decorated, too (some with four-posters). It's pretty good value and three-for-two-night deals (midweek, low season) are a bargain. Parking. **£115**

★ **L'Enclume** Cavendish St, LA11 6PZ ☎015395 36362, ⓦlenclume.co.uk. At one of the Lake's most celebrated restaurants (see page 234) you can complete the whole sybaritic experience with a stay in one of sixteen smallish but highly individual rooms which come in three different

categories. These mix French antique furniture and country-chic character with designer fabrics, restful colours and excellent bathrooms – a couple of rooms overlook gardens and priory, while others are located nearby in two other village buildings, one right next door to their associated *Rogan & Company* brasserie (see page 235). Most rooms are rated as standard, while the suites (including large Art Deco suite with wet room and village views) run up to £219. Closed first two weeks in Jan. Parking. **£159**

Perfect English 7 The Square, LA11 6QB, bookings through Cavendish Arms, ☎015395 36240, ⓦthecavendisharms.co.uk. The high-end gift- and home furnishings shop in the square has three very nice B&B rooms above, which you access up a spiral staircase and via a private balcony. It's a contemporary space – muted colours, claw-foot baths, restored fireplaces – with breakfast either served continental-style in your room or as a full English a short walk away in the *Cavendish* (see above). Parking. **£100**

EATING

SEE MAPS PAGES 224 AND 232

If you're coming on the gourmet trail it's essential to book ahead for the stellar experience of *L'Enclume*, though there are plenty of other local **foodie outlets**, from the artisan producers in the Unsworth Yard development (near the church) to Holker's stately home café and food hall. The increasingly popular **Cartmel Food Market** is held in the village square on the third Friday of the month.

Cartmel Cheeses 1 & 2 Unsworth's Yard, LA11 6PN ☎015395 34307, ⓦcartmelcheeses.co.uk. There are up to fifty artisan British and French cheeses on display in this cheery cheese emporium, so you're bound to find something you like. They're happy to shave off a taste or two of anything you fancy – the local choice is Holker Farm's St James, a raw ewes' milk cheese made just a couple of miles from the shop. The cheese shop also owns the adjacent *Cartmel Bakehouse* (same hours), where you can stock up on fancy handmade bread, including sourdough – that's lunch sorted. Mon–Sat 9.30am–5pm, Sun 10am–4.30pm.

★ **Cartmel Village Shop** The Square, LA11 6QB ☎015395 36280, ⓦcartmelvillageshop.co.uk. The village shop is a model of its kind – the spiritual home of Cumbrian sticky toffee pudding, and supplier of lovely deli things, local produce and takeaway sandwiches. There's also a small upstairs café, so you can enjoy a slap-up, sit-down, eat-in, sticky-toffee-pudding feast (served with cream or ice cream), as well as other snacks and lunch treats (dishes £4–7). Shop Mon–Sat 9am–5pm, Sun 10am–4.30pm; café Mon–Sat 9.30am–4pm, Sun 10.30am–3.30pm.

Courtyard Café Holker Hall, Cark-in-Cartmel, LA11 7PL, 2 miles west of Cartmel ☎015395 53907; Holker Food Hall ☎015395 53908, ⓦholker.co.uk. The café at

the stately home (see page 233) is an excellent place for breakfast (until noon), lunch or tea, especially on fine days when you can sit outside in the courtyard. Most dishes are under £9 and much of the produce is from the estate, with a large selection also sold in the adjacent Holker Food Hall (same opening hours), from shorthorn beef, oak-smoked farm cheese and the local salt-marsh lamb to gourmet sausages and damson gin. Regional producers' markets are also held here, usually on the first Sun of each month. Late March to early Nov Wed–Sun 10.30am–5pm.

Hazelmere Café 1–2 Yewbarrow Terrace, Grange-over-Sands, LA11 6ED, 3 miles east of Cartmel ☎015395 32972, ⓦthehazelmere.co.uk. For the finest local cuppa head over to the seaside at Grange, where the award-winning *Hazelmere* dishes up single-estate teas in bone china cups alongside traditional meals (potted shrimps, bangers and mash; meals £7–16), and cakes and bread from its own bakery. Café daily 10am–5pm; bakery Mon–Sat 8.30am–5pm, Sun 9.30am–4.30pm.

★ **L'Enclume** Cavendish St, LA11 6PZ ☎015395 36362, ⓦlenclume.co.uk. Cartmel's medieval blacksmiths (*enclume* is French for anvil) could only have dreamt of food so fine. Chef Simon Rogan's ideas are simply extraordinary, with artfully constructed dishes presented in up to thirteen courses, depending on the menu – an oyster cracker, dry aged pork, wilted kale and honey wine, or raw Cornish mackerel in coal oil are typical examples, while other dishes are accompanied by intensely flavoured jellied cubes, mousses or foams, or suffused with wild herbs, hedgerow flowers and exotic roots. It's clever, contemporary cooking and one of England's most critically acclaimed, Michelin-starred experiences. Set lunch from £65, going up to £155 for "The Menu" at lunch or dinner. Book as far in advance as possible, and even then you might need to be flexible with dates. Tues–Sun noon–1.30pm & 6.30–9pm.

★ **Rogan & Company** Devonshire Square, LA11 6QD ☎ 015395 35917, ⓦ roganandco.co.uk. Simon Rogan's casual-dining Cartmel offshoot – in a classy space carved from a sixteenth-century building – is in no sense a substitute for eating at *L'Enclume*, though it still boasts one

Michelin star. The gastro-bistro menu (terrine of own farm pork with caper jam, roasted valley partridge with beetroot and cherry) is beautifully presented and impeccably sourced (the local butcher and milkman get a salute on the blackboard), while prices are reasonable – most mains hover around £25, or it's just £18 for the two-course set lunch. Mon & Thurs–Sat noon–1.45pm & 6–9pm, Sun noon–2.30pm; also open Wed May–Oct.

Ulverston and around

First-time visitors will be pleasantly surprised by **Ulverston**, a close-knit market town on the Furness peninsula that formerly prospered on the cotton, tanning and iron ore industries. The cutting of Britain's shortest, widest and deepest canal in 1796 allowed direct shipping access into town and boosted trade with the Americas and West Indies, while exports from the heart of the Lake District (from wooden bobbins and linen to copper and slate) passed out through Ulverston and made it wealthy. Today it's an attractive place, with dappled grey limestone cottages and a jumble of cobbled alleys and traditional shops zigzagging off the central Market Place; it also boasts a good number of attractions both in town and nearby.

In the immediate vicinity of Ulverston is an area marketed to visitors as the "**Lake District peninsulas**" – just don't expect any lakes, although there are plenty of varied family attractions, from **zoo** and ruined **abbey** to the fascinating local museum in the neighbouring town of **Barrow-in-Furness**. Walkers also know the town as the start of the **Cumbria Way**, the seventy-mile footpath from Ulverston to Carlisle.

Hoad Monument

Easter–Oct Sun & public hols 1–5pm • Free • Follow Church Walk from the end of King St, past the parish church

What looks like a lighthouse high on a hill to the north of town is the **Hoad Monument**, built in 1850 to honour locally born **Sir John Barrow**, a former Secretary of the Admiralty who did much to promote British exploration, particularly the attempt to find the Northwest Passage. The monument is open to the public when the flag's flying, and the walk to the top grants fine views of Morecambe Bay, the town and – to the north – the distant lakeland fells. The monument also forms part of a good eleven-mile circular **walk** from town, taking in other local landmarks and the local coast – pick up a leaflet from the town tourist office.

Market Hall

New Market St, LA12 7LJ • Mon, Tues & Thurs–Sat 9am–5pm • ☎ 01229 582183, ⓦ ulverstonmarket.co.uk

Ulverston's **Market Hall** is the centre of commercial life, while stalls set up in **Market Place** and surrounding streets every Thursday and Saturday for the busy outdoor market, held since the thirteenth century – the granting of the town charter, by Edward I, is still celebrated here every autumn during Ulverston's Charter Festival. There's also a bustling **farmers' market** on the third Saturday of each month, and Ulverston comes over all Dickensian at the end of November with a good-natured Christmas market in and around the Market Place.

Laurel and Hardy Museum

Brogden St, LA12 7AH • Easter–Sept daily 10am–5pm; Oct–Easter Tues & Thurs–Sun 10am–5pm • £5, family ticket £10 • ☎ 01229 582292, ⓦ laurel-and-hardy.co.uk

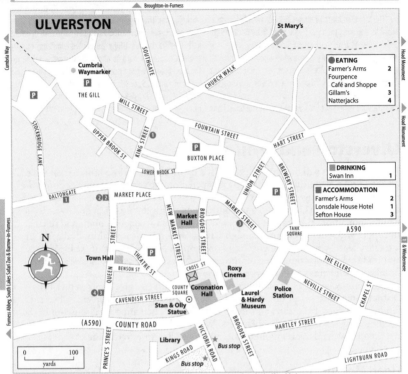

Ulverston's most famous son is Stan Laurel (born Arthur Stanley Jefferson), the whimpering, head-scratching half of Laurel and Hardy. The duo are celebrated in an endearing collection of memorabilia at the **Laurel and Hardy Museum**, which you'll find behind Coronation Hall; you enter through the Roxy Cinema, formerly a theatre and music hall. Information boards and cases of mementoes are set up on one of the Roxy's old stages, including a copy of Stan's birth certificate (June 16, 1890, in Foundry Cottages, Ulverston), which lists his father's occupation as "comedian" – young Arthur Stanley could hardly have become anything else. Once you've read the stories and picked your way through the eccentric showcase of hats, beer bottles, photos, models, puppets, press cuttings and props, you can sit yourself down and enjoy screenings of the original films. Stan and Olly also appear, leaning on a lamppost, in a celebratory **statue** just outside the front of Coronation Hall.

Conishead Priory

Conishead Priory, LA12 9QQ, 2 miles southeast of Ulverston on A5087 • World Peace Temple Mon–Sat 11am–5pm, Sun noon–5pm (closed 2 weeks in May and 4 weeks from mid-July); grounds daily dawn–dusk; guided tours Sat & Sun 2.30pm • Free; guided tours £3.60 • ☎ 01229 584029, ⊛ manjushri.org

Just outside town, the dramatic Victorian Gothic mansion that is **Conishead Priory** stands on a site originally occupied by a twelfth-century Augustinian priory. It's now a residential Buddhist centre, and the house and specially built **World Peace Temple** are open for visits – the latter features the largest bronze Buddha statue cast in the West – while seventy acres of woodland grounds provide a peaceful place for a stroll. A beautifully restored conservatory **café** has outdoor seating in spring and summer. Just beyond Conishead Priory, at **Bardsea**, there's paddling when the tide is in, scenic views across Morecambe Bay and a pub in the village for refreshments.

South Lakes Safari Zoo

Broughton Rd, Dalton-in-Furness, LA15 8JR, 3 miles southwest of Ulverston on A590 Barrow road • Daily April–Oct 10am–5pm, Nov–March 10.30am–4pm • £16.50, under-15s free; reduced prices in winter • ☎ 01229 466086, ⓦ southlakessafarizoo.com • Bus #6 or #X6 from Ulverston to Melton Top, or 20min uphill walk from Dalton-in-Furness train station; free parking

Whatever you feel about zoos, you're likely to be positively surprised by the **South Lakes Safari Zoo**. An award-winning conservation organization, it relies for the most part on ditches and trenches (not cages) and is split into separate habitat areas, from Australian bush to tropical rainforest. It's quite something to encounter free-roaming kangaroos or hand-feed a giraffe in rural Cumbria, while the Sumatran tiger-feeding (encouraging them to climb and jump for their meal) is unique in Europe.

Furness Abbey

Manor Rd, Barrow-in-Furness, LA13 0PJ, 6 miles southwest of Ulverston off A590 • April–Sept daily 10am–6pm; Oct daily 10am–5pm, Nov–March Sat & Sun 10am–4pm • £6; EH • ☎ 01229 823420, ⓦ english-heritage.org.uk/visit/places/furness-abbey • Buses #X6 and #6 between Ulverston and Barrow pass nearby; free parking

Cumbria's wealth used to be concentrated at mighty **Furness Abbey**, which at the peak of its influence owned much of southern Cumbria. Founded in 1124, the Cistercian abbey ran sheep farms on the fells, controlled fishing rights, produced grain and leather, smelted iron, dug peat for fuel and manufactured salt and even beer. It became such a prize that the Scots raided it twice, though it survived until April 1536 when Henry VIII chose it to be the first of the large abbeys to be dissolved. The roofless red-sandstone arcades and pillars have been a popular tourist attraction since the early nineteenth century – Wordsworth was very taken with the "mouldering pile". A small **visitor centre** at the site contains some rare examples of effigies of armed knights with closed helmets and crossed legs (only seven others have ever been found intact). Then you can borrow an audioguide from the reception desk to guide you around the massive slabs of stone-ribbed vaulting and richly embellished arcades.

Barrow Dock Museum

North Rd, Barrow-in-Furness, LA14 2PW, 10 miles southwest of Ulverston, A590 • Wed–Sun 11am–4pm • Free • ☎ 01229 876400, ⓦ dockmuseum.org.uk • Bus #X6 or #6 from Ulverston, or signposted from Barrow train station; free parking at museum

The gruff, industrial shipbuilding town of Barrow-in-Furness was once one of England's busiest ports. Despite a significant amount of town-centre regeneration it scarcely figures on anyone's Lake District itinerary, though the excellent **Barrow Dock Museum** is definitely worth a visit. Located in the dried-out graving dock where ships were once repaired, the striking-looking museum tells the history of Barrow, which is also the history of modern shipbuilding, while popular family events are held here every summer.

ARRIVAL AND DEPARTURE   ULVERSTON AND AROUND

By car Ulverston is around 11 miles west of Cartmel, 17 miles southwest of Windermere town, or 24 miles from Kendal; the turn-off from the M6 for Ulverston is junction 36. There are pay-and-display car parks off Market St and at The Gill.

By train Ulverston train station, on the Cumbrian Coast line, is a few minutes from the centre – walk up Prince's St and turn right at the main road for County Square. There are hourly services from Manchester/Preston/Lancaster to

Ulverston, Dalton and Barrow-in-Furness (timetables at ⓦ tpexpress.co.uk) and to and from Carlisle/Barrow and Preston/Lancaster (ⓦ northernrailway.org).

By bus Buses arrive on Victoria Rd, near the library. Main service from the Lakes is the #618 (Mon–Sat 5 daily) from Windermere, via Bowness, Newby Bridge and Haverthwaite to Ulverston (35min). The #X6 from Kendal (Mon–Sat hourly, 4 on Sun) runs to Ulverston (1hr) and then on to Dalton and Barrow.

INFORMATION AND ACTIVITIES

Bike rental Velo Bikes, Lightburn Industrial Estate, west from the centre on Lightburn Rd (Mon–Sat 9am–5.30pm; ☎ 01229 581116, ⓦ velobikes.co.uk) rents bikes for £25/ half day, £40/day – they also have info on local cycle routes, including the 72-mile Cumbria Way Cycle Route (ⓦ cumbriawaycycleroute.co.uk) which shadows the hiking route to Carlisle.

Cumbria Way A waymarker spire at The Gill, at the top of Upper Brook St, signals the start of the 70-mile walk to Carlisle. The first night's stop is Coniston, 15 miles away.

Tourist information There are leaflet stands at the Laurel and Hardy Museum (see page 235), the railway station, Booths supermarket and elsewhere, but the best source is via ⓦ ulverston.com.

ACCOMMODATION   SEE MAPS PAGES 224 AND 236

★ **Bay Horse** Canal Foot, LA12 9EL, 1.5 miles east of Ulverston ☎ 01229 583972, ⓦ thebayhorsehotel.co.uk. This cosy old dog-friendly inn on the Leven estuary lulls you with gorgeous views and good Cumbrian cuisine (see below). Nine cream-and-fawn rooms are comfortable rather than cutting-edge, but some open out onto a sea-view terrace (£120) so you don't even need to get out of bed to see the water and watch the birds swooping. From town, follow the A590 and turn off at the signpost for Canal Foot, running through an industrial estate to reach the inn, by the last lock on the Ulverston canal (or a 30min walk). Parking. **£100**

Farmer's Arms 3 Market Place, LA12 7BB ☎ 01229 584469, ⓦ the-farmers-ulverston.co.uk. The town's finest pub offers a choice of accommodation: three nicely turned-out en-suite rooms upstairs, with bold colour schemes and large beds; six self-catering cottages with contemporary furnishings and fitted kitchens in the town centre, just a couple of hundred yards from the pub (two or three bedrooms; £120–150); and more self-catering in

a converted former pub nearby (£120). A hearty breakfast (not included) is served at the pub. Parking. Pub rooms **£85**

Lonsdale House Hotel 11 Daltongate, LA12 7BD ☎ 01229 582598, ⓦ lonsdalehousehotel.co.uk. Business-like rooms in a Georgian townhouse (no surprise that each has a trouser-press and some have the regulation four-poster), but the best part is the private walled garden at the back – rooms overlooking this tend to escape any street noise. Afternoon tea and sundowner drinks are available in the garden, and there's also a cellar bistro and bar. Parking. **£90**

Sefton House 34 Queen St, LA12 7AF ☎ 01229 582190, ⓦ seftonhouse.co.uk. Amiable B&B in an attractive town-centre Georgian house that also holds Ulverston's best café (see page 240). Four of the five clutter-free rooms (doubles and twins) have their own neat little en-suites with one sharing a bathroom (£60). Local restaurants and pubs are just a step away, but you'll find it hard to resist a nightcap and a natter downstairs in the café before heading up to bed. Car parks are a short walk away. **£65**

EATING   SEE MAPS PAGES 224 AND 236

★ **Bay Horse** Canal Foot, LA12 9EL, 1.5 miles east of Ulverston ☎ 01229 583972, ⓦ thebayhorsehotel. co.uk. Best posh night out is down at the *Bay Horse*, where dinner (open to non-guests; reservations essential) is served in the candlelit conservatory – proper steaks, lakeland lamb, game in season and fresh fish, book-ended by home-made bread and truffles. Meanwhile, the snug Victorian-style bar – all hunting pictures, heavy drapes and padded seats – serves up a varied lunchtime menu and an evening light bites menu, from sandwiches to grills (£8–16), along with a comprehensive range of vegetarian options. A few drinks tables outside by the canal lock round off the picture. Lunch Tues–Sun noon–2pm; dinner daily 7.30pm for 8pm.

★ **Farmer's Arms** 3 Market Place, LA12 7BB ☎ 01229 584469, ⓦ the-farmers-ulverston.co.uk. More wine bar and restaurant than pub (with wicker chairs, sofas and newspapers), and the best place in town for a convivial drink and a reasonably priced meal. It's open from breakfast onwards, and food ranges from sandwich lunches and traditional bar meals to pricier blackboard specials (£10–

15). Fish and seafood is always a good choice – perhaps a big bowl of mussel and langoustines, Whitby scampi or seared scallops with black pudding. Daily 9am–11pm; kitchen 9am–3pm & 5–8.30pm.

Fourpence Café and Shoppe 16 King St, LA12 7DZ ☎ 01229 583131, ⓦ fourpencecafe.co.uk. Eccentric bric-a-brac shop that even many locals don't realize is also a café, serving excellent home-made lemonade and sandwiches, chowder, hot-filled jacket potatoes (or sweet potatoes, if you'd rather), rarebits, hot beef chilli and stacks more (all £5–8). They also offer delicious vegetarian and fish soups; check the blackboard for daily specials. Simple food, but it's all made freshly to order and the friendly service makes for a relaxed meal. Mon, Tues & Thurs–Sat 10am–4pm, Sun 11am–3pm; Nov to mid-Feb closed Sun.

★ **Gillam's** 64 Market St, LA12 7LT ☎ 01229 587564, ⓦ gillams-tearoom.co.uk. A traditional tearoom (with summer terrace garden) that's wholly organic, Fair Trade and veggie, and has no truck with the microwave. They're serious about their drinks, whether you want a single-estate oolong or pot of Ethiopian Yirgacheffe, while food

(mushrooms on toast, veggie quiche and the like, £6–10) is locally sourced. They also have a specialist grocers and deli next door. Tues–Sat 9am–5pm, Sun 10am–4pm.

★ **Natterjacks** 34 Queen St, LA12 7AF ☎ 01229 582190. Other cafés are all shutting for the day when *Natterjacks* opens – and Ulverston's first night-time café is a real hit with the local arts and music crowd, who come for artisan coffee and home-made organic cakes and cookies (£1–2) or a local ale or glass of wine. Occupying the opened-out ground floor of a townhouse B&B, it has a real American coffee-house feel (courtesy of Boston-born Valerie) with its mix-and-match furniture, art-hung walls and piano in the corner. All sorts meet here, from local ukulele group to book club. Mon–Fri 5–10pm.

DRINKING

SEE MAP PAGE 236

Swan Inn Swan St, LA12 7JX ☎ 01229 582519, ⊛ the swaninnulverston.co.uk. The real-ale place – ten cask ales and three ciders served at any one time, in a refurbished old pub with beer garden (and roaring open fire for winter) on the edge of town. Mon–Thurs 3.30–11.30pm, Fri & Sat noon–midnight, Sun noon–11pm.

ENTERTAINMENT AND FESTIVALS

Ulverston bigs itself up as the "Festival Town", but to be fair there's a major celebration of one kind or another almost every month. Highlights are May's **Flag Fortnight** – with the whole town draped in flags and banners – and September's **Charter Festival**, which culminates in a spectacular lantern procession. There are also arts and music festivals, an annual carnival, and a very popular **walking** festival held at the end of April, with ten days of outdoor events, from one-mile strolls to all-day hikes (see page 34). **Coronation Hall** County Square, LA12 7LZ ☎ 01229 587140, ⊛ corohall.co.uk. The local cultural centre – "the Coro" to locals – for theatre, opera, concerts and all sorts of community and festival events, including the annual beer festival every Sept.

DIRECTORY

Doctor Local doctors are based at the Community Health Centre, Stanley St (☎ 01229 484045).
Hospital The nearest full hospital is in Barrow-in-Furness (Furness General Hospital, Dalton Lane; ☎ 01229 870870, ⊛ uhmb.nhs.uk).
Pharmacies Boots, 32 Market St (☎ 01229 582049); J. Hewitt, 10 Market Place (☎ 01229 582003).
Police station Ulverston Market Hall (Mon, Tues, Thurs & Fri 9am–1pm; ☎ 101, ⊛ cumbria.police.uk).
Post office County Square (Mon–Sat 9am–5.30pm).
Swimming pool Lakes Leisure Ulverston, Priory Rd (☎ 01229 584110, ⊛ better.org.uk). Public admission usually mornings and evenings during termtime, otherwise all day, but call or check the website for specific times. There's also a gym, bowling green, astroturf pitch and Cumbria's biggest tennis centre.

Whitehaven and around

Some fine Georgian houses and an impressively busy harbour mark out the centre of **Whitehaven**, one of the few grid-planned towns in England and easily the most interesting destination on Cumbria's west coast. A mere fishing village of 250 people in the early seventeenth century, within a hundred years Whitehaven had boomed fifty-fold as the Lowther family exploited the local coal seams and expanded the harbour. Later economic expansion was as much due to the slave trade and the town spent a brief period during the eighteenth century as one of Britain's busiest ports, importing sugar, rum, spices, tea, timber and tobacco.

Town and harbour regeneration has wrought handsome changes in Whitehaven, whose Georgian streets and neatly painted houses make it one of Cumbria's most distinguished towns. Indeed the harbour sits at the heart of a renaissance project that has spruced up the quayside with promenades, sculptures and heritage trails. The **Crow's Nest**, a 130ft-high tower, lit at night, is the dramatic centrepiece of the bustling marina. As a whole, the town provides a good day out, with a lively **market** every Thursday and Saturday, as well as three excellent **museums** and an outstanding **bookshop**.

Around Whitehaven, some coastal stretches north and south might just persuade you to stay longer. A day at the beach is always an option, and the cliffs and sands at **St Bees** are a honeypot on warm summer days. North of Whitehaven the train runs up

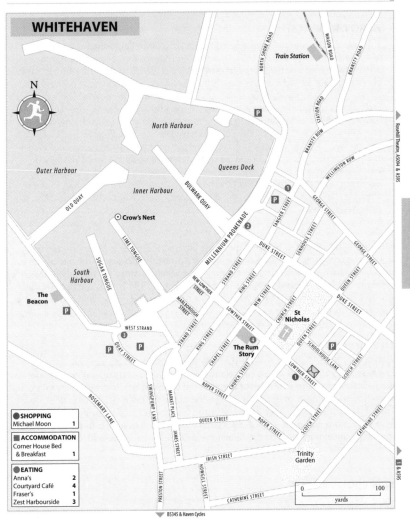

WHITEHAVEN

N

North Harbour

Outer Harbour

Inner Harbour

Queens Dock

South Harbour

Crow's Nest

The Beacon

WEST STRAND

OLD QUAY

LIME TONGUE

SUGAR TONGUE

QUAY STREET

BULWARK QUAY

MILLENNIUM PROMENADE

MARLBOROUGH STREET

STRAND STREET

NEW LOWTHER STREET

STRAND STREET

KING STREET

CHAPEL STREET

The Rum Story

LOWTHER STREET

NEW STREET

CHURCH STREET

St Nicholas

TANGIER STREET

DUKE STREET

SENHOUSE STREET

QUEEN STREET

GEORGE STREET

GEORGE STREET

DUKE STREET

QUEEN STREET

SCHOOLHOUSE LANE

SCOTCH STREET

SCOTCH STREET

CATHERINE STREET

LOWTHER STREET

ROPER STREET

CHURCH STREET

MARKET PLACE

ROSEMARY LANE

SWINGPUMP LANE

JAMES STREET

QUEEN STREET

IRISH STREET

PRESTON STREET

HOWGILL STREET

CATHERINE STREET

ROPER STREET

Trinity Garden

Train Station

NORTH SHORE ROAD

WAGON ROAD

BRANSTY ROAD

STATION ROAD

BRANSTY ROW

WELLINGTON ROW

BRANSTY ROW

Rosehill Theatre, A5094 & A595

7

B & A595

B5345 & Haven Cycles

● SHOPPING
Michael Moon   1

■ ACCOMMODATION
Corner House Bed
& Breakfast   1

● EATING
Anna's   2
Courtyard Café   4
Fraser's   1
Zest Harbourside   3

0   100
yards

the coast as far as **Maryport** before heading inland for Carlisle, but to see the best of the Solway Firth coast you really need a car, in which case you can potter up as far as the little resort of **Silloth**, stopping where you want for bracing walks and sweeping coastal views.

The Beacon

West Strand, CA28 7LY • Tues–Sat 10am–4.30pm, Sun 11am–4pm; also open Mon during school hols • £7 • ☎ 01946 592302, ⓦ thebeacon-whitehaven.co.uk • Pay-and-display parking outside museum

Best place for Whitehaven's local history is **The Beacon**, an enterprising museum on the harbour that resembles a squat lighthouse. There are interactive exhibitions on all floors, covering themes from slaving to smuggling, with a special emphasis on the local characters who have shaped the town, from the iron ore miners known as the "Red

HERO OR PIRATE?

That's the question the Whitehaven Beacon poses about **John Paul Jones**, so-called "Father of the American Navy", who attacked Whitehaven in 1778. A couple of centuries ago, the answer would have very much depended on which side you stood during the American War of Independence (or, as Americans know it, the Revolutionary War). Jones had been born in Scotland and first sailed as an apprentice out of Whitehaven, where he served on merchant and slaving ships. Later, in America, he joined the revolutionary Continental Navy and, while harrying British shipping, conceived a plan to assault the port of his apprenticeship. It would have been a mighty coup against one of Britain's biggest ports, but, let down by a drunk and mutinous crew, he damaged only one of the two hundred boats in dock, though he did spike Whitehaven's defensive guns. In the United States his reputation ebbed and flowed with the years after his death in 1792, and not until 1913 was he granted full honours as a naval hero; in Britain, for most of that time, he was always viewed as a mere pirate. To chase down the story in Whitehaven – and decide which side you're on – visit the exhibit at The Beacon (see below).

Men" (after the colour of the dust they were covered in) to the nineteenth-century ship rescue company, the "Rocket Brigade". It's probably also one of the few places in the UK to champion nuclear power, using "The Sellafield Story" to trace the industry's development from original weapons research during the 1940s. You can easily spend a couple of hours here, teaching yourself how to build a ship, tie a knot or dress like a Roman centurion.

The Rum Story

Lowther St, CA28 7DN • Mon–Sat 10am–4.30pm • £9.95, family ticket £25.95 • ☎ 01946 592933, ⓦ rumstory.co.uk

The Rum Story is housed in the eighteenth-century shop, courtyard and warehouses of the Jefferson rum family. It's one of a number of places in Whitehaven where you could happily spend an hour or so, discovering what made the town tick in days gone by. You'll learn all about the town's links with the Caribbean and the family's rum business, with digressions along the way on associated topics, whether it's life in the British Navy, the temperance movement or the hideousness of the slaves' Middle Passage. There's an interesting **café**, too (see page 244).

St Nicholas Centre

Lowther St, CA28 7DG • Mon–Fri 10am–3.30pm, Sat 10am–4pm • Free • ⓦ whitehavenparish.co.uk

The prominent seventeenth-century **church of St Nicholas** succumbed to a fire in 1971 and all that stands today is its tower, with a lovely garden outside surrounding the former nave. **George Washington's grandmother**, Mildred Gale, wife of a Whitehaven merchant, lies buried here – there's a copy of the burial register and a commemorative plaque displayed inside the tower, which now serves as the **St Nicholas Centre**, a volunteer-run café, community centre and chapel. Someone will doubtless suggest you climb the tower's narrow, twisting stone staircase to an upper gallery where the church silver is on display, as are the internal workings of the tower clock.

St Bees Head and St Bees village

Five miles south of Whitehaven • Bus #20 from Whitehaven stops in St Bees village and also runs right to the beach, though the last one back is in the early afternoon; there are later services on the train

Five miles south of Whitehaven, the lighthouse on the sandstone cliffs of **St Bees Head** marks the start of Alfred Wainwright's 190-mile Coast-to-Coast walk. The beach below is one of the finest on the coast, wide and sandy, though a bit exposed on windy days, and there's a massive car park, an even-bigger holiday camp and a bucket-and-spade café. **St Bees village** itself is rather nicer, set half a mile inland with two or three old pubs within walking distance of the train station and a twelfth-century priory.

Lake District Coast Aquarium

South Quay, Maryport, CA15 8AB • Daily 10am–5pm • £8.95, children £5.95, family ticket £25.95 • ☎ 01900 817760, ⓦ coastaquarium. co.uk • Maryport can be reached easily on the scenic Cumbrian Coast line (see page 21)

North of Whitehaven, past Workington, it's a fourteen-mile drive (the last part along the Solway Firth coast) to **Maryport**, another eighteenth-century port with a restored harbour and marina, this one featuring the **Lake District Coast Aquarium**. It's a handy rainy-day attraction (children love the fish-feeding sessions and nautical adventure playground), and there's also free entry to the shark exhibition and film in the aquarium's Wild Solway Centre.

Solway Coast Discovery Centre

Liddell St, Silloth, CA7 4DD • April–Sept Mon, Wed & Fri 9.30am–12.30pm & 1–4pm, Sat 10am–2.30pm; Oct–March Mon, Wed & Fri 12.45–4pm, Sat 11am–1pm • Free • ☎ 016973 33055, ⓦ solwaycoastaonb.org.uk • Buses (ⓦ reays.co.uk) run from Maryport to Silloth (Mon–Sat about 5 daily)

Silloth, thirteen miles north of Maryport, is the Solway Firth's nicest small resort with its cobbled streets, seafront green and promenade, salt marshes and dunes. The **Solway Coast Discovery Centre** here is a good family-friendly attraction, delving into the history and environment of this area of outstanding natural beauty. There's also a tourist office and local art gallery, open the same times as the centre.

ARRIVAL AND DEPARTURE   **WHITEHAVEN AND AROUND**

By car Whitehaven is on the A595, around 15 miles (or a 30min drive) from Cockermouth, or 17 miles from Ravenglass. There's limited-time disc-zone parking in town (pick up a disc from local shops); for longer stays you're better off following signs to a central car park.

By bus Buses use a variety of stops around town – catch services going south from Duke St, including #20 to St Bees (Mon–Sat 5–6 daily; 25min); or north from Lowther St, including #600 to Cockermouth (Mon–Sat 3–5 daily; 30min) and Carlisle (1hr 30min).

By train There's a roughly hourly service south to St Bees, Ravenglass, Millom and Barrow, or north via Maryport to Carlisle (timetables on ⓦ northernrailway.co.uk). From Whitehaven's train station, you can walk around the harbour to The Beacon in less than 10min.

PEOPLE AND PLACES: I'LL CRY IF I WANT TO

If you want to know what's going on in Whitehaven, just go along to the Thursday or Saturday market and keep an ear out for official **Town Crier**, Rob Romano. The weekly "Town Shout" is just one of the Town Crier's duties, along with welcoming dignitaries, opening fairs and fetes, talking to local schools and, once a year, reading out the Lammas Fair Proclamation in the marketplace – something that's been done since 1672, when Charles II first granted the market charter to the town. How did Rob get to be Town Crier in the first place? "Well, I don't mind dressing up and I don't mind shouting," admits Rob, though just as important to him is the chance to promote the joys of Whitehaven to the wider world. Although London-born, Rob married a Whitehaven girl and has lived here since 1974, becoming Town Crier in 2001. "I'll get involved in anything that helps put a bit of polish on a cracking little town," he says, and to that end in his official capacity he welcomed the Queen and Prince Philip on their visit in 2008. Ask this most indefatigable booster of Whitehaven if there's any downside at all to being Town Crier and he'll only admit to one thing – apparently, the costume gets a bit too hot at times.

INFORMATION AND ACTIVITIES

Coast-to-Coast The start of the famous Coast-to-Coast walk across England starts at St Bees Head, 5 miles south of Whitehaven. The first day's walking is a break-yourself-in 14 miles to Ennerdale Bridge, and many choose to stay the night in Whitehaven or St Bees beforehand so as to get an early start. Latest updates on the route can be found at ⓦ wainwright.org.uk/coast-to-coast.

Cycling Whitehaven itself is the start of the 140-mile C2C cycle route to Sunderland/Newcastle (ⓦ c2c-guide.co.uk). A metal cut-out, protruding from the harbour slipway, marks the spot – it's traditional for C2C cyclists to dip their front wheel in the water before starting.

Tourist information There's no tourist office in Whitehaven; the best source of information is Western Lake District Tourism (☎ 01539 822222, ⓦ western-lakedistrict. co.uk).

ACCOMMODATION

SEE MAPS PAGES 224 AND 241

Corner House Bed & Breakfast Foxhouses Rd, CA28 8AD, 0.5 mile south of the centre near Corkickle train station ☎ 01946 696357, ⓦ thecornerhousebandb. co.uk. Beautiful mix of period wooden floors, sash windows, bold wallpaper and modern amenities in this cosy, immaculately maintained Victorian villa. The six rooms are all en suite (cheaper options have wet rooms with shower, but no bath), owners Leisa and Dave can't do enough for their guests, and the generous breakfast features local free-range eggs. Town is a 10min walk away, or a quick ride on the bus. Parking. **£85**

Moresby Hall Moresby, CA28 6PJ, 2 miles north of Whitehaven ☎ 01946 696317, ⓦ moresbyhall.co.uk. Quality accommodation in a very attractive Grade I listed manor house, where you can stroll the lawns and walled gardens, or sit in the orangery and enjoy the views. A dozen or so grand rooms with all the trimmings (robes, posh toiletries, iPod docks) keep you well rested – the nicest have carved 7ft four-poster beds, though the others are equally cheery and bright and will save you around £30 a night. You're out of town, but there's dining (open to non-residents) from Mon to Sat, as well as supper platters available, and glam fine-dining nights on Fri and Sat nights (advance reservations required). Parking. **£180**

EATING

SEE MAP PAGE 241

Anna's Unit 1, Millennium Promenade at Duke St, CA28 7UJ ☎ 01946 695454, ⓦ annaswhitehaven.co.uk. A cheery harbourfront café with sea views that does a nice line in sweet and savoury crêpes, sandwiches, wraps, salads and deli platters (£5–9); a fabulous evening menu is available Thurs to Sat primarily focused on small sharing plates (£7–9) and tapas (around £7 each or four for £25). Tues, Wed & Sun 10am–6pm, Thurs 10am till 10.30pm, Fri & Sat till 11.30pm.

Courtyard Café The Rum Story, Lowther St, CA28 7DN ☎ 01946 592933. The café in the rum museum (see page 242) is an interesting place, set under a glass roof and furled sailcloth in the old Jefferson stables. It serves toasties, sandwiches, baked potatoes, salads and cakes (£1.75–6) – not forgetting rum sundaes, rum tea bread, rum coffee and rum hot chocolate. Daily 10am–4.30pm.

Fraser's 32 Tangier St, CA28 7UZ ☎ 01946 62622. Cumbria's best fish and chips? Many would say so – it's been a fixture in town for more than forty years, and all the fish is sourced from sustainable fishing grounds. Around £7–8 if you eat in, or cheaper if you get a takeaway and walk down to the harbourfront for a marina view. Mon–Sat 11am–8pm.

Zest Harbourside 8 West Strand, CA28 7LR ☎ 01946 66981, ⓦ zestwhitehaven.com. Rock up to this splendid harbourfront establishment for superior butties and burgers, pizza and pasta and more substantial mains like beef, ale and mushroom pot pie – the only drawback is that, despite the tables for drinks, you can't eat outside. Sun–Thurs 11.30am–9pm, Fri & Sat till 9.30pm.

ENTERTAINMENT

Rosehill Theatre Moresby, CA28 6SE, 1 mile north of Whitehaven, signposted off A595 ☎ 01946 692422, ⓦ rosehilltheatre.co.uk. Newly refurbished, this enterprising local theatre is the venue for classical and contemporary music, drama and arthouse films. It was founded by a Hungarian émigré, arts enthusiast and textile designer, Sir Nicholas Sekers – where else in Cumbria can boast a silk-lined theatre?

SHOPPING

SEE MAP PAGE 241

Michael Moon 19 Lowther St, CA28 7AL ☎ 01946 99010/599010, ⓦ moonsbookshop.co.uk. There are certain places you just shouldn't miss and Michael Moon's bookshop is one, a bookworm's secondhand treasure trove with thirteen rooms full of books inside a higgledy-piggledy house. There is, supposedly, a mile of shelves holding books on every conceivable subject, and if you want to know anything about western Cumbria and Whitehaven in particular, Michael's your man. Easter–Dec Mon–Sat 9.30am–5pm; Jan–Easter Mon, Tues & Thurs–Sat 9.30am–5pm.

Cockermouth

Cockermouth, midway between the industrial coast and Keswick at the confluence of the Cocker and Derwent rivers, dominates the flat vales that leach out of the northwestern fells. There's a lot to admire about the town – impressive Georgian facades, tree-lined streets and riverside setting – and there's no shortage of local attractions, not least the logical first stop on the **Wordsworth trail**, namely the house where the future poet was born.

Main Street and Market Place

Walk along **Main Street** and Cockermouth immediately reveals its quirky, traditional charms and independent shops. In the space of a few hundred yards you could as easily buy a rack of lamb as an antique sherry barrel. The whiff of hops in the air from Jennings brewery is ever-present, while down **Old Kings Arms Lane** (60 Main St) modern businesses are now housed in the former stables and lodgings of an old coaching inn. This is where you'll also find the **Cockermouth History Wall**, an outdoor display that tells the story of the town, from the Romans to the disastrous floods of 2009 (see page 246). Over the river in **Market Place** (with monthly farmers' markets) there are more reminders of bygone days, from the pavement plaque teaching you the basics of talking Cumbrian to the traditional facade and mahogany counter inside **J.B. Banks**, ironmongers in the town since 1836.

Wordsworth House

Main St, CA13 9RX • Mid-Feb to Oct daily except Fri 11am–5pm, last admission 4pm, admission by timed ticket in peak periods • £8.80, family ticket £22; NT • ☎ 01900 824805, ⊛ nationaltrust.org.uk/wordsworth-house-and-garden

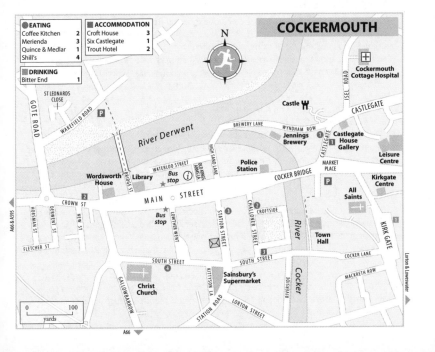

At the western end of Main Street is the **Wordsworth House**, a handsome Georgian building that was the birthplace of all five Wordsworth children, including William (1770) and Dorothy (1771). It's a house suitable for the professional man that Wordsworth's father was, though he only rented it from his employer, Sir James Lowther, for whom he spent much of his time away on business. The children, too, though happy in the house, were often sent to their grandparents in Penrith, and when Wordsworth's father died in 1783 – with the children already either away at school or living with relations – the family link with Cockermouth was broken. The building has been beautifully restored, but rather than a pure period-piece it's presented as a functioning eighteenth-century home – with a costumed cook willing to share recipes in the kitchen and a clerk completing the ledger with quill and ink. In around half the rooms you're encouraged to touch the items on display – children can dress up in one of the bedrooms – or lend the servants a hand, while the walled kitchen garden beside the river has been planted with fruit, vegetables and herbs that would have been familiar to the Wordsworths. It's an education, in the best sense, and a really excellent visit.

7

Jennings Brewery

Brewery Lane, CA13 9NE • Tour 1.30pm: Feb Thurs–Sat; March–June & Oct–Dec Wed–Sat; July–Sept Mon–Sat • £9.50 • ☎ 01900 820362, ⓦ jenningsbrewery.co.uk

Jennings have been brewers in the town since 1874, though it's no longer an independent brewery – it's been owned by Marston's since 2005. Nonetheless, the name remains a potent one in the Lakes and you don't have to step far to sample their product, available in any local pub. Or you can take the ninety-minute-long **brewery tour**, which ends with a free tasting in the bar.

AFTER THE DELUGE

Though many lakeland towns have been prone to winter **flooding** over the years, abnormal rainfall has caused havoc in recent times. In November 2009, the centre of Cockermouth turned into a disaster zone as storm waters surged through the streets, reaching over 8ft high in parts, and more than two hundred people had to be rescued, many by helicopter; in nearby Workington, a local policeman was killed as a bridge collapsed. Virtually every house and business along Main Street, Market Place and around was badly damaged, along with Wordsworth House, Jennings Brewery, the *Trout Hotel* and many other local landmarks and attractions. Today, plaques on walls show the rather alarming high-water mark (there's one on the *Black Bull* pub).

December 2015 saw another major event, Storm Desmond, which broke the UK record for the amount of rainfall in 24 hours. Keswick was badly hit – despite flood walls having been built along the river since 2009, trees, rocks and debris off the fells – and not a few caravans, swept along by raging waters – blocked bridges and saw the town centre inundated. Yet they were luckier than settlements around nearby Ullswater: Pooley Bridge saw its namesake collapse (though recovery teams soon had a temporary replacement constructed), and two-street Glenridding was lucky not to have been wiped off the map. Further south, the A591 was badly damaged and closed for months between Keswick and Grasmere.

While many businesses have lost everything, one positive side of these events is the extraordinary local spirit and enterprise shown by the communities involved: after the 2009 flooding Cockermouth, in particular, was back on its feet within the year – indeed Main Street, after the restoration of its shop facades, looked better than it had for decades. But if serious floods become an annual event, it's difficult to imagine how the region will cope long-term, as insurance companies raise their premiums or simply refuse to cover local homes and businesses.

HERDWICK SHEEP

The hardiest of indigenous British sheep breeds is the **Herdwick**, its name derived from the "herdwyck" (or sheep pasture) on which it was raised in medieval times. Other sheep breeds are more numerous but it's the grey-fleeced (black when young), white-faced Herdwick that's most characteristic of the Lake District – and which, in many ways, echoes the enduring struggle of lakeland hill farmers. The sheep live out on the inhospitable fells for almost the whole year – most are so good at foraging they never require additional feed. They are territorial, knowing their own "heafs" or particular grazing areas on the fells, and are historically concentrated in the central and western fells. The National Trust has been instrumental in maintaining the breed on its own farms by obliging tenants to keep Herdwicks. Beatrix Potter was also a keen sheep-farmer and encouraged the breed on the farms she left to the Trust on her death. Partly, the emphasis on maintaining the numbers of Herdwicks is to do with heritage: much of the existing lakeland landscape has been created for and around them, from the intensively grazed fields of the valley bottoms to the dry-stone walls further up the fells. But there's also an economic imperative not to let upland sheep-farmers (guardians of much of the landscape) go to the wall without a fight.

Despite low wool prices, there's a renewed interest in locally sourced Herdwick wool products (from carpets to thermal insulation), while many farmers sell on their flocks to restaurants and suppliers as high-quality meat. Cockermouth sees an annual celebration of all things woolly in June's **Woolfest** (Ⓦ woolfest.co.uk), while during the Lake District's summer agricultural shows, the **Herdwick Sheep Breeders' Association** (Ⓦ herdwick-sheep.com) hands out prizes to the healthiest and best-looking sheep – their website also has a list of working Herdwick farms with B&B accommodation.

7

Castlegate House Gallery

Castlegate, CA13 9HA • Mon, Wed & Fri 10am–4pm, Thurs & Sat 10am–5pm, Tues & Sun by appointment • Free • Ⓣ 01900 822149, Ⓦ castlegatehouse.co.uk

It's always worth checking to see what's on at **Castlegate House Gallery**, a Georgian mansion that lies opposite the entrance to Cockermouth Castle – itself a private residence and closed to the public. The house and sculpture garden exhibits changing shows of contemporary paintings, sculpture, ceramics and glass, specializing in the work of accomplished regional artists, mostly from the north of England and Scotland.

ARRIVAL AND INFORMATION

COCKERMOUTH

By car Cockermouth is 15 miles northwest of Keswick. The A66 bypasses the town to the south; turn in on either the B5292 (Whinlatter Pass road) or A5086 (from Loweswater and Ennerdale). The car park over the river off Wakefield Rd is the best place to park, since parking on Main St is limited to an hour (and you need to display a disc in your car, available from local shops).

By bus All buses stop on Main St, with the most useful service the #X4/X5 (hourly, Sun every 2hr) from Penrith (1hr 30min) and Keswick (35min).
By taxi A. & K. Taxis (Ⓣ 01900 823665).
Tourist office 88 Main St (Mon–Fri 10am–4pm, Wed till 5pm, Sat & bank hols 10am–2pm; Ⓣ 01900 822634, Ⓦ cockermouth.org.uk).

ACCOMMODATION

SEE MAPS PAGES 224 AND 245

Cockermouth makes a handy base for exploring the **western Lakes** – it's not far from Loweswater, Ennerdale Water and Buttermere – and it's less self-consciously touristy and outdoorsy than nearby Keswick, so a night or two here makes a pleasant change. Accommodation is pretty varied too, from local hostel and riverside hotel to Georgian B&Bs and boutique farmhouse stays.
Croft House 6–8 Challoner St, CA13 9QS Ⓣ 01900 827533, Ⓦ croft-guesthouse.com. A stylish revamp of

a Georgian townhouse on a quiet residential street. It's decidedly chintz-free – contemporary furnishings and maplewood floors throughout its seven rooms – while the owners offer daily specials, veggie and vegan alternatives for breakfast as well as Fair Trade coffee and tea. Parking. **£75**
Old Homestead Byresteads Farm, Hundrith Hill Rd, CA13 9TW, off B5292 2 miles southeast of Cockermouth Ⓣ 01900 822223, Ⓦ theoldhomestead.co.uk. Wake to

the sight of pedigree sheep grazing outside your window on this 180-acre farm, whose original farmhouse (from 1624) has been authentically restored using traditional lime plaster, cobbles, oak and stone. This adds up to serious country-chic – spacious rooms (some are king-sized) feature underfloor heating, walk-in showers, carved pine beds, leather chairs and sofas, and sweeping views down the Lorton Valley. Drawback? B&B is most commonly only available during the week, since it's also rented out as a ten-bedroom holiday house. Parking. **£70**

★ **Six Castlegate** 6 Castlegate, CA13 9EU ☎ 01900 826786, ⓦ sixcastlegate.co.uk. This period-piece house has been completely refurbished – the lofty Georgian proportions, impressive carved staircase and oak panelling remain, but the half-dozen rooms are contemporary-country in style with coordinated fabrics in soft colours,

good bathrooms with walk-in power-showers and rooftop and hill views. You'll save £10 in the two smaller standard rooms, and there's also a neat single (£55) in the "Butler's Pantry". Permit available for nearby parking. **£90**

Trout Hotel Crown St, CA13 0EJ ☎ 01900 823591, ⓦ trouthotel.co.uk. On the banks of the Derwent – and thoroughly refurbished after flooding in 2015 – this is the top choice in Cockermouth, well known among the fishing fraternity and a really fine place for a few restful days away. It retains something of a traditional aspect with its ornate staircase, panelled bar and silver-service restaurant, but service is familiar and friendly, the rooms are large and modern, and there's also a contemporary bar and courtyard bistro, *The Terrace*. Rates vary – river and garden views are pricier – but two-night weekend deals (including dinner) and other special offers can be a real bargain. Parking. **£130**

EATING
SEE MAP PAGES 224 AND 245

You'll find most of the **cafés and restaurants** in town spread along Main Street and up and around Market Place.

Coffee Kitchen 40 Challoner St, CA13 9QU ☎ 01900 824474, ⓦ thecoffeekitchen.co.uk. Best place in town for your java fix is this two-storey, bare-boards-and-sofas coffee house where they really know their beans and brews. There's food too – cakes, muffins, soups, dips, bacon rolls and sandwiches on home-made artisan bread, all for around £2.50–5. Mon–Sat 8am–6pm.

★ **Merienda** 7a Station St, CA13 9QW ☎ 01900 822790, ⓦ merienda.co.uk. Bright and breezy café-bar – it's Spanish for "snack" – with an arty feel, own-blend coffee and food that puts the emphasis on locally sourced and Fair Trade products. Expect anything from a scrambled egg and smoked salmon breakfast to a steak sandwich on home-made onion bread or meze platter (dishes £3–8). The evening menu ranges from tapas-style snacks, such as tempura king prawn tacos, to such dishes as baked trout (mains around £15). Mon–Thurs 8am–9pm, Fri & Sat 8am–10pm, Sun 9am–9pm.

Quince & Medlar 13 Castlegate, CA13 9EU ☎ 01900 823579, ⓦ quinceandmedlar.co.uk. Gourmet vegetarians have long made a beeline for this elegant Georgian house where dinner is a romantic, candlelit affair. The menu offers creative meat-free cuisine – fancied-up nut roasts,

cassoulet, smoked cheese roulade, stuffed filo parcels and so on; the vegetarian and vegan tasting menus (£30) comprise some highly original small plates. Reservations advised. Wed–Sat 6.30–10pm.

Shill's 11 South St, CA13 9RU ☎ 01900 823000, ⓦ shillsofcockermouth.co.uk. Excellent ground-floor deli specializing in fine wine, cheese and meats with an easy-going, comfortable yet smart café upstairs. Get in early and start the day with a simple coffee or full English (£9.95), or plump for lunch or dinner of tapas, sharing dishes and fuller meals (£6–16). Mon–Wed 9.30am–5pm, Thurs–Sat 9am–10.30pm.

★ **Wellington Farm Café** Wellington Farm, CA13 0QU, off A66/A5086 roundabout, 1 mile southwest of Cockermouth ☎ 01900 822777, ⓦ wellingtonjerseys.co.uk. The Stamper family farm on the edge of town has a great tearoom and farm shop – not only are there fine views from the terrace and tasty home-made food, but also you can get award-winning ice cream made with the milk from the farm's pedigree Jerseys. Dubbs Moss wetland and woodland reserve is just a short walk away, so you can park up for a stroll (bring wellies or boots). At the roundabout, take the exit signposted for "Mitchell's" agricultural market and the farm. Daily 10am–5pm.

DRINKING
SEE MAPS PAGES 224 AND 245

There are lots of **places to drink** in Cockermouth – this is the home ground of the Jennings brewery, remember – including a couple of contemporary bars occupying handsomely restored Georgian buildings on Market Place. However, best **pub** by far is the *Bitter End*, an independent microbrewery bravely taking on Jennings on its home patch.

★ **Bitter End** 15 Kirkgate, CA13 9PJ ☎ 01900 828993, ⓦ bitterend.co.uk. The nicest, cosiest pub in town also contains Cumbria's smallest brewery, producing great ales like Lakeland Golden, Farmers, Cockersnoot and Cuddy Lugs.

Ask for a taster if you're not sure which to choose, as staff are happy to extol the virtues of their brews. The food is really popular – get here early if you want to eat – ranging from bistro favourites (steak and ale pie, fish and chips) to a daily specials list that could include wild mushroom lasagne or oven-roast cod. The meat is sourced from Cumbrian farms, and most mains are £10–13 (up to £20 for the steaks). Mon & Tues 4–11pm, Wed–Fri noon–11pm, Sat & Sun 11am–11pm; kitchen Mon–Fri noon–2pm & 4–9pm; Sat & Sun noon–9pm.

Royal Yew Dean, CA14 4TJ, 5 miles south of Cockermouth ☎ 01946 861342, ⓦ royalyew.co.uk. The *Bitter End* people are also behind this handsome gastropub, a short drive out into the country. The beer's good, of course (including their own Yew Tree Ale), and the bistro-style menu is a similar mix of classics and specials, such as home-made Wagyu beef lasagne and pork belly in apple cider (mains £12–16). The Super Seven lunch menu (all dishes for £7) is terrific value. Mon–Thurs & Sun 11.30am–10.30pm, Fri & Sat 11.30am–11pm; kitchen daily 11.30am–9pm.

ENTERTAINMENT

Kirkgate Centre Kirkgate, CA13 9PJ ☎ 01900 826448, ⓦ kirkgatearts.org.uk. The local arts venue is a converted Victorian school run entirely by volunteers, featuring a wide-ranging programme of theatre, cinema, music and the arts.

DIRECTORY

Laundry DIY Wash & Dry, Meadow Bank, Windmill Lane (daily 8.30am–6.30pm; ☎ 01900 827219).
Pharmacies Allison, 31 Main St (☎ 01900 822292); Boots, 56–58 Main St (☎ 01900 823160).
Police station Europe Way (Mon–Sat 9am–1pm; ☎ 101, ⓦ cumbria.police.uk).

Post office Cumbria Co-op, 12 Station St (Mon–Fri 8am–5.30pm, Sat 9am–3pm).
Swimming pool Cockermouth Leisure Centre, Castlegate Drive (☎ 01900 823596, ⓦ better.org.uk), has a gym and a climbing wall as well as a swimming pool.

7

Penrith and around

Penrith – four miles from Ullswater and sixteen east of Keswick – is a handsome, bustling market town in the Eden Valley, paved and built in red sandstone, which immediately sets it apart from the stone villages of south Cumbria.

The town also has a long pedigree and a **historic significance** greater than anywhere else in the Lakes. Probably Celtic in origin, it was the capital of the independent kingdom of Cumbria until 1070, and from the thirteenth century onwards was a thriving market town on the main north–south trading route. The medieval **castle** might now be in ruins, but the **market** is still going strong, and Penrith's beguiling kernel of winding alleys, open squares and traditional shops can easily occupy half a day.

There's lots to see **around Penrith**, too – you'll be surprised by how many offbeat attractions, including a **prehistoric stone circle**, are within easy reach – and it wouldn't be out of the question to spend an extra day or two exploring the region. This is very definitely not the hills, crags and waters of the Lake District, but the rolling countryside of the **Eden Valley** has its own gentle beauty that's worth getting to know. You can't rely on public transport to construct any kind of tour, but with a bike or car you'll be able to complete a satisfying circuit (some attractions fall naturally together), with the possibility of having a good lunch somewhere suitably rural on the way.

Penrith Castle

Castle Park, CA11 7JQ, opposite the train station • Daily: April–Sept 7.30am–9pm; Oct–March 7.30am–4.30pm • Free • For Beacon Hill, walk down into town, then head up Sandgate and Fell Lane to Beacon Edge (20min), turn left and follow the signposted right turn up through the woods

The major historic relic, **Penrith Castle**, was built as a bastion against Scottish raids from the north, and served as one of the northern headquarters of Richard III. The immaculately kept sandstone ruins sit within a formal park at the top of town – come at sunset to see the warm colours of the walls and towers at their best. Traditionally, warnings of attack or – in Napoleonic times – of possible invasion instead came from the north side of town, from **Beacon Hill**, which is worth the hour's stroll, there and back, to take in more expansive views of Penrith and the fells beyond.

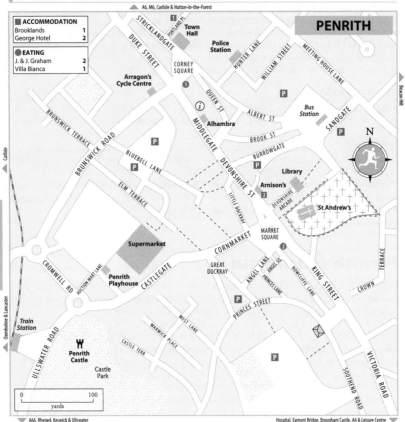

PENRITH

■ ACCOMMODATION
Brooklands	1
George Hotel	2

● EATING
J. & J. Graham	2
Villa Bianca	1

▼ A66, Rheged, Keswick & Ullswater

Hospital, Eamont Bridge, Brougham Castle, A6 & Leisure Centre ▼

Market Square and around

Market Square, CA11 7BS • Farmers' market March–Dec third Tues of month 9.30am–2.30pm

Come to Penrith on market day, Tuesday, if you want to get to grips with the local economy. The narrow streets, arcades and alleys off **Market Square** – including the old **Corn Market** and the open space of **Great Dockray** – provide traditional shopping for stalwart Cumbrian families, in the butchers' shops, fishmongers, outfitters, grocers and agricultural feed merchants. There's a really good **farmers' market**, too, held on the third Tuesday of every month (except Jan & Feb), while tradition also rears its head in the stately **George Hotel** – where Bonnie Prince Charlie spent the night in 1745 – and **Arnison's**, the yesteryear drapers and milliners. The shop stands on the site of the town's old Moot Hall, owned in the eighteenth century by Wordsworth's grandparents. The young William and Dorothy often stayed here and their mother died in the house in 1778 (she's buried in St Andrew's churchyard, though the grave isn't marked).

St Andrew's church

St Andrew's Place, CA11 7XX • Mon–Sat 9am–5pm • Free

St Andrew's church (possibly designed by Nicholas Hawkmoor, and built 1720–22) sits back from Market Square in a spacious churchyard surrounded by handsome Georgian houses, some of them now cafés and galleries. The soaring tower – a local landmark – is the oldest part of the church, dating from medieval times, while out in the churchyard an even older relic, the so-called "Giant's Grave", is actually a collection of pre-Norman crosses and "hogsback" tombstones.

Brougham Castle

Moor Lane, CA10 2AA • April–Sept daily 10am–6pm; Oct daily 10am–4pm; Nov–March Sat & Sun 10am–4pm • £5.70, family ticket £14.80; EH • ☎ 01768 862488, ⓦ english-heritage.org.uk/visit/places/brougham-castle

You could walk to the nearest local site, **Brougham Castle**, a mile and a half south of Penrith in a pretty spot by the River Eamont. It's a far more impressive ruin than Penrith's own castle, and you can climb the towering sandstone keep, in which you'll find remnants of Roman tombstones used as building material, plundered from an earlier Roman fort on this site.

Brougham Hall

7

Brougham, CA10 2DE, 2 miles south of Penrith on B6262 • Daily 10am–5pm, though hours sometimes vary; café 9am–4.30pm • Donation requested • ☎ 01768 868184, ⓦ broughamhall.co.uk • From Penrith follow signs for A6 to Shap and cross Eamont Bridge; parking is free

Combine a visit to Brougham Castle with nearby **Brougham Hall**, an unusual fourteenth-century fortified country house that's slowly being restored – it has a rather remarkable sixteenth-century carved-oak main door that's still in daily use. Within the encircling walls and battlements are various craft outlets and businesses, from brewery and photography studio to ceramicist and stonemason, plus a small café with castle courtyard tables that's open every day.

Rheged

Redhills, on the A66, 0.5 mile west of the M6 (junction 40) • Daily 10am–5.30pm • Free; cinema: £6.50, family ticket £21 • ☎ 01768 868000, ⓦ rheged.com • Parking is free; bus #X4/X5 (between Penrith and Keswick) stops at the centre

Rheged – a Cumbrian "visitor experience", just outside Penrith – is a good place to bring children, especially if it's pouring down outside. Sited in a disused limestone quarry, and billed as Europe's largest earth-covered building, it's designed to blend in with the surrounding fells, which it does admirably – from the main road you wouldn't know it was there. The name comes from the ancient kingdom of Cumbria, which once stretched from Strathclyde in Scotland as far south as Cheshire.

An impressive atrium-lit underground visitor centre fills you in on the region's history, while you'll also find souvenir shops, galleries displaying arts and crafts, seasonal exhibitions and events, workshops and demonstrations. There's a farmers'

ROUND TABLES AND STONE CIRCLES

Devoted stone-chasers and druid-fanciers can have a whale of a time around Penrith, tracking down mysterious standing stones and earthworks. Nearest to town, just south of Eamont Bridge, by the A6, **King Arthur's Round Table** is actually a prehistoric circular earthwork with a wide ditch; another, **Mayburgh**, just a few hundred yards away, still has a standing stone in the middle. Both are at least 3000 years old and point to the presence of a significant prehistoric population in these parts. Most impressive of all, though, is the site of **Long Meg and her Daughters**, six miles northeast of Penrith, just outside Little Salkeld, off the A686. Standing outside the "daughters" (a ring of stones almost 400ft in diameter, the largest stone circle in Cumbria), Long Meg herself is the tallest stone at 12ft high and has a profile like the face of an old woman.

market here, too, held on the last Sunday of the month throughout winter. More specifically for children there are indoor and outdoor play areas, plus a Making Space zone where kids can engage in pottery painting, block printing and the like. The staple visit, though, is for the big-screen **3D cinema**, showing family-friendly movies and landscape spectaculars.

There's also an atrium **café**, though the finer dining is at the horseshoe bar of the contemporary "**food hall**" known as *Taste*, which specializes in regional Cumbrian foods and dishes. If you can't find something here to take home (sticky toffee pudding, smoked venison, Cumbrian cheese, damson gin), you're not trying.

Little Salkeld Watermill

Little Salkeld, CA10 1NN, 6 miles northeast of Penrith, off A686 • Free; tours £2, courses from £75/day • Feb–Dec daily except Wed 10.30am–4pm • ☎ 01768 881523, ⍟ organicmill.co.uk • 1.5 miles from Langwathby train station

The prettily sited **Little Salkeld Watermill** not only has a mill shop and organic bakery – where they specialize in stoneground wheat, rye, barley and spelt flours – but also a wholefood veggie tearoom, so it's a good target for lunch or afternoon tea. To learn more about how they operate, take one of the mill tours or, better still, sign up for one of their milling, oven-building or bread-making courses which run throughout the year.

Hutton-in-the-Forest

Hutton-in-the-Forest, CA11 9TH, 6 miles northwest of Penrith on B5305 (Wigton road) • House Easter to early Oct Wed, Thurs, Sun & bank hols 11.30am–4pm; gardens and grounds Easter–Oct Sun–Fri 10am–5pm • House and gardens £11.50; gardens only £7 • ☎ 017684 84449, ⍟ hutton-in-the-forest.co.uk

Hidden away in rolling farm- and parkland northwest of Penrith, the stately pile of **Hutton-in-the-Forest** is open for house tours and strolls in the magnificent gardens, grounds and woodland. There's also a seasonal calendar of "meet the gardener" tours and guided gamekeeper walks, plus plant and food fairs, garden shows and open-air theatre. The tearoom is open when the house is open, but you might also want to make a point of visiting the *UpFront* gallery and coffee shop (see page 254), which is just up the road from the main entrance to the house.

ARRIVAL AND DEPARTURE

PENRITH AND AROUND

Penrith positions itself as one of the main gateways to the Lake District; reasonable enough given that it's a stop on the London–Scotland train route and lies just off the M6 motorway and A66 to Keswick.

By car Driving in off the M6, take junction 40 – there's disc parking on town-centre streets (discs available from the tourist office and elsewhere), a large car park off Brunswick Rd and others signposted around town, though spaces are

hard to come by on Tues (market day).

By bus The bus station is on Albert St, behind Middlegate, and has regular services to Patterdale/Windermere (#508), and Keswick and Cockermouth (#X4/X5).

By train Trains from Manchester, London, Glasgow and Edinburgh pull into Penrith station, opposite the castle and a 5min walk down into Market Square. You can also access the scenic Settle-to-Carlisle Railway (⍟ settle-carlisle.

POTTY PENRITH

Potfest (⍟ potfest.co.uk), Europe's biggest ceramics show, takes place in Penrith over two consecutive weekends (late July/early August). First up is **Potfest in the Park**, with ceramics on display in marquees in front of Hutton-in-the-Forest country house, as well as larger sculptural works laid out in the lovely grounds. This is followed by the highly unusual **Potfest in the Pens**, which sees potters displaying their creations in the unlikely setting of the covered pens at Penrith's cattle market, just outside town on the A66. Here, the public can talk to the artists, learn about what inspires them and even sign up for free classes.

co.uk) at nearby Langwathby, 5 miles to the northeast – there's a bus from Penrith out to the station.

By taxi Town Taxis (☎ 01768 868268); Eden Taxis (☎ 01768 865432).

INFORMATION AND ACTIVITIES

Bike rental Arragon's Cycle Centre, 2 Brunswick Rd (from £25/day; Mon–Fri 9am–5.30pm, Sat 9am–5pm; ☎ 01768 890344, ⓦ arragons.com).

Tourist office Middlegate (March–Sept Mon–Sat 10am–5pm, Sun 11am–4pm; Oct–Feb Mon–Sat 10am–4pm; ☎ 01768 867466, ⓦ visiteden.co.uk).

ACCOMMODATION   SEE MAPS PAGES 224 AND 250

If you're aiming for the Lakes themselves it doesn't make much sense to stay in Penrith, with Ullswater and Keswick both less than half an hour away. But there's a good enough choice if you fancy a night in town, and some very nice options in the surrounding countryside – the Lowther Estate's *George and Dragon* gastro-inn at Clifton (see page 217) is also close to town. The bulk of the standard **B&Bs** line noisy Victoria Road, the continuation of King Street, a 2min walk south of Market Square. Portland Place has a rather more refined row of **guesthouses**.

★ **Askham Hall** Askham, CA10 2PF, about 4 miles south of Penrith off the Helton road ☎ 01931 712350, ⓦ askhamhall.co.uk. Red-stone manor house set in a huge acreage which includes landscaped gardens, farm animals, an oak-beamed "party barn", a spa and a pool. The fifteen bedrooms are tastefully decorated with modern furnishings (they've avoided heavy hangings and gone for a light colour scheme) and offer period touches, from four-posters in the enormous Pele Tower rooms to antique fireplaces in the smaller but perfectly formed standard doubles. Most also have nice country views. The garden café is good for a light lunch, or you can dine on seasonal local fare at their excellent restaurant (set three-course meals £55). **£180**

Brooklands 2 Portland Place, CA11 7QN ☎ 01768 863395, ⓦ brooklandsguesthouse.com. A very handsome 1870s townhouse that's been lovingly restored. Seven colour-coordinated rooms have country pine furniture and small but snazzy bathrooms: three are rated superior, one with a four-poster, one with Victorian bedstead and leather sofa, and a third more contemporary bedroom dressed up as a suite. Rooms at the rear overlooking the churchyard are the quietest. On-street parking outside. **£95**

★ **Crake Trees Manor** Crosby Ravensworth, CA10

3JG, 15 miles southeast of Penrith, A6 via Shap or M6 junction 39 ☎ 01931 715205, ⓦ craketreesmanor. co.uk. It takes more effort to reach than most, but this gorgeous barn conversion B&B in the nearby Eden Valley is emphatically worth it. There are B&B rooms in the stylish, galleried family home, and another suite above the courtyard, all with slate floors, antique beds, serious showers and fluffy wrap-me-up towels. Or book the wonderfully cosy and romantic "Shepherd's Hut", a hand-built reclaimed-oak-and-steel bolthole for two that stands a short way from the house in the meadows – it's got a cute little wood-burner and a teeny veranda for your evening sundowner. Help yourself to hot drinks and Ruth's home-made biscuits in the house, where a fantastic Aga-cooked breakfast (and evening meals by arrangement) are taken around an enormous oak table. Two further options are pods (aka "Hen Houses") with sleeping benches and mattresses that sleep three or four, and the self-catering "Brew House" cottage (sleeping two), though there's a three-day minimum-rental period (£260) for this. The great community-run *Butchers' Arms* pub is nearby, or it's a 25min drive to Penrith. Parking. Shepherd's hut **£80**, pods from **£40**, doubles **£100**

George Hotel Devonshire St, CA11 7SU ☎ 01768 862696, ⓦ thegeorgehotelpenrith.co.uk. The traditional choice in Penrith is this atmospheric old coaching inn right in the centre. Refurbishment has brought most of the rooms up to three-star standard and, though some can be a bit of a squeeze, the gloriously old-fashioned public areas compensate – there are cosy wood-panelled lounges with roaring fires, rustic bric-a-brac and armchairs you could hibernate in. The traditional bar and restaurant is the sort of place where Cumbrian ladies-who-lunch come to take tea and sip sherry. Parking. **£120**

EATING   SEE MAPS PAGES 224 AND 250

Penrith is a solid country **dining** kind of place, though nearby village **gastropubs** have raised the bar a bit. There are also several out-of-town tearooms and coffee houses that each offer a different reason for a country drive with lunch or afternoon tea at the end of it.

J. & J. Graham 6–7 Market Square, CA11 7BS ☎ 01768 862281, ⓦ jjgraham.co.uk. This famous grocer's-cum-deli has been supplying the good folk of Penrith for more than two hundred years. There's pretty much anything you

could want here, all beautifully presented, and the cheese counter and bread racks in particular are stellar – don't go anywhere else for superior picnic supplies. Mon–Sat 8.30am–5.30pm.

★ **La Casa Verde** Larch Cottage Nurseries, Melkinthorpe, CA10 2DR, 4 miles south of Penrith, off A6 ☎ 01931 712404, ⓦ larchcottage.co.uk. This is a lovely place for lunch – a Mediterranean-style garden café set among the plants, shrubs, ruined sandstone walls and arches, gardens and grottoes of the charming Larch Cottage Nurseries. There are seats inside and out, and a menu that ranges from home-made tarts, *bruschette* or a pasta of the day to good, crispy Italian pizzas (dishes £8–14), all finished off by home-made cakes. Afterwards, there's another easy hour to be spent browsing the specialist gardens and plant collections. Nurseries daily 9am–4.45pm (4.15pm in winter); lunch served noon–3pm.

UpFront Gallery & Coffee Shop Unthank, Hutton-in-the-Forest, CA11 9TG, 6 miles northwest of Penrith on B5305 (Wigton road) ☎01768 484538, ⓦup-front. com. Changing exhibitions in the gallery – housed in converted seventeenth-century farm buildings – provide one reason for a visit, though the rustic coffee shop is a destination in its own right. It's a veggie place, with bakes,

crumbles, chillis and pies (£6–9) alongside the usual soups, sandwiches and cakes, and you can sit outside in the summer. The gallery is also the base for owner John Parkinson's other passion, his puppet theatre (see page 254). Tues–Sun 10am–4.30pm.

Villa Bianca Corney Square, CA11 7PX ☎01768 210826, ⓦvillabiancahotelrestaurant.co.uk. Cheery Italian restaurant in characterful cottage surroundings. Friendly service and decent prices (£7–15) for pizza (the "Villa Bianca" comes with rocket and Parma ham) and pasta make this a good choice for fill-me-up dining, though meat and fish mains – like fresh salmon steak baked in garlic and white wine – are pricier at £12–20. Mon–Fri 5.30–9.30pm, Sat 6–9.30pm; also Sun April–Sept.

ENTERTAINMENT

The town is the regional arts and music hub, with **Eden Arts** (ⓦedenarts.co.uk) the place to find out about concerts, events, exhibitions and festivals. These include performances hosted by the venerable **Penrith Music Club** (ⓦpenrithmusicclub.com), with classical concerts and recitals held monthly (Sept–April) in Penrith Methodist Church.

Alhambra Middlegate, CA11 7PT, next to the tourist office ☎01768 862400, ⓦpenrith-alhambra.co.uk. The local cinema usually shows arthouse and indie films on Sun nights.

Penrith Playhouse Auction Mart Lane, CA11 7JG,

top of Castlegate ☎01768 867466, ⓦpenrithplayers. co.uk. Penrith's member-run theatre stages productions throughout the year, and also hosts regular rock, folk and blues gigs in the Playhouse bar sponsored by Plug & Play (usually first Sun of month; ⓦplug-play.co.uk).

UpFront Gallery Puppet Theatre Unthank, Hutton-in-the-Forest, CA11 9TG, 6 miles northwest of Penrith on B5305 (Wigton road) ☎01768 484538, ⓦup-front. com. John and Elaine Parkinson's rural gallery and coffee shop is home to theatre designer John's puppet theatre, with special productions – fairy tales to puppet circus – staged every Christmas, Easter and school summer holiday.

DIRECTORY

Hospital Penrith New Hospital, Bridge Lane, Penrith (☎01768 245555, ⓦcumbriapartnership.nhs.uk).

Pharmacies Boots, 3 Grahams Lane, Penrith (☎01768 862735); Lightfoot's, 8 Middlegate, Penrith (☎01768 862695).

Police station Hunter Lane, Penrith (Mon–Sat 9am–1pm;

☎101, ⓦcumbria.police.uk).

Post office Crown Square, Penrith.

Swimming pool Penrith Leisure Centre, Southend Rd (☎01768 863450, ⓦbetter.org.uk), has a swimming pool, climbing wall, gym, bowling and café.

7

7

SCRAMBLING ALONG PINNACLE RIDGE

Contexts

History

The Lake District remained a land apart for centuries, its features – rugged and isolated – mirrored in the characteristics of its inhabitants. Daniel Defoe thought it "eminent only for being the wildest, most barren and frightful of any that I have passed over" – and, as he went on to point out, he'd been to Wales so he knew what he was talking about. Two factors spurred the first waves of tourism: the reappraisal of landscape brought about by such painters as John Constable and the writings of William Wordsworth and his contemporaries, and the outbreak of the French Revolution and its subsequent turmoil, which put paid to the idea of the continental Grand Tour. Later, as tourism to the Lakes was cemented by the arrival of the railway, Wordsworth – while bemoaning mass travel – wrote in his *Guide to the Lakes* that he desired "a sort of national property, in which every man has a right and interest who has an eye to perceive and a heart to enjoy". His wish finally came true in 1951 when the government established the Lake District as England's largest National Park. It has subsequently become one of the most visited parts of England.

Early times

Geologically speaking, the Lake District is extremely old. The rocks which make up the Skiddaw and Blencathra massif consist of 500-million-year-old slate, while 100 million years later occurred the immense volcanic activity which shaped the high central mountains. The granite outcrops visible at Ennerdale and Eskdale were formed 350 million years ago. Later still, a tropical sea covered the region (320 million years ago) whose shell remains formed the ubiquitous limestone and sandstone.

At the heart of the region is Scafell, the remnant of a volcanic dome that had already been weathered into its present craggy shape before the last **Ice Age**, when glaciers flowed off its flanks to gouge their characteristic U-shaped valleys. As the ice withdrew, moraines of sediment dammed the meltwater, creating the main lakes, all of which radiate from Scafell's hub – Wordsworth, in a famous image, described them as immense spokes. The gentler terrain to the south was formed after this main burst of activity, with subsequent mini ice ages (the last around twelve thousand years ago) gouging out smaller tarns, flattening the valley bottoms and modifying the shape and scale of the mountains. Consequently, the Lake District as it appears today comprises a huge variety of terrains and geological material within a compact region.

c10,000 BC	**c4000 BC**	**c2000 BC**
Last Ice Age sculpts Lake District landscape	Neolithic settlers begin to clear upland forests	Creation of stone circles, such as Castlerigg

The first humans

Before **Neolithic peoples** began to colonize the region more than five thousand years ago, most of the now bare uplands were forested with pine and birch, while the valleys were blanketed with thickets of oak, alder, ash and elm. As these first settlers learnt to shape flints into axes, they began to clear the upland forests for farmland – remnants of shaped stone axes have been found in so-called "factory" sites on Pike of Stickle (in Langdale) and on the slopes of Scafell. During the later **Stone and Bronze ages**, the subsistence existence of Lake District settlers is unlikely to have changed much. Their hunter-gatherer lifestyle was augmented by early stock-rearing and planting, though evidence of their lives is sketchy. Bronze tools and weapons have been found (around Ambleside, Keswick and St John's in the Vale), though few burial or settlement sites have been pinpointed.

By the third century BC, **Celtic peoples** from the south and east were pushing into the region. From their hillfort settlements (like that on Carrock Fell) they exploited the local metal deposits and employed advanced farming techniques. Sophisticated religious practices (including burial) and basic systems of law and communal defence (against raiders from the north) were established features of their lives by the time the Romans arrived in Britain in 55 BC.

The Romans and Celts

The **arrival of the Romans** in the north of England after 69 AD led to the first large-scale alteration of the region's landscape. **Hadrian's Wall**, from the Tyne to the Solway Firth – marking the northern limit of the Roman Empire – was completed by 130 AD. Associated with the wall were roads, forts and supply routes which cut through the heart of the Lakes. There are the remains of fortresses still to be seen at Hardknott Pass and at Waterhead, near Ambleside, while Roman roads can be traced between Kendal and Ravenglass and, most obviously, from Troutbeck to Brougham (near Penrith) along the ridge known as High Street.

Throughout the Roman period the Lake District was essentially a **military zone**, policed by auxiliaries (recruited from all parts of the Roman Empire) rather than true legionaries. However, around the bases grew **civilian settlements** as at Ambleside – which formed the basis of later towns and villages. Lead mining was first practised

---

THE LAKE DISTRICT'S STONE CIRCLES

The dramatic stone circles at **Castlerigg** (near Keswick), **Little Salkeld** (near Penrith) and **Swinside** (near Duddon Bridge) are among the region's most important historic sites – but, despite years of investigation and scholarship, their **purpose** is still frustratingly unclear. Some have suggested they had a time-keeping function or were used for religious purposes, others that the circles were a commercial focus or meeting place. What's clear is the high degree of cooperation between people required to erect the stones in the first place – and, clearer still, as you stand there marvelling today, the overpowering effect such constructions must have had on early peoples whose lives and horizons were otherwise restricted.

---

55 BC	**120–140 AD**	**4th–6th centuries**
Romans arrive in Britain, arriving in the north of England by 69 AD	Construction of Hardknott Roman Fort	Collapse of Roman rule; arrival of Christianity in Cumbria

during Roman times, while upland forests continued to be replaced by agricultural land as cereal crops were planted to supply the various permanent settlements. At Ravenglass, on the Cumbrian coast, are the extant remains of a bathhouse, part of a fort which survived until the fourth century.

In the face of constant raids and harassment, England had become irrevocably detached from what remained of the Roman Empire by the start of the fifth century AD. The original **Celtic inhabitants** of the northwest had never fully abandoned their traditions in the face of Roman might, and surviving Celtic place names (Derwent, Blencathra) indicate strong local ties. Indeed, from the Celts comes the word they used to describe themselves – *Cymry* – from which derives the modern place-name Cumbria. **Christianity** secured an enduring toehold in the region too. St Kentigern (or Mungo), the Celtic missionary, founded several churches in the region, passing through Crosthwaite in Keswick in 553 AD.

The Saxon and Norse invasions

The **Saxon invasion** of England's south and east during the sixth century initially had little impact on the Lake District, which slowly fell under the control of the newly established **Kingdom of Northumbria**. However, place-name evidence does suggest that Saxon farmers later settled on the lakeland fringes – names ending in "ham" and "ton" betray a Saxon influence, as does the suffix "-mere" attached to a lake.

A greater impact was made by **Norse (ie Norwegian) Vikings** during the ninth and tenth centuries. Although they eventually supplanted much of the native lakeland population, it would be wrong to see the Norse arrival as a violent invasion. Unlike the Danes, who had sacked Lindisfarne on the east coast in 793, the Norse invasion was less brutal, with Viking settlers (rather than warriors) gradually filtering into the Lake District from their established bases in Scotland, Ireland and the Isle of Man. They farmed the land extensively and left their indelible mark on the northern dialect – dale, fell, force, beck, tarn, ghyll and the suffix "-thwaite" (a clearing) all have Norse origins. Physical remains are scarce, the finest example being the splendid Norse cross in the churchyard at Gosforth, which combines pagan and Christian elements in a style reminiscent of similar crosses in Ireland and the Isle of Man. By the end of the eleventh century, wherever they originated, lakelanders were living in small farming communities in recognized shires, or administrative districts, whose names survived for the next nine hundred years: Cumberland and Westmorland.

However, the region began to be disputed in a burgeoning number of turf wars between rival kingdoms. **Dunmail**, a Cumbrian warlord, was defeated in battle in 945 by the Saxon **King Edmund**, who granted control of the region to the kings of Scotland. This heralded six hundred years of political manoeuvring between Scottish kings keen to push the border south and, after the Conquest, Norman rulers intent upon holding the line at Carlisle. The Lakes themselves, and their farming communities, were largely left alone as the opposing armies marched north and south, but the northern and western lowlands became a cross-border battleground. Castles at Cockermouth, Penrith and Kendal attest to the constant political threat, while raiding "**reivers**" or local clans made the borderlands ungovernable.

7th century	9th–10th centuries	945
Lake District part of the Kingdom of Northumbria	Vikings settle in the region, leaving their mark on place names	Cumbrian warlord Dunmail defeated by Saxon King Edmund

DIGGING IN AND DIGGING OUT

Although centuries of farming and agriculture had already sculpted the countryside, the first industrial changes wrought upon the landscape came with the advent of **mining**. Plumbago, or **graphite**, had been discovered in Borrowdale early in the sixteenth century and in 1564 Elizabeth I gave royal assent to an Anglo-German venture to exploit the ore – invaluable for pencil-making, glazing, black-leading iron weapons (to stop them rusting) and making casting moulds for cannon bore and shot. German miners settled in Keswick, while locals found employment in providing lodging, transport and charcoal. Later, **copper** mining took hold in the Keswick and Coniston areas, while **slate** quarrying in Borrowdale had always taken place on a local basis and was to boom in later centuries. You can still see traces of this early industrial heritage, particularly at Honister, whose working slate mine traces its ancestry back several hundred years.

Medieval and Elizabethan times

By medieval times, most of the Lake District's **traditional industries** had been firmly established. The native breed of sheep, the Herdwick, had proved itself a hardy species since at least Roman times, surviving harsh winters on the fells, while in summer cropping the wild flowers on the hills and preventing the regeneration of the woodland. **Religious houses** bordering the Lake District, such as Furness Abbey in the south, Carlisle in the north and St Bees in the west, came to hold large rural areas, establishing outlying farms – or "granges" – which further exploited the land. The **wool** produced found its way into markets throughout Europe and beyond, with **packhorse routes** meandering across the region to and from market towns such as Kendal, Keswick, Penrith and Cockermouth. The monks also maintained woods, or **coppices**, whose timber they used to produce charcoal (for iron smelting) and bark (used in tanneries).

The **Dissolution of the Monasteries** in 1536 had little effect on these industries. The new Crown tenants and the emerging "**statesman**" **farmers**, who bought their own smallholdings, merely continued the age-old practices, denuding the uplands further with every passing year. Indeed, for most people, **domestic life** probably altered very little for three hundred years – clothes were still produced locally, while primitive agricultural methods and poor land kept yields relatively low. The general diet was largely unchanged since Viking times, based around oatmeal cakes or porridge, bread and cheese – potatoes weren't widely cultivated until the eighteenth century. Increasingly, however, houses were being built of durable stone (rather than turf and timber) and many of the Lake District's farms and cottages – including notable examples such as Townend at Troutbeck – can trace their origins back as far as the seventeenth century.

The Picturesque and the Romantic

Until the eighteenth century, it was difficult to persuade the wider world – or at least fashionable England – that the Lake District had anything to offer. Indeed, the old county of Cumberland (containing the northern part of the Lake District) was viewed as a dangerous, unstable corner of the kingdom, too close to lawless Scotland for

1124	11th–15th centuries	16th century
Foundation of Furness Abbey; rise of medieval trades	English and Scottish borderlands in constant state of turmoil; castles built at Kendal, Penrith and Cockermouth	Graphite mining is the first industry established in Borrowdale; Keswick later becomes a major pencil-making town

comfort. William, Duke of Cumberland, the "butcher" son of George II, put down the Jacobite rebellion of 1745, and the fortified towers and castles on the lakeland periphery tell their own story of border raids and skirmishes.

A sea change occurred with the advent of the so-called **Picturesque Movement** in the late eighteenth century, when received notions of beauty shifted from the classical to the natural. Vivid, irregular landscapes were the fashion among writers and artists, and it was with a palpable sense of excitement that the era's style arbiters discovered such landscapes on their doorstep. The poet **Thomas Gray** made the first of two visits in 1767 and recorded his favourable impressions in his journal (published in 1775), while in 1778 **Thomas West** produced the first guidebook dedicated solely to the region, waxing lyrical about the "Alpine views and pastoral scenes in a sublime style". These, and a dozen other books or treatises touching on the Lake District published during the 1770s, merely reinforced the contemporary Romantic view that contact with nature promoted artistic endeavour and human development. **Thomas Gainsborough**, **J.M.W. Turner** and, later, **John Constable** were all eager visitors to the Lakes, and all drew inspiration from what they saw. The first visitors were encouraged to view the mountains and lakes in a methodical manner – from particular "stations" (ie viewpoints) and through a "claude glass" (or convex mirror) to frame the views.

The pre-eminent Romantic, **William Wordsworth**, was born in Cockermouth in 1770, moving to Dove Cottage outside Grasmere in 1799 and, in 1813, to nearby Rydal Mount. He became the centre of a famous, if fluctuating, literary circle – not only one of the so-called **Lake Poets** with **Samuel Taylor Coleridge** and **Robert Southey**, but also friend of the critic, essayist and opium eater **Thomas De Quincey** and of the writer **John Wilson** ("Christopher North" of *Blackwood's Magazine*).

The eighteenth and nineteenth centuries

The **Industrial Revolution** didn't so much pass the Lake District by as touch its periphery. Carlisle was a cotton-manufacturing town of some repute, while the coastal ports became important shipping centres and depots for nearby coal and iron industries. Georgian Whitehaven was one of Britain's busiest ports for a time in the late eighteenth century; Barrow-in-Furness is still an important shipbuilding town.

Within the Lakes themselves, sheep farming remained the mainstay of the economy. Textile production still tended to take the form of homespun wool, as it had for centuries. However, the manufacture of wooden **bobbins** for the northwest's cotton mills later became an important local industry. There were also improvements in farming as turnips were introduced widely as a crop, which meant that cattle and sheep could be kept alive throughout the winter. Meanwhile, the French Revolution and the ensuing **Napoleonic Wars** (1803–15) not only precluded European travel (in part explaining the growing popularity of the Lakes with the English gentry) but also pushed food prices higher. As a consequence, farmers began to reclaim the once-common land of the hillsides, a tendency sanctioned by the General Enclosure Act of 1801. Most of the region's characteristic dry-stone walls were built at this time.

Copper mining at Coniston became increasingly important, as did **slate quarrying** at Honister Pass and around Elterwater. The still-visible scars, shafts and debris on the Old Man of Coniston and at Honister Pass are evidence of these booming trades.

18th century	1778	1799
Economic expansion; Whitehaven becomes one of Britain's busiest ports	Thomas West writes the first "guidebook" to the Lakes	William Wordsworth moves to Dove Cottage in Grasmere

Transport and communications improved slowly. Roads and packhorse routes that had been barely altered since Roman times saw improvement following the passing of the Turnpike Acts in the 1750s. High passes opened up to the passage of stagecoaches, while England's burgeoning canal system reached Kendal in 1819. The **railway age** arrived late, with early railway lines associated with the mining and quarrying industries. The first passenger line, in 1847, connected Kendal with Windermere – and prompted a furious battle with the elderly Wordsworth who, having spent years inviting appreciation of the Lake District by outsiders, now raged against the folly of making the region easier to visit. Not only was it easier to visit, but after 1869 the Lake District even had its very own indigenous candy to sweeten the teeth of visitors – **Kendal Mint Cake**, a peppermint sweet that's been the mainstay of climbing expeditions ever since. It's still made in Kendal today.

With the passing of Southey (1843) and Wordsworth (1850), the mantle of local literary endeavour passed to writer **Harriet Martineau**, who lived at Ambleside between 1845 and 1876, and to social philosopher and critic **John Ruskin**, who settled at Brantwood near Coniston in 1872.

The twentieth century: protecting the Lake District

Two thousand years of farming and two hundred years of industrialization began to take their toll on the region. John Ruskin's unsuccessful campaign to prevent the damming of Thirlmere was just one example of an increased **environmental awareness** which manifested itself most obviously in the **creation of the National Trust** in 1895. Ruskin's disciple, Octavia Hill, and a Keswick clergyman, Canon Rawnsley, were the Trust's cofounders (with Rawnsley its first secretary) – Brandlehow Woods on Derwent Water's western shore was the Trust's first purchase in the Lakes (1902). The Trust is now the largest landholder in the Lake District, gaining early impetus from the generous bequests of **Beatrix Potter**, who has probably done more than anyone after Wordsworth to popularize the region through her children's stories.

WORDS IN TIME

William Wordsworth, naturally, started it all – not just with his poetry, which brought the realities and wonders of Lake District life to a wider audience, but also with his own *Guide to the Lakes*, a mature distillation of all his thoughts on nature and beauty. This was first published in 1810 and had gone through four further editions by 1835, thus inspiring a seemingly endless succession of nineteenth-century men and women of letters, who promptly continued to visit or take a house, pronounce upon and then **write** about the region. Sir Walter Scott, Percy Bysshe Shelley, Matthew Arnold, Alfred (Lord) Tennyson, Thomas Carlyle, George Eliot, Charlotte Brontë, Ralph Waldo Emerson and Nathaniel Hawthorne all spent various periods in the Lake District and left their own records of their impressions. Few survive the literary test of time, save perhaps Charles Dickens and Wilkie Collins, who came to the Lakes together and climbed Carrock Fell, a trip recounted in Dickens' amusing *Lazy Tour of Two Idle Apprentices* (1857).

1847	**1850**	**1872**
Passenger railway line links Kendal with Windermere, marking the arrival of the modern age of tourism	Death of William Wordsworth	John Ruskin moves to Brantwood, Coniston

The **formation of the Forestry Commission** in 1919 presented another threat to the natural landscape as afforestation gathered pace, turning previously bare valleys and fellsides into thick conifer plantations. Successful environmental battles in the 1930s limited the scope of the plantations, but afforestation is still an emotive subject today.

Similarly, **water extraction** had long fuelled fears for the landscape. The Lake District has been used as a water source for northwestern England since Thirlmere was dammed in 1892. Construction at Haweswater in the 1930s raised the water level there by 90ft – and drowned a village in the process. (Ennerdale Water still supplies the coastal towns and as late as 1980 there were serious proposals to raise levels there and at Wast Water in an attempt to drain more water for industrial use.)

Legal protection of the Lake District was, therefore, long overdue by the time of the establishment in 1951 of the **Lake District National Park**, spreading over 885 square miles. For the first time, there was to be direct control over planning, building and development within the Lake District, as well as systematic maintenance of the footpaths, bridleways, dry-stone walls, open land and historic monuments. The widely recognized National Park emblem – the outline of Great Gable – was adopted in 1953, and the Queen made the first royal visit to the park in 1956.

The National Park: the first fifty years

The establishment of the National Park didn't, of course, end the threats to the social and natural environment of the Lake District, but it did provide the framework to defend the region from mass commercialism and development. Even so, many of the current problems facing the National Park were signalled in its earliest years.

As the privations of the postwar years were reduced, the number of leisure visitors increased dramatically. The first dedicated car park, at Tarn Hows, was established in 1954, while traffic in the National Park doubled in the five years upto 1959. The number of caravan sites increased and there were early worries about litter on the fells and other obtrusive irritants. In the 1960s, speed restrictions were imposed on Derwent Water, Ullswater and Coniston for the first time and the first full-time park warden was employed as tourism to the Lakes became a year-round phenomenon. The house at **Brockhole**, near Windermere, was acquired in 1966 and opened in 1969 as the country's first National Park Visitor Centre. Meanwhile, in 1974, centuries of tradition were abandoned when local government reorganization resulted in the scrapping or reduction of the old counties of Cumberland, Westmorland and Lancashire: the Lake District became part of the new county of **Cumbria**.

During the 1970s and 1980s, **conservation** became the new watchword as visitor numbers steadily increased. Car park charges were introduced for the first time, to provide revenue and deter drivers; meanwhile, footpath erosion had become a major problem in many areas. Attempts were made to educate visitors about the impact of their presence on the lakes and landscape – information centres were opened at Keswick, Bowness Bay and Seatoller among others, while 10mph limits were imposed on craft using Derwent Water, Ullswater and Coniston. Cars were kept out of ancient villages such as Hawkshead, whose centre became pedestrianized, and the centre of Ambleside became the Lakes' first formal conservation area.

1895	1905	1951
Creation of the National Trust; it purchases its first land on Derwent Water in 1902	Beatrix Potter buys Hill Top farmhouse; she donates the land to the National Trust on her death	Establishment of Lake District National Park

However, the underlying fragility of the park's ecosystem was exposed in 1986, after the accident at the nuclear power station at Chernobyl in the Soviet Union. Radioactive fallout contaminated Cumbrian soil, acting as a reminder – if one were needed – of the danger on the Lakes' own doorstep presented by the presence of the **Sellafield nuclear-reprocessing plant**, near Ravenglass, symbol of all that threatens the local environment.

Great strides were made during the 1990s to address some of the most fundamental problems facing the National Park. Coordinated traffic management and erosion control schemes were formulated, which began to have a significant effect on the environment. In 1993, Bassenthwaite became the first lake in Britain to be declared a National Nature Reserve and, in the same year, the **Lake District Environmentally Sensitive Area (ESA)** was established to protect traditional buildings and landscapes. Upland farmers – struggling with the downturn in their industry, and affected by the BSE crisis and other health scares – were given grants to maintain dry-stone walls and hedgerows, renovate traditional buildings and stock wild-flower meadows.

The Lakes today

The National Park celebrated its centenary in 2001, and extended its boundaries by 3 percent in 2016, gaining an extra 27 square miles – just a year later the Lake District was inscribed as a UNESCO World Heritage Site, thus increasing its profile even further. There's no doubt that the park has been a force for good – for example, defending the lakes from over-exploitive water extraction and preventing mass development in scenic areas. But, at times, it seems as if it's fighting a battle with the wider problems facing rural England as a whole. **Conservation** is now seen as fundamental to the National Park's well-being, the future challenge being to extend the same protection to lakeland traditions and the way of life.

Farming and the countryside

In the Lake District, the unproductive nature of much of the land means that **hill farming** is basically undertaken at subsistence level, and would hardly be possible at all without European Union and central government subsidies. Cumbria was also hardest hit of all the English counties by the **foot-and-mouth crisis** of 2001, which badly affected tourism as visitors were asked to keep away from infected areas. Although many Cumbrian farms subsequently restocked, replacing the thousands of animals slaughtered in the government's programme to contain the disease, not all businesses survived. The truth is, there were probably too many farms trying to make a living in inauspicious economic circumstances (a deep-rooted problem for British farming as a whole) and no amount of diversification – from camping barns to pony rides – could save some businesses from going under.

Sustainable development

Another flashpoint is the necessary **development restrictions** imposed by the National Park Authority, the National Trust (which owns a quarter of the land) and the district councils. At the same time, second-homers from the towns and

1955	1969	1974
Alfred Wainwright publishes the first of his hand-drawn walking guides	Brockhole opens – Britain's first dedicated National Park Visitor Centre	New county of Cumbria is declared

cities ("off-comers" in the local parlance) push up **housing** prices, thus forcing the lakeland youth away from home and from the land – in line with other rural British holiday regions, it's estimated that up to a fifth of all Lake District houses are second or holiday homes (and in some places, like Coniston, this figure is much higher still). However, the National Park has an affordable housing strategy in place, while **employment** initiatives are working to provide more opportunities for local people, not just in tourism and hospitality, but also in the retail, small business and technology industries. The establishment of the **University of Cumbria** in 2007 (with campuses in Carlisle, Penrith, Ambleside and elsewhere) also means more sustainable educational and training opportunities for the region.

In some ways, the National Park is simply too successful for its own good. At its first meeting in 1951, the authority dealt with fifteen planning applications. Today, it deals with more than 1200 a year. A local population of just 41,000 is swamped by annual **visitor numbers** topping fifteen million (even more if you include all Cumbria), with all the traffic and environmental pressure that that entails – it's estimated that 82 percent of visitors currently arrive in the National Park in a private motor vehicle. Expanded bus services, the promotion of cycling and an integrated **transport strategy** are starting to have some effect, but it's a long haul to persuade people to leave their cars at home.

The Coronavirus (Covid-19) pandemic hit the UK hard from March 2020, causing 1259 deaths as of late April 2021 in Cumbria, out of the whole UK total of 127,000 at the same point in time. As the first wave receded in summer 2020 and with international travel limited, the Lakes were even more of a honeypot for visitors than usual, causing pleas for consideration from local residents. At the time of writing, 2021 is expected to be another bumper year for staycations, following the release from a third national lockdown but with overseas travel still uncertain.

Environment and conservation

Around 350 **voluntary rangers** help manage the environment (patrolling lakeshores, maintaining footpaths, planting trees, restoring hedgerows and rebuilding stone walls), but they are faced with an exponential increase in leisure activities which impinge directly upon the Park's habitats – such as mountain-biking, ghyll-scrambling, 4x4 safaris and watersports. The long-running saga of **speed restrictions** on Windermere presented the park authorities with the classic dilemma of balancing business needs with those of the environment. Watersports companies and related businesses fought a long campaign against the restriction, but since 2005 powered craft on England's largest lake have been restricted to 10mph. Other initiatives point the way to a greener future for the lakes, including the solar-powered Coniston Launch and the projects currently under way to improve the **water catchment** areas at Bassenthwaite and Windermere. However, the disastrous **floods** that hit Cumbria in the winters of 2009 and 2015 – badly affecting places like Cockermouth and Keswick, were a salutary reminder that nature cannot always be controlled.

On the land, the 2005 CRoW Act, giving a statutory "right to roam" across open countryside, has provided new rights for the public while safeguarding the landscape and wildlife. More than fifty percent of the National Park area is open for public

2001	2015	2016
Foot-and-mouth crisis has a devastating effect on Cumbrian farming and tourism	Storm Desmond leads to catastrophic flooding in Cumbria	National Park boundaries extended by three percent

access: more than two thousand miles of **paths and bridleways** are virtually all clear of obstructions and many have been made suitable for wheelchair users and pushchairs. **Erosion control** is well in hand on all the most popular walking routes under the "Fix the Fells" initiative.

The Lake District Environmentally Sensitive Area (ESA), set up in 1993 and covering almost the entire National Park, provided the initial supportive framework for traditional farm buildings to be restored, hedges and orchards replanted, and moorland and riverbanks protected. It has recently been superseded by the **Environmental Stewardship** scheme. In addition, more than one hundred Sites of Special Scientific Interest (SSSIs) cover another sixteen percent of the Park, and there are eight National Nature Reserves (NNRs), and another eighty-odd Regionally Important Geological Sites. Projects designed to preserve some of the Lake District's most **threatened species** (such as the red squirrel, otter and the water vole) are increasingly successful, and new native woodlands are being established. The **Wild Ennerdale** project (returning parts of the valley to a more "natural", pre-plantation state) is an excellent example of contemporary conservation in action, while the presence of ospreys at Bassenthwaite and elsewhere is further evidence of success.

2017	2020–2021
Lake District becomes UNESCO World Heritage Site	Covid-19 pandemic travel caution and restrictions further increase popularity of lakeland holidays

Books

We've highlighted a selection of books below which will give you a flavour of Lake District life, past and present, as well as the impressions of the visitors, writers and poets who have toured and settled in the region. As a glance in any bookshop will show you, there are hundreds of Lake District titles available. We've concentrated on those of interest to the general reader (which discounts most of the academic literary criticism of the Lake Poets) and those most useful to the non-specialist visitor – for rare historical monographs, mountain-climbing guides, lavish limited-edition pop-up Beatrix Potter books and other arcana, consult a specialist bookshop or Amazon. Books Cumbria (ⓦbookscumbria.com) is a very handy source for locally published, out-of-print, rare or otherwise esoteric books about the Lake District and Cumbria. For walking, climbing, scrambling and cycling guides, look no further than Cicerone (ⓦcicerone.co.uk).

LAKELAND LIFE, HISTORY AND NATURE

Richard Askwith *Feet in the Clouds*. If you've ever been passed on a mountain by wiry people running uphill, very quickly, and wondered quite how barmy they must be – here's your answer. Askwith's painful and obsessive quest to join the ranks of the hardest-of-the-hard fell runners manages to be both insightful and funny at the same time. It's a sports book, certainly, but only in the same way as *Fever Pitch* or *Touching the Void*.

Hunter Davies *A Walk Around the Lakes; London to Loweswater; Strong Lad Wanted for Strong Lass*. The journalist, biographer and author Davies takes every opportunity to plug the Lakes in print. His account of a walk around the region is an entertaining mix of anecdote, history and reportage, while in *London to Loweswater* (and inspired by J.B. Priestley's *English Journey* of 1934) Davies spends a year travelling from London to his Lake District home, reflecting on his own past and the state of the nation. *Strong Lad Wanted for Strong Lass*, meanwhile, is his wry account of growing up in Carlisle in the 1950s.

W.M.W. Fowler *Countryman's Cooking*. A former RAF pilot, failed Eskdale mink farmer and all-round bounder, Fowler stuffed this corker of a read – first published in the 1960s – with rants against the government, tall stories and outrageously "old-fashioned" views (such as how to lure female pastry cooks with bottles of gin). In between is a useful, well-written guide to traditional British cookery, full of hands-on practical advice – even if it is blatantly intended, as Fowler puts it, "for men".

A.H. Griffin *A Lifetime of Mountains; The High Places; The Coniston Tigers;* and others. The veteran lakelander climber, writer, journalist and *Guardian* newspaper country diarist, Harry Griffin (1911–2004) produced a dozen volumes

that range around the fells with a keen eye for nature and tradition. Although the early books, written in the 1960s and 1970s, are mostly out of print (*Inside the Real Lakeland*, *In Mountain Lakeland*, *Pageant of Lakeland* etc), the best of his *Guardian* diary pieces are collected in *A Lifetime of Mountains*, his weekly features for the *Lancashire Evening Post* are included in *The High Places*, and *The Coniston Tigers* is a climbing and walking memoir recalling seventy years of mountain adventure.

Norman Nicholson *The Lakers; Portrait of the Lakes; The Lake District: An Anthology*. Cumbria's best-known poet turned to prose with his informed, sympathetic studies of lakeland life, history, geology and people. The comprehensive *Anthology* is a joy, with extracts from writings of every period since the first visitors, and incorporating dialect verse, legends, letters and journals.

★ **John Pepper** *Cockley Beck*. Pepper happened upon a farm cottage in the Duddon Valley in the early 1980s, and spent several winters there, later writing a lyrical tribute to the countryside and local community that was first published in 1984 (with a new edition in 2006). Inspired in parts by Henry David Thoreau's account of a solitary rural retreat in *Walden*, it's a reflective, philosophical book that soon attracted the epithet "classic".

Nikolaus Pevsner *Cumberland and Westmorland*. The regional edition of Pevsner's renowned architectural guide to the old counties of England. First published in 1967 (when there was still a Cumberland and Westmorland, rather than Cumbria) and detailing every church, hall, house and cross worth looking at.

James Rebanks *The Shepherd's Life*. Oxford-educated Rebanks might not be your idea of a typical Lake District shepherd, but his family has farmed the Cumbrian fells since records began and there's nobody better qualified to write about life on the land. His down-to-earth descriptions in this highly acclaimed 2015 memoir are something of an antidote to Wordsworthian romanticism – the pages reek of sheep, sweat and family struggles – though blunt opinions of townies (and their dogs) have won him a few critics.

William Wordsworth *Guide to the Lakes*. The old curmudgeon's guide to the Lakes went through five editions between 1810 and 1835. This facsimile of the last, and definitive, edition is full of his prejudices (on the "colouring" of buildings, the shape of chimneys, forestation, the railway, the great unwashed) and timeless scenic observations.

John Wyatt *The Shining Levels*. Billed as "the story of a man who went back to nature", this was originally published in 1973 (and later reissued in 1993). John Waytt was brought up in industrial Lancashire but disowned city life to become a forest-worker, living in a woodsman's hut in the Lakes (he was later Head Warden for the National Park). Sleeping by the fire, coppicing, rabbit-hunting, searching for wild berries and nuts, adopting a roe deer – three decades later it reads as a heartfelt rural lament.

LANDSCAPE AND PHOTOGRAPHY

★ **Bill Birkett** *A Year in the Life of… the Langdale Valleys; Buttermere; Borrowdale; the Duddon Valley*. Birkett is well known as a climber and walker, but he's also a respected mountain writer and photographer. Here he turns his camera on the lakeland valleys in his own backyard to provide stunning photographic essays of the seasonal landscapes, interspersed with features on local history, heritage, farming and nature.

Gilly Cameron Cooper *Beatrix Potter's Lake District*. A beautifully produced coffee-table book, presenting Potter as naturalist, farmer and conservationist, as well as seeking out the places that inspired her stories. The excellent photography is from the National Trust (with map references to help you track down the locations), and Potter watercolours and illustrations are also reproduced, plus images from the 2006 *Miss Potter* film about her life.

WALKING GUIDES

Bill Birkett *Complete Lakeland Fells; Lakeland Fells Almanac; Exploring the Lakes and Low Fells*. The *Complete* edition is the definitive, modern fell-walking reference guide from a leading Cumbrian mountain writer and photographer: classic walks to the top of 541 separate fells for all levels. The *Almanac* distils the *Complete* fells into 129 circular walks taking in the tops, with maps, times and route details. Less adventurous walkers can tour the lake perimeters, tarns, valley bottoms, viewpoints and low fells in his company, too, using eighty easy-to-follow, half-day circular routes laid out clearly over two small-format hardback volumes of *Exploring the Lakes and Low Fells*.

Ian and Krysia Brodie *The Cumbria Coastal Way*. The first available guidebook to the 150-mile Cumbria Coastal

---

CLASSIC GUIDEBOOKS

The first **guidebook** to the Lake District was written in the late eighteenth century and dozens more followed as the region opened up to people of leisure. Most of the earliest guides are long out of print, but a trawl through the stock in any local secondhand/ antiquarian bookshop throws up old copies of other classic publications. They make interesting souvenirs, while you'll often find that the landscapes described have hardly changed in more than a century.

The earliest lakeland writings were contained in the journal of the poet **Thomas Gray**, first published as part of **Thomas West**'s *Guide to the Lakes in Cumberland, Westmorland and Lancashire* (1778). In 1810, **William Wordsworth** wrote down his own observations, appearing in the most complete form as his *Guide to the Lakes* (1835), which, alone of all the historic guides, is still in print. His friend in later life, the writer and political observer **Harriet Martineau** of Ambleside, produced her own *Complete Guide to the English Lakes* (1855). Fifty years later, **W.G. Collingwood**'s *The Lake Counties* (1902) set new standards of erudition, while **Canon H.D. Rawnsley** (cofounder of the National Trust) also found time to produce a multitude of lakeland volumes: *Round the Lake Country* (1909) is typical. Between 1904 and 1925, in the days before cheaply available colour photography, landscape watercolourist **Alfred Heaton Cooper** illustrated guidebooks for A. & C. Black; the Lake District titles are fairly easy to come by, as are the four lakeland books illustrated by his son **William Heaton Cooper**, starting with *The Hills of Lakeland* (1938). *The Lake Counties* (1937) volume in **Arthur Mee**'s classic "King's England" series is widely available too.

Way (Morecambe Bay to the Solway Firth), which runs around the southern lakeland peninsulas and up the west Cumbrian coast to the Scottish border. Essential for day-walkers (the route can be walked in sections) and long-distance hikers alike.

Anthony Burton *The Cumbria Way*. This is the best guide to pack for the 72-mile Cumbria Way (Ulverston to Carlisle), which cuts right through the heart of the Lake District National Park. Durable format, clear walking instructions, Ordnance Survey map extracts, plus history and anecdotes.

★ **Frank Duerden** *Best Walks in the Lake District*. First published in 1986, but thoroughly revised in 2006, the forty well-conceived walks in this hefty pocket guide range from easy strolls to major full-day hikes in every area of the Lakes, complete with historical and descriptive background notes. Only sketch maps are included, but the walking instructions are very detailed, and it's particularly good on the dozen or so strenuous "horseshoe" routes that are among the Lake District's finest walks.

Eileen and Brian Evans *Short Walks in… North Lakeland; South Lakeland; West Lakeland*. A three-volume series of pocket-sized guides which cover fifty half-day (four- to eight-mile) walks in each lakeland region, concentrating on the lower fells, valleys and woodlands. Some classic routes are included, but the emphasis is more on out-of-the-way tracks and secluded areas.

John and Anne Nuttall *The Tarns of Lakeland, Vol.1 (West)* and *Vol. 2 (East)*. Wainwright walked fells; the Nuttalls tackle tarns (mountain lakes), the "little specks of blue", in their own words – hundreds of them, across the Lake District, linked by forty walks in each volume that range from easy to hard. Obsessive? Clearly so, but you'll soon be seduced by the clear, hand-drawn route maps and walk details, handsome line drawings and interesting asides and anecdotes.

Pathfinder Guide *Lake District Walks; More Lake District Walks*. The best general guides for the day-pack: two slim volumes of walks, graded from short and easy to challenging and long, with useful accompanying text and clear Ordnance Survey map extracts.

★ **W.A. Poucher** *The Lakeland Peaks*. First published in 1960 and updated intermittently, Walter Poucher's classic guide for fell-walkers and peak-baggers has almost as many fans as the Wainwright volumes. The pocket-sized guide details 142 routes up fourteen separate mountain groups, accompanied by Poucher's impressive black-and-white landscape photographs (on which are superimposed the various summit routes).

★ **A. Wainwright** *A Pictorial Guide to the Lakeland Fells* (7 vols); *The Outlying Fells of Lakeland; Lakeland Sketchbooks* (5 vols). Wainwright's *Pictorial Guide* is his masterpiece: seven beautifully produced, small-format volumes of handwritten notes and sketches (written between 1952 and 1966) guiding generations of walkers up the mountains of the Lake District. Wainwright refused any revision during his lifetime and the originals still stand as remarkable works, though all seven volumes have now been revised and updated by Chris Jesty (between 2005 and 2009) to take account of changing routes and landscapes. *The Outlying Fells* scooped up lower, lesser fells on the perimeter of the Lakes, and there are also five volumes of pen-and-ink *Lakeland Sketchbooks* from the late 1960s and early 1970s. New interest has seen all sorts of spin-off publications, from *Twelve Favourite Mountains* to *Wainwright's TV Walks*, while Wainwright himself produced other large-format titles (most with superb photography by Derry Brabbs) holding forth on the majesty of lakeland mountains, passes and valleys.

LAKELAND NOVELS

Melvyn Bragg *Without A City Wall; The Silken Net; The Second Inheritance; For Want of a Nail; The Maid of Buttermere; The Cumbrian Trilogy; The Soldier's Return; A Son At War; Crossing the Lines*. The writer, broadcaster, professional Cumbrian (born in Wigton) and butt of Dame Edna Everage – "Don't write any more, Melvyn dear, or we'll never catch up" – Bragg is at his best in *The Maid of Buttermere*, a fictionalized romantic tragedy involving one of the Lakes' most enduring heroines. *The Soldier's Return* and its sequels, *A Son At War* and *Crossing the Lines*, all very moving portraits of small-town life in the years after World War II, draw heavily on the experiences of his own family in Wigton. Other novels also lovingly explore the Cumbrian past and present, notably *The Cumbrian Trilogy* (comprising *The Hired Man*, *A Place in England* and *Kingdom Come*), which traces the lives of four generations of a Cumbrian family through the twentieth century.

★ **Sarah Hall** *Haweswater; The Carhullan Army; How to Paint a Dead Man*. Hall's lyrical first novel, *Haweswater*, delves graphically into the lives of a simple farming community in the 1930s, as the remote village of Mardale is destined to be flooded to create Haweswater reservoir. Different kinds of passions run high in *The Carhullan Army*, an extraordinary near-future novel about female freedom fighters set in a dystopian Cumbria, with Penrith and the bleak northern fells a backdrop to violence and betrayal. Meanwhile, in *How to Paint a Dead Man*, a Cumbrian artist is one of four connected voices that make up an intriguing novel exploring art and illusion.

★ **Reginald Hill** *The Stranger House*. Prolific crime-writer Hill – creator of book and TV detective duo Dalziel and Pascoe – goes back to his native Cumbria in a hugely entertaining thriller. Two strangers arrive in the remote village of "Illthwaite" in "Skaddale", pursuing personal histories but soon becoming enmeshed in a web of past religious intrigue, child abuse, ghosts and murder. Hill claims the titular inn at the heart of the novel (the

WAINWRIGHT, ON THE BOX AND IN YOUR EAR

In 2012, a new generation of walkers was introduced to the Lake District fells by the BBC's **Wainwright Walks** series, presented by Julia Bradbury (available on DVD in two volumes). Ten of his favourite fells are featured, from Haystacks to Helvellyn, including some fantastic aerial photography. The gravelly voice of Wainwright in the series was actor Nik Wood-Jones, who also narrates **Wainwright: The Podcasts**, a book with maps plus downloadable CD to eight classic Wainwright walks – you can hear highlights of the walks on the Cumbria Tourism website (⦿golakes.co.uk).

Stranger House), isn't based on any particular hostelry, but the setting is clearly the western valleys of Eskdale and Wasdale, with their isolated churches, old halls, mountain tarns and Viking crosses.

Val McDermid *The Grave Tattoo*. What if *Bounty* mutineer Fletcher Christian didn't die on Pitcairn Island, but returned in secret to his native Lake District? And what if he told his tale to his childhood friend William Wordsworth – both were born in Cockermouth – who produced an epic poem on the subject, never yet found but potentially worth millions? Psychological thriller writer McDermid takes a few literary and historical facts and mixes them up with a dollop of speculation, intrigue and forensic science to produce a contemporary Lake District mystery that never quite shifts into top gear.

Magnus Mills *All Quiet on the Orient Express*. Strange goings-on in an unnamed lakeland community as the outsider-narrator is slowly sucked into the confused relationships of the hard-to-fathom locals. Great, and increasingly sinister, fun.

Hugh Walpole *Rogue Herries; Judith Paris; The Fortress; Vanessa*. Largely forgotten now, Walpole was a successful writer by the time he moved to the Lake District in 1923. He immersed himself in the local history to produce these four volumes covering two hundred years of the rip-roaring lives and loves of the Herries clan – too flowery for today's tastes but full of lakeland lore and life.

CHILDREN'S BOOKS

Beatrix Potter *The Tale of Peter Rabbit; The Tale of Jemima Puddle-duck; The Tale of Squirrel Nutkin*; and many more. Rabbits, pigs, hedgehogs, mice and ducks in lakeland stories of valour, betrayal, adventure and romance. The original 23 titles – 24 since *Kitty in Boots* was discovered and published in 2016 – have been ruthlessly merchandised since Potter's day, as colouring books, pop-up volumes, foam-filled fabric books, wallpaper, board games, diaries, calendars, etc – while the Renee Zellweger/Ewan McGregor biopic *Miss Potter* (about her life and the writing of the first book, *The Tale of Peter Rabbit*) spawned even more spin-offs, from movie editions to audio CDs.

★**Arthur Ransome** *Swallows and Amazons; Swallowdale; Winter Holiday; Pigeon Post; The Picts and the Martyrs*. Ransome's innocent childhood stories of pirates and treasure, secret harbours and outdoor camps, summer holidays and winter freezes still possess the power to entrance. The series starts with *Swallows and Amazons* (first published in 1930), and there's no better evocation of the drawn-out halcyon days of childhood. Read the books alongside Christina Hardyment's *Arthur Ransome & Captain Flint's Trunk*, a companion guide and "voyage" in search of the people, places, boats and other influences behind the stories.

PEOPLE

Juliet Barker *Wordsworth: A Life*. Gets right to the emotional heart of her subject's life and loves. Barker manages to make the irascible man of letters seem more human, even more likeable, as a consequence, and the evenly paced account of his quiet death, which came in 1850, is a moving read.

John Batchelor *John Ruskin: No Wealth But Life*. This book provides the best background material yet on Ruskin's life for the non-academic reader. The subtitle is Ruskin's own evaluation of "wealth" and Batchelor conveys well Ruskin's journey from precocious child to visionary and moralist.

★**A.S. Byatt** *Unruly Times*. Authoritative, insightful study of Wordsworth and Coleridge "in their times", which charts their relationship, ideas, work and family situations against a lively backdrop of contemporary politics, society and culture.

Roland Chambers *The Last Englishman*. Contemporary interest in children's author Arthur Ransome stems largely from the gradually revealed evidence that, long before he wrote the books that made his name, he had spent years in Russia (1917–24) as a foreign correspondent, Bolshevik apologist and, ultimately, spy. This biography, subtitled *The Double Life of...*, is a spirited investigation of the complexities of this "simplest of men".

Hunter Davies *Wainwright: The Biography; William Wordsworth*. Davies turns his informal, chatty style upon two of the Lake District's biggest enigmas. Hard biographical detail aside, there's not much to learn about the character of either man that a close reading of their respective works won't tell you already – but then that's not Davies' fault.

Thomas De Quincey *Confessions of an English Opium-Eater; Recollections of the Lakes and the Lake Poets.* Tripping out with the best-known literary drug-taker after Coleridge – "Fear and Loathing in Grasmere" it isn't, but neither is the *Confessions* a simple cautionary tale. The famous *Recollections* collected together magazine features De Quincey wrote in the 1830s, providing a highly readable, often catty, account of life in the Lakes with the Wordsworths, the Coleridges and Southey.

★ **Richard Holmes** *Coleridge: Early Visions; Coleridge: Darker Reflections.* The supreme account of the troubled genius of Coleridge, who emerges from Holmes's acclaimed two-volume biography as an animated intellectual and creative poet in his own right as well as the catalyst for Wordsworth's poetic development.

Kenneth R. Johnston *The Hidden Wordsworth.* For "hidden" read "young", as Johnston's controversial book focuses on the creation of the poet by examining his early life and work in exhaustively researched detail. The book ends in 1807 with more than half of Wordsworth's life yet to run, but the argument is that "his young life was his most important life". And along the way are sprinkled the controversies, with Wordsworth variously touted as lover, rebel and – most contentiously – spy.

Kathleen Jones *A Passionate Sisterhood.* Welcome feminist take on the lives of the sisters, wives and daughters of the Lake Poets, whose letters and journals reveal not quite the rustic idyll we've been led to expect by the poetry.

Linda Lear *Beatrix Potter: The Extraordinary Life of a Victorian Genius.* Potter's is a life that's been largely overlooked by serious biographers, possibly down to snobbery about the perceived literary value of her works. But as this definitive biography makes abundantly clear, not only was she a pioneer children's writer (one of the first to see the potential in tie-in merchandising) but also an accomplished scientist, innovative farmer, businesswoman and conservationist.

Mark Storey *Robert Southey: A Life.* Although he's little known now, in his day Southey was a major man of letters, author of 45 books, and expert on Brazil, Portugal and Spain. He was thought of primarily as a poet, his reputation established by *Joan of Arc* and subsequent epics and by his appointment as Poet Laureate. Despite his poetry, however, what has endured most is his clear, plain prose style – thought "perfect" by Byron – and his biographical history of Nelson.

★ **Frances Wilson** *The Ballad of Dorothy Wordsworth.* Dorothy is put centre-stage in this excellent, gripping biography of the often-overlooked sister of the sage. It's extremely perceptive, especially on the deep emotional ties between poet brother and supportive sister that led from affection via "strange fit of passion" to breakdown, depression and death.

Dorothy Wordsworth *The Grasmere Journals; Home at Grasmere.* Was she a poet in her own right? Judge for yourself from the sharply observed descriptions of nature and day-to-day Grasmere life contained in the *Journals*. *Home at Grasmere* lets you see the debt Wordsworth owed his sister by placing journal entries and completed poetry side by side.

POETRY

Samuel Taylor Coleridge *Selected Poems; The Complete Poems; Critical Edition of the Major Works.* Final texts of all the poems in varying editions: the Penguin *Selected* (edited by his biographer Richard Holmes) also includes extracts from Coleridge's verse plays and prefaces; the Penguin *Complete* edition includes unfinished verses.

Norman Nicholson *Collected Poems.* The bard of Cumbria – who lived all his life in Millom, on the coast – produced five books of verse by the time of his death in 1987, collected here. He writes beautifully and movingly of his country, its trades, its past and its people.

William Wordsworth *The Prelude; Lyrical Ballads; Poetical Works; Selected Poems.* There are dozens of editions of the works of Wordsworth on the market, but these are the current pick. The major poems, sonnets and odes are all collected in *Selected Poems* (Penguin), which has the advantage of being a cheap, pocket-sized edition. For the full text of major works, you'll need *Lyrical Ballads* and *The Prelude* (both Penguin) – the latter presenting the four separate texts of 1798, 1799, 1805 and 1850. (Wordsworth revised his original, 1798 text three times, the last published after his death.) *Poetical Works* (OUP) contains every piece of verse ever published by Wordsworth.

Habitats of the Lake District

The Lake District National Park covers 912 square miles, or nearly 590,000 acres. For such a relatively small region it has a highly varied landscape, geology and climate, and possesses a unique combination of spectacular mountains, rugged fells, pastoral and wooded valleys, and tarns, lakes and rivers. This section gives a general introduction to the region's various habitats, including a rundown of the threats posed by modern agricultural methods and human encroachment. Each habitat description includes brief details of the flora and fauna found there, while some of the more prominent nature reserves in the National Park are also covered. For more information about local habitats and wildlife, don't miss the exhibits at the Lake District Visitor Centre at Brockhole (see page 61).

Woodland and forest

There is more **native woodland** in the Lake District than in any other upland National Park in Britain. The most widespread type, sessile-oak woodland, occurs on the acid rocks that make up most of the Lake District, with birch, rowan, hazel and holly also present alongside the dominant oak. On limestone it's ash woodland that dominates, though elm, hazel, silver birch, yew and rowan might also be present. The woodlands provide food, shelter and breeding sites for many different birds and animals, from the buzzard to the wood mouse, while common plants include bluebell, primrose, wood anemone, cowslip and wild daffodil. Shrubs such as blackthorn and buckthorn are typical. In more acidic soil, bilberry, wavy hair and other grasses, ferns and bracken are common, shrubs less so. Woodlands in **Borrowdale** are particularly important for their lichens and their rich moss and liverwort communities, which depend upon high rainfall and humidity.

Five thousand years ago, nearly all of Britain was covered in woodland but over time it was cleared for settlement and agriculture. Although there's little, if any, true natural forest, or "wildwood", remaining in the Lakes, there are sites that have been continually wooded for at least the past four hundred years, which are known as **ancient semi-natural woodland**. The continuity of woodland cover over such a long period of time has allowed a rich flora and fauna to develop. **Roudsea Wood NNR**, on the southern fringes of the National Park (a mile southwest of Haverthwaite village), is a good example of this kind of habitat, featuring a large variety of trees, ferns and woodland birds. East of Windermere, near Staveley, **Dorothy Farrer's Spring Wood** shows the continuing benefit of coppicing (cutting trees, often hazel, back to a stump) in ancient seminatural woodland. The tree canopy is periodically opened up, allowing more light to reach the woodland floor and encouraging the growth of plants and fungi. The National Park also contains the highest-altitude woodland in England and Wales, including the **Eskdale and Birkrigg woods** in the Newlands Valley, which are both thought to be descended from original wildwood.

Conifer plantations occupy large areas of the Lake District. They often contain fast-growing, nonindigenous tree species such as spruce and pine, which are favoured by commercial timber growers but support only a limited range of wildlife. They are, however, used by several birds of prey, including the sparrowhawk, goshawk and merlin, and provide refuge, feeding and nesting areas for the native red squirrel. Recent moves towards more varied planting and felling patterns are producing a mosaic of smaller stands of different-aged trees, seen for example in plantations at **Thirlmere** and in **Grizedale Forest**. These are more botanically diverse and of much greater value to wildlife. For example, young plantations often harbour small mammals such as voles and mice which, in turn, are a food source for kestrels and owls. Other coniferous plantations worth visiting include **Dodd Wood**, four miles north of Keswick (harbouring red squirrels and various birds of prey, including the Lake District ospreys) and **Thornethwaite Forest** (buzzard and sparrowhawk), while in **Ennerdale** the "Wild Ennerdale" project is encouraging a more natural approach to the evolution of valley and forest – alongside the resident roe deer, red squirrel and badger, wild cattle have been introduced to some of the cleared plantation land.

Overgrazing by stock and deer is the greatest cause of decline in the natural regeneration of broad-leaved woodlands, so in some areas woodland management schemes (providing stock-proof fencing or undertaking coppicing and so on) are being practised. Other threats are posed by the **ornamental species** introduced by the Victorians, such as rhododendron and laurel, which have escaped from the private gardens for which they were originally intended. Their dense canopy prevents light from reaching the woodland floor, while the roots produce toxic chemicals that prevent other plants from growing.

Grassland

Before people began to clear the forests for agriculture and settlement, open grassland was a rare feature below the tree line. Most grasslands have been created by humans and grazing animals. Some areas have been drained, ploughed and re-seeded with "improved" grass mixtures for agriculture and so have limited wildlife value. Others remain as unimproved pasture, which supports a greater diversity of plants and animals.

Acid grassland is common on upland sheep pasture where high rainfall, coupled with a long history of burning and grazing, has favoured this relatively species-poor habitat. However, the invertebrate species associated with grasslands provide a vital food source for birds such as the skylark and meadow pipit, along with small mammals

---

PROTECTING A UNIQUE LANDSCAPE

Today's landscape and habitats within the Lake District National Park are heavily protected and maintained for future generations. There are currently eight **National Nature Reserves (NNR)**, more than a hundred **Sites of Special Scientific Interest (SSSI)**, three **RAMSAR** sites (an internationally important wetland designation), two **European Special Protection Areas (SPA)** and 23 candidate **Special Areas of Conservation (cSAC)**. In addition, in an attempt to combat the threat of agricultural intensification, the Lake District National Park was designated an **Environmentally Sensitive Area (ESA)** in 1993, and is now covered by the government's **Environmental Stewardship** scheme. By providing them with financial incentives, farmers are encouraged to reduce chemical inputs such as fertilizers and pesticides; to safeguard and restore hedges, dry-stone walls, traditional farm buildings and archeological remains; and to take care of wildlife habitats such as flower-rich hay meadows, heather moor, wetlands and native woodland. At the same time, the National Park Authority works closely with organizations such as the **Cumbria Wildlife Trust** (w cumbriawildlifetrust.org.uk), **Friends of the Lake District** (w friendsofthelakedistrict.org. uk), **Natural England** (w gov.uk/government/organisations/natural-england), the **National Trust** (w nationaltrust.org.uk) and the **Royal Society for the Protection of Birds** (w rspb.org.uk) to monitor important habitats and ensure they are protected and maintained for future generations.

such as mice and voles. Acid grasslands often contain small areas of richer habitat in the form of wet flushes, springs and mires where many interesting plants, such as the insectivorous sundew and butterwort, can be found.

Calcareous grassland occurs on the limestone outcrops in the Lake District, which were formed during the last Ice Age when huge glaciers scoured the bedrock. In limestone areas this created a smooth, flattened surface, which is characteristic of **limestone pavements**. Weathering and runoff from rainwater widened and deepened any cracks in the rock, giving rise to a complex pattern of solid blocks called **clints**, separated by fissures (sometimes several feet deep) known as **grikes**. These habitats form distinctive niches for a range of plants and animals. For instance, rare ferns thrive in the deep grikes, while above you may catch a glimpse of the Duke of Burgundy or other rare butterflies.

The flattened area of limestone known as limestone pavement is a nationally rare habitat of international importance and, outside Britain, it's found in only a few other areas of Europe. However, commercial exploitation of limestone pavement (to build walls, gateposts and decorative rockeries) has led to large-scale destruction of this fragile habitat and, today, most pavement in England is protected. Cumbria holds 36 percent of Britain's limestone pavement and examples at **Whitbarrow NNR** are some of the finest in Britain. Here, just to the southeast of Cartmel Fell and Bowland Bridge in the Winster Valley, the limestone ridge of Whitbarrow Scar is dominated by the rare blue moor grass, but also contains the hart's tongue fern, dog's mercury, yellow rockrose and limestone bedstraw, as well as the rarer dropwort, dark-red helleborine and rigid buckler fern. Uncommon orchids and distinctive plants, such as crested hair-grass, can also be seen, along with four species of fritillary butterfly, plus the grayling, northern brown argus and common blue butterfly.

Hay meadows support a rich variety of wild flowers and tall-growing grasses, and provide nectar for invertebrates. Their richness is maintained by the fact that plants can flower and set seed before mowing, enabling them to be dispersed during summer hay-making. Unfortunately, many hay meadows have been lost over the years with the intensification of agriculture. The move away from hay-making towards silage production (which requires an earlier cut and often relies on the input of artificial fertilizer) has led to a considerable loss of species diversity. However, farmers are now being encouraged to take care of traditional hay meadows, which can sometimes support more than a hundred different species of flowering plant.

Upland heath

Heathland is an open habitat dominated by dwarf shrubs like heather. Such areas were originally cleared for agriculture but their poor acidic soils made them unsuitable for farming – the acid-tolerant heather, therefore, was able to colonize the land. These open habitats are particularly important for insects, and more than 170 species of butterfly and moth have been identified at **Rusland Moss NNR** in the south of the National Park (three miles north of Haverthwaite village), along with numerous spiders, flies, beetles, birds and reptiles.

Large areas of upland heath have traditionally been managed as shooting estates. A diverse age structure of vegetation is maintained through systematically burning strips of heather to promote seed germination and encourage the growth of new shoots. This practice ensures a constant food supply for birds, such as the red grouse (found only in Britain), and provides an important breeding ground for the short-eared owl as well as Britain's smallest bird of prey, the merlin.

Heathland needs careful management to prevent it reverting to woodland. This is commonly achieved through stock grazing. However, if stocking densities are too high, the regeneration of heather cannot keep pace with the consumption of young shoots by the sheep, and the heather dies back.

Mires

The cool, wet climate of the Lake District provides ideal conditions for the development of peat, and the area is considered to be of national importance for both the extent and quality of its **mires**. Peat is characteristic of waterlogged conditions and consists of partially decomposed plant material. In areas where soil microorganisms cannot complete their natural breakdown processes due to highly acidic conditions and a lack of oxygen, organic remains accumulate as peat. Many mires are nutrient-poor ecosystems, unsuitable for farming. The vegetation depends almost entirely on dilute nutrient supplies present in rainwater and atmospheric dust. Mosses and liverworts flourish, along with many species of lichen and dwarfed forms of heathers and sedges.

Blanket mire (ie where there's a blanket covering of peat) is a scarce habitat, particularly important for breeding moorland birds such as red grouse, golden plover and merlin. Extensive areas remain on some of the flatter fell-tops within the National Park, where you'll find cross-leaved heath, purple moor grass, cotton grass, bog asphodel, sundew and sphagnum moss. Small fragments of **raised mire** (flattish, boggy areas of deep peat) also occur within the National Park, such as **Meathop Moss SSSI**, which supports a wide range of plants, more than two hundred species of moth and butterfly (including the large heath butterfly), and several species of dragonfly and damselfly. At **Roudsea Mosses NNR** (a mile southwest of Haverthwaite village), a raised mire provides a breeding site for more than fifty species of bird including woodcock, curlew, greater spotted woodpecker and reed bunting. **Dubbs Moss**, a small reserve just to the southwest of Cockermouth, is a mostly wet mixture of mire, fen, meadow and woodland, with plenty of mosses and ferns in evidence.

Unfortunately, artificial drainage of sites, coupled with the increased demand for peat by gardeners, has led to a widespread decline of this wetland habitat. However, attempts are being made to raise gardeners' awareness of alternatives for soil conditioning (such as home-made compost), and steps are being taken to protect and manage existing mires more sympathetically. In areas where rare plants such as the bog orchid have been found, grazing has been controlled.

Lakes, tarns and rivers

The iconic **lakes and tarns** were formed in the last Ice Age by huge glaciers gouging out depressions, which were later filled by meltwater and rain. They vary considerably in size, depth and nutrient status, but between them support an exceptional variety of aquatic plants and animals. However, the lakeshore habitat is a fragile "soft shore" environment that is highly susceptible to erosion. Trampling feet, livestock grazing and waves from passing boats can lead to soil and organic material being washed away. Over time a reedy shoreline may begin to resemble a pebble beach, which contains only a fraction of the invertebrate species and little or no aquatic vegetation.

The deep, cold, clear lakes of **Buttermere**, **Ennerdale** and **Wast Water** have only a restricted range of plants and animals, but these include some rare crustaceans specifically adapted to nutrient-poor environments. In contrast, lakes such as **Windermere** and **Bassenthwaite** – with their wooded shorelines, shallow bays and reedbeds – provide valuable nesting haunts for swans, grebes, ducks, geese and other birds. **Esthwaite Water** is the most nutrient-rich of the lakes, supporting white and yellow water lilies and rare pondweeds as well as nesting grebes, plus wild rainbow and brown trout. Windermere is of national importance for wintering wildfowl, while Bassenthwaite Lake is very rich in aquatic plants (including the scarce, floating water plantain) and is one of only two lakes in Britain known to support the rare fish, vendace – the other, **Derwent Water**, also attracts various wintering wildfowl, including the pochard and tufted duck. In 2001, the first pair of ospreys to nest in northern England for 150 years bred near the shores of Bassenthwaite Lake, and ospreys continue to return – three chicks were reared for the first time in 2006 and others have been reared every year since.

Many of the **rivers** within the National Park are of considerable ecological importance. The significant populations of fish, together with other species such as native crayfish, freshwater pearl mussel, water vole and otter, reflect the generally high standards of water quality. The fast-flowing upland **streams** provide ideal conditions for birds such as dippers, and yellow and grey wagtails.

Rock and scree

Glacial activity has produced a wide variety of crags, knolls, ledges and other rock features. In some places, steep-sided **gills** cut deeply into the fellsides. These ravines provide a damp, sheltered environment and are largely inaccessible to grazing animals, which enables them to support many unusual plants. Steep rocky cliffs, known locally as **crags**, support a mixture of lowland plant species and the more distinctive arctic-alpine flora (including yellow, purple and mossy saxifrage and alpine lady's mantle). Sheltered **rock ledges** and **screes** provide a habitat for tall herbs and ferns (including the parsley fern, common in the Lake District, but fairly rare elsewhere) along with many mosses, liverworts and flowering plants.

Crags and ledges also provide a habitat for a varied range of bird species, including stonechat, wheatear and ring ouzel, and nest sites for the buzzard, raven and peregrine falcon. The population of peregrine falcons, in particular, suffered a huge decline during the 1950s and 1960s due to widespread use of pesticides and illegal persecution. Their numbers dropped to just six pairs in Cumbria, though over the last twenty years they have made a considerable recovery and the Lake District today supports the highest density of peregrines anywhere in Europe. The very high fells (particularly in Langdale) are also the only place you'll spot the mountain ringlet butterfly, Britain's only true alpine butterfly.

Coastal environments

Five sites of international importance for nature conservation are located on the coast of the National Park, while on its southern boundary the National Park encompasses small parts of the **Duddon Estuary** and **Morecambe Bay**. These extensive areas support huge numbers of breeding and wintering birds, for which they are awarded special European protection – RAMSAR status. Depending on the time of year, you're likely to see flocks of knot, dunlin and oystercatcher, plus grey and ringed plover, curlew, greenshank, spotted redshank, mallard, shelduck and wigeon.

In the west, the National Park's coast stretches from **Drigg Local Nature Reserve** (SSSI) for twelve miles south to **Silecroft**. Large numbers of the natterjack toad are found here along with the palmate, great crested and smooth newt, and the common lizard, while other important species include the adder and the slow-worm. More than two hundred plant species are found in the coastal habitats, from sea campion, sea beet and sea kale established on the shingle beaches to typical salt-marsh plants such as glasswort and sea arrowgrass. On the dunes, marram grass and lyme grass help stabilize the sand, while in the hollows, or "slacks", of the dune systems (sometimes filled with fresh or sea water) rarer species such as creeping willow, marsh pennywort and various other marsh orchids can often be found. Shingle and dune habitats also provide breeding areas for five species of tern and large colonies of gulls. The **Hodbarrow** nature reserve, near Millom – a habitat fashioned from a former iron-ore-mining site – sees a huge variety of coastal bird species, including great crested grebe, tufted duck, shelduck, oystercatcher and ringed plover, as well as birds of prey such as the kestrel, sparrowhawk and barn owl.

This feature is based on literature kindly provided by the Lake District National Park Authority.

Climbing in the Lake District

Two centuries ago, no one climbed rocks for fun. That's not to say that people didn't go up mountains, but they would never have thought of themselves as climbers or what they were doing as a sport. Shepherds, soldiers and traders ventured onto high ground, but only with good reason. Mountains were the stuff of myth and legend – useless to farmers, dangerous to travellers, largely unknown and often feared. Daniel Defoe, writing of the Lake District in the 1720s, thought the region's mountains "had a kind of inhospitable terror in them"; and Dr Johnson, some fifty years later, was "astonished and repelled by this wide extent of hopeless sterility". But revolution was afoot in the late eighteenth century, as much in man's perception of the natural world as in politics, and two new influences were making themselves felt upon the landscapes of Europe: Romanticism and the urge for scientific discovery.

Early steps

In August 1786, Mont Blanc in the French Alps (the highest summit in Western Europe) was climbed for the first time by a young Chamonix doctor, **Michel-Gabriel Paccard** and his porter **Jacques Balmat**. Given that only eighty years previously a serious attempt had been made to seek out and classify "alpine dragons", Paccard's climb was both a mountaineering *tour de force* and a triumph of scientific rationalism over superstition.

In England it was the artistic, rather than the scientific, community which began to influence the general attitude towards the Lake District's own, lesser, mountain range. **The Picturesque Movement**, precursor of Romanticism, had made the depiction of landscape fashionable and, by the 1760s, various English artists were making good money out of the developing public taste for mountainous scenery. Idealized prints of Derwent Water by Thomas Smith and William Bellers proved both popular and profitable, while in 1783 the renowned artist Thomas Gainsborough visited the Lakes and produced three well-received works (including one of the Langdale Pikes).

Capturing the prevailing Romantic spirit, other visitors published successful accounts of their lakeland expeditions, and in the writings of **William Gilpin**, **Thomas West** and novelist **Mrs Ann Radcliffe** are found the first descriptions of mountains as objects to be climbed (primarily for the "picturesque" views from the top). But the relatively easy ascent of Skiddaw aside (which could be conquered on horseback), most Lake District mountaintops were still well off-limits. It took the energy and vision of an opium-riddled, rheumatic poet to transform the way people regarded lakeland crags and cliffs.

Coleridge and the birth of rock climbing

If Wordsworth was the great walker in the Lake District, then **Samuel Taylor Coleridge** was the pioneer of rock-climbing. In August 1802, setting off from his home in Keswick, he made a nine-day solo tour – which he dubbed his "circumcursion" – taking in the peaks and valleys of the central and western Lakes in a hundred-mile circuit. Coleridge was escaping a troubled marriage and an ebbing literary career and, recording his travels in his journal and in a series of letters to his beloved "Asra" (Wordsworth's sister-in-law, Sara Hutchinson), he became the sport's first great writer.

Coleridge's was a wild spirit and it was with a real sense of exhilaration that he found himself on the top of Scafell on the fifth day of his tour. In a famous passage from his journal he records his hair-raising descent, dropping down the successive ledges of **Broad Stand** by hanging over them from his fingertips. In this manner, he soon found himself in a position where: "... every Drop increased the Palsy of my Limbs ... and now I had only two more to drop down, to return was impossible – but of these two the first was tremendous, it was twice my own height, and the Ledge at the bottom was so exceedingly narrow, that if I dropt down upon it I must of necessity have fallen backwards and of course killed myself". A moment's reflection brought respite: "I know not how to proceed, how to return, but I am calm and fearless and confident."

This ability to overcome the body's response to fear is a quality all climbers must possess, and Coleridge's breathless account marks him out as a true mountaineer. He revelled in the activity for its own sake and in his "stretched and anxious state of mind" he discovered calm and an escape from the cares of home.

Wasdale and the Victorian climbers

For the most part, the Lake District crags were largely ignored by daring English gentlemen climbers and their professional guides. Mountaineering meant Alpine glaciers and snow ridges, and most Alpinists regarded lakeland rock climbers as mere "chimney sweeps" and "rock gymnasts". But change was in the air. A handful of more broad-minded climbers began to gather for winter practice at **Wasdale Head**, from where Coleridge had set off for Scafell in 1802. On the whole they were professional men from the industrial cities or academics, with the time and energy to indulge their passion for the mountains. From their ranks came the Cambridge classicist and unlikely sporting revolutionary **Walter Parry Haskett Smith**, who began to record his routes, guiding those who might choose to follow his footsteps and handholds. The visitor's book at the **Wastwater Hotel** (now the *Wasdale Head Inn*) became the lakeland climber's bible, and the hotel doubled as the rock climbers' clubhouse.

An almost chivalrous code developed among the climbers: comradeship tempered the excesses of competition and bar-room bragging was not tolerated. These men found in climbing an escape from the demands of their professions, families and society, and a few days spent at Wasdale each year was an excuse for the sort of behaviour not usually associated with the staid lives of Victorian gentlemen. After a hard day on the crag, there were often evening gymnastic revelries: the "billiard room traverse" – circling and leaving the room without touching the floor – or the "passage of the billiard table leg", completed by climbing beneath the table and around a table leg.

In 1886, Haskett Smith made the first ascent of **Napes Needle**, that slender pillar of rock that rises on the southern flank of Great Gable. This was no simple gully scramble, nor could it be rationalized as merely an alternative route to a fell top. This was climbing pure and simple, and climbing for its own sake at that. If one climb set the standard for a new sport, this was it. The route is short, but exposed, and is still many a novice's first lakeland climb. Haskett Smith did it alone, unroped and in nailed boots, at the end of a full day in the hills. (He later repeated this pioneering climb on its fiftieth anniversary, when he was a sprightly 76-year-old.)

Haskett Smith's exploits didn't go unnoticed. **Owen Glynne Jones**, the son of a Welsh carpenter, was teaching at the City of London School when, in 1891, he saw a photograph of Napes Needle in a shop on the Strand and within a fortnight had climbed it during his Easter holidays. He was a bold, brash man ("The Only Genuine Jones", as he called himself), who climbed ferociously well and pioneered several physically demanding routes, eagerly taking up the right of first ascenders to name new climbs (a tradition that remains to this day) – "Jones's Route Direct" on Scafell owes its name to him.

Jones came to dominate lakeland climbing in the 1890s, doing much to publicize the new sport in the process. In 1897, his book, *Rock Climbing in the English Lake District*, was published, including thirty magnificent full-page photographs by Keswick brothers and photographers **George and Ashley Abraham**. Jones's accompanying descriptions of the routes included **grades** allocated according to the difficulty of the climb – from Easy to Severe. This was the first attempt to put some order into what had been, until now, a sport without classification, and Jones's basic grading framework still stands, although there are now some twenty intermediate and additional grades.

Danger and progress on the fells

Jones was killed in a fall in the Alps in 1899 and his death highlighted the dangers facing the early climbers. Their **specialist equipment** was basically limited to nails arranged in varying patterns on the sole or around the edge of the boot to help grip the rock. Heavy hemp ropes (as used when crossing crevasse-strewn Alpine glaciers) were of dubious benefit on lakeland crags. Two or more climbers might rope themselves together but, as the rope itself was not attached to the rock (as it is today), the chances of surviving a fall were slim. Put bluntly, it was "one off, all off" and the tragic results can be seen in St Olaf's graveyard at Wasdale Head, where three headstones mark the graves of a roped party who fell together from the Pinnacle Face of Scafell in 1906.

Some measure of organization came to lakeland rock-climbing with the establishment in 1907 of the **Fell and Rock Climbing Club (FRCC)** of the English Lake District. Ashley Abraham became its president, with honorary memberships granted to Haskett Smith, Cecil Slingsby (a great lakeland climber on Scafell and Gable, and probably the first Englishman to learn the art of skiing) and Norman Collie (an experienced climber in Skye, the Alps, the Rockies and the Himalayas, who also found time to discover the gas neon and develop the first practical application of the X-ray). The Fell and Rock, as the club came to be known, not only promoted safer climbing techniques but helped usher the sport out of the Victorian age with its revolutionary acceptance of women members (something the more established Alpine Club didn't do until after World War II).

Meanwhile, lakeland climbers continued to push at the boundaries of possibility. **Siegfried Herford** (Welsh-born but with a German mother) began climbing in 1907, and his eventual ascent of **Central Buttress** on Scafell in the spring of 1914 was a landmark climb, requiring a new grade to be added to the grading framework – it was so tough that no one else repeated the climb for seven years.

A democratic sport

By the **mid-1930s**, climbing had become a popular, rather than a specialist, pastime. Partly, this was because it was now a safer sport than it had been: rubber-soled gym shoes were worn in dry weather rather than nailed boots, and rope techniques had improved markedly. But, more importantly, what had once been the preserve of daring gentlemen was now open to all – better road access, more holiday time and the establishment of youth hostels and rambling clubs all brought new faces (known as "crag rats") onto the crags.

Jim Birkett, a quarryman from Langdale, and **Bill Peascod**, a Workington coal miner, were typical of the new breed of climber. Birkett was a reserved man and a traditionalist, who kept climbing in nailed boots long after his contemporaries had abandoned them. On May 1, 1938, he pioneered his first classic route on **Scafell East Buttress**, calling it "May Day". This was followed by "Gremlin's Groove" on the same face and two other classics on **Esk Buttress** ("Afterthought" and "Frustration"), before Birkett turned his attention to **Castle Rock** in Thirlmere, climbing what was then known as the Lakeland Everest in April 1939 by a route he called "Overhanging Bastion". Meanwhile, the more extrovert Peascod was making similar advances in

Buttermere, with routes such as "Eagle Front", climbed in June 1940, followed by nine other new routes of a similarly severe standard in 1941.

Popularity and professionalism

By the **1960s**, thanks to the conquest of Everest, climbing rode high in the public conscience. Men like **Joe Brown** and **Chris Bonington** became household names – although they were better known for their achievements in the Alps and Himalayas than for any of the notable lakeland routes they had also created.

By the **1970s**, an increasing number of professional climbers were taking a new approach to their sport, training as hard as any top athlete in order to push the boundaries still further. Typical of this single-minded athleticism were the exploits of the Yorkshireman **Pete Livesey**, whose great lakeland season came in 1974. In **Borrowdale** alone he put up four routes of such a magnitude that many at first thought them impossible without using "aid" (pitons, ropes or other artificial help on the rock). But Livesey maintained the tradition of so-called "free climbing" (whereby equipment is used only to provide safety in the event of a fall), thus proving it was simply another psychological barrier that had to be broken. Soon others were climbing even more "impossible" routes than Livesey. **Bill Birkett** – son of the Langdale climber, Jim – undertook some audacious climbing in the Patterdale area, most notably on **Dove Crag**, in the 1970s and 1980s. And today, **Dave Birkett**, Bill's nephew, has a reputation as one of the world's finest adventure climbers, creating new standards right back in the heart of the Lakes, where many of his routes (graded Extreme 9, about as tough as it gets) have been unrepeated by other climbers.

Modern equipment and challenges

Climbing equipment has developed alongside the athletic professionalism. Nailed boots and gym shoes have given way to specialized climbing shoes, first developed in the 1950s by the French climber Pierre Allain (and known by his initials as PAs). Where Haskett Smith would have climbed in tweeds, modern climbers don multicoloured Lycra leggings: chalk bags hang from belts, ready to dry sweat-dampened fingers, along with a battery of safety chocks and slings, placed in the rock to give the nylon rope a secure anchor point in the event of a fall. Despite the severity of today's climbing, accidents are few and far between, since a securely placed sling or "runner" (through which the rope is clipped) holds anyone whose ambition out-runs their ability. There was a move towards "**aid climbing**" in the Lakes in the 1960s, when pitons and screws were used to assist an ascent, but it was largely frowned upon and today nearly all lakeland climbers climb "**free**"; that is, by their own efforts alone. It's a technique championed by Cumbria's latest young gun, adventure climber and BASE jumper Leo Houlding – one of a bunch of young British climbers (including Ian Parnell, Andy Kirkpatrick and Airlie Anderson) scaling crags and peaks from Yosemite to Patagonia.

The number of climbers on the Lake District's crags has increased to such an extent that queues now form on popular routes in the summer. But there are still **challenging routes** to be discovered alongside the classics on Gable and Scafell. Hikers, meanwhile, have the history of climbing all around them. Take a walk up from the *Wasdale Head Inn* and the very names of the features around the Great Napes on Great Gable – Sphinx Ridge, Needle Gulley and Napes Needle itself – are all attributable to the pioneer climbers. You may not know it, and it will not be listed by the Ordnance Survey, but on Scafell Crag you could pass by "Botterill's Slab" (1903, F.W. Botterill), "Pegasus" (1952, A. Dolphin & P. Greenwood) or "The White Wizard" (1976, C.J.S. Bonington & N. Estcourt), and find climbers on each. All are finding something different in the challenge of hand and foot on rock, and all are, in their own way, conquering the impossible. In that, nothing has changed.

William Wordsworth: a life

Wordsworth was of a good height, just five feet ten, and not a slender man… Meantime his face … was certainly the noblest for intellectual effects that, in actual life, I have seen.

Thomas De Quincey, *Recollections of the Lake and Lake Poets*

William Wordsworth and the Lake District are inextricably linked, and in the streets of Grasmere, Hawkshead and Cockermouth, and the fells surrounding Ullswater, Borrowdale and the Duddon Valley you're never very far away from a house or a sight associated with the poet and his circle. His birthplace, houses, favourite spots and final resting place are all covered in the Guide, together with anecdotes about, and analysis of, his day-to-day life, his poetry and personal relationships. Below, a general biographical account of Wordsworth's life is provided to place the various sites and accounts in context.

Childhood, school and university

William Wordsworth was **born in Cockermouth** (April 7, 1770), the second eldest of four brothers and a sister, Dorothy. His father, John, was agent and lawyer for a local landowner, Sir James Lowther, and the family was comfortably off, as the surviving Wordsworth home in Cockermouth attests. The children spent much time with their grandparents in Penrith – William even attended a school there – and when their mother Ann died (she was only 30) in 1778, the family was split up: Dorothy was sent to live with relations in Halifax in Yorkshire, while William and his older brother Richard began life at the respected **grammar school in Hawkshead**, lodging with **Ann Tyson** and going back to Penrith or Cockermouth in the holidays. On his father's death in 1783, William and the other children were left in relative poverty as the Lowthers refused to pay John Wordsworth's long-owed salary (indeed, it was almost twenty years before the debt was honoured).

At school in Hawkshead, Wordsworth (now supported by his uncles) flourished, storing up childhood experiences of ice-skating, climbing, fishing and dancing that would later emerge in his most celebrated poetry. In 1787, finished with school and clutching new clothes made for him by Ann Tyson and the already devoted Dorothy, Wordsworth went up to **St John's College, Cambridge**, where his uncles intended that he should study to become a clergyman. His academic promise soon fizzled out. Despite a bright start – to his evident amusement, De Quincey later recalled that Wordsworth briefly became a "dandy", sporting silk stockings and powdered hair – he abandoned his formal studies and left in 1790 without distinction and with no prospect of being ordained. His uncles were furious, but Wordsworth had other plans for his future.

In France

A walking tour through **France and the Alps** in the summer of 1790 excited the young, idealistic Wordsworth who had grand thoughts of being a poet. His interest was fired by the contemporary revolutionary movements of Europe. The Bastille had fallen the previous year and Wordsworth's early republicanism flowered. ("Bliss was it in that dawn to be alive, but to be young was very Heaven!") He returned to France in 1791 where he met one **Annette Vallon**, with whom he fell in love – she became pregnant, giving birth to their child, Caroline, in December 1792. But by this time, Wordsworth had returned to England, to oversee the publication, in 1793, of his first works,

Descriptive Sketches (inspired by his revolutionary travels) and the lakeland reverie *An Evening Walk*. When war broke out between England and France in 1793 Wordsworth was unable to return to France or to Annette; they didn't meet again until 1802.

Depressed by the events of the Terror in France, which rather dented his revolutionary enthusiasm, Wordsworth alternated between fretting and idling in London and making walking tours around England. He thought he might become a teacher and shared Dorothy's oft-expressed dream of setting up home together and devoting his life to poetry – something that at last seemed possible when a small, but unexpected, bequest from the dying **Raisley Calvert**, the brother of an old schoolfriend, gave him just enough to live on.

The Lyrical Ballads and Germany

William and Dorothy moved to **Dorset** in 1795 (where they'd been offered a house), and William became acquainted with a fiery, widely read, passionate young critic and writer. **Samuel Taylor Coleridge** had read and admired Wordsworth's two published works and, on meeting Wordsworth himself, was almost overcome with enthusiasm for his ideas and passions. There's no doubt that they inspired each other and the Wordsworths moved to **Somerset** to be near Coleridge – "three people, but one soul", as Coleridge later had it. Here they collaborated on what became the **Lyrical Ballads** (1798), a work which could be said to mark the onset of English Romantic poetry and which contained some of Wordsworth's finest early writing (quite apart from Coleridge's *The Rime of the Ancient Mariner*): not just the famous *Lines Written above Tintern Abbey*, but also snatches later incorporated into *The Prelude* (Wordsworth's great autobiographical work, unpublished during his lifetime – Wordsworth only ever knew it as the "Poem on my own Life"). It's hard to see today quite how unusual the *Lyrical Ballads* were for their time: conceived as "experiments", the mixture of simple poems with a rustic, natural content and longer narrative works flew right in the face of contemporary classicism. Sales and reviews were universally poor.

Wordsworth, Dorothy and Coleridge went to **Germany** in 1798, during which time their joint idea for a long autobiographical, philosophical work began to gel in Wordsworth's mind. He produced a first version of *The Prelude* in Germany, along with the affecting "Lucy" poems (including *Strange fits of passion have I known*), which some say pointed to an unnatural passion for his sister. It was certainly an unusual relationship: Dorothy devoted herself entirely to William (her favourite brother since childhood) and his work; she kept house for him, walked with him, listened to his poems, transcribed and made copies of them, and he wrote passionate poems about nameless women who could be no one else but Dorothy. But there's no evidence – to be blunt – that she slept with him, despite the claims of some critics.

Grasmere

In 1799 William and Dorothy moved to **Grasmere** (and Coleridge followed), in the search both for conducive natural surroundings in which Wordsworth's work could flourish and for somewhere they could survive on a restricted budget. William was to spend the last two-thirds of his life in and around the village.

Brother and sister first moved into **Dove Cottage** where they remained until 1808, a period in which Wordsworth established himself as a major poet. A new edition of the *Lyrical Ballads* (1801) appeared, including some of the poems he'd written in Germany together with his first major Grasmere poems, such as *The Brothers* and *Michael*, based on local stories and characters. This edition also included its famous **preface** expounding his theories of poetry (against "inane phraseology"; for simple, natural, emotive language), which many critics found arrogant. Wordsworth was at his most productive in the years to 1805, resulting in the publication of *Poems in Two Volumes*

(1807), containing the celebrated odes to *Duty* and *Immortality*, the Westminster Bridge sonnet, the *Daffodils* poem (untitled when first published) and a hundred other new poems and sonnets. A third edition of *Lyrical Ballads* appeared, and he had also found time to expand and complete a second version of *The Prelude*. All this early work set new standards in poetry: questioning the nature of perception, challenging contemporary prejudices and orchestrating a highly original vision of the human soul within nature.

Dorothy, meanwhile, kept a **journal** recording life at Dove Cottage, which has become a classic in its own right. Her skilled observations of the local people and landscape prompted some of William's best-known work, most famously the "Daffodils" stanzas – Wordsworth relied heavily on her journal for the famous images of the flowers dancing and reeling in the breeze.

Marriage and money

Wordsworth's dire financial position slowly improved. His sales and reviews weren't getting any better (Byron trashed most of *Poems in Two Volumes*) but the Lowthers finally stumped up the debt owed to William's long-dead father. This allowed him to marry an old childhood friend from Penrith, **Mary Hutchinson**, in 1802, having first travelled with Dorothy to France to make amends with his first love Annette; Wordsworth later provided an annuity for Annette and their young daughter. Outwardly, the **marriage to Mary** seemed precipitous and passionless and scholars have speculated about Wordsworth's motives, though letters between William and his wife (discovered in the 1970s) tend to scotch the myth that he was marrying out of duty. **Children** followed – John, Dorothy (always known as Dora), Thomas, Catherine and William – though Catherine and then Thomas, both infants, succumbed to mortal illnesses in the same tragic year of 1812.

Dove Cottage became too small for comfort as the family grew. His wife's sister, Sara Hutchinson, was a permanent fixture, as was Coleridge (by now separated from his wife) and his visiting children. The Wordsworths moved to other houses in Grasmere (Allan Bank and the Old Rectory), and then in 1813 finally settled on **Rydal Mount**, a gracious house two miles south of the village. Here William lived out the rest of his life, supported for some years by his salaried position as **Distributor of Stamps for Westmorland** (good fortune, caused, as De Quincey noted, by the current incumbent distributing "himself and his office into two different places"). It was hardly a sinecure – he had to travel through the county, collecting dues and granting licences, work which he undertook assiduously – but it brought him in £200 a year.

The Rydal years

Wordsworth may have already written his finest poetry, but after the move to Rydal he was at the peak of his fame. Over the years, the literary world made its way to his door, a procession recorded in detail by the critic and essayist **Thomas De Quincey** who first made the pilgrimage to Grasmere to meet his hero in 1807. After a long friendship interrupted by disagreements, De Quincey's frank series of articles on Wordsworth and his family in 1839 (later published as *Recollections of the Lakes and the Lake Poets*) caused an irreparable rift. **Coleridge**, too, was *persona non grata* after a falling-out in 1810, though the two old friends did come to some kind of an accommodation in later life, and *The Prelude* remained dedicated to him.

There were family setbacks. The death of William's brother, John, in 1805 had affected him deeply (and led later to a burgeoning religious faith); after 1828, his beloved sister Dorothy suffered a series of depressive illnesses, which incapacitated her mind for most of the rest of her long life; and Sara Hutchinson – who had so besotted Coleridge and who had lived with them for thirty years – died of the flu in 1835.

Wordsworth continued to be productive, at least in the early Rydal years. *The Excursion* (1814), long enough in itself, was conceived as part of an even longer philosophical work to be called "The Recluse", which he never completed. His first *Collected Poems* appeared the following year, together with *The White Doe of Rylstone*; but it wasn't until *Peter Bell* (1819) and *The River Duddon* sonnets (1820) that sales and reviews finally flourished. His *Vaudracour and Julia* (1819) also had deep significance: a tale of seduction, it was a fictionalized account of his affair with Annette.

As Wordsworth grew older he lost the radicalism of his youth, becoming a loud opponent of democracy, liberalism and progress. Political developments in France and the threat of the mob and the Reform Bill at home appalled him. His views on nature and the picturesque had led him to produce his own descriptive **Guide to the Lakes** ("for the minds of persons of taste"), at first published anonymously (1810) to accompany a book of drawings; its later popularity (a final, fifth edition, appeared in 1835) did much to advertise the very charms of the region he was keen to preserve. In the end, fulminating against the whitewashed houses and fir plantations he thought were disfiguring the Lakes, Wordsworth retreated to his beloved garden at Rydal Mount.

Apart from the rare crafted sonnet or couplet, Wordsworth's later work was largely undistinguished. The third major revision of *The Prelude* had been completed in 1838; the poem didn't see the light of day until after his death, when Mary gave it a name and handed it over for publication. But in 1843, on the death of Robert Southey and at the age of 73, Wordsworth's position as Grand Old Man of the literary establishment was confirmed by his appointment as **Poet Laureate**.

After his **death in 1850**, William's body was interred in St Oswald's churchyard in Grasmere, to be later joined by Dorothy (1855) and by his wife Mary (1859).

Small print and index

A ROUGH GUIDE TO ROUGH GUIDES

Published in 1982, the first Rough Guide – to Greece – was a student scheme that became a publishing phenomenon. Mark Ellingham, a recent graduate in English from Bristol University, had been travelling in Greece the previous summer and couldn't find the right guidebook. With a small group of friends he wrote his own guide, combining a contemporary, journalistic style with a thoroughly practical approach to travellers' needs.

The immediate success of the book spawned a series that rapidly covered dozens of destinations. And, in addition to impecunious backpackers, Rough Guides soon acquired a much broader readership that relished the guides' wit and inquisitiveness as much as their enthusiastic, critical approach and value-for-money ethos. These days, Rough Guides include recommendations from budget to luxury and cover more than 120 destinations around the globe, from Amsterdam to Zanzibar, all regularly updated by our team of roaming writers.

Browse all our latest guides, read inspirational features and book your trip at **roughguides.com**.

Rough Guide credits

Editor: Rachel Lawrence and Sarah Clark
Cartography: Katie Bennett
Picture editor: Aude Vauconsant

Head of DTP and Pre-Press: Rebeka Davies
Head of Publishing: Sarah Clark

Publishing information

Eighth Edition 2021

Distribution

UK, Ireland and Europe
Apa Publications (UK) Ltd; sales@roughguides.com
United States and Canada
Ingram Publisher Services; ips@ingramcontent.com
Australia and New Zealand
Booktopia; retailer@booktopia.com.au
Worldwide
Apa Publications (UK) Ltd; sales@roughguides.com

Special Sales, Content Licensing and CoPublishing
Rough Guides can be purchased in bulk quantities
at discounted prices. We can create special editions,
personalised jackets and corporate imprints tailored to
your needs. sales@roughguides.com.
roughguides.com

Printed in Poland

A catalogue record for this book is available from the
British Library

The publishers and authors have done their best to
ensure the accuracy and currency of all the information
in **The Rough Guide to The Lake District**, however,
they can accept no responsibility for any loss, injury, or
inconvenience sustained by any traveller as a result of
information or advice contained in the guide.

Help us update

We've gone to a lot of effort to ensure that this edition of
The Rough Guide to The Lake District is accurate and up-
to-date. However, things change – places get "discovered",
opening hours are notoriously fickle, restaurants and
rooms raise prices or lower standards. If you feel we've got
it wrong or left something out, we'd like to know, and if
you can remember the address, the price, the hours, the
phone number, so much the better.

Please send your comments with the subject line
"Rough Guide The Lake District Update" to mail@
uk.roughguides.com. We'll credit all contributions and
send a copy of the next edition (or any other Rough Guide
if you prefer) for the very best emails.

ABOUT THE AUTHOR

Jules Brown first visited the Lake District when he was 9 years old; all he can remember is that
it was raining. Aged 15 he slept out in the fields having spent his youth hostel money on beer.
When he was 36 he got stuck up Jack's Rake. And when he was 47 he took his two young sons
up their first fell – all they can remember is that it was raining. Between times, Jules has also
written Rough Guides to Scandinavia, Sicily, Hong Kong, Washington DC, Barcelona, Spain,
Portugal, England and Britain, as well as researching and editing many others.

This edition was updated by Norm Longley. Norm has spent most of his working life in eastern
Europe – he is the author of the Rough Guides to Slovenia and Romania – but more recently has
turned his hand to home shores, contributing to the Scotland, Wales and Ireland guides. He lives
in Somerset and can occasionally be seen erecting marquees on The Rec in Bath.

Photo credits
(Key: T-top; C-centre; B-bottom; L-left; R-right)

Index

Map symbols

The symbols below are used on maps throughout the book

International boundary		★	Bus stop	⟋	Viewpoint
County boundary		🏛	Stately home	⟩⟨	Bridge/pass
Chapter division boundary		⊤	Gardens	P	Parking
Motorway		🛢	Petrol station	⛰	Hills/mountains
Pedestrianized road		⌂	Abbey	⚓	Swimming pool
Road		♟	Museum	🐾	Animal park
Footpath		⠶	Ruin	🦃	Bird park
Railway		♔	Castle	⚱	Distillery
Unpaved road		✉	Post office	⛪	Church
Ferry route		✚	Hospital		Building
National park boundary		⊛	Watermill	⊞	Cemetery
Tourist railway		🌊	Waterfall		Park
Tourist office		⛺	Campsite		Beach
Statue		▲	Mountain peak		Marshland
Point of interest		⌒	Cave		

Listings key

- Accommodation
- Eating
- Drinking/nightlife
- Shopping